D0585842

Working Memory
and Education

Working Memory and Education

EDITED BY

Susan J. Pickering

ELSEVIER

AMSTERDAM • BOSTON • HEIDELBERG • LONDON
NEW YORK • OXFORD • PARIS • SAN DIEGO
SAN FRANCISCO • SINGAPORE • SYDNEY • TOKYO

Academic Press is an imprint of Elsevier

Academic Press is an imprint of Elsevier
30 Corporate Drive, Suite 400, Burlington, MA 01803, USA
525 B Street, Suite 1900, San Diego, California 92101-4495, USA
84 Theobald's Road, London WC1X 8RR, UK

This book is printed on acid-free paper. ∞

Library of Congress Cataloging-in-Publication Data
Application submitted

British Library Cataloguing-in-Publication Data
A catalogue record for this book is available from the British Library.

ISBN 13: 978-0-12-554465-8
ISBN 10: 0-12-554465-0

For information on all Academic Press publications
visit our Web site at www.books.elsevier.com

Printed in the United States of America
06 07 08 09 10 9 8 7 6 5 4 3 2 1

Contents

v

6. DECONSTRUCTING WORKING MEMORY IN DEVELOPMENTAL DISORDERS OF ATTENTION

Kim Cornish, John Wilding, and Cathy Grant

7. WORKING MEMORY AND DEAFNESS: IMPLICATIONS FOR COGNITIVE DEVELOPMENT AND FUNCTIONING

Madeleine Keehner and Joanna Atkinson

8. WORKING MEMORY IN THE CLASSROOM

Susan E. Gathercole, Emily Lamont, and Tracy Packiam Alloway

9. ASSESSMENT OF WORKING MEMORY IN CHILDREN

Susan J. Pickering

10. SOURCES OF WORKING MEMORY DEFICITS IN CHILDREN AND POSSIBILITIES FOR REMEDIATION

Meredith Minear and Priti Shah

Contributors

Tracy Packiam Alloway, Department of Psychology, Science Laboratories, University of Durham, Durham, United Kingdom

Joanna Atkinson, University College, London, United Kingdom

Alan Baddeley, Department of Psychology, University of York, York, United Kingdom

Rebecca Bull, Department of Psychology, University of Aberdeen, Kings College, Aberdeen, United Kingdom

Kate Cain, Psychology Department, Lancaster University, Lancaster, United Kingdom

Kim Cornish, Department of Educational Psychology, McGill University, Montreal, Quebec, Canada

Peter F. de Jong, Department of Education, University of Amsterdam, Amsterdam, The Netherlands

Kimberly Andrews Espy, University of Nebraska—Lincoln

Susan E. Gathercole, Department of Psychology, University of York, York, United Kingdom

Cathy Grant, Nottingham, United Kingdom

Madeline Keehner, Department of Psychology, Curtin University of Technology, Perth, Western Australia

Emily Lamont

Meredith Minear, Department of Psychology, Washington University, St. Louis, Missouri

Gary Phye, Department of Psychology, Iowa State University, Ames, Iowa

Susan J. Pickering, Graduate School of Education, University of Bristol, Bristol, United Kingdom

Priti Shah, Department of Psychology, University of Michigan, Ann Arbor, Michigan

H. Lee Swanson, School of Education, University of California, Riverside, Riverside, California

John Wilding, Royal Halloway College, University of London, Egham Hill, Egham, Surrey, United Kingdom

Acknowledgments

Many people have contributed to the creation of this book. First, I would like to thank the contributing authors, without whom there would be no book. I would like to thank all the contributors for their cheerful correspondence and tolerance of delays, as well as the fantastic work that they each carry out in the area of working memory and education.

I would also like to thank my colleagues at the Graduate School of Education and Department of Experimental Psychology, University of Bristol, for their helpful comments on the chapters of the book. Special thanks goes to my PhD student, Marcus Witt, for being pedantic about grammar and reading through the chapters when my eyes had long stopped seeing what was actually there. Finally, this book would not have been possible without the love and support of my family. Thank you.

Introduction

There are two main reasons why this book was written. The first concerns the growing interest in applying detailed theoretical knowledge about cognition, and in particular the study of working memory, to our understanding of how children perform in educational settings. Although research in this area has been carried out for some years now, there has recently been a significant increase in the number of research groups that investigate working memory with respect to educational attainment. During the last decade, many papers have been published in academic journals on this topic, each one providing further important details about working memory and children's academic functioning. Journal papers are an extremely important source of knowledge for many; however, their audience tends to be restricted to academics and, more specifically, to academics in the particular audience to which the journal is directed (e.g., psychology, education). In the course of my own work I have found the task of gathering all the research on working memory and education very time consuming. There is no one place where information like this exists altogether. This book, then, was an attempt to bring together in one place the research that has been published in specific and detailed research studies in academic journals for the benefit of readers from a range of backgrounds. This latter point is one that I shall return to later in this introduction.

The second reason why this book was created is based on the publication of a test battery for measuring working memory in children. In 2001, Sue Gathercole and I created the Working Memory Test Battery for Children (WMTB-C). The test is described in some detail in numerous chapters of this book, so only a brief mention is made here. The test was designed to be a theoretically based assessment tool for use by psychologists and specialist teachers. It departed from a number of existing batteries of memory tests in that it linked very clearly to a well-established model of working memory—the model originally developed by Baddeley and Hitch in 1974. Although we have included some background information about the test and the research that underpins it in the test manual, space constraints prevented us from providing users of the test with detailed information about the concept of working memory and the growing body of research that suggests its importance in children's educational functioning. This book was therefore developed to act as a companion to the WMTB-C and its manual and to provide those users of the test with much more information about the working memory performance of children and its relevance to the classroom.

Before providing an introduction to the 10 chapters of the book, it is probably worth reflecting on the two major concepts to which the book has devoted itself: working memory and education.

Readers of this book will realize that the term *education* has been conceptualized in this book in rather a traditional way. Each chapter confines itself largely to reporting research with children of school age, although research with adults has also proved useful in developing our understanding of working memory structures and functions. Moreover, the educational domains that have been described in this book include reading, reading comprehension, and arithmetic, all of which are traditional school subjects across much of the world. At present, there is much debate about what education means. Education is extremely broad, and increasingly we are moving away from traditional conceptualizations of education as being the teaching and learning of skills such as reading and arithmetic, by children, in classrooms. Although acknowledging that education is much more than what children do in classrooms, this book has used this more traditional view of education as its focus. We know that education is something that is increasingly being viewed as a lifelong issue and that there is much to learn apart from reading and mathematics. This book is designed to provide a starting point for bringing cognitive psychology and educational practice together. It is hoped that it will serve as a source of inspiration for those interested in carrying out investigations of working memory in adults and children in a wide range of educational domains.

Having given some thought to what we mean by the term education, we shall now consider what we mean by *working memory*. Although it was not specifically requested that the contributors of this book provide a description of working memory before describing the research in each area, many of them did. In addition, the first chapter of the book is devoted to a detailed description of the working memory model by Alan Baddeley himself. As the reader works his or her way through the chapters, it should become apparent that there are converging and diverging views about what exactly working memory is. Is this a major problem for a book such as this? The answer to this question, in my view, is "no."

The concept of working memory is both reassuringly simple and frustratingly complex. Some readers of this book may already be familiar with the terms *short-term memory*, *long-term memory*, and perhaps even *working memory* before they begin reading. Each one of these terms lends itself to an intuitively straightforward conceptualization of others' and one's own memory performance in daily life. When these terms are used in an everyday context, however, different people often use them in different ways. I have had a number of conversations with parents who describe their children as having a poor short-term memory, going on to qualify this with a tale of how the child in question constantly fails to remember things that they have done the day before. Psychology offers a different perspective on this issue, however. Many scientists would argue that remembering something from a day ago would actually involve long-term memory (perhaps in addition to short-term memory).

Things become more complex still when we examine short-term memory and working memory. Are they both the same thing? The answer to this question might well be both yes and no. Immediate memory—one's ability to encode and then output information over very short periods (probably seconds)—has been studied over a number of years and by researchers located all over the world. Two important features of academic research are as follows: 1) different researchers have different views (theories, models) of particular concepts, and 2) our knowledge and understanding of these concepts is ever changing in the light of new research findings. What implications does this have for our concepts of short-term memory and working memory? The answer lies with the somewhat differing conceptualizations that researchers in this area have about what exactly short-term memory and working memory are. Some of these (often quite subtle) differences are reflected in the chapters of this book. However, it was a pleasant surprise to me to see exactly how much convergence was apparent across chapters. Although the WMTB-C is based on the Baddeley and Hitch model of working memory, contributors to this book were not specifically instructed to discuss their work within this framework. It is an indication of how helpful this model has been, therefore, that most, if not all, of the chapters draw on it heavily in the course of their discussions.

In their simplest terms, working memory and short-term memory are overlapping concepts. In the Baddeley and Hitch model, a dynamic working memory system allows us to simply store information for short periods (using the two slave systems of the system: the phonological loop and the visuo-spatial sketchpad) and also manipulate that information while it is being stored (using the central executive, probably acting in conjunction with one or more of the slave systems). The simple storage of information is often called short-term memory. When some form of active processing is going on in addition to the storage of information, this is much more likely to be conceptualized as working memory activity. Thus, the dynamic working memory model provides us with a mechanism for both short-term and working memory processes.

Further complexity is added to the concept of working memory in terms of the type of information that is being stored in the memory system. The Baddeley and Hitch model provides specified components for dealing with visuo-spatial and verbal information. However, I am often asked, "What about temporary storage of nonspeech sounds, smells, tastes, movements, and other types of stimulation that regularly occur in our world?" To my knowledge, there is no comprehensive model of working memory that can provide an answer to this question. The Baddeley and Hitch model, like other theories and models of memory functioning, has begun its description of working memory with the evidence that was already in existence (namely data on verbal and visual memory) and set about investigating these phenomena more thoroughly. Only time will tell us whether the study of olfactory working memory, for example, will prove to be experimentally tractable in the same way as verbal and visual working memory.

The lively research activity that surrounds working memory may provide further specification to the Baddeley and Hitch model, or it may eventually cause us to abandon the model altogether. This prospect does not seem very likely at present because, so far, the model has survived more than 30 years' worth of academic challenges very well indeed. That is not to say that there are not other descriptions of how working memory may be organized. By its very nature, a cognitive process such as working memory is entirely abstract. We cannot see it, and therefore cannot check which explanation is correct. We can only manipulate it experimentally and observe the behavioral manifestations of our hypothesized system at work. In recent years, we have begun to be able to correlate such behavioral observations with data from brain scanning studies to provide neuroanatomical evidence on working memory functioning. For those readers interested in understanding more about the research on working memory and the different explanations that have been proposed, a good book to read is an edited volume by Jackie Andrade (2001) called *Working Memory in Perspective* (Hove: Psychology Press).

THE ORGANIZATION OF THIS BOOK

The current volume consists of 10 chapters, and these chapters have been arranged so that related topics are located close to one another. The first chapter was written by Alan Baddeley and is designed to provide an introduction to the concept of working memory as embodied in the model developed by Alan and his colleague Graham Hitch and subsequently modified over the last 30 years. In this chapter, the reader is presented with a description of the three established components of the model and the experimental data that support their existence. At the end of the chapter, a fourth working memory component, the episodic buffer, is discussed. This new component brings the reader up-to-date with the cutting edge of research on this memory model. Our knowledge and understanding of this new component is at a very early stage, and for this reason it is not discussed to any significant extent in other chapters of this book. Future discussions of working memory may include much more significant references to this new component, however.

Chapters 2, 3, and 4 have been grouped together to allow the reader to assess the role of working memory in reading (decoding print), reading comprehension, and arithmetic—our three traditional school domains. Chapter 2 is written by Peter de Jong, a researcher with a long-standing interest in the role of working memory in spoken language and literacy. In this chapter he makes a distinction between short-term verbal memory (simple storage of phonological information) and working memory (the storage and processing of information in memory), arguing that it is the latter, rather than the former, that appears to be related to children's skills in decoding print. This chapter is followed by a discussion of the other major component of the reading process—reading comprehension. In Chapter 3, Kate Cain describes how researchers have tried to understand the processes at work when we read text and make an attempt to understand what we are reading. Text comprehension is much more complex than we might think. Much of what we read is not a literal account of what is being presented, and we as readers need to work hard to make sense of what we see. Working memory appears to play a major role in this process, and this chapter provides us with a number of accounts as to why this might be the case.

Chapter 4 concerns itself with research that has found a link between working memory and performance in the domain of arithmetic. This area of research has shown a significant increase in interest over recent years, and consequently our understanding of the cognitive processes that might promote or constrain good arithmetic performance is better than ever. In this chapter, Rebecca Bull and Kimberly Andrews Espy discuss their own research, and that of others, in which the role of working memory in different types of arithmetic processing has been investigated.

Chapters 5, 6, and 7 share a common aim to discuss working memory in populations in which some aspect of functioning related to education is impaired. In Chapter 5, H. Lee Swanson shares some of his work on the role of working memory in children with learning disabilities (i.e., children who show deficits in their academic and cognitive functioning). After describing what is meant by the term *learning disabilities* (LD), this chapter discusses how a method of dynamic assessment of working memory has been applied to children with LD. Dynamic assessment departs from more traditional forms of cognitive assessment by creating a role for the examiner as a provider of support in each of the working memory tasks. In many ways, therefore, this approach uses the Vygotskian concept of the *zone of proximal development* and collects measures from a child in terms of what they can achieve by themselves and what they can achieve with the aid of probes from the examiner. It appears that children with LD do not all score in the same way on such dynamic assessment tasks, and moreover, the differences exhibited by the children may be of great use when planning remedial interventions.

Chapter 6 presents a discussion of the role of working memory in disorders of attention. In this chapter, Kim Cornish, John Wilding, and Cathy

Grant discuss the findings from a set of related studies of children with impaired attention. In line with previous research, the results from their studies suggest that the central executive component of working memory is of greatest relevance to these populations. This component of working memory is the least understood and most complex, not least because it appears to serve a number of separable but related functions. By applying common research methods to children with different types of attentional problem, Cornish and her colleagues have been able to learn more about these populations and about the central executive itself. Indeed, this chapter is one of a number of chapters that include detailed analyses of central executive functions (see also Chapters 2 and 4). By placing the detailed theorizing contained in Chapter 6 alongside that contained in the other chapters, we begin to witness exciting new developments in our understanding of the structures and functions of the working memory system, which might not have been possible without this book.

In Chapter 7 Madeleine Keehner and Joanna Atkinson discuss how working memory has been found to operate in children who are deaf. Research that has applied measures of working memory functioning to this population has found some startling results, many of which relate to the effect on cognition of being skilled in sign language. Because spoken language has been found to play a significant role in the operation of working memory in hearing children, the working memory status of children who cannot hear is of particular interest in understanding how working memory is organized. In this chapter readers will see that, because sign language is now being recognized more and more as a true language, so also is its role in working memory processes. In addition, the implications of using sign language for the balance of phonological and visuo-spatial skills in deaf children are also hugely relevant for psychologists, educators, and others.

Chapters 8, 9, and 10 bring together the findings of some recent research on the assessment and remediation of working memory. In Chapter 8, Susan Gathercole, Tracy Alloway, and Emily Lamont present the findings from their research on working memory in the classroom. Using a combination of working memory assessments and classroom observation, they provide a detailed description of how working memory problems might manifest themselves in school. This chapter describes how working memory limitations may constrain learning opportunities and are illustrated with detailed descriptions of three children with significant working memory problems. Professor Gathercole and her colleagues also go on to consider how teachers and classroom support staff might attempt to meet the needs of children, such as those described, within the classroom context. This chapter provides a very readable account and is full of information that is sure to appeal to teachers and others.

Chapter 9 was written by me. It aims to provide the reader with a review of some important issues in the assessment of working memory. As mentioned earlier, space constraints in the manual for the WMTB-C prevented a detailed description of the subtests in the battery. Users of the WMTB-C may find themselves thinking, "What does this test measure?" or "Why has this child scored in this way on this subtest?" It is hoped that this chapter will provide some useful information on what each subtest is designed to measure and what other cognitive skills may have a bearing on the scores that a particular child will achieve. Also included in this chapter is a brief discussion of some of the research that we have carried out using the WMTB-C with children with developmental disorders. This research suggests that working memory may be a useful tool for making distinctions between different kinds of learning problems, even when multiple problems appear to occur together in the same child (as is often the case). Moreover, at the individual level, standardized profiles of working memory performance can provide educators with important information about the child's working memory performance in comparison to his or her peers and, moreover, where their relative strengths and weaknesses lie. This information can be very helpful when planning remedial interventions for children with learning problems.

Indeed, remediation of working memory is the topic of Chapter 10. In this chapter, Meredith Minear and Priti Shah present a comprehensive review of the different types of remedial intervention that have been carried out with children. This is a very new area of research but one that is sure to attract a lot of attention in the coming years. That is not to say that teachers have not been remediating working memory problems before now. Skilled and experienced teachers will almost certainly have been using a range of creative interventions with children whose memories are poor. What have been lacking, however, are scientific investigations of the efficacy of such approaches. Evidence is now being collected from different interventions ranging from repeated practice on a memory task to the administration of medication. This chapter establishes how these types of approaches have been used with children with a range of educationally relevant problems and what outcomes have been observed.

HOW TO READ THIS BOOK

There is a limit to what can be achieved in one book. This book is not, for example, designed to be an educational manual. It does not (with the exception perhaps of Chapters 8 and 10) provide the reader with suggestions for things that can be done in class on Monday morning. During the development of this book decisions were made about the intended audience and, therefore, structure and tone of the book. The aim was to steer a middle ground. As an academic psychologist previously based in a department of psychology and who now works in a school of education, I am keenly aware of the opportunities and pitfalls of bringing different disciplines together. Psychology and education have a long history of coexistence and, to some extent, collaboration. The commitment of the book's contributors to applying work from mainstream experimental cognitive psychology to practical issues in education is, I believe, an indication of the willingness of psychologists and educationalists to work together for the greater good of children and the development of knowledge.

It is my hope that this book reaches different readers, including academic researchers in psychology, education, and related fields; teachers and trainee teachers; students of psychology and other related disciplines; and professional psychologists, such as educational psychologists. Numerous chapters are clearly written in an academic style; a number of chapters contain reported statistical outcomes, which some readers may find daunting. This particular approach has been taken because, for many of the intended readers, this is exactly the sort of information that they are looking for. For those that are less experienced in reading work in this style, please do not be put off. At the end of each chapter there is a Summary Box. Here each chapter author has summarized the key points from his or her chapter. If you are feeling daunted by a chapter, begin first by reading the summary, and take some time to digest the message that it is telling you. If you feel that you would like to learn more about a topic, you can then begin to read the chapter itself. Also, don't forget that the References at the end of each chapter contain a list of resources have been referred to in the chapter. If you want to follow up on any of the information that is presented in the chapters, you can look for the original reference in the References and obtain the work yourself. Happy reading, and, of course, while you are reading, make sure that your working memory is functioning to help you!

CHAPTER

1

Working Memory: An Overview

ALAN BADDELEY

University of York

One might imagine that cognitive psychology and the study of education would be close companions, with the study of learning and memory providing a theoretical basis for the study of education. I'm sad to say that is not the case. There have, of course, been psychologists concerned with cognition who have been extremely influential in the educational field; Piaget and Bruner are notable examples. However, neither of these has had a major impact on, or drawn from, mainstream cognitive psychology, at least over the last two or three decades. The problem has not been one of mutual antagonism, at least not by cognitive psychologists, who I am sure would be delighted to see their work influencing education; rather, the problem has been failure to address common problems using mutually understandable concepts. Certainly, there are some notable exceptions, with topics such as reading, with institutions like the Learning Research and Developmental Center at the University of Pittsburgh, and with individuals such as John Bransford (1979) providing good examples. In general, however, those studying the cognitive psychology of learning and memory have tended to stay relatively close to the laboratory, and as far as I can ascertain, those studying education stay relatively close to the classroom.

This certainly proved true in my case; as a newly appointed director of a Medical Research Council (MRC) unit, I initially proposed to concentrate on the basic skills of reading, writing, and arithmetic because of their relevance to education. This was firmly discouraged by the relevant MRC committee who declared it beyond their remit. I therefore chose neuropsychology as a more appropriately medical area of applied research for my newly acquired unit. I have, however, retained my interest in the application of psychology to education, and for that reason I welcomed the invitation from my colleague Susan Pickering to contribute to this book.

My main qualification for contributing to the book is that of a cognitive psychologist, involved over the last two or three decades in developing the concept of working memory (WM). Theoretical concepts can potentially be useful to practitioners on at least three levels. First, they may provide a broad understanding of the processes underlying practice, in this case education; second, such understanding can, in turn, be used to develop better methods of assessment that will allow teaching or remedial strategies to be optimally targeted. Third, the concepts may contribute to a better understanding of the whole process of teaching and, one hopes in due course, help to improve educational methods more generally. The latter two applications require more knowledge of the current educational scene than I possess. I shall therefore limit myself to attempting to give a clear account of our current knowledge of WM, leaving the application of such knowledge in the remainder of this book to my better qualified colleagues.

I regard scientific theories as if they are maps, providing a broad overview of an area, emphasizing some features, and leaving others unspecified. A given theoretical map will depend on the purpose for which it was developed and, of course, on the level of detail. The classic map of the London underground, for example, is extremely useful to the traveler despite the fact that it lacks great detail and departs from strict geographic accuracy. It is, however, important that maps with different functions, such as street maps and tube maps, can be cross-linked. The same applies to scientific theories; psychological theories of memory often are expressed in terms of flow diagrams that may suggest a series of rigidly separate modules. At an atomic level, however, although the brain is somewhat modular in structure, there are multiple complex neural connections between the modules, making modularity a matter of degree rather than absolute. The theory I will be describing is expressed in a series of flow diagrams. Nonetheless, it shows significant compatibility with neuropsychological evidence from patients who are brain damaged and have cognitive impairments and is increasingly closely linked with neuroimaging and electrophysiological approaches. At the same time, it provides a broad qualitative framework for understanding practical problems ranging from child development (Baddeley & Hitch, 1974; Gathercole & Adams, 1994) to dementia (Baddeley, Baddeley, Bucks, & Wilcock, 2001) and from intelligence (Mackintosh, 1998) to anesthesia (Andrade, 2001).

Within a general theory, there are likely to develop a number of more specific models. Models are an attempt to give a more detailed account of phenomena, possibly expressed mathematically or in terms of a computer program. A number of competing models may occur within the same theoretical framework. For example, Burgess and Hitch (1999), Page and Norris

(1998), and Henson (1998) all give somewhat different accounts of the way in which the phonological loop component of WM stores the order in which items are presented. I regard the existence of competing models as a healthy state of affairs, likely to prompt a search for new evidence aiming to decide between them, hopefully leading to the eventual convergence of the various accounts.

HOW MANY KINDS OF MEMORY?

Until the late 1950s, most accounts of memory treated it as a single unitary faculty. At about that time, however, John Brown (1958) in England and Peterson and Peterson (1959) in the United States observed that small amounts of information would be rapidly forgotten if the participant was prevented from rehearsing that information. To account for their data, they proposed a short-term memory (STM) system that operated using different rules from long-term memory (LTM). This view was resisted strongly (Melton, 1963), leading to a lively controversy and to the subsequent generation of a great deal of further evidence during the mid-1960s (see Baddeley, 1997, Chapter 3 for a review).

Perhaps the most convincing evidence came from a comparison between two types of neuropsychological patients. Patients suffering from the classic amnesic syndrome appeared to be unable to commit new material to memory, as measured either experimentally or in terms of their everyday life. A patient with amnesia, such as case H.M. studied by Milner (1966), would not, for example, be able to tell you what he had for breakfast that day, would not know whether you had met him before, and would not be able to learn his way around a new environment or to keep track of current events. Such a patient would in effect be locked in the present. However, the functioning of STM could be intact, allowing the patient to hear and repeat back a telephone number and to recall, for instance, the most recent item of a word list that had been presented (Baddeley & Warrington, 1970). A patient with exactly the opposite pattern, namely, preserved LTM and impaired STM, was described by Shallice and Warrington (1970). The presence of two complementary sets of patients provided a "double dissociation"—a pattern of results that allows one to rule out a simple interpretation of memory task performance in terms of the relative difficulty of the two sets of STM and LTM tasks.

By the late 1960s, evidence seemed to be accumulating in favor of a clear separation between STM and LTM. A number of models were proposed, with the most influential being that of Atkinson and Shiffrin shown in Figure 1.1 (1968). It was assumed that information came in from the environment, was processed by a series of temporary sensory memory systems (that are perhaps best regarded as part of the process of perception), and then fed into a limited capacity short-term store (STS). This was assumed to act as a

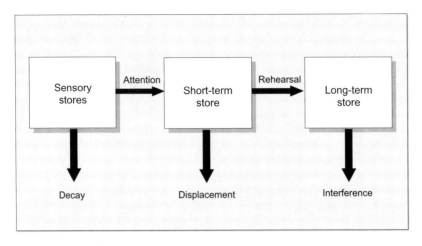

FIGURE 1.1

The model of memory proposed by Atkinson and Shiffrin. Information is assumed to come in from the environment and pass through brief perceptual stores into a short-term memory system. This is assumed to act as a working memory, necessary for feeding information into and out of the more durable long-term memory store.

WM—that is, a system for holding information and allowing it to be used to perform a wide range of cognitive tasks, including transfer into, and retrieval from, LTM. Such transfer was assumed to depend entirely on how long an item resided in the STS.

Although the model gave a good account of a wide range of data and a precise account of some of the authors' own results, it encountered two problems. The first of these concerned the learning assumption. There was little evidence to suggest that simply holding an item in the STS would facilitate learning, and there was considerable evidence that degree of learning depended on the way in which information was processed by the participant. In particular, elaborate semantic encoding (involving the meaning of memory items) appeared to lead to much more learning than simply concentrating on the sound of the word presented or its visual appearance when written. Craik and Lockhart (1972) proposed a theoretical framework that became known as *levels of processing*. Rather than thinking in terms of different stores, they suggested that it would be more profitable to emphasize methods of encoding, with deeper and more detailed encoding leading to more durable memory. They and others produced extensive evidence for the importance of rich semantic coding for long-term learning. Although the details of their framework are certainly open to criticism (e.g., Baddeley, 1978; see Craik, 2002, for a response), there is no doubt that the concept of processing level gives a simple account of a very robust phenomenon, which is, incidentally, of great relevance to educational practice. Deeper

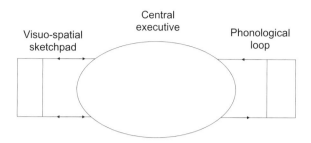

FIGURE 1.2

The three-part model of working memory proposed by Baddeley and Hitch (1974). Temporary visual and verbal stores are controlled by an attentional system.

understanding is likely to give rise to much better subsequent retention than repeated presentation at a more superficial level.

In addition to this criticism of their long-term learning assumption, Atkinson and Shiffrin also had problems in accounting for data from neuropsychological studies of STM. In particular, their model would suggest that patients with serious disruption of the STS should find great difficulty in feeding information into and out of LTM. Furthermore, given the importance assigned to this store as a WM, such patients should encounter wide-ranging difficulties in their everyday life. In fact, they did not; one worked as a very efficient secretary, a second was a taxi driver, and a third ran a family and a shop.

At about this time, my colleague, Graham Hitch, and I began a 3-year research project concerned with the relationship between STM and LTM. We did not have access to patients with STM; instead we tried to simulate this condition using our student participants (Baddeley & Hitch, 1974). It was generally agreed that the classic digit span task, whereby a participant hears and repeats back strings of numbers increasing in length, places heavy demands on STM. We therefore required our participants to carry out tasks demanding reasoning, learning, or comprehending while at the same time holding and repeating back sequences of numbers. We argued that as the sequence length increased, the amount of uncommitted STM remaining should diminish, resulting in an increasing degree of interference with our various tasks. We did indeed find this, but the disruption was far less dramatic than we had anticipated. For example, our reasoning task required participants to verify sentences purporting to describe the order of two letters (e.g., *A is not preceded by B: B-A*, for which the response should be *False*). Participants given an eight-digit number to retain should have been at the limit of their STM capacity and should fail the task. They did take about 50% longer to perform the verification, but they were no less accurate. We concluded that the idea of a unitary store was too simple and proposed instead the three-component model shown in Figure 1.2.

At the center of our model was a limited capacity attentional control system, which we termed the *central executive*. This was assisted by two subsidiary slave systems: one, the *phonological* (or *articulatory*) *loop*, was capable of holding and rehearsing sound and speech-based information, whereas the other, the *visuo-spatial sketchpad*, performed a similar service for visual material. We suggested that digit recall, used as a secondary task in our studies, relied principally on the phonological loop, together with a contribution from the central executive. As the length of the remembered sequences increased, the demands on the executive would increase, thus resulting in a growing degree of general impairment. We proposed that even long digit sequences were not sufficient to fully use the executive and made little demand on the sketchpad, with the result that the effect of the concurrent task was never catastrophic. We proposed that the patients with impaired STM described by Shallice and Warrington (1970) had a deficit that was limited to the phonological loop, an assumption that received subsequent support from the study of an Italian patient with a very pure phonological STM deficit (Vallar & Baddeley, 1984).

Somewhat tentatively, Graham Hitch and I published our model in 1974, since which time it has survived remarkably well, providing a simple but robust base for a wide range of studies of WM. The value of the model, I believe, has stemmed directly from its simplicity, which has led to the development of a battery of basic methodological tools that can be applied widely. Simplicity does, of course, have its disadvantages. It forms the main criticism of the model by contributors to the book by Andrade (2001), in which a number of younger investigators were invited to comment on the strengths and weaknesses of the Baddeley and Hitch model. I remain unrepentant on the issue of detailed specification and see it as one of the jobs of those using the model to make their own contribution, either by filling in the missing parts or producing a better model.

The three components of the Baddeley and Hitch model will be discussed in turn, followed by a brief account of some more recent developments.

The Phonological Loop

The loop was assumed to have two components, namely, a store that is capable of holding phonological information over a matter of seconds before the memory trace fades or is refreshed by the second component. This is assumed to involve subvocalization, whereby inner speech is used to rehearse the items, successively retrieving them from the store and feeding them back by means of articulation, hence the term "articulatory loop." Short sequences such as three digits will take less than a second to rehearse, with the result that the first digit will not have faded by the time the last digit has been spoken, and hence performance can be maintained indefinitely. As the length of sequence increases, a point is reached whereby it is impossible to rehearse all the digits rapidly enough to avoid losing one or more as a result of trace decay. This process provides a simple account of why we have a limited digit span.

A second function of the articulatory process is to convert visually presented material into a phonological code by subvocal naming. Thus there is little difference in memory span for digits that are presented visually or auditorily because participants tend to covertly speak the visual digits and convert them into a phonological code. This process of subvocal naming can be prevented by requiring the participant to continuously repeat some irrelevant utterance, such as the word "the," a process known as articulatory suppression—a simple but very useful methodological tool (Murray, 1965).

One of the clearest markers of the use of the phonological store is the *phonological similarity effect*. Conrad (1964), studying the recall of visually presented single consonants, noted that errors tended to involve consonants that sounded, rather than looked, similar. Hence, *V* was liable to be misremembered as *B* and *F* as *X*. When participants were required to remember sequences of consonants, they made far more errors with phonologically similar lists such as *T, P, G, V, D* than with dissimilar sets such as *K, W, Y, R, F* (Conrad & Hull, 1964). A similar effect occurs for words, with a sequence such as *man, cad, cap, mat, can* being recalled perfectly on only about 20% of occasions, compared with about 80% for *pit, day, cow, pen, sup*. This is not a general similarity effect; a sequence of adjectives that are similar in meaning but different in sound such as *big, huge, large, wide, tall* is only slightly less well recalled than a dissimilar list such as *old, wet, strong, smooth, thin* (Baddeley, 1966a). In addition, the effect is limited to STM, so when the task is designed in such a way as to involve LTM (e.g., by doubling the length of the sequences and presenting them over a number of learning trials), meaning becomes all-important and sound becomes irrelevant. In short, the loop relies on sound, whereas LTM is more likely to rely on meaning (Baddeley, 1966b).

The clearest marker of the articulatory rehearsal process is the word-length effect (Baddeley, Thomson, & Buchanan, 1975). Whereas participants recall about 80% of sequences of single-syllable words correctly, performance drops to around 50% if word length is increased to produce sequences of polysyllabic words such as *refrigerator, tuberculosis, university, electricity, opportunity*. This fits the model neatly, on the assumption that longer words take longer to articulate during rehearsal, allowing a greater degree of trace decay and resulting in poorer performance. Studies that measure articulation time for words of different length provide supporting evidence for this hypothesis, and additional support is obtained from the observation that participants who articulate more rapidly show better STM performance (e.g., Baddeley et al., 1975). Further evidence for this interpretation comes from a comparison of digit span across different languages where digits differ in their mean syllable length, from around one in English to more than two in Arabic. Average articulation time increases as a function of the number of syllables, and mean digit span decreases. The most rapid articulation and highest spans recorded so far were found in Chinese, for which it is possible to combine two digits into a single syllable (Hoosain & Salili, 1987). There is, incidentally, evidence that speed of articulation across languages is associated with capacity for mental arithmetic, although it is important to note that phonological loop performance is not the principal determinant of mental arithmetic ability (Hitch & McAuley, 1991).

Although Baddeley and Hitch underlined the importance of speed of articulation during rehearsal, Cowan et al. (1992) have stressed the importance of time taken to articulate items *during recall*; longer sequences take longer to recall and therefore allow more forgetting. This is certainly the case, and at least one study (Dosher & Ma, 1998) has suggested that the word-length effect may actually be entirely attributable to recall delay. A more recent study, in which output delay was carefully controlled (Baddeley, Chincotta, Stafford, & Turk, 2002), suggests that both rehearsal and output are important, as the phonological loop would predict.

The phonological loop model assumes that forgetting is a result of simple trace decay within the store. This is not an essential feature of the model, but it does have the advantage of simplicity over interpretations dependent on the assumption that later syllables interfere with the retention of earlier items, which then need to specify the mechanism by which such interference operates. Baddeley et al. (1975) supported the trace decay view with just one study, in which they required participants to remember sequences of two-syllable words that had either short vowels (e.g., *cricket*, *bishop*) or long vowels (e.g., *Friday*, *harpoon*). As predicted by the trace decay hypothesis, performance on the long vowels, which presumably allowed more forgetting during rehearsal and output, led to poorer performance. A number of studies have contested this finding, replicating it with the particular word-set initially used but not with other groups of words (Caplan, Rochon, & Waters, 1992; Lovatt, Avons, & Masterson, 2002). Some of these studies have been criticized by Baddeley and Andrade (1994) on the grounds of inappropriate measures of spoken duration and confounding effects of phonological similarity. These criticisms have, in turn, been rejected (Waters & Caplan, 1996). A 2003 study by Mueller, Seymour, Kieras, and Meyer (2003) uses more carefully developed measures of both articulation rate and phonological similarity, applying them to their own data and to the various sets of words used in the literature. Mueller and colleagues conclude that the combined effects of spoken duration and phonological similarity give a precise account of all of the available data, hence supporting a trace decay interpretation of forgetting within the phonological loop. However, it seems unlikely that this controversy is fully resolved. Fortunately, although the question of whether forgetting in STM results from trace delay or interference is of great theoretical interest, this issue does bear on the practical value of the phonological loop model.

A number of theorists have proposed an entirely different interpretation of the word-length effect, arguing that long words have more syllables, each of which is liable to be forgotten, therefore increasing the overall probability of forgetting (Brown & Hulme, 1995; Neath & Nairne, 1995). Of course, a five-syllable word is not five times as liable to forgetting as a monosyllabic word, particularly under standard (closed set) conditions where the same set of 8 or 10 words is used repeatedly within an experiment. This is presumably because participants can reconstruct the partly forgotten word from its surviving fragments, a process called *redintegration*. This explanation, however, introduces the further complexity of deciding just how these two processes of forgetting and reconstruction interact. Such an interpretation has to be further constrained to explain how articulatory suppression completely removes the word-length effect. In addition to this, the number of syllables would also predict that polysyllabic words should be more subject to forgetting, regardless of whether they are surrounded by short or long words. Data by Cowan, Baddeley, Elliott, and Norris (2003) indicated that this is not the case.

Further evidence for this distinction between storage and rehearsal comes from a range of studies involving neuroimaging of the brain while performing various tasks, some involving phonological storage and others involving articulation. Paulesu, Frith, and Frackowiak (1993) used positron emission tomography (PET) to study the blood flow in the brain associated with these two aspects of the phonological loop. They identified two areas within the left hemisphere as being implicated in phonological STM: an area between the temporal and parietal lobes, Brodman Area (BA) 40, was associated with storage, and a more frontal area (BA44 and BA6) was identified as the articulatory rehearsal component. These findings were consistent with evidence from earlier studies involving patients with lesions with the temporo-parietal area being associated with the STM deficits described earlier, whereas damage to the more frontal region (also known as Broca's area) was known to be linked to problems of speech production (Vallar & Papagno, 2002). Extensive research by Smith, Jonides, and colleagues has provided further support for these conclusions (see Smith & Jonides, 1997, for a review).

At present, therefore, despite some lively and intriguing controversy, the phonological loop model seems to be surviving well and providing a simple and robust account of a wide range of studies. Does it matter? Are these controversies any more than storms in a rather small academic teacup? If patients with grossly defective phonological loop function are able to live normal lives, is the phonological no more than a pimple on the anatomy of cognitive psychology, as James Reason (personal communication) has suggested? Having devoted considerable time and effort to studying the loop, I clearly regard this as a crucial question.

The opportunity to tackle the question occurred when an Italian colleague, Guiseppe Vallar, invited me to study a very pure case of impaired

STM in a young woman who had suffered a left-hemisphere stroke. Her memory for digit sequences was limited to one or two items at most, whereas her long-term learning ability seemed normal, as was her language capacity, except under conditions where immediate memory was involved (Basso, Spinnler, Vallar, & Zanobio, 1982). We began by testing her capacity to comprehend complex sentences. She did, indeed, show an impairment but only when comprehension depended on literal retention of the beginning of a long sentence to understand the end.

We then explored the hypothesis that the phonological loop may have evolved to facilitate the process of learning language. The adult patients studied so far would have already acquired language and hence would have found the loss of the loop far less debilitating. However, if this was the case, we might expect that our patient would have great difficulty in learning a new language. We tested this hypothesis by attempting to teach our patient the vocabulary of a foreign language, Russian. We required her to learn the Russian equivalent of eight words in her native language—for example, *rose-svieti*. For comparison purposes, we attempted to teach her eight arbitrary pairs of words (e.g., *horse-castle*), where learning was expected to be based on their meaning rather than their sound. When compared to a group of normal participants matched for age and education, her learning rate for pairs of known words was unimpaired, whereas she completely failed to master any of the pairs involving Russian words (Baddeley, Papagno, & Vallar, 1988). We were also able to simulate this result in normal people by disrupting the operation of the loop. When we interfered with the use of the phonological loop either by articulatory suppression (Papagno, Valentine, & Baddeley, 1991), or by manipulating word length and phonological similarity (Papagno & Vallar, 1992), foreign language vocabulary acquisition was seriously delayed, whereas the rate of learning to associate native language word pairs was unaffected.

At that point we had only studied the acquisition by adults of a second language. We therefore went on to study children's acquisition of their first language. In one study, Gathercole and Baddeley (1990) tested a subgroup of children with specific language impairment (SLI). They were 8 years old and had normal nonverbal intelligence, but they had the language of 6 year olds. When we tested their memory, we found a particular weakness for sound mimicry, a component of the Goldman-Fristoe-Woodcock (1974) test that requires the participant to hear a nonsense word (usually monosyllabic) and then repeat it back. To investigate this further, we developed a nonsense word repetition test that required children to hear and repeat back nonsense words ranging in length from one to four, and subsequently five, syllables (Children's Test of Nonword Repetition, CNRep; Gathercole & Baddeley, 1996). We compared the children in our 8-year-old SLI group with children matched for age and nonverbal intelligence and with a group of 6-year-old children who were matched with our SLI group for level of language development. We found that our SLI group was worse than their age-matched controls and were substantially worse than the 6 year olds. In fact, their performance was at a level that would be expected in 4 year olds. We found no evidence for an obvious hearing deficit or poorer articulation, concluding that their deficit probably lay in the capacity of the phonological store.

Our SLI study therefore gave further support to the view that the phonological loop might be important in first language learning, at least in cases where the system was seriously reduced in capacity. That does not, of course, necessarily mean that it sets a limit for language development across the population as a whole. To investigate this, we began by testing a range of 4- to 5-year-old children who were just starting school (Gathercole & Baddeley, 1989). In addition to nonsense word repetition, we used the Raven's Progressive Matrices test (Raven, 1984) to measure nonverbal intelligence and a receptive vocabulary test, the British Picture Vocabulary Scale (Dunn & Dunn, 1982), which involves presenting the child with sets of four pictures. The name of one picture is spoken, and the child is required to point to the appropriate picture. We observed correlations of .525 and .572 between receptive vocabulary and nonsense word repetition for 4 and 5 year olds, respectively, and a weaker correlation with nonverbal intelligence ($r = .388$ and $.322$). We have since replicated our correlation between CNRep performance and vocabulary many times with children ranging from ages 3 to 13 years, consistently finding a healthy association between the two measures, a correlation that remains when differences in intelligence are statistically removed (Baddeley, Gathercole, & Papagno, 1998).

Correlation does not, of course, necessarily imply causation, and one might plausibly argue that possession of a good vocabulary helps one repeat novel nonsense words, rather than the reverse. Evidence for this was produced by Gathercole (1995), who divided the nonsense words from the CNRep test into two sets, depending on whether they had a letter structure that was similar to English (e.g., fermicate) or dissimilar (skiticult). Both high- and low-vocabulary children performed consistently better on the wordlike items, suggesting that language habits in LTM were proving a useful aid to storing unfamiliar verbal items. However, when the children were tested again a year later, their *increase* in vocabulary over the year was predicted much more effectively by performance on the non–wordlike items. This pattern of results is consistent with a two-component view of nonsense word repetition. Performance is certainly supported by language habits. However, it is the capacity to repeat non–wordlike nonsense words (for which the contribution from prior language habits is low) that predicts future learning.

One possible explanation is to assume that the phonological store is relatively free of the influence of language habits, in contrast to the articulatory rehearsal process that depends heavily on existing knowledge. One might argue that this is a useful way to set up the system because if the store were excessively dependent on old habits, it would have difficulty registering novel material without distorting it, hence failing to provide a good mechanism for learning new words.

Further evidence in favor of this view was serendipitously provided in a series of studies that initially had the very practical aim of adapting the CNRep task for use with children with articulatory difficulties. This involved changing the testing procedure from recall to recognition and replacing the complex nonsense words with a series of consonant–vowel–consonant (CVC) syllables, some of which formed real words (e.g., *hat, dog, bed*) and some formed nonsense words (e.g., *mip, lod, tep*). The child would hear a sequence of items, which was then repeated either in exactly the same order or with the order of two of the items switched. Children were also asked to *recall* the sequences of CVC items using the more standard STM procedure. Recall led to a large advantage in performance for the words sequences over the nonsense word sequences. However, when the recognition procedure was used, the difference in performance between the two sets of CVCs virtually vanished (Gathercole, Frankish, Pickering, & Peaker, 1999). These results are again consistent with the suggestion that the phonological loop contains a memory store that is relatively free of the influence of language habits and is sufficient for serial recognition, without the need for rehearsal. Recall, in contrast, depends on a secondary articulatory component that depends crucially on prior linguistic knowledge.

Before moving on, we should consider an alternative interpretation of our results, proposed by Snowling, Chiat, and Hulme (1991). They suggest that both nonsense word repetition and vocabulary development stem from a common underlying capacity for phonological processing. There have, of course, been a whole range of suggestions linking dyslexia to more basic processes (Beaton, 2004), and if dyslexia, why not more basic skills such as vocabulary acquisition? For example, dyslexia has been attributed both to impairment of the capacity to detect sudden auditory transitions (e.g., Tallal, Stark, & Mellits, 1985) and to problems of phonological awareness (PA). PA is the capacity to reflect on the phonological structure of language, as revealed by, for example, the ability to detect rhymes, to delete initial phonemes (e.g., remove the *m* from *man* to produce *an*), or to transpose phonemes as in Spoonerisms (e.g., hear *dear queen*, say *queer dean*).

There is no doubt that phonological awareness correlates with reading performance (Beaton, 2004). However, the evidence seems to suggest that in the case of more complex tasks, PA benefits from the skills acquired during reading, rather than the reverse (Morais, Alegria, & Content, 1987). Our own data indicate that both nonsense word repetition and PA are associated with reading performance but contribute independently, whereas only nonsense word repetition makes a substantial independent contribution to vocabulary (Gathercole, Willis, & Baddeley, 1991).

I suspect, therefore, that phonological awareness is not simply a unitary function. That does not, of course, mean that some other more basic aspect of phonological processing might not be at the root of both the phonological store and nonsense word repetition. Tallal et al.'s (1985) hypothesis of detection of rapid transitions presents one candidate. Both this measure and nonword repetition were used by Bishop, North, and Donlan (1995) in a study of the genetic contributors to language development. They studied pairs of identical and nonidentical twins, selected such that one of the pair had been identified as having delayed language development. They found a clear association between nonsense word repetition and language that appeared to be strongly heritable, whereas they found a much less clear genetic link with impaired detection of rapid auditory transitions.

Is the phonological loop important only for vocabulary acquisition? Although the evidence is less extensive, it also appears to contribute to syntactic development (Baddeley, Gathercole, & Papagno, 1998), presumably because this also depends on the capacity to hold sequences of speech sounds during the learning process.

As mentioned previously, the phonological loop appears to contribute to the development of reading skills, probably in a number of different ways, ranging from learning letter–sound correspondences, through sound blending, possibly up to the level of text comprehension (see Chapters 2 and 3 of this book for detailed discussion of these issues). It is important to emphasize, however, that for none of these functions is it likely that poor phonological loop capacity is the sole determining factor. Limited phonological loop capacity may, therefore, be compensated by strengths in other capacities.

In conclusion, the simple concept of a phonological store, together with a subvocal articulatory system, would seem to give a good account, not only of normal functioning within the laboratory, but also of a range of neuropsychological and developmental deficits. Evidence suggests that the system is involved in both native language acquisition and second language learning in children and adults. Although the evidence is less strong, the phonological loop appears to contribute to the acquisition of grammar and to the early stages of reading (Baddeley et al., 1998).

The Visuo-Spatial Sketchpad

The visuo-spatial sketchpad is a system that parallels the phonological loop but has proved less easy to study; we do not have a rich and standardized set of stimuli such as those provided by language, nor have robust phenomena such as the phonological similarity and word-length effects been identified. It seems likely that the system will play an important role in the acquisition of our visual and spatial knowledge of the world: What color is a banana? How does a bicycle work? How do you play a DVD? How can I find my way around my hometown? Whereas we have many tests of language at the levels of phonology, individual word meaning, and text comprehension, we appear to lack well-developed measures of visuo-spatial world knowledge.

There are, however, compensating features to the study of visuo-spatial WM. First, it can be studied in animals, allowing detailed examination of memory at the single-cell level by investigators such as Patricia Goldman-Rakic (1988), who has used single-cell recording in awake monkeys to investigate the anatomic basis of their visual WM. We also know a great deal about vision and visual attention, and these fields are beginning to encompass the study of visual WM. For example, Luck, and Vogel (1997) report that immediate memory is limited to four objects, but they also find that within each object, subjects can encode multiple dimensions, with little attentional cost. However, when the various visual features are bound together to form integrated objects rather than bundles of separate features, their retention over time may depend on the attentional resources that are available (Wheeler & Treisman, 2002).

Within the multi-component tradition, work had tended to focus on the role of WM in imagery. My own early work stemmed from an experience while on sabbatical leave in California. I became interested in American football and listened to the Stanford—UCLA game on the radio while driving along the freeway. I had a very clear image of the state of the game but noticed with alarm that my steering had become erratic. I switched to music and survived to investigate the phenomenon on my return.

We chose a task that required participants to recall sequences of spoken sentences. Half the time the sentences could be remembered by using an imagery strategy, whereas for the rest of the sequences this was not possible. We did not have access to a driving simulator, so we attempted to interfere with imagery using a pursuit rotor. This requires the participant to keep a stylus in contact with a moving spot of light, with performance measured by time on target. We found that subjects could successfully recall eight sentences using imagery and six using a purely verbal strategy. However, when we required our subjects to combine memory with tracking, the imagery condition was dramatically impaired and the verbal condition was unaffected (Baddeley, Grant, Wight, & Thomson, 1975). We went on to demonstrate that the *spatial* component of the tracking task, rather than its *visual* aspect, was crucial. To produce a spatial but nonvisual task, subjects were blindfolded and required to point to a moving sound source. This disrupted performance on the imagery rather than the verbal task, whereas a visual but nonspatial task involving judging the brightness of a wide field of light tended to show the opposite effect (Baddeley & Lieberman, 1980).

We concluded that the sketchpad was a spatial rather than a visual system. Our conclusion was premature; it was true of the task we had chosen, but it was not true of all tasks involving visual imagery. Robert Logie (1995) required his subjects to learn to associate pairs of objects by imagining them interacting—for example, an elephant driving a tank. He found that imagery led to better recall than verbal rehearsal but that this effect was removed by visual rather than spatial activity—for instance, by observing a series of pictures or even color patches. Subsequent work by Quinn and McConnell (1996) showed that this visual rather than spatial type of imagery may be disrupted by stimuli as simple as a pattern of flickering dots. This result has certainly been replicated, but it is still not entirely clear what process or mechanism is specifically targeted by the flickering visual noise field (Andrade, Kemps, Weriner, May, & Szmalec, 2002).

The distinction between the visual and spatial aspects of the sketchpad is reflected in performance on two simple psychological tasks. The first of these, the so-called Corsi blocks task (Milner, 1971), involves presenting the subject with an array of nine cubes arranged at quasi-random locations on a board placed between the tester and the participant. The tester begins by tapping two of the blocks in sequence and then asking the participant to imitate the sequence. The sequence of blocks gradually increases to a point at which performance breaks down. This length is the Corsi span; in adults it is usually about five, roughly two less than span for digits.

A simple test of visual, rather than spatial, STM is provided by pattern span (Della Sala, Gray, Baddeley, Allamano, & Wilson, 1999). In this, the participant is initially presented with a 2 × 2 matrix, with two of the four cells filled. After 3 seconds this is removed from view and the participant is asked to respond by indicating which cells were filled in the stimulus matrix, using an empty 2 × 2 matrix. The size of the matrix is increased by two cells every three trials, with half of the cells of each matrix being randomly filled. Pattern span is determined by the maximum number of cells that the participant can accurately recall, usually about 14–16 in a normal adult. Della Sala et al. (1999) have contrasted the Corsi blocks and pattern span tasks, showing that Corsi span is more disrupted by the requirement to perform a spatial task between presentation and recall than when a visual task is interposed. Exactly the opposite occurs in the case of pattern span. Della Sala et al. also identified and reported individual neuropsychological patients showing contrasting deficits—in one case a deficit in Corsi but not pattern span, whereas the other showed the reverse pattern. Although there is growing agreement on the need to fractionate the sketchpad, there is less unanimity on how to characterize this difference. I have drawn a distinction between visual and spatial (see also Logie, 1995), whereas others such as Pickering, Gathercole, Hall, and Lloyd (2001) suggest that the crucial difference may be between *dynamic* (rather than spatial) and *static* (rather than pattern) aspects of visual WM. Yet other studies suggest the possibility of a third kinesthetic or motor dimension (Smyth & Scholey, 1996; Smyth & Pendleton, 1990). A review of the cognitive fractionation of visuo-spatial WM is provided by Pickering (2001a).

A further possible characterization is proposed by Jonides, Smith, and colleagues (e.g., Smith, Jonides, & Koeppe, 1996) who make the distinction between memory for *objects* (visual) and *location* (spatial), relating their findings to earlier neuroanatomical work on monkeys carried out by Mishkin, Ungerleider, and Macko (1983), who find separate visual processing pathways for *what* and *where* information. Jonides et al. (1993) use functional magnetic resonance imaging (fMRI) to study the pattern of activity within the brain during visuo-spatial memory tasks. A typical experiment might involve showing a participant an array of marked locations on an open visual field, followed after a delay by a circle (Jonides et al., 1993). The participant's task is to decide whether the circle coincides with one of the locations presented. The anatomical pattern of activation observed is somewhat more complex than the pattern of activation associated with the phonological loop. It involves areas within the occipital lobe (usually associated with the earlier stages of vision), the parietal lobe (associated with spatial and motor coding), and the frontal and prefrontal areas (usually regarded as important for executive control). Activation tends to be predominantly in the right hemisphere, unlike the loop (Smith et al., 1996).

What function is served by the visuo-spatial sketchpad? The capacity for spatial visualization has, of course, been studied psychometrically for many years, using tasks such as block counting, in which a two-dimensional representation of a pile of blocks is presented and the participant is required to work out how many blocks are involved, including those that are occluded from sight. There is evidence to suggest that such spatial processing tasks are able to predict likely success in occupations such as architecture or engineering and may be related to other more everyday activities, such as learning one's way around a new town (Mackintosh, 1998). Within the WM tradition, people have begun to explore the creative use of imagery (e.g., Pearson, 2001), often using tasks in which participants need to manipulate basic shapes such as circles, triangles, or letter D shapes so as to create novel representations, which then must be demonstrated to the tester.

Application to educational issues is still at a relatively early stage. However, a promising start has been made in studying the development of visuo-spatial WM (see Pickering, 2001b, for a review).

The Central Executive

The central executive is the most important, complex, but least understood component of WM. For the first few years, we concentrated almost entirely on the loop and sketchpad, on the grounds that these presented more tractable problems than the central executive. We treated the executive as if it were simply a pool of general processing capacity that could perform virtually any function. In short, we treated it as if it were a homunculus, a little person who ran things and whose activity could be used to explain all the issues that lay beyond the limits of the two subsystems. I regard this as a defensible, indeed sensible, strategy, provided one realizes that the homunculus does not provide an explanation but simply marks the existence of a whole range of further questions. Provided one them attempts to tackle these questions, one can hopefully remove the homunculus' jobs one by one until they eventually can be made redundant. We still have a long way to go with this process, but we have made a start.

I began (Baddeley, 1986) by adopting a model of attentional control first proposed by Norman and Shallice (1986). This proposes that action is controlled at two levels. The first of these depends on highly overlearned habits controlled by well-established routines or schemata, which are triggered virtually automatically by environmental stimuli. Driving your car along a familiar route would be an example. We need, however, to have a way of coping with nonroutine occurrences such as finding our way to an unfamiliar part of town or deciding what action to take on meeting a traffic jam. Norman and Shallice (1986) propose that this aspect of control depends on a second component, the *supervisory attentional system* (*SAS*), which is capable of intervening, modulating habits, and creating novel solutions.

Norman's interest in the model stemmed from a concern to understand slips of action. He explains these in terms of failure to adequately monitor and modify habitual patterns—for example, when we set off to the supermarket on a Saturday morning but find ourselves absent-mindedly driving to work. Shallice's concern was more for the application of the model neuropsychologically. He proposed that patients with bilateral damage to the frontal lobes were exhibiting impairment in functioning of the SAS, resulting in failure to control action. Hence, such a patient might tend to perseverate excessively, either in terms of actions or speech. One such patient—for example (Baddeley & Wilson, 1988), describing the accident leading to his brain damage (which he could almost certainly not actually remember)—got into a perseverative loop whereby he described apologizing to the driver of the lorry he crashed into, who in turn apologized to him, who apologized to the driver, who again apologized, and so on. Paradoxically, the same patients may show what appears to be the opposite of perseveration, extreme distractibility, with attention being captured by whatever stimuli occur (Shallice, 1988). Such stimulus-dependent behavior sometimes may result in *utilization* behavior. This involves responding to available objects by using them, however inappropriately. Examples range from simply drinking someone else's coffee to responding to the sight of a hypodermic needle by injecting the doctor. Shallice (1988) argues that each of these represents a failure of the SAS to control action.

The simple distinction between control by habit and by a limited-capacity attentional system has continued to be a useful one, giving a good account of some very interesting recent developments in social psychology. The control of behavior by habits and schemata is well illustrated by the work of John Bargh and his colleagues, who take what they describe as a determinist view of social behavior, emphasizing the extent to which it is controlled implicitly by attitudes and habits that are environmentally cued, often without our being aware of them (Bargh & Ferguson, 2000). A good example is that of social imitation, as when flocks of birds or shoals of fish respond to each others' movement in such a way as to make it appear as if the flock or shoal is a single entity. At the human level, unconscious imitation may frequently be observed in social interaction, when two people conversing adopt the same body posture—for example, by both folding their arms. In one experiment, a participant was asked to perform a joint task with a confederate of the experimenter, who was instructed to adopt a series of predetermined bodily actions, such as stroking the chin. Videos of the participant were then studied by independent judges. They observed significantly more imitative chin stroking in the experimental group that in control participants. In another study, the confederate intentionally imitated the posture of the participant while performing a joint task. When participants were later asked to evaluate the confederate, those who had imitated the participant were judged more positively than those who had not (Chartrand & Bargh, 1999).

Other experiments have used an implicit priming procedure, in which attitudes or goals are activated by requiring subjects to process apparently unrelated material—for example, putting together scrambled words to make sentences, where the words might or might not prime a particular action. It was somewhat surprising that working with words that are related to age, such as *grey*, *wrinkled*, and *forgetful*, significantly increased the time taken by participants to walk from the experimental room to the elevator after the experiment, when compared to participants who had manipulated neutral words (Bargh, Chen, & Burrows, 1996). In another series of experiments, participants were primed with words that were either striving and aggressive or peaceful and cooperative before going on to what appeared to be another experiment. This involved a computer-based game in which the participant was responsible for one of a number of companies fishing in a lake with limited fish stocks. Those primed with aggressive words were more likely to adopt a competitive rather than a cooperative strategy (Chartrand & Bargh, 2002).

Bargh and Ferguson (2000) offer what at first sight appears to be a hard-line determinist interpretation of their data, arguing that most, if not all, human behavior is the result of unseen stimuli implicitly activating automatic habits and attitudes. However, Bargh (personal communication, 2005) emphasizes that he does not wish to present the view that behavior is, for example, predetermined, but simply to assert that it is explicable in terms of its precursors in just the same way as physical phenomena are in principle explicable. If we accept this point, as I assume the majority of scientists will, then the question becomes one of the relative contribution of such habitual influences compared with actions determined by reflective and conscious processes. Within Shallice's model, this becomes a question of balance between actions based on schemata and those reflecting the SAS, or—within a WM framework—the central executive.

Bargh is an ingenious experimenter who has proved himself capable of setting up experimental paradigms in which quite different behavior can be induced without the conscious awareness of his participants. Just how typical such situations are, however, remains an entirely open question. My own view is that action is usually determined at multiple levels operating simultaneously. Driving a car, for example, involves scanning the road ahead while interpreting a red light as a stop signal, maintaining a safe distance from the car in front, and possibly chatting to a passenger at the same time. Meanwhile, actions of the hands will steer the car and, where appropriate, change gear. Other essential bodily actions are also occurring; some, such as breathing, are automatic but potentially under direct control, whereas others, such as the beating of the heart, are usually not. Thus most control while driving is likely to be delegated to lower levels of control, while the central executive is probably attending to something else, such as a conversation or making plans for the weekend ahead. The executive needs, of course, to be able to switch immediately to deal with any emergency.

So what has social psychology to say about the central executive or SAS? Work by Baumeister and colleagues is of particular relevance here. Baumeister is interested in the self and in self-control (Baumeister, Bratslavsky, Muraven, & Tice, 1998; Baumeister & Heatherton, 1996). He accepts that much of behavior is habitual but emphasizes the crucial importance of the capacity to override habits. He uses the analogy of a car, suggesting that for almost 95% of the time cars go straight ahead, but a car that is not capable of turning is not likely to be a very successful one. Baumeister uses a range of different methods to study self-control. He has, for example, developed a brief questionnaire in which respondents are asked about such characteristics as their capacity to pursue goals with persistence or to resist petty temptations. Preliminary studies using the questionnaire have shown it to be highly related to a number of real-world indicators, ranging from proneness to excessive drinking, through to level of grade point averages in students. Baumeister stresses the strong link between his self-control measure and important aspects of lifestyle and life satisfaction, finding that other potential predictors such as measures of self-esteem appear to show a much weaker correlation with the capacity to cope (Baumeister, Campbell, Krueger, & Vohs, 2003).

It is suggested that self-control demands effort, and the source of this effort can be depleted through use, as muscle can become fatigued. Baumeister and colleagues have carried out a number of studies that tend to support this view. In one experiment, participants were shown videos that would be likely to evoke strong positive and negative emotions in the viewer (Muraven & Baumeister, 2000). One group of participants was instructed to inhibit such emotions, whereas a second was free to express them. This was followed by an apparently unrelated experiment conducted by another experimenter, in which participants had to persevere in attempting to solve anagrams that were, in fact, insoluble. Those who had inhibited their emotions gave up significantly more rapidly. Muraven and Baumeister (2000) cite other work indicating that resisting a stressor such as excessive crowding, intermittent loud bangs, or bad smells, results in reduced perseverance on subsequent unrelated tasks, as if the capacity for self-control had been depleted. Although it is hard to be certain that other variables, such as disenchantment with psychologists in general, may not play a part in these findings, nevertheless they do open up a very important practical aspect of understanding the processes of executive control.

Fractionating the Executive

Faced with the issue of how to make progress in pensioning off the homunculus, I decided to try to fractionate it, splitting off a number of components, which I felt we might then be able to study more easily. I began (Baddeley, 1996) by postulating a number of features that I assumed would be likely to be necessary for virtually any executive control system. These features included the capacity to focus attention, to divide it, to switch it, and to link WM with LTM. Most of the studies we had carried out up to that point involved the capacity to focus attention, so we extended our range to study the division of attention, in particular focusing on a specific patient group—those suffering from Alzheimer's disease (AD). My colleagues and I were successful in showing that, whereas normal aging had little impact on the capacity to divide attention *per se*, this ability was clearly impaired by AD, a result that could not be simply attributed to the greater difficulty of the task-sharing condition (Baddeley, Baddeley, Bucks, & Wilcock, 2001). Attempts within the dual-task paradigm to study attention switching gave some support to the possibility that this might be a separate function but somewhat unexpectedly also emphasized the role of the phonological loop as a useful verbally based control mechanism (Baddeley, Chincotta, & Adlam, 2001). Our results were thus consistent with the emphasis by Luria (1968) and Vygotsky (1962) on the use of language to control and direct behavior. Finally, the attempt to study the relation between WM and LTM proved particularly productive in causing the three-component WM model to be modified by the introduction of a fourth subsystem, the *episodic buffer*, as will be described later in this chapter.

Anatomically, there is general acceptance of the importance of the frontal lobes in the executive control of behavior. Such evidence initially came from patients with frontal-lobe lesions (Shallice, 1988) but has more recently been supplemented by neuroimaging studies. There is extensive evidence of the involvement of the frontal lobes in many executive processes, including control and rehearsal within the phonological loop, and the encoding of information into long-term memory, both of which tend to involve left frontal areas (Henson, 2001; Owen, 1997). Retrieval or monitoring of retrieval, or both, however, appear to have more of a right frontal focus (Tulving, Kapur, Craik, Moscovitch, & Houle, 1994). The ventral part of the right frontal area also appears to be involved in more emotional and motivational aspects of control (Tranel, 2002). Some rather basic issues, however, remain undecided, with Shallice arguing for potentially separable anatomic locations for each of a wide range of executive functions, whereas Duncan and Miller (2002) emphasize the extent to which many apparently very different executive functions appear to depend on the same right frontal area. I am sure that neuroimaging will, in due course, play an important role in helping us understand executive control, but I doubt that we have yet reached a point at which unequivocal conclusions can be drawn.

Individual Differences in Working Memory

Probably the most active area of behavioral research on the executive aspects of WM has stemmed from studies based on individual differences in the capacity to combine the storage and processing of information. A classic study by Daneman and Carpenter (1980) required participants to read aloud a series of sentences and then recall the last word of each. An example might be as follows:

> It was a terrible winter and everyone died except for a single dog.
> The economy improved, and more and more people were able to take longer and longer holidays.
> The sailor who brought the parrot home found it irritated his wife, and he eventually sold the bird.

The participant should then recall *dog, holidays, bird*. WM span is determined by the number of sentences that can be successfully processed and their final words recalled (usually between two and five). Daneman and Carpenter showed that this span correlated quite highly with the capacity of their university student participants to comprehend prose passages. Other studies have shown that it is not essential to use prose material; Turner and Engle (1989) developed a broadly equivalent measure, operation span, in which the sentences were replaced by arithmetic calculations, again followed by words that had to be recalled.

This original finding has been replicated many times (Daneman & Merikle, 1996), and it has proved successful in predicting a wide range of real-world cognitive skills from reading to learning a computer language and from spelling to playing bridge (Engle, 2001). Kyllonen and Christal (1990) found a close association between performance on a battery of such WM tasks and performance on reasoning tasks of the type conventionally used to measure intelligence. It will come as no surprise therefore to find that variants of the Daneman and Carpenter task have been used with some considerable success within an educational context, as described in a number of the chapters of this book.

Although there is no doubt about the practical usefulness of WM span, it is still far from clear exactly what it is measuring and how. In recent years, a number of groups have attempted to tackle this question, in studies that are implicitly concerned with fractionating WM, and as such are complementary to the approaches already described.

One difficulty in attempting to pick apart the contributing factors to performance on a complex task such as WM span lies in the problem of collinearity. A participant who is strong in one component may often be strong on others, leading to high levels of intercorrelation and making the influence of each difficult to tease apart. A common method of analysis is to perform a stepwise regression, whereby the various candidate test measures contributing to performance on a given task (such as prose comprehension) can be compared, leading to the identification of which measure is the best unique predictor, followed by the next best, and so on. A low correlation between a given test and the criterion measure (e.g., comprehension) *could* mean that the test is sampling a capacity that is only weakly related to comprehension. However, it may be that the correlation is low simply because the measure of a crucial capacity is unreliable. Executive tests tend to be inherently unreliable because they attempt to tap processes that have evolved to cope with novel situations. Usually, reliability is achieved by repeating the measure in question, preferably many times, making most tests an aggregation of many items. However, if the same executive task is used repeatedly, it is likely to become increasingly automatic and hence less and less dependent on executive processing. Thus, attempts to make an executive test more stable and reliable will tend to make it less valid as a measure of the ability to deal with novel problems (Rabbitt, 1997).

A number of ingenious statistical techniques have been applied to this problem, of which the most promising would currently appear to be latent variable analysis. This involves starting with a hypothesis as to what underlying processes might reasonably be expected to be important. Several separate measures of each process are then devised, resulting in a battery of tests. A large sample of participants is then tested, and a confirmatory factor analysis is used to check that the expected clustering of tests into separable subgroups does indeed occur. The next step is to abstract the common component from these clusters, using that to build a statistical model of the way that the various components are interrelated. This method has the advantage of allowing existing knowledge to guide subsequent research in a way that is relatively robust to problems of unreliability in the individual measures because it is the common core that is abstracted and used.

These and related measures have been applied by a range of groups (e.g., Engle, Tuholski, Laughlin, & Conway, 1999; Hitch, Towse, & Hutton, 2001; Kane, Bleckley, Conway, & Engle, 2001; Miyake, 2001; Miyake, Friedman, Rettinger, Shah, & Hegerty, 2001). Their results first of all appear to confirm the broad structure of WM as comprising an executive controller and two systems involved in temporary storage, one principally verbal and the other visuo-spatial. Work is now going ahead on attempting to use this approach to fractionate the executive. Friedman and Miyake (2004), for example, have examined the hypothesis that the principal method of executive control is through the process of inhibition (Engle, 1996). The concept of inhibition is widely used but measured in a number of different ways. Friedman and Miyake found that tests of inhibition that attempt to measure the capacity to prevent an inappropriate but habitual response, such as occurs in the Stroop task, correlate highly with inhibitory measures based on the ability to persevere against distraction, whereas both differ from susceptibility to retroactive interference (an inhibitory process in the memory domain reflecting competition between wanted memory and competing memory traces). It is still too early to know whether these findings will replicate across laboratories and whether their initial appearance of mapping onto findings with other materials will persist. The future of this approach, however, does seem promising.

The Episodic Buffer

All the work described so far can be seen as fitting broadly within the original three-component Baddeley and Hitch model. However, over the years, a number of phenomena have emerged that do not fit the pattern, at least if one assumes, as did Baddeley and Logie (1999), that the executive is purely an attentional system with no storage function. This attentional assumption was made for reasons of theoretical parsimony because it was felt that otherwise the WM system was just too flexible to generate testable hypotheses. It did, however, lead to difficulties, which were brought to a head by a study of a very pure but densely amnesic patient, KJ, who despite his amnesia was able to recall most of a complex paragraph comprising more than 25 idea units. This was clearly well beyond the capacity of either the phonological loop or the visuo-spatial sketchpad. It did not appear to reflect LTM, in that after a brief delay, his performance dropped to zero. How was he holding the material?

A study of immediate and delayed prose recall in a range of patients with amnesia indicated that only a small subsample were able to do relatively well on immediate prose recall (Baddeley & Wilson, 2002). What characterized these patients was a high level of preserved intelligence, good executive processes, or both. We suggested that comprehending a prose passage might involve creating and elaborating a representation of the content in long-term memory, much in the way that Kintsch and van Dyck (1977) have suggested. In the case of normal participants, the structure will be held together by LTM, but in the absence of this, executive processes are required to maintain it, which in turn demands constant attention. Once attention is withdrawn, forgetting rapidly ensues. Such unexpectedly preserved capacities are not limited to prose recall. Tulving (personal communication, 1999) describes an extremely densely amnesic patient who retains the capacity to play bridge. When invited by Tulving to do so, he not only proved capable of remembering the trump suit and which cards had gone but played so sufficiently well as to win the rubber!

Our puzzle as to how to fit this into the existing model also applies some less striking but perhaps more important aspects of normal remembering. For example, memory span for unrelated words is about 5, compared to 15 words for sentences (Brener, 1940). This is usually explained in terms of Miller's (1956) concept of chunking, whereby LTM is used to bind together clusters of items, with span being set by number of chunks rather than number of items. In the case of sentences, each chunk is likely to comprise several words. We are, however, left with the question: Where are these chunks held within the WM model?

We have emphasized the problem of interfacing WM and LTM, but the model has similar problems in specifying how the phonological and visuo-spatial subsystems might interact. Although memory for letters is primarily dependent on phonological coding, under certain circumstances, evidence of visual coding of a virtually presented letter sequence also occurs (e.g., Logie, Della Sala, Wynn, & Baddeley, 2000). This seems to imply some form of common code that combines the two, but the three-component model has no way of achieving this, given that the executive is no longer assumed to have storage capacity.

To account for these and a range of other related problems, a fourth component was proposed, namely the episodic buffer (Baddeley, 2000). The episodic buffer is assumed to be a temporary storage system that uses a multi-dimensional code to create integrated representations based on information from perception, the subsystems of WM, and LTM. It is episodic in the sense of holding together integrated episodes, and it is a buffer in the sense of a limited capacity system that provides the interface between inputs having a range of different codes. It is, furthermore, assumed to be dependent on the central executive for control and, finally, to allow retrieval through conscious awareness. Its role in the current model of WM can be seen in Figure 1.3. At present, access from the subsystems is assumed to

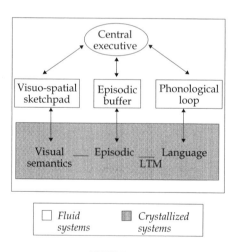

FIGURE 1.3

The current multi-component model of working memory. In addition to the three components proposed by Baddeley and Hitch, its links with long-term memory are specified, and a new component, the episodic buffer, is added. This is assumed to coordinate information from the various subsystems and to be the basis of conscious awareness.

come through the executive. We intend to investigate this and other assumptions and may modify the model in due course.

The episodic buffer is assumed to be a temporary representation accessible to conscious awareness. Rather than simply reflecting activated LTM, it is thought to play a constructive role in binding information together in chunks. Together with the central executive, it is believed to play an important role in measures of WM span. As such, it brings the Baddeley and Hitch model more in line with a range of alternative models that have tended to focus on executive processes, rather than on the subsystems, but does so without abandoning the general model that has proved so fruitful in those areas. Its ultimate success, however, is likely to depend on its capacity to generate practical ideas and new knowledge.

In the meantime, the episodic buffer serves the valuable function of moving the study of multi-component WM beyond the stage of fractionation and isolation of components, on to the question of how the components work together and link into long-term memory. A better understanding of this system should enable us to identify and help children with limitations in one or more components of their WM and may help people optimize the way they acquire new information and use it productively.

Summary Box

- Human memory comprises an alliance of separable systems.
- Working memory is one of these, providing the temporary storage that underpins our capacity for complex thought. It may be divided into the following:
  - The phonological loop, a system for holding and manipulating sound and speech
  - The visuo–spatial sketchpad, which performs a similar role for non-verbal material
  - The central executive, an attentional control system that selects and operates strategies
- Individuals differ in the capacity of their various working memory sub-systems in ways that influence scholastic achievement.
- In recent years an additional component of the episodic buffer has been proposed.
- This is assumed to link the component of working memory with long-term memory and to be the basis of conscious awareness.

References

Andrade, J. (1995). Learning during anaesthesia: A review. *British Journal of Psychology, 86*(4), 479–506.

Andrade, J. (2001). *Working Memory in Perspective*. Hove: Psychology Press.

Andrade, J., Kemps, E., Wernier, Y., May, J., & Szmalec, A. (2002). Insensitivity of visual short-term memory to irrelevant visual information. *Quarterly Journal of Experimental Psychology, 55*, 753–774.

Atkinson, R. C., & Shiffrin, R. M. (1968). Human memory: A proposed system and its control processes. In K. W. Spence (Ed.), *The psychology of learning and motivation: Advances in research and theory. Vol. 2* (pp. 89–195). New York: Academic Press.

Baddeley, A. D. (1966a). Short-term memory for word sequences as a function of acoustic, semantic and formal similarity. *Quarterly Journal of Experimental Psychology, 18*, 362–365.

Baddeley, A. D. (1966b). The influence of acoustic and semantic similarity on long-term memory for word sequences. *Quarterly Journal of Experimental Psychology, 18*, 302–309.

Baddeley, A. D. (1978). The trouble with levels: A re-examination of Craik and Lockhart framework for memory research. *Psychological Review, 85*, 139–152.

Baddeley, A. D. (1986). *Working Memory*. Oxford: Oxford University Press.

Baddeley, A. D. (1996). Exploring the central executive. *Quarterly Journal of Experimental Psychology, 49A*(1), 5–28.

Baddeley, A. D. (1997). *Human memory: Theory and Practice* (2nd ed.). Hove, Sussex: Psychology Press.

Baddeley, A. D. (2000). The episodic buffer: A new component of working memory? *Trends in Cognitive Sciences, 4*(11), 417–423.

Baddeley, A. D., & Andrade, J. (1994). Reversing the word-length effect: A comment on Kaplan, Rochon and Waters. *Quarterly Journal of Experimental Psychology, 47A*, 1047–1054.

Baddeley, A. D., Baddeley, H. A., Bucks, R. S., & Wilcock, G. K. (2001). Attentional control in Alzheimer's disease. *Brain, 124*, 1492–1508.

Baddeley, A. D., Chincotta, D., & Adlam, A. (2001). Working memory and the control of action: Evidence from task switching. *Journal of Experimental Psychology: General, 130*, 641–657.

Baddeley, A. D., Chincotta, D., Stafford, L., & Turk, D. (2002). Is the word length effect in STM entirely attributable to output delay? Evidence from serial recognition. *Quarterly Journal of Experimental Psychology, 55A*, 353–369.

Baddeley, A. D., Gathercole, S. E., & Papagno, C. (1998). The phonological loop as a language learning device. *Psychological Review, 105*(1), 158–173.

Baddeley, A. D., Grant, S., Wight, E., & Thomson, N. (1975). Imagery and visual working memory. In R. Dornic (Ed.), *Attention and performance. Vol. V*, pp. 205–217. Hillsdale, NJ: Lawrence Erlbaum Associates.

Baddeley, A. D., & Hitch, G. J. (1974). Working memory. In G. A. Bower (Ed.), *Recent advances in learning and motivation. Vol. 8*, (pp. 47–89). New York: Academic Press.

Baddeley, A. D., & Lieberman, K. (1980). Spatial working memory. In R. S. Nickerson (Ed.), *Attention and performance. Vol VIII.* (pp. 521–539). Hillsdale, NJ: Lawrence Erlbaum Associates.

Baddeley, A. D., & Logie, R. H. (1999). Working memory: The multiple component model. In A. Miyake & P. Shah (Eds.), *Models of working memory: mechanisms of active maintenance and executive control.* (pp. 28–61). Cambridge: Cambridge University Press.

Baddeley, A. D., Papagno, C., & Vallar, G. (1988). When long-term learning depends on short-term storage. *Journal of Memory and Language, 27*, 586–595.

Baddeley, A. D., Thomson, N., & Buchanan, M. (1975). Word length and the structure of short-term memory. *Journal of Verbal Learning and Verbal Behaviour, 14*, 575–589.

Baddeley, A. D., & Warrington, E. K. (1970). Amnesia and the distinction between long- and short-term memory. *Journal of Verbal Learning and Verbal Behavior, 9*, 176–189.

Baddeley, A. D., & Wilson, B. (1988). Frontal amnesia and the dysexecutive syndrome. *Brain & Cognition, 7*(2), 212–230.

Baddeley, A. D., & Wilson, B. A. (2002). Prose recall and amnesia: Implications for the structure of working memory. *Neuropsychologia, 40*, 1737–1743.

Bargh, J. A. (2005). Bypassing the will: toward demistifying the non-conscious control of social behaviour. In R. R. Hassin, J. S. Uleman, & J. A. Bargh (Eds.), *The new unconscious.* (pp. 37–58). Oxford: Oxford University Press.

Bargh, J. A., Chen, M., & Burrows, L. (1996). Automaticity of social behaviour: Effects of trait construct and stereotype priming on action. *Journal of Personality and Social Psychology, 71*, 233–244.

Bargh, J. A., & Ferguson, M. J. (2000). Beyond behaviorism: On the automaticity of higher mental processes. *Psychological Bulletin, 126*(6), 925–945.

Basso, A. H., Spinnler, G., Vallar, G., & Zanobia, E. (1982). Left hemisphere damage and selective impairment of auditory verbal short-term memory: A case study. *Neuropsychologica, 20*, 274.

Baumeister, R. F., Bratslavsky, E., Muraven, M., & Tice, D. M. (1998). Ego-depletion: Is the active self a limited resource? *Journal of Personality and Social Psychology, 74*, 1252–1265.

Baumeister, R. F., Campbell, J. D., Krueger, J. L., & Vohs, K. D. (2003). Does high self-esteem cause better performance, interpersonal success, happiness, or healthier lifestyles? *Psychological Science in Public Interest, 4*(1).

Baumeister, R. F., & Heatherton, T. F. (1996). Self-regulation failure: An overview. *Psychological Enquiry, 7*, 1–15.

Beaton, A. A. (2004). *Dyslexia, reading and the brain.* Hove: Psychology Press.

Bishop, D. V. M., North, T., & Donlan, C. (1995). Genetic basis of specific language impairment: Evidence from a twin study. *Developmental Medicine and Child Neurology, 37*, 56–71.

Bransford, J. D. (1979). *Human cognition: learning, understanding and remembering.* Belmont, CA: Wadsworth Publishing Company.

Brener, R. (1940). An experimental investigation of memory span. *Journal of Educational Psychology, 26*, 467–483.

Brown, G. D. A., & Hulme, C. (1995). Modelling item length effects in memory span: No rehearsal needed? *Journal of Memory and Language, 34*, 594–621.

Brown, J. (1958). Some tests of the decay theory of immediate memory. *Quarterly Journal of Experimental Psychology, 10*, 12–21.

Burgess, N., & Hitch, G. J. (1999). Memory for serial order: A network model of the phonological loop and its timing. *Psychological Review, 106*, 551–581.

Caplan, D., Rochon, E., & Waters, G. S. (1992). Articulatory and phonological determinants of word-length effects in span tasks. *Quarterly Journal of Experimental Psychology, 45A*, 177–192.

Chartrand, T. L., & Bargh, J. A. (1999). The chameleon effect: The perception-behavior link and social interaction. *Journal of Personality and Social Psychology, 76*, 893–910.

Chartrand, T. L., & Bargh, J. A. (2002). Non-conscious motivations: Their activation, operation and consequences. In A. Tesser, D. A. Stapel, & J. V. Wood (Eds.), *Self and motivation: Emerging psychological perspectives.* (pp. 13–41). Washington, DC: American Psychological Association.

Conrad, R. (1964). Acoustic confusion in immediate memory. *British Journal of Psychology, 55*, 75–84.

Conrad, R., & Hull, A. J. (1964). Information, acoustic confusion and memory span. *British Journal of Psychology, 55*, 429–432.

Cowan, N., Baddeley, A. D., Elliott, E. M., & Norris, J. (2003). List composition and the word length effect in immediate recall: a comparison of localist and globalist assumptions. *Psychonomic Bulletin & Review, 10*(1), 74–79.

Cowan, N., Day, L., Saults, J. S., Keller, T. A., Johnson, T., & Flores, L. (1992). The role of verbal output time and the effects of word-length on immediate memory. *Journal of Memory and Language, 31*, 1–17.

Craik, F. I. M. (2002). Levels of processing: Past, present . . . and future? *Memory, 10*, 305–318.

Craik, F. I. M., & Lockhart, R. S. (1972). Levels of processing: A framework for memory research. *Journal of Verbal Learning and Verbal Behavior, 11*, 671–684.

Daneman, M., & Carpenter, P. A. (1980). Individual differences in working memory and reading. *Journal of Verbal Learning and Verbal Behaviour, 19*, 450–466.

Daneman, M., & Merikle, P. M. (1996). Working memory and language comprehension: A meta-analysis. *Psychonomic Bulletin & Review, 3*, 422–433.

Della Sala, S., Gray, C., Baddeley, A., Allamano, N., & Wilson, L. (1999). Pattern span: A means of unwelding visuo-spatial memory. *Neuropsychologia, 37*, 1189–1199.

Dosher, B. A., & Ma, J. J. (1998). Output loss or rehearsal loop? Output-time versus pronunciation-time limits in immediate recall for forgetting-matched materials. *Journal of Experimental Psychology: Learning, 24*(2), 316–335.

Duncan, J., & Miller, E. K. (2002). Cognitive focus through adaptive neural coding in the primate prefrontal cortex. In D. T. Stuss & R. Knight (Eds.), *Principles of frontal lobe function.* (pp. 278–291). Oxford: Oxford University Press.

Dunn, L. M., & Dunn, L. M. (1982). *British Picture Vocabulary Scale.* Windsor: NFER-Nelson.

Engle, R. W. (1996). Working memory and retrieval: An inhibition-resource approach. In J. T. E. Richardson, et al. (Eds.), *Working memory and human cognition.* New York: Oxford University Press, pp. 89–119.

Engle, R. W. (2001). What is working memory capacity? In H. L. Roediger, J. S. Nairne, I. Neath, & A. M. Surprenant (Eds.), *The nature of remembering: Essays in honor of Robert G. Crowder.* (pp. 297–314). Washington, DC: American Psychological Association.

Engle, R. W., Tuholski, S. W., Laughlin, J. E., & Conway, A. R. A. (1999). Working memory, short-term memory, and general fluid intelligence: A latent variable approach. *Journal of Experimental Psychology: General, 128*, 309–331.

Friedman, N. P., & Miyake, A. (2004). The relations among inhibition and interference control functions: A latent variable analysis. *Journal of Experimental Psychology: General* (133), 101–135.

Gathercole, S. E. (1995). Is nonword repetition a test of phonological memory or long-term knowledge? It all depends on the nonwords. *Memory and Cognition, 23*, 83–94.

Gathercole, S. E., & Adams, A. M. (1994). Children's phonological working memory: Contributions of long-term knowledge and rehearsal. *Journal of Memory & Language, 33*, 672–788.

Gathercole, S. E., & Baddeley, A. D. (1989). Evaluation of the role of phonological STM in the development of vocabulary in children: A longitudinal study. *Journal of Memory & Language, 28*, 200–213.

Gathercole, S. E., & Baddeley, A. D. (1990). Phonological memory deficits in language-disordered children: Is there a causal connection? *Journal of Memory and Language, 29*, 336–360.

Gathercole, S. E., & Baddeley, A. D. (1996). *The children's test of nonword repetition.* London: Psychological Corporation UK.

Gathercole, S. E., Frankish, C. R., Pickering, S. J., & Peaker, S. M. (1999). Phonotactic influences on short-term memory. *Journal of Experimental Psychology: Learning, Memory & Cognition, 25*, 84–95.

Gathercole, S. E., Willis, C. S., & Baddeley, A. D. (1991). Differentiating phonological memory and awareness of rhyme: Reading and vocabulary development. *British Journal of Psychology, 82*, 387–406.

Goldman, R., Fristoe, E. M., & Woodcock, R. W. (1974). *Auditory skills test battery.* Circle Pines, MN: American Guidance Service Inc.

Goldman-Rakic, P. W. (1988). Topography of cognition: Parallel distributed networks in primate association cortex. *Annual Review of Neuroscience, 11*, 137–156.

Henson, R. (2001). Neural working memory. In J. Andrade (Ed.), *Working memory in perspective.* (pp. 151–174). Hove: Psychology Press.

Henson, R. N. A. (1998). Short-term memory for serial order: The Start-End Model. *Cognitive Psychology, 36*, 73–137.

Hitch, G. J., & McAuley, E. (1991). Working memory in children with specific arithmetical learning difficulties. *British Journal of Psychology, 82*, 375–386.

Hitch, G. J., Towse, J. N., & Hutton, U. M. Z. (2001). What limits working memory span? Theoretical accounts and applications for scholastic development. *Journal of Educational Psychology: General, 130*(2), 184–198.

Hitch, G. J., Towse, J. N., & Hutton, U. (2001). What limits children's working memory span? Theoretical accounts and applicaions for scholastic development. *Journal of Experimental Psychology: General, 130*, 184–198.

Hoosain, R., & Salili, F. (1987). Language differences in pronunciation speed for numbers, digit span, and mathematical ability. *Psychologia, 30*(1), 34–38.

Jonides, J., Smith, E. E., Koeppe, R. A., Awh, E., Minoshima, S., & Mintun, M. A. (1993). Spatial working memory in humans as revealed by PET. *Nature, 363*, 623–625.

Kane, M. J., Bleckley, M. K., Conway, A. R. A., & Engle, R. W. (2001). A controlled-attention view of working-memory capacity. *Journal of Experimental Psychology: General, 130*(2), 169–183.

Kane, M. J., Bleckley, M. K., Conway, A. R. A., & Engle, R. W. (2001). A controlled-attention view of working-memory capacity. *Journal of Experimental Psychology: General, 130*(2), 169–183.

Kintsch, W., & van Dyck, T. (1971). Toward a model of text comprehension and production. *Psychological Review, 85*, 63–94.

Kyllonen, P. C., & Christal, R. E. (1990). Reasoning ability is (little more than) working memory capacity. *Intelligence, 14*, 389–433.

Logie, R. H. (1995). *Visuo-spatial working memory.* Hove: Lawrence Erlbaum Associates.

Logie, R. H., Della Sala, S., Wynn, V., & Baddeley, A. D. (2000). Visual similarity effects in immediate serial recall. *Quarterly Journal of Experimental Psychology, 53A*(3), 626–646.

Lovatt, P. J., Avons, S. E., & Masterson, J. (2002). Output decay in immediate serial recall: speech time revisited. *Journal of Memory & Language, 46*, 227–243.

Luck, S. J., & Vogel, E. K. (1997). The capacity of visual working memory for features and conjunctions. *Nature, 390*, 279–281.

Luria, A. R. (1968). The directive function of speech in development and dissolution, Parts I & II. In R. C. Oldfield & J. C. Marshall (Eds.), *Penguin modern psychology readings: Language.* Harmondsworth, UK: Penguin Books, pp. 70–82 & 353–366.

Mackintosh, N. J. (1998). *IQ and human intelligence.* Oxford: Oxford University Press.

Melton, A. W. (1963). Implications of short-term memory for a general theory of memory. *Journal of Verbal Learning and Verbal Behavior, 2*, 1.21.

Miller, G. A. (1956). The magical number seven, plus or minus two: Some limits on our capacity for processing information. *Psychological Review, 63*, 81–97.

Milner, B. (1966). Amnesia following operation on the temporal lobes. In C. W. M. Whitty & O. L. Zangwill (Eds.), *Amnesia.* (pp. 109–133). London: Butterworths.

Milner, B. (1971). Interhemispheric differences in the localization of psychological processes in man. *British Medical Bulletin, 27*, 272–277.

Mishkin, M., Ungerleider, L. G., & Macko, K. O. (1983). Object vision and spatial vision: Two cortical pathways. *Trends in Neurosciences, 6*, 414.

Miyake, A. (2001). Individual differences in WM: introduction to the special section. *Journal of Experimental Psychology: General, 130*, 163–168.

Miyake, A., Friedman, N. P., Rettinger, D. A., Shah, P., & Hegarty, P. (2001). How are visuospatial working memory, executive functioning, and spatial abilities related? A latent-variable analysis. *Journal of Experimental Psychology: General, 130*(4), 621–640.

Morais, J., Alegria, J., & Content, A. (1987). The relationship between segmental analysis and alphabetic literacy: An interactive view. *Cahiers de Psychologie Cognitive/Current Psychology of Cognition, 7*, 415–438.

Mueller, S. T., Seymour, T. L., Kieras, D. E., & Meyer, D. E. (2003). Theoretical implications of articulatory duration, phonological similarity, and phonological complexity in verbal working memory. *Journal of Experimental Psychology: Learning, Memory, and Cognition, 29*, 1353–1380.

Muraven, M., & Baumeister, R. F. (2000). Self-regulation and depletion of limited resources: Does self-control resemble a muscle? *Psychological Bulletin, 126*, 247–259.

Murray, D. J. (1965). The effect of white noise upon the recall of vocalized lists. *Canadian Journal of Psychology, 19*, 333–345.

Neath, I., & Nairne, J. S. (1995). Word-length effects in immediate memory: Overwriting trace-decay theory. *Psychonomic Bulletin & Review, 2*, 429–441.

Norman, D. A., & Shallice, T. (1986). Attention to action: Willed and automatic control of behaviour. In R. J. Davidson, G. E. Schwarts, D. Shapiro (Eds.), *Consciousness and self-regulation. Advances in research and theory. Vol. 4* (pp. 1–18). New York: Plenum Press.

Owen, A. M. (1997). The functional organisation of working memory processes within the human lateral frontal cortex: The contribution of functional neuroimaging. *European Journal of Neuroscience, 9*, 1329–1339.

Page, M. P. A., & Norris, D. (1998). The primacy model: A new model of immediate serial recall. *Psychological Review, 105*, 761–781.

Papagno, C., Valentine, T., & Baddeley, A. D. (1991). Phonological short-term memory and foreign language vocabulary learning. *Journal of Memory and Language, 30*, 331–347.

Papagno, C., & Vallar, G. (1992). Phonological short-term memory and the learning of novel words: The effect of phonological similarity and item length. *Quarterly Journal of Experimental Psychology, 44A*, 47–67.

Paulesu, E., Frith, C. D., & Frackowiak, R. S. J. (1993). The neural correlates of the verbal component of working memory. *Nature, 362*, 342–345.

Pearson, D. G. (2001). Imagery and the visuo-spatial sketchpad. In J. Andrade (Ed.), *Working memory in perspective*. (pp 33–59). Hove: Psychology Press.

Peterson, L. R., & Peterson, M. J. (1959). Short-term retention of individual verbal items. *Journal of Experimental Psychology, 58*, 193–198.

Pickering, S. J. (2001a). Cognitive approaches to the fractionation of visuo-spatial working memory. *Cortex, 37*, 470–473.

Pickering, S. J. (2001b). The development of visuo-spatial working memory. *Memory, 9*, 423–432.

Pickering, S. J., Gathercole, S. E., Hall, M., & Lloyd, S. A. (2001). Development of memory for pattern and path: Further evidence for the fractionation of visual and spatial short-term memory. *Quarterly Journal of Experimental Psychology, 54A*, 397–420.

Quinn, G., & McConnell, J. (1996). Irrelevant pictures in visual working memory. *Quarterly Journal of Experimental Psychology, 49A*(1), 200–215.

Rabbitt, P. (1997). Introduction: methodologies and models in the study of executive function. *Rabbitt, P. (Ed) Methodology of frontal and executive function*. Hove, Psychology Press, pp. 1–38.

Shallice, T. (1988). *From neuropsychology to mental structure*. Cambridge: Cambridge University Press.

Shallice, T. (2002). Fractionation of the supervisory system. In D. T. Stuss & R. Knight (Eds.), *Principles of frontal lobe function*. (pp. 262–277). Oxford: Oxford University Press.

Shallice, T., & Warrington, E. K. (1970). Independent functioning of verbal memory stores: A neuropsychological study. *Quarterly Journal of Experimental Psychology, 22*, 261–273.

Smith, E., Jonides, J., & Koeppe, R. A. (1996). Dissociating verbal and spatial working memory using PET. *Cerebral Cortex, 6*, 11–20.

Smith, E. E., & Jonides, J. (1997). Working memory: A view from neuroimaging. *Cognitive Psychology, 33*, 5–42.

Smyth, M. M., & Pendleton, L. R. (1990). Space and movement in working memory. *Quarterly Journal of Experimental Psychology, 42A*, 291–304.

Smyth, M. M., & Scholey, K. A. (1996). Serial order in spatial immediate memory. *Quarterly Journal of Experimental Psychology, 49A*, 159–177.

Snowling, M., Chiat, S., & Hulme, C. (1991). Words, nonwords, and phonological processes: Some comments on Gathercole, Willis, Emslie and Baddeley. *Applied Psycholinguists, 12*(3), 369–373.

Tallal, E., Stark, R. E., & Mellits, E. D. (1985). Identification of language-impaired children on the basis of rapid perception and production skills. *Brain and Language, 25,* 314–322.

Tranel, D. (2002). Emotion, decision making, and the ventromedial prefrontal cortex. In D. T. Stuss & R. T. Knight (Eds.), *Principles of frontal lobe function.* (pp. 338–353). Oxford: Oxford University Press.

Tulving, E., Kapur, S., Craik, F. I. M., Moscovitch, M., & Houle, S. (1994). Hemispheric encoding/retrieval asymmetry in episodic memory—positron emission tomography findings. *Proceedings of the National Academy of Sciences, USA, 91*(6), 2016–2020.

Turner, M. L., & Engle, R. W. (1989). Is working memory capacity task-dependent? *Journal of Memory and Language, 28,* 127–154.

Vallar, G., & Baddeley, A. D. (1984). Fractionation of working memory. Neuropsychological evidence for a phonological short-term store. *Journal of Verbal Learning and Verbal Behaviour, 23,* 151–161.

Vallar, G., & Papagno, C. (2002). Neuropsychological impairments of verbal short-term memory. In A. D. Baddeley, M. D. Kopelman, & B. A. Wilson (Eds.), *Handbook of memory disorders. 2nd ed.* (pp. 249–270). Chichester: Wiley.

Vygotsky, L. S. (1962). *Thought and language* (E. Hanfmann & G. Vakar, Trans.). Cambridge, MA: MIT Press.

Waters, G. S., & Caplan, D. (1996). The measurement of verbal working memory capacity and its relation to reading comprehension. *Quarterly Journal of Experimental Psychology, 49A,* 51–79.

Wheeler, M. E., & Treisman, A. M. (2002). Binding in short-term visual memory. *Journal of Experimental Psychology: General, 131,* 48–64.

CHAPTER 2

Understanding Normal and Impaired Reading Development: A Working Memory Perspective

PETER F. DE JONG

University of Amsterdam

The importance of learning to read is well recognized in modern literate societies. In the early school grades, major parts of the curriculum are devoted to reading or reading-related activities. Special efforts are made to identify children at risk for reading problems. Remediation and special education are provided for those that lag behind. The negative effects of illiteracy and impaired reading ability for the individual and for society at large seem to be widely acknowledged.

Learning to read involves the acquisition of word-decoding ability—that is, the ability to identify single words and the ability to comprehend written text. In the early phases of reading acquisition, when text comprehension seems dependent on the ability to identify the words in the text, these abilities are highly related. As reading acquisition proceeds, the relationship between the two tends to weaken. Nevertheless, in all phases of reading acquisition, word decoding and reading comprehension can be clearly separated. Therefore, it is generally believed that the cognitive and environmental determinants of word decoding and reading comprehension are partly different (e.g., de Jong & Leseman, 2001; Snow, 1991). In this chapter, the focus is on the acquisition of word decoding. Chapter 3 of this book devotes itself to the discussion of reading comprehension.

Optimal reading instruction, successful early identification of reading problems, and effective methods of remediation depend, at least in part,

Working Memory and Education

on an understanding of the cognitive determinants of normal and impaired reading development. In the last decade, Baddeley and Hitch's (1974; Baddeley, 1986) model of working memory (WM) has proved successful in enhancing our understanding of individual and developmental differences in a wide range of cognitive abilities such as language learning (Baddeley, Gathercole, & Papagno, 1998), reading comprehension (Daneman & Carpenter, 1980; Leather & Henry, 1994), mathematics (Fürst & Hitch, 2000), and reasoning (Kyllonen & Christal, 1990). In this chapter, the model will be used to analyze normal and impaired reading development.

The chapter is organized as follows. In the first section the task of the beginning reader is briefly described. This task analysis is used as a starting point to consider how the various components of WM might be involved in reading acquisition. The role of the phonological loop, here denoted as *verbal short-term memory* (STM), is described in the next section. A distinction is made between its role in the acquisition of letter knowledge and its role in reading. In the third section, the involvement of the central executive in reading acquisition is considered. In the last section the value of a WM perspective for the understanding of normal and impaired reading development is considered.

LEARNING TO READ: THE TASK

In skilled readers word identification is generally quick and accurate. The sight of a word's written form is often sufficient for the immediate activation of its pronunciation in memory. Such rapid and accurate word identification is believed to depend on orthographic knowledge, a system of associations between phonology and orthography at the word and the subword level (Ehri, 1998; Perfetti, 1992; Share, 1995). In beginning readers this system has not yet been sufficiently developed. Their word identification tends to be error prone, effortful, and slow. Becoming a skilled reader requires the acquisition of orthographic knowledge.

To start reading, the beginning reader has to acquire two abilities. First, the beginning reader has to learn that there is a systematic correspondence between the written and the spoken form of words. In alphabetic orthographies, phonemes in the spoken form are represented by letters. The beginning reader has to understand this alphabetic principle and to acquire the basic letter–sound correspondences of the orthography. However, this is not sufficient to enable the identification of a word. To make a connection between the letters in the written word form and the phonemes in its spoken counterpart, a reader should also be able to recognize phonemes in spoken words. Although a written word is just a sequence of letters, a spoken word cannot be regarded as a series of separate phonemes. The phonemes in words are bonded or coarticulated. As a result, there are no clear boundaries between the sound patterns of the individual phonemes in a spoken word. In addition, because of coarticulation, the sound of a particular phoneme is not constant throughout different words, but it is affected by the surrounding phonemes in a word. For example, the sound features of the /b/ in *bed* are different from the /b/ in *bath*. As a result, a beginning reader has to learn to abstract phonemes from a range of sounds.

The acquisition of letter-sound knowledge and the ability to detect and manipulate phonemes in spoken words (phoneme sensitivity or phonological awareness) have been regarded as the twin foundations of early reading development (Byrne, 1998). There is good evidence that these abilities develop in tandem as soon as a minimum level of letter knowledge is acquired (e.g., Bowey, 1994; Johnston, Anderson, & Holligan, 1996). Similarly, there is probably an interactive relationship between early reading ability and the development of phonological sensitivity.

When orthographic knowledge has not been sufficiently developed to read words by sight, a different strategy is used to identify a word. One prominent strategy is decoding or phonological recoding (Ehri, 1998; Share, 1995). This is the sequential translation of letters into sounds and the blending of these sounds into the spoken form of the word. Successful phonological recoding seems dependent on letter-sound knowledge and a minimum of phonological sensitivity. The method is obviously very useful in languages such as Dutch, German, or Turkish, with orthographies in which the mapping of graphemes to phonemes is fairly consistent. In countries with a transparent orthography, phonological recoding is often explicitly instructed. The English orthography, however, is very inconsistent, especially with respect to the pronunciation of the vowel (Treiman et al., 1995). For example, in Dutch the vowel *a* in the words *hand (hand), ball (bal),* and *cat (kat)* has a similar sound, whereas in English the vowel sound is different in each word (Landerl, Wimmer, & Frith, 1997). Therefore, in addition to phonological recoding, English beginning readers also tend to use strategies that exploit analogies to existing words to identify a new word (e.g., Goswami, 1993, 2002).

The importance of phonological recoding, but possibly also of some other reading strategies, is that it provides the beginning reader with a self-teaching mechanism for the identification of new words. According to Share (1995), each successful phonological recoding of a new word associates its written form with its spoken counterpart and thus provides the opportunity to acquire orthographic knowledge. In normal readers, after only a few successful encounters with a novel word, a long-term association between its written and spoken form is established. Whether phonological recoding actually leads to word-specific knowledge, as Share contends, or to more general orthographic knowledge can be debated. However, there is mounting evidence to suggest that the development of a system of connections between phonology and orthography is dependent on the repeated and successful reading of (novel) words (Cunningham, Perry, Stanovich, & Share, 2002; Ehri & Saltmarsh, 1995; Share, 1999).

THE ROLE OF VERBAL SHORT-TERM MEMORY

Verbal STM is a system for the temporary storage of verbal information (e.g., Baddeley, Gathercole, & Papagno, 1998). In Baddeley's WM model the system is denoted as the phonological loop (see Chapter 1). However, individual differences in the capacity or functioning of this system are most often referred to as verbal STM capacity, or sometimes more briefly as verbal STM. In the remaining part of this chapter the term verbal STM will be used, and in general, the context should be sufficient to clarify whether the term refers to the system or to individual differences in the capacity of the system.

In the normal course of development, the learning of letter names and sounds precedes learning to read words. Letter knowledge in kindergarten has been found to be one of the best predictors of later reading ability (e.g., de Jong & van der Leij, 1999; Share, Jorm, MacLean, & Mathews, 1984; Lonigan, Burgess, & Anthony, 2000; Scarborough, 1998; Wagner, Torgesen, & Rashotte, 1994). In many respects, learning letter names and sounds can be conceived as the acquisition of relatively novel sound patterns (Share, 1995). Baddeley et al. (1998) have suggested that verbal STM supports the learning of new words and is especially suited to the temporary storage of unfamiliar sound sequences. Therefore, the acquisition of letter knowledge seems a natural starting point to consider the role of verbal STM in learning to read. Next, I consider the relationship between verbal STM and reading ability.

Acquisition of Letter Knowledge

Given the importance of letter knowledge for later reading, there is surprisingly little research about the factors that affect its acquisition. One notable exception is a series of studies by Treiman and colleagues (Treiman, Tincoff, Rodriguez, Mouzali, & Francis, 1998; Treiman, Wheatherston, & Berch, 1994; but see also Share, 2004). For middle-class children in North America (unlike those in many European countries), the acquisition of letter names usually precedes the learning of their sounds. This gave Treiman et al. (1998) the opportunity to examine whether the knowledge of a letter's name might aid in the learning of its sound. In English, for some of the letters, such as the *b* or the *f,* the sound is in the name. For other letters, such as the *y* (*wai*) or *h,* this is not the case. If verbal STM is involved in the learning of new letter sounds, it is to be expected that the former, more "wordlike" letter sounds are easier to learn than the latter, less "wordlike" letter sounds (e.g., Gathercole, 1995; Gathercole & Baddeley, 1990).

In their first study, Treiman et al. (1998) examined letter name and letter-sound knowledge in a large sample of children aged 3.5 to 7 years old. As predicted, knowledge of letter sounds that were embedded in a letter's name was larger than knowledge of letter sounds where this was not the case. The result was probably not because of other, for example, visual, properties of the letters. In contrast to letter-sound knowledge, the knowledge of a letter's name was unrelated to the involvement of a letter's sound in its name. In a second, more controlled study, Treiman et al. (1998) provided further evidence of children's use of letter knowledge in the acquisition of their sounds. Preschool children were taught the sounds of 10 letters for which the names had already been learned. Each child was given three learning trials within a week. On each trial all the letters and their sounds were presented. Despite the briefness of this training, letter-sound knowledge of letters *for which the sound was in the name* had increased substantially from pre- to post-test. For the other letters, the training did not have an effect.

The results of Treiman et al.'s study (1998) clearly suggest that verbal STM is involved in the learning of letters. However, this does not imply that individual differences in verbal STM affect individual differences in the development of letter knowledge. Generally, studies on the cognitive abilities that affect individual differences in the development of letter knowledge are scarce, and most of these studies have been concerned with the role of more general language skills (e.g., Storch & Whitehurst, 2002). An exception is a study by Lonigan, Burgess, and Anthony (2000). They examined the effect of phonological sensitivity on letter knowledge. Phonological sensitivity is the ability to detect and manipulate the sound units of one's oral language, and it is of interest here because it tends to be highly related to verbal STM (e.g., de Jong & van der Leij, 1999; Wagner et al., 1994). Two groups of preschool children were included in the study. The older group was followed over a period of 1 year, starting at the age of 5 years. In this group a significant relationship was found between phonological sensitivity on the first occasion and letter knowledge 1 year later. However, phonological sensitivity did not make an additional contribution to the prediction of letter knowledge at the second occasion after letter knowledge on the first occasion was taken into account. The children in the older group already had a fair amount of letter knowledge at the start of the study. This was presumably not the case in the younger age group, which was first tested at the age of 3.5 years and retested at the age of 5 years. In this group, phonological sensitivity at age 3.5 appeared to be related to letter knowledge at the age of 5 years. In addition, an independent effect of oral language skills was found. Given a relationship between phonological sensitivity and verbal STM, the Lonigan et al. (2000) study gives some support, albeit indirectly, for a relationship between verbal STM and the acquisition of letter knowledge.

More direct evidence for this relationship comes from a 2004 study by de Jong and Olson (2004). A group of 77 Dutch children was followed from the autumn of their first kindergarten year to the end of their second year in kindergarten. In Dutch education, kindergarten encompasses 2 years. In the autumn of the first year the mean age of the children was approximately

TABLE 2.1
Incremental Percentages of Variance Predicting Letter
Knowledge in the Second Year of Kindergarten from the
Fall of the First Year

Step	Predictor	2nd Fall	2nd End
1	Age	3.6^a	2.3
2	Block design	6.5^b	5.3^b
3	Vocabulary	3.3	5.7^c
4	Nonword Repetition	6.9^b	9.8^c
3	Nonword Repetition	9.4^c	13.7^c
4	Vocabulary	0.8	1.8
	R^2	20.3	23.1

Note: Results for Letter Knowledge (Fall) are based on $N = 77$,
for Letter Knowledge (End) on $N = 76$.
[a] $p < .10$
[b] $p < .05$
[c] $p < .01$

4 years and 6 months. Letter knowledge at this age was assumed to be neg-ligible because in the Netherlands letter knowledge is mainly acquired at school; alphabet books are rarely found in Dutch families. Studies indicate that Dutch children know on average between four and six letters at the beginning of the second year in kindergarten (e.g., Aarnoutse, van Leeuwe, & Verhoeven, 2000). Therefore, this study, starting almost 1 year earlier, was assumed to have begun well before the development of letter knowledge.

The Dutch version of the nonword repetition test (de Jong & van der Leij, 1999) was used as a measure of verbal STM. Letter knowledge involved a mixture of letter-name and letter-sound knowledge. Substantial correlations were found between nonword repetition in the autumn of the first kinder-garten year and letter knowledge in the autumn and at the end of the second year (0.39 and 0.44, respectively). To examine whether this relationship was specific or the result of the relationship of nonword repetition to more general abilities as nonverbal intelligence and vocabulary, a series of hier-archical regression analyses was conducted. The results are presented in Table 2.1.

In the first set of hierarchical regression analyses, the effect of nonword repetition on letter knowledge in the fall of the second year was considered. After age, nonverbal intelligence (Block design), and vocabulary were con-trolled, nonword repetition entered in Step 4 described a significant amount of additional variance in letter knowledge. Because there is substantial evi-dence that STM, reflected by nonword repetition, is involved in the develop-ment of vocabulary (e.g., Baddeley, Gathercole, & Papagno, 1998), the additional effects of nonword repetition on letter knowledge might actually be larger. To examine this possibility, nonword repetition was also entered before vocabulary in the analysis. As expected, in this analyses nonword rep-etition appeared to describe even more variance in letter knowledge. It is

interesting that vocabulary, entered at Step 4, did not add any significant variance after nonword repetition was taken into account. The second set of
analyses, predicting letter knowledge at the end of the second year, revealed
a similar pattern of results (see Table 2.1).

The results of this study suggest that verbal STM is involved in the development of letter knowledge. Individual differences in STM had a specific
effect. Of course, this single study does not permit a straightforward causal
interpretation of this effect. In addition, the results suggest that the effects
of more general language skills on the acquisition of letter knowledge are
probably due to the fact that individual differences in these skills also reflect
individual differences in phonological processing ability. This does not necessarily imply that verbal STM affects the development of both oral language
skills and letter knowledge. The results of this study are entirely compatible with the alternative hypothesis that growth in oral language skills, in particular vocabulary, is a driving force in phonological development and also
in STM (Brown & Hulme, 1996; Fowler, 1991; Metsala & Walley, 1998; Storch
& Whitehurst, 2002). Following this view, however, these results do suggest
that vocabulary development is not the only factor that influences phonological development. If this were the case, no additional effect of verbal STM
on the acquisition of letter knowledge would have been found after vocabulary was controlled for.

Although there is good reason to assume a role for verbal STM in the
acquisition of letter knowledge, it should be noted that this role might be
limited. Nonword repetition described approximately 15–19% of the variance in letter knowledge; all cognitive variables together described 23% at
most. Probably, in normally developing children, most of the individual
differences in letter knowledge are the result of differences in the child's
environment (e.g., Whitehurst & Lonigan, 1998).

This might not be the case for children with dyslexia. Several studies have
demonstrated that children with dyslexia have problems with early letter
learning (Pennington & Lefly, 2001; Snowling, Gallagher, & Frith, 2003). Children that later turned out to have reading impairments were found to have
less letter knowledge in kindergarten than their normally reading peers.
Dyslexia is highly heritable, and the effects of environmental factors are
small (e.g., Gayan & Olson, 1993). In addition, children with dyslexia have
been regularly found to have problems in STM and perform at a lower level
on the nonword repetition test (Brady, 1997; see later in this chapter).
Accordingly, the finding of a specific relationship between verbal STM and
letter knowledge can readily explain the delay in the acquisition of letter
knowledge in children with dyslexia.

STM and Reading

The importance of verbal STM for early reading development seems obvious
when the requirements of phonological recoding are considered. Letters are
sequentially converted into sounds, and the latter have to be temporarily

stored until the last letter has been translated. Then, the full sequence of sounds can be blended into a word. The temporary storage of letter sounds involves, almost by definition, verbal STM.

The relationship between individual differences in verbal STM and reading ability is well documented (see for reviews Brady, 1997; Elbro, 1996; Wagner & Torgesen, 1987). For further interpretation of this relationship, however, two issues have to be addressed. The first issue concerns the causal nature of the relationship. Support for a causal interpretation requires longitudinal studies in which verbal STM is shown to make an additional contribution to reading development when other plausible causes are controlled for (Wagner et al., 1994). Wagner et al. (1994) have argued that many longitudinal studies have failed to take account of the progress in reading at a prior point in time (the autoregressive effect) on the subsequent development of reading. In these studies, the causal nature of the relationships is hard to interpret.

The second issue is whether the relationship between verbal STM and reading ability is specific. Because verbal STM is related to other phonological abilities, its relationship with reading ability might be the result of a common underlying ability or, put slightly differently, a result of association with the primary causal agent of reading acquisition. The most likely agent for reading is phonological sensitivity or awareness. The alternative possibility is that the effects of the verbal STM can be distinguished from the effects of other phonological abilities. Several, mostly cross-sectional, studies have found that verbal STM and phonological sensitivity made independent contributions to reading acquisition, although their common contribution is generally larger (Hansen & Bowey, 1994; Leather & Henry, 1994; Rohl & Pratt, 1995).

The number of longitudinal studies in which both issues have been addressed is scarce. Wagner et al. (1994, 1997) examined the effects of phonological sensitivity and verbal STM on learning to read in English in a longitudinal study from kindergarten through fourth grade. In contrast to all previous studies, Wagner et al. considered relations among factors—that is, compound scores of at least two tests. Such scores are believed to give a better, and less task-specific, reflection of the construct of interest. The verbal STM factor was measured by an oral digit span task and a memory for sentences task. In their first report of this study (Wagner et al., 1994), covering 1-year time periods to the end of second grade, and in their second report (Wagner et al., 1997), covering 2-year periods to the end of fourth grade, phonological sensitivity was found to have an effect on reading achievement after prior reading acquisition and vocabulary were controlled. Verbal STM did not, however, have an additional effect.

A similar factor study was carried out by de Jong and van der Leij (1999) with children learning to read Dutch. The study started in kindergarten and continued until the end of second grade. Because Dutch has a transparent orthography, which is relatively easy to learn, reading was operationalized as reading *fluency* (i.e., accurate and rapid reading). Wagner et al. (1994, 1997) considered reading accuracy. Indicators of verbal STM were word span, nonword repetition, and a complex word span task with a visual processing component. The results showed that both phonological sensitivity and verbal STM at a prior point in time were substantially related to later reading fluency. Generally, however, the relationship of reading with phonological sensitivity was stronger than with verbal STM. In the time period from kindergarten to the end of first grade, neither verbal STM nor phonological sensitivity had an additional effect on reading, when more general abilities and letter knowledge were controlled. In contrast, in the time period from the beginning of first grade to the end of second grade, both phonological abilities had an additional effect on reading, after prior reading, nonverbal intelligence, and vocabulary had been controlled. However, the additional contribution of verbal STM could be fully accounted for by phonological sensitivity, whereas the latter remained to have a small additional effect when verbal STM was controlled. Thus, verbal STM did not have an independent effect on reading acquisition.

Both longitudinal studies suggest that individual differences in phonological sensitivity are more important for reading acquisition than individual differences in verbal STM. The relationship of verbal STM to reading ability seems mainly the result of its association with phonological sensitivity. A similar conclusion has been reached by Pennington et al. (Pennington, Van Orden, Kirson, & Haith, 1991) with respect to impaired reading development. These authors observed that for children with dyslexia problems in phonological sensitivity are more severe and consistent than their problems in verbal STM. Pennington et al. (1991) concluded from their review that there is "stronger support for problems in phoneme awareness being a primary deficit in dyslexia than problems in verbal STM" (p. 183). Impairments in verbal STM in children with dyslexia are best conceived as "correlated and contributing symptoms" (p. 183).

The subordinate role of verbal STM in reading acquisition seems to be at odds with its involvement in the process of phonological recoding. Although speculative, there might be at least two reasons why individual differences in verbal STM might not be a driving force in reading development. One reason could be that individual differences in phonological recoding ability are not very important because it is used far less than supposed. This would especially apply to children learning to read in an opaque orthography, such as English, but it does not seem very likely in children that have to master a transparent orthography. As a consequence, the relation between verbal STM and reading should be lower in an opaque orthography than in a transparent orthography. Such a result has not yet been reported. Another possible reason for the moderate role of individual differences in verbal STM is that phonological recoding imposes a memory load that is well within the memory span of most beginning readers. This reason is more likely because early reading usually starts with one-syllable words of two to three phonemes. In addition, phonotactic and lexical constraints on (recoded) phoneme sequences might further reduce this memory load. When learning proceeds, longer words have to be read, which, in principle, could impose a larger memory load. However, larger words often consist of one-syllable words or word forms, such as morphemes, so that by this time phonological recoding is probably no longer at the level of grapheme–phoneme translation. The identification of longer words is aided by orthographic knowledge, acquired through the reading of the one-syllable words.

Although individual differences in verbal STM might not be so important for reading acquisition, the following question remains: Which underlying abilities account for its relation with reading? From Baddeley's (1986) model of verbal STM, two possible underlying abilities can be derived. One is phonological memory, the ability to hold phonological information in the phonological store; the other is speech rate, which is an indicator of rehearsal speed (i.e., the time needed to refresh decaying information in the phonological store).

These underlying abilities can only explain the relationship between verbal STM and reading if they are also related to reading. For speech rate, the evidence is mixed. In some studies including samples of normal children, substantial relationships have been found between speech rate and reading abilities (McDougall, Hulme, Ellis, & Monk, 1994; Muter & Snowling, 1998). In these studies, speech rate could fully account for the relationship between verbal STM and reading and appeared to be the better predictor. In the majority of studies, however, speech rate hardly appeared to be related to reading ability (Cutting & Denckla, 2001; Hansen & Bowey, 1994; see also Stanovich, Nathan, & Zolman, 1988). These disparate results are hard to explain. More consistent results have been found in studies with children with dyslexia. Differences in verbal STM between normal and dyslexic readers tended to remain when speech rate was taken into account, although the differences did decrease (McDougall & Donohoe, 2002; Roodenrys & Stokes, 2001). Thus, speech rate explains part of the verbal STM impairment of children with dyslexia.

As part of a follow-up of their earlier longitudinal study (de Jong & van der Leij, 1999), de Jong and van der Leij (2002) examined the role of speech rate in reading acquisition. As outlined before, the study concerned reading fluency and not reading accuracy. Because both reading fluency and speech rate involve speed, a higher correlation might be expected than reported in previous studies. The results did not support this prediction. The concurrent correlation of speech rate with reading fluency at the end of first grade was 0.17, and its correlation with reading fluency 2 years later was 0.20. It is interesting that another ability that involves speed, serial rapid naming (in this case the rapid naming of a series of well-known objects), was highly correlated with reading fluency.

TABLE 2.2
Correlations of Word Span and Speech Rate with
Reading Fluency

Grade 1 Cognitive Ability	Reading Fluency	
	End of Grade 1	End of Grade 3
Word span	0.38^a	0.29^a
Speech rate	0.14^b	0.19^b

N = 139
$^a p < .01$
$^b p < .05$

For various reasons, de Jong and van der Leij (2002) did not include a measure of verbal STM. Therefore, the possibility remains that the low association between speech rate and reading fluency was observed because reading fluency was also only slightly related to verbal STM. To examine this possibility, a supplementary analysis of these data was done to examine the relationships among speech rate, word span, and reading. The correlations for the observed variables are presented in Table 2.2.

The results are straightforward. The correlation of reading fluency with word span is substantially higher than its correlation with speech rate. The correlation between word span and speech rate was 0.33 ($p < .01$), which has been found before (e.g., McDougall et al., 1994; Muter & Snowling, 1998). Subsequent regression analyses revealed that speech rate did not explain any variance in reading fluency after nonverbal intelligence and vocabulary were controlled, whereas word span did.

In sum, there is no solid evidence that speech rate can account for the relationship between verbal STM and reading ability in normal readers. There is, however, some evidence that speech rate explains part of the differences in verbal STM between dyslexic and normal readers.

The other ability that could underlie the relation of verbal STM with reading ability is phonological memory. Currently, nonword repetition is one of the most popular measures of the ability to hold phonological information in the phonological store. Part of its popularity is probably a result of the assumption that the task seems less dependent on rehearsal than memory span tasks. In normal readers, substantial relationships have been found between nonword repetition and reading ability (e.g., de Jong & van der Leij, 1999; Gathercole, Willis, & Baddeley, 1991; Muter & Snowling, 1998). In addition, there is consistent evidence that children with dyslexia have problems with nonword repetition (e.g., Brady, 1997; Messbauer & de Jong, 2003; Roodenrys & Stokes, 2001; Snowling, 2000; van Bon & van der Pijl, 1997). In the remainder of this section, impairments in phonological memory in children with dyslexia are discussed.

These impairments in children with dyslexia can be the result of a problem in the encoding of phonological information (e.g., Brady, 1997). In an early study, Shankweiler, Liberman, Mark, Fowler, and Fisher (1979) tested whether verbal memory span differences between normal and poor readers were the result of differences in the amount of phonological coding. They hypothesized that if dyslexic readers make less use of this type of coding, their span performance would be less affected by the phonological similarity of the items than the span performance of normal readers. Both groups of readers were administered span tasks with rhyming and non-rhyming letters. As predicted, normal readers performed better on the non-rhyming task, whereas the performance of the dyslexic readers was similar on both span tasks. However, the results of this study have been severely disputed (e.g., Hall et al., 1983; Johnston, 1982) because, as acknowledged by Shankweiler et al., both span tasks were probably too difficult for the group of children with dyslexia.

An alternative explanation for an impairment in the phonological store is a deficiency in the support from long-term memory (LTM). A growing number of studies have shown that the availability of phonological information in LTM can support the retention and reconstruction of phonological codes in phonological memory (e.g., Gathercole, 1995; Hulme, Maughan, & Brown, 1991; Hulme, Roodenrys, Brown, & Mercer, 1995). A possible deficiency in the availability of long-term phonological knowledge in children with dyslexia fits nicely with the dominant hypothesis of the primary cause of dyslexia, the phonological deficit hypothesis (Snowling, 2000). According to this hypothesis, most of the problems experienced by children with dyslexia in phonological processing stem from a single underlying deficit. This common deficit is conceived as impoverished and less detailed long-term phonological representations of spoken words. The most important consequence of impoverished phonological representations is an impairment in the development of phonological sensitivity and subsequently in learning to read. However, another consequence might be an insufficient support from LTM for the coding of sound sequences in the phonological store.

Two effects of long-term knowledge on phonological memory are well documented. The lexicality effect reflects the larger span for words than for nonwords. The wordlikeness effect denotes the positive correlation between the capacity of verbal STM for nonwords (both span and nonword repetition) and the wordlikeness of the nonwords. Both effects have been studied in normal children and in children with dyslexia. van Bon and van der Pijl (1997) administered a nonword repetition test with high and low wordlike nonwords to groups of poor and normal Dutch readers. As expected, poor readers were found to be worse in nonword repetition than were normal readers. However, both groups were similarly affected by the wordlikeness of the nonwords. Low wordlike nonwords were repeated less well than high wordlike nonwords by both groups. It is interesting that differences in nonword repetition between the groups disappeared when phoneme sensitivity was controlled for. This finding is in accordance with the hypothesis that individual differences in nonword repetition and in phoneme sensitivity reflect a common underlying ability.

The results of van Bon and van der Pijl (1997) on the nonword repetition task were replicated in a study by Roodenrys and Stokes (2001) with English readers. The performance of the dyslexic readers appeared to be lower than the performance of the normal readers, but both groups were similarly affected by the wordlikeness of the nonwords. Roodenrys and Stokes (2001) also examined the effects of long-term knowledge on memory span performance. Both the effects of lexicality (words or nonwords) and of wordlikeness (high or low wordlike nonwords) were considered. As expected, the memory spans of the children with dyslexia were lower than the span of the normal readers. Also, a lexicality effect and a trend toward a larger memory span for high wordlike nonwords than for low wordlike nonwords were found. As on the nonword repetition task, the groups did not differ in their susceptibility to wordlikeness. In addition, the results indicated that both groups had a similar lexicality effect. The latter result is not in accordance with the findings of McDougall and Donohoe (2002). In their study, the dyslexic readers showed a larger lexicality effect than the normal readers. This was because the children with dyslexia performed worse on the nonword span task but not on the word span task with high-frequency words. In contrast, Roodenrys and Stokes (2001) found a smaller word span in the group of children with dyslexia, supporting the findings of several other studies.

Do the results of these studies refute the hypothesis that the impairment in phonological memory of children with dyslexia is (partly) a result of a deficiency in the support from long-term phonological representations? The answer should be "no" because the assumptions underlying these studies might be wrong. For example, the expectation of a difference in susceptibility for the wordlikeness effect is based on the assumption that LTM representations affect the short-term representation of high wordlike words but not the temporary representation of low wordlike words. However, because the cut-off between high and low wordlike nonwords is arbitrary, it seems more reasonable to assume a difference in degree of support from LTM. Accordingly, the same processes underlie individual differences in phonological memory for high and low wordlike words, just as similar processes are assumed to underlie performance on more and less difficult items of the Raven Progressive Matrices test (e.g., Carpenter, Just, & Shell, 1990). A similar argument can be made with respect to the lexicality effect. The same redintegrative processes might underlie phonological memory for both words and nonwords (see for example Roodenrys & Hinton, 2002). Thus, the results of these studies are entirely compatible with the hypothesis that children with dyslexia have an impairment in the long-term representation of the phonological features of words. Such low-quality representations provide less support for the coding and reconstruction (redintegration) of information in the phonological store, irrespective of whether this information concerns words, high wordlike nonwords, or low wordlike nonwords.

So far, the relationship between verbal STM and reading seems to be better accounted for by the capacity of phonological memory, the ability to code and reconstruct phonological information in the phonological store, than by speech rate. Empirically and theoretically, the relationship between phonological memory and reading can be easily understood through its strong relationship with phonological sensitivity and the common underlying ability that both are assumed to reflect. (In contrast, evidence for a substantial relationship between speech rate and phonological sensitivity is mixed.) This common ability is assumed to reflect the quality of phonological representations in LTM and thus emphasizes LTM as a prime source of individual differences in phonological memory. However, an independent influence of differences in the quality of verbal short-term phonological representations should not be excluded. In addition, there is evidence to suggest that low-quality, long-term phonological representations might result from deficits in speech perception (e.g., Brady, 1997).

THE ROLE OF THE CENTRAL EXECUTIVE

The central executive (CE) is thought to be a limited capacity system for the regulation and control of processes in WM (e.g., Baddeley, 1986; Miyake, Friedman, Emerson, Witzki, & Howerter, 2000). The system is often associated with attention control (Baddeley, 1986; Kane & Engle, 2003), assumed to be necessary for the temporary storage of information while processing continues.

As stated earlier, beginning readers often have to resort to the slow and effortful process of phonological recoding. During this process, grapheme–phoneme conversion rules have to be activated in LTM (Siegel, 1993); the activation and application of the more complex rules might not be automatic in beginning readers. In addition, the sequential conversion of graphemes to phonemes evidently requires the temporarily storage of sounds while subsequent graphemes are translated. Early reading seems, therefore, to involve verbal STM, and requires the ability to store and process phonological information simultaneously. The latter is a function attributed to the CE.

Several studies have shown that individual differences in the capacity of the CE, often referred to as WM capacity, and individual differences in verbal STM capacity are related but distinct (e.g., Conway, Cowan, Bunting, Therriault, & Minkoff, 2002; Engle, Tuholski, Laughlin, & Conway, 1999). In many studies WM capacity has been found to have a stronger relation with reading *comprehension* than verbal STM capacity (Daneman & Merikle, 1996). Far fewer studies have been concerned with differences in the relationships of verbal STM and WM capacity with word *decoding*.

In most studies on reading comprehension and WM, complex span tasks have been used to assess WM capacity (see Chapter 3). A classic complex span task is Daneman and Carpenter's (1980) reading span task. This task requires the reading of sentences (the processing component) while, simultaneously, storing the last words of these sentences (the storage component). After a number of sentences, the last words have to be reproduced in the order in which they appeared. Variations of the reading span task have been devised with different processing components such as listening (Siegel & Ryan, 1989), counting (Case, Kurland &, Goldberg, 1982) and arithmetic (Turner & Engle, 1989). The key measure in all these complex span tasks is the amount of information that can be stored while processing continues.

An early study by Leather and Henry (1994) provided some evidence that, as in reading comprehension, WM capacity is more strongly related to individual differences in word decoding than verbal STM. In a group of second-grade normal readers, both a listening and a counting span task appeared to explain additional variance in reading ability after word span was taken into account. More recently, Kail and Hall (2001) reported a similar finding. However, the possibility remains that in dyslexic readers, being at the extreme end of the reading ability distribution, a deficit in WM capacity mainly reflects an impairment in the temporary storage of verbal information. This issue initiated a number of studies on the WM deficits of children with dyslexia.

In the first study (de Jong, 1998), a group of 10-year-old children with dyslexia was compared with a group of age-controlled normal readers and a group of younger normal readers with the same reading age on simple and complex span tasks. The simple span tasks were a digit and a word span task. Complex span tasks were a reading span, a computation span, and a counting span task. Some of the key results of this study are displayed in Figure 2.1.

The dyslexic readers (DYS) performed worse than the age-matched normal readers (CA) on all the simple and complex span tasks. The differences between the dyslexic readers and the group of reading-age controls (RA) were not significant. More importantly, when lower performance on the simple span tasks of the children with dyslexia were controlled for, the differences with their normal reading peers on the complex span tasks remained. More recently, similar results have been found in other studies (e.g., Swanson & Ashbaker, 2000; Willcutt et al., 2001). This suggests that the deficits in WM capacity of the children with dyslexia do not stem from their impairments in verbal STM.

The finding of a generally lower performance on all complex span tasks, irrespective of the type of processing required, was in accordance with the results of an earlier study by Siegel and Ryan (1989). They found that children with dyslexia performed worse than their normal reading peers on a complex span task with a language component (Listening span) and an

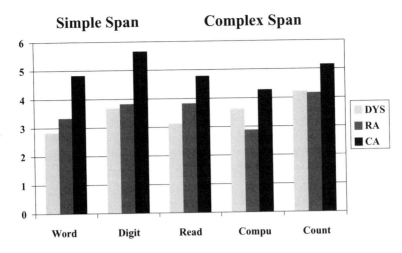

FIGURE 2.1

Performance of dyslexic readers (DYS), normal age-matched readers (CA), and reading-matched younger readers (RA) on simple and complex span tasks. (Read = Reading span; Compu = Computation span; Count = Counting span.)

arithmetic component (Counting span) (see also Swanson, 1993). These findings are in line with the hypothesis that the WM deficits of children with dyslexia reflect a domain-independent impairment in the capacity to store and process information simultaneously. However, there is the alternative hypothesis that WM deficits of children with dyslexia are the result of deficiencies in rapid information processing. This hypothesis was not supported by the results of de Jong (1998). Deficits in complex span were not always accompanied by deficits in processing speed. For example, the children with dyslexia had a similar counting speed as the normal readers. In addition, complex span differences between the dyslexic group and the group of normal readers did not disappear when various measures of processing speed (reading, counting, computation) were taken into account.

Although these results suggested that children with dyslexia have a deficit in WM capacity, it was not clear from this study whether this deficit is specific to reading disability or might also be a characteristic of other learning disabilities. For example, several studies had shown that children with arithmetic difficulties might also have impairments in WM capacity (Hitch & McAuley, 1991; Siegel & Ryan, 1989). To pursue this issue, a small study was carried out involving 36 children with reading disabilities who differed in the severity of their accompanying arithmetic disability (de Jong & Korbee, 1998). Thus, the main aim of this study was to investigate the effect of arithmetic disability on complex span performance when reading (dis)ability was controlled for.

First, however, the group of children with dyslexia was split into a regular dyslexic group, with a mean lag in reading ability of 2 years, and a dyslexic group, with more severe reading disabilities, having a mean lag of 3 years. Both groups were matched for age and verbal intelligence. The comparison of these two dyslexic groups was carried out to show that the complex span tasks in this study were sufficiently sensitive to reveal group differences in performance. The underlying assumption for this comparison was that reading ability is a continuum and that differences in WM capacity can be found between relatively less and relatively more able readers along the entire continuum. The group of regular children with dyslexia was matched for reading age with a group of 18 younger normal readers.

In Figure 2.2a the mean scores of the three groups on the listening span (Siegel & Ryan, 1989) and the counting span (Case, Kurland, & Goldberg, 1982) are displayed. On both tasks, the performance of the group of children with severe dyslexia was significantly lower than the performance of the other two groups. The result shows once more that the impairment in WM capacity of children with dyslexia is not affected by the domain (language or arithmetic) of the processing component of the complex span task. However, it should be mentioned that the severe dyslexic group had a lower arithmetic ability than the regular dyslexic group. Potentially, the lower performance of the former group on the complex span tasks could be because of their lower arithmetic ability.

Two further results of this study seem to be inconsistent with this alternative explanation. First, the reading-age control group also had a lower arithmetic ability than the regular dyslexic group. Nevertheless, these groups did not differ significantly in complex span performance. The second inconsistent result stems from a comparison of two groups of dyslexic readers that differed in arithmetic ability but were matched on reading ability, age, and vocabulary. The group of 19 children with dyslexia with severe arithmetic disabilities had a similar mean lag in reading and arithmetic ability of approximately 2 years and 6 months. The 17 children with dyslexia in the group with mild arithmetic disabilities had a discrepancy between their reading and arithmetic ability. As in the group with severe arithmetic disabilities, this group had a lag in reading ability of 2 years and 6 months, but their lag in arithmetic ability was only 1 year and 2 months. Despite this difference in arithmetic ability, the groups did not differ significantly in performance on the listening and the counting span task (see Figure 2.2b).

Thus, the findings of this study suggest that deficits in complex span performance are specific to reading disabilities. Differences in arithmetic ability did not appear to affect WM capacity when differences in reading ability were controlled for. At first sight, the results seem to be at odds with those of a few other studies in which children with arithmetic disabilities, but normal reading, appear to have impaired complex span performance (e.g., McLean & Hitch, 1999; Siegel & Ryan, 1989; see also Bull & Scerif, 2001, in a normal sample). However, in all of these studies deficient performance

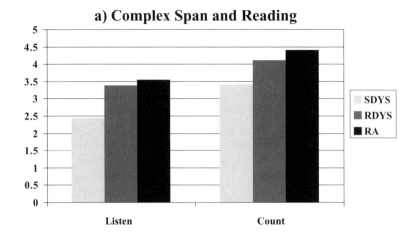

a) Complex Span and Reading

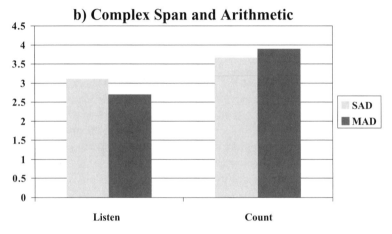

b) Complex Span and Arithmetic

FIGURE 2.2

Complex span performance (Listening and Counting span) of groups of severely dyslexic (SDYS), regular dyslexic (RDYS), and reading-age controls (RA) in panel (*a*) and of groups of children with dyslexia with severe arithmetic difficulties (SAD) or with mild arithmetic difficulties (MAD) in panel (*b*).

was found on complex span tasks that had a numeric processing component (counting span or addition span). This suggests that the impaired complex span performance of children with arithmetic disabilities might be specifically related to the numeric domain. Whether this impaired performance reflects a domain-specific deficit in WM capacity or, alternatively, results from deficits in the processing of numeric information, as, for example, suggested by Hitch and McAuley (1991, see also Bull & Johnston, 1997), is not yet clear. In contrast, current results suggest that children with dyslexia have a deficit in WM capacity that encompasses the language and the numeric domain. Whether this deficit extends to the domain of visual WM is also unclear because none of the studies have included a visual span task. The WM capacity deficit of children with dyslexia is neither a result of problems in verbal memory span, nor of processing speed impairments and seems to be independent of accompanying arithmetic difficulties.

Current evidence suggests that the CE is not a single unified system (e.g., Baddeley, 1996; Miyake et al., 2000). Complex span tasks reflect only one of its components. In adults, Miyake et al. (2000) showed that at least three separate CE factors should be distinguished: inhibition, switching, and updating. Willcutt et al. (2001) found similar factors in a group of children. Complex span performance primarily reflects updating, the ability to control and update information in WM. *Inhibition* corresponds to the ability to suppress dominant responses deliberately. *Switching* or *shifting* refers to the ability to alternate between different tasks, task sets, or operations. Given this multi-component structure of the CE, the question arises whether children with dyslexia also show impairments on components of the CE other than updating—that is, in inhibition and shifting.

To date, there are some indications that children with dyslexia might have a slight impairment in inhibition (Willcutt et al., 2001). Willcutt et al. (2001) examined all three CE functions in a group of children with dyslexia with and without attention deficit/hyperactivity disorder (ADHD) problems. They found a clear dissociation in the pattern of performance of the children with dyslexia and the children with ADHD. As in other studies, the performance of the children with dyslexia was impaired on the complex span tasks. In addition, a trend toward a lower performance of children with dyslexia on inhibition tasks was found. In contrast, the children with ADHD were grossly impaired on the inhibition tasks but not on the updating tasks. Neither children with dyslexia nor the children with ADHD differed from the normal children on tasks meant to reflect the ability to switch.

Comorbidity of dyslexia and ADHD is well documented. However, dyslexia is also often accompanied by arithmetic disabilities (Geary, 1993). In recent years, several studies have reported a relationship between the CE functions of switching and inhibition and arithmetic ability (e.g., Bull, Johnston, & Roy, 1999; Bull & Scerif, 2001; McLean & Hitch, 1999). Recently, van der Sluis, de Jong, and van der Leij (2004) examined inhibition and switching in children with dyslexia. To determine whether possible impairments are specifically related to reading disability, van der Sluis et al. used a full 2 × 2 (reading by arithmetic disability) design. Thus, the study involved four groups: children without learning disabilities (normal), children with reading disabilities (RD), children with arithmetic disabilities (AD), and children with reading and arithmetic disabilities (RAD).

A problem with most current executive function tasks is that tasks supposed to reflect different functions also tend to differ in other respects. For example, the Stroop task, assumed to require inhibition, differs widely from the Wisconsin Card Sorting test, which is often used to measure switching ability. To overcome this task impurity problem (Miyake et al., 2000), van der Sluis et al. (2004) manipulated inhibition and switching in the same basic task. This task was the rapid naming of geometric objects, randomly ordered in five rows of eight figures. The objects were a square, a circle, a triangle, and a diamond.

In the inhibition condition, each geometric figure contained a smaller geometric figure in its center. For example, a circle was placed in the center of a square. The task was to name the smaller geometric form (circle) and ignore the larger object (square). In the switching condition, each geometric object had a digit inside. Both digit and object had the same color. However, depending on the color (blue or yellow) either the digit or the object had to be named. Finally, an object-naming task that required both inhibition and switching was administered. In this task, as in the inhibition condition, each geometric figure contained a smaller geometric form inside. As in the switching condition, either the inner or the outer object had to be named depending on the color. In addition to these object-naming tasks, the Trail Making task was included. This task is supposed to reflect switching (e.g., McLean & Hitch, 1999).

On each of the four object-naming tasks, the time to name the 40 objects was recorded. Analyses indicated that compared to the basic object-naming task, inhibition, switching, and inhibition plus switching significantly decreased naming speed. Next, scores for inhibition (Objects-I), switching (Objects-S), and switching plus inhibition (Objects-IS) were derived by subtraction of the time needed for the basic task. The switching score on the Trail Making task was the difference between Trail B, the switching condition, and Trail A, the nonswitching condition. The mean score for each of the groups on these four tasks is presented in Figure 2.3.

Figure 2.3 shows that differences among the groups on Objects-I and Objects-S were minimal. Statistical analyses confirmed that none of these differences was significant. On the Objects-IS and the Trails the differences between groups with and without arithmetic disabilities seem most pronounced. The former group performed at a lower level than the latter group. Statistical analyses revealed a main effect of arithmetic but it did not show an effect of reading or a significant interaction of reading and arithmetic. The latter indicates that the performance of the children with both disabilities is just the sum of their deficits in reading and arithmetic.

With respect to dyslexia, the interpretation of these results is fairly straightforward. Children with dyslexia (RD and RAD) did not show an inhibition or switching impairment. Note, however, that the object-inhibition task probably did not require the suppression of an automatic response. However, it certainly did demand selective attention, which is also consid-

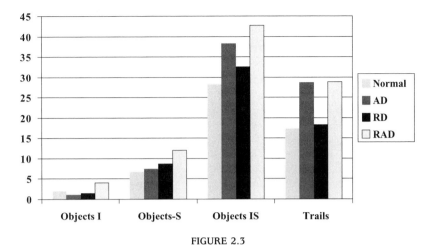

FIGURE 2.3

Object naming and trail making speed for children with arithmetic disabilities (AD), children with reading disabilities (RD), children with reading and arithmetic disabilities (RAD), and children without learning disabilities (Normal). (Object-I = object naming with inhibition; Objects-S = object naming with switching; Objects-IS = object naming with switching and inhibition.)

ered to be a function of the CE (see Baddeley, 1996), and might be considered a weaker form of inhibition. Fortunately, van der Sluis et al. also included a task that was a better reflection of inhibition ability (not displayed in Figure 2.3). In this task, the number of similar digits had to be named, whereas the digit number had to be suppressed (see Bull & Scerif, 2001). For example, the stimulus "222" would require the response "three." Children with dyslexia performed at a level similar to the normal children on this task, suggesting, once more, the absence of inhibition problems.

Sidestepping reading and reading disabilities for a moment, the results of this study also suggest that the Trail Making task might not be a simple measure of switching ability. The children with arithmetic disabilities performed at a similar level to the children without arithmetic disabilities on the "pure" inhibition and switching tasks (Objects-I and Objects-S) but performed at a lower level on the Objects-IS and the Trail Making task. The Objects-IS required both switching and inhibition, although the latter might be better conceived as resistance to interference. Such a dual requirement might also be involved in the Trail Making task. At the moment that the subject has to make a switch to the other category, there might also be some interference of the previous category. A similar argument can be made with respect to the Wisconsin Card Sorting task. Accordingly, the key requirement of these tasks might not be the ability to switch as such but to alternate between task sets in the face of competing stimuli.

To summarize this section, the major deficit in WM capacity for children with dyslexia is in updating—that is, the control and updating of verbal information in WM—although recent evidence suggests that this deficit is not consistently found across studies (e.g., van der Sluis, van der Leij, & de Jong, 2005). The deficit does not depend on the type of processing, and it seems not to result from deficiencies in processing efficiency or deficits in verbal STM. Moreover, current evidence suggests that updating problems are specific to dyslexia. In children with ADHD or arithmetic disabilities, these problems are virtually absent or domain specific. Deficits in switching and inhibition of children with dyslexia are less pronounced and might even be absent.

CONCLUSION

Learning to read starts with the acquisition of letter knowledge and the development of sensitivity for phonemes in spoken words. Verbal STM might be involved in the learning of letter-sound correspondences because letter names and letter sounds can be regarded as novel sound structures. In this chapter some empirical evidence is provided for a relationship between verbal STM and the acquisition of letter knowledge.

Verbal STM and phoneme sensitivity are highly related. Whether verbal STM has a specific effect on the development of phoneme sensitivity is not yet clear. For the time being, both abilities can best be conceived as manifestations of the quality of the phonological representations of spoken words. Phoneme sensitivity seems the better indicator of this common underlying ability.

This view is in accordance with the subordinate role of verbal STM in the development of reading. Although verbal STM is clearly involved in phonological recoding, the evidence suggests that individual differences in verbal STM are not causally related to individual differences in the development of normal reading. Neither does a verbal STM deficit seem to be the cause of dyslexia. A deficit in verbal STM is more likely to be a correlate. One of the main candidate causes of dyslexia is a deficit in phonological sensitivity. The relationship of verbal STM with reading ability can best be understood through its relationship with phonological sensitivity and the common underlying ability that they both reflect.

Phonological recoding probably also requires the CE. Indeed, a relationship between updating, mainly conceived as complex span performance, and reading ability has regularly been found. There is little evidence for the causal nature of this relationship. Children with dyslexia tend to have a major CE deficit in the updating of verbal information. Impairments in other CE components are only minor or nonexistent.

The general conclusion is that the role of WM in the acquisition of single-word reading is limited. Deficits in WM do not seem to be the prime cause of dyslexia. However, this certainly does not imply that WM deficits in people with dyslexia should be further neglected. These deficits might have consequences for the acquisition of other cognitive abilities, such as spelling, syntactic awareness, and reading comprehension (e.g., Shankweiler, Crain, Brady, & Macaruso, 1992).

Adopting a WM perspective has been very useful in helping us to pinpoint and understand the specific impairments of children with dyslexia. In addition, these impairments appear to be nicely differentiated from the WM deficits of children with arithmetic disabilities. More generally, it seems worthwhile to use the WM perspective to characterize developmental disorders, including learning disabilities and socio-emotional problems. A characterization of disorders in terms of intact and impaired components of WM could highlight similarities and differences in the cognitive profile of disorders and provide further hypotheses about their origins. A general description of disorders along the components of WM might stimulate new comparisons—for example, between WM deficits in ADHD and arithmetic ability—and might reveal overlap in impairments between two disorders, which could imply a common cause and comorbidity (see Chapter 9 for further discussion of this issue). Finally, but no less important, such a classification can show patterns of dissociations of intact and impaired functions, thus providing a further validation of the different components of WM.

Summary Box

- The acquisition of letter-sound knowledge and the ability to detect and manipulate phonemes in spoken words are the twin foundations of early reading development (Byrne, 1998).
- Verbal STM is found to affect the acquisition of letter knowledge, which is understandable because letter names and letter sounds can be conceived as novel words.
- Phonological recoding, the sequential translation of letters into sounds and the blending of these sounds into the spoken form of the word, serves as a self-teaching mechanism for learning to read (Share, 1995).
- Phonological recoding clearly involves verbal STM, but there is no evidence that individual differences in verbal STM have a causal influence on individual differences in reading acquisition.
- The relationship between verbal STM and reading ability can best be understood through its strong relationship with phonological sensitivity and the common underlying ability that both are assumed to reflect.

- There is evidence to suggest that children with dyslexia have a deficit in the updating function of the CE. This deficit encompasses the language and numeric domain and is not a result of deficiencies in processing efficiency or deficits in verbal STM.
- Impairments in other functions of the CE in children with dyslexia, in particular inhibition and switching, are only minor or even absent.
- Deficits in WM (verbal STM and CE) do not seem to be a prime cause of dyslexia, but they can best be regarded as a correlate.
- A WM perspective has proved very useful in pinpointing and understanding the specific impairments of children with dyslexia and in differentiating their impairments from the WM deficits of children with other learning disabilities, such as arithmetic disabilities.
- A characterization of disorders in terms of intact and impaired components of WM could highlight similarities and differences in the cognitive profile of disorders and provide further hypotheses about their origins.

References

Aarnoutse, C., van Leeuwe, J., & Verhoeven, L. (2000). Ontwikkeling van beginnende geletterdheid [Development of beginning literacy]. *Pedagogische Studiën, 77*, 307–325.

Baddeley, A. D. (1986). *Working memory.* Oxford, England: Clarendon Press.

Baddeley, A. (1996). Exploring the central executive. *The Quarterly Journal of Experimental Psychology, 49A*, 5–28.

Baddeley, A., Gathercole, S., & Papagno, C. (1998). The phonological loop as a language learning device. *Psychological Review, 105*, 158–173.

Baddeley, A. D., & Hitch, G. J. (1974). Working memory. In G. H. Bower (Eds.), *The psychology of learning and motivation* (Vol. 8, pp. 47–90). New York: Academic Press.

Bowey, J. A. (1994). Phonological sensitivity in novice readers and nonreaders. *Journal of Experimental Child Psychology, 58*, 134–159.

Brady, S. A. (1991). The role of working memory in reading disability. In S. A. Brady & D. P. Shankweiler (Eds.), *Phonological processes in literacy* (pp. 129–151). Hillsdale, NJ: Lawrence Erlbaum Associates.

Brady, S. A. (1997). Ability to encode phonological representations: An underlying difficulty of poor readers. In B. A. Blachman (Ed.), *Foundations of reading acquisition and dyslexia: Implications for early intervention* (pp. 21–47). Mahwah, NJ: Lawrence Erlbaum Associates.

Brown, G. D. A., & Hulme, C. (1996). Nonword repetition, STM, and word age-of-acquisition: A computational model. In S. E. Gathercole (Ed.), *Models of short-term memory* (pp. 129–148). Sussex, UK: Psychology Press.

Bull, R., & Johnston, R. S. (1997). Children's arithmetical difficulties: Contributions from processing speed, item identification, and short-term memory. *Journal of Experimental Child Psychology, 65*, 1–14.

Bull, R., Johnston, R. S., & Roy, J. A. (1999). Exploring the roles of the visual-spatial sketch pad and central executive in children's arithmetical skills: Views from cognition and developmental neuropsychology. *Developmental Neuropsychology, 15*, 421–442.

Bull, R., & Scerif, G. (2001). Executive functioning as a predictor of children's mathematics ability: Inhibition, switching, and working memory. *Developmental Neuropsychology, 19*, 273–293.

Burgess, S. R., Hecht, S. A., & Lonigan, C. J. (2002). Relations of the home literacy environment (HLE) to the development of reading-related abilities: A one-year longitudinal study. *Reading Research Quarterly, 37*, 408–426.

Burgess, S. R., & Lonigan, C. J. (1998). Bidirectional relations of phonological sensitivity and prereading abilities: Evidence from a preschool sample. *Journal of Experimental Child Psychology, 70*, 117–141.

Byrne, B. (1998). *The foundation of literacy.* Sussex, UK: Psychology Press.

Carpenter, P. A., Just, M. A., & Shell, P. (1990). What one intelligence test measures: A theoretical account of the processing in the Raven Progressive Matrices Test. *Psychological Review, 97*, 404–431.

Case, R., Kurland, D. M., & Goldberg, J. (1982). Operational efficiency and the growth of short-term memory span. *Journal of Experimental Child Psychology, 33*, 386–404.

Conway, A. R. A., Cowan, N., Bunting, M. F., Therriault, D. J., & Minkoff, S. R. B. (2002). A latent variable analysis of working memory capacity, short-term memory capacity, processing speed, and general fluid intelligence. *Intelligence, 30*, 163–184.

Cunningham, A. E., Perry, K. E., Stanovich, K. E., & Share, D. L. (2002). Orthographic learning during reading: Examining the role of self-teaching. *Journal of Experimental Child Psychology, 82*, 185–199.

Cutting, L. E., & Denckla, M. B. (2001). The relationship of serial rapid naming and word reading in normally developing readers: An exploratory model. *Reading and Writing, 7–8*, 673–705.

Daneman, M., & Carpenter, P. A. (1980). Individual differences in working memory and reading. *Journal of Verbal Learning and Verbal Behavior, 19*, 450–466.

Daneman, M., & Merikle, P. M. (1996). Working memory and language comprehension: a meta-analysis. *Psychonomic Bulletin & Review, 3*, 422–433.

de Jong, P. F. (1998). Working memory deficits of reading disabled children. *Journal of Experimental Child Psychology, 70*, 75–96.

de Jong, P. F., & Olson, R. K. (2004). Early predictors of letter knowledge. *Journal of Experimental Child Psychology, 88*, 254–273.

de Jong, P. F., & Leseman, P. P. M. (2001). Lasting effects of home literacy on reading achievement in school. *Journal of School Psychology, 39*, 389–414.

de Jong, P. F., & Korbee, L. (1998). Working memory capacity in reading disabled children with and without arithmetic disabilities. Unpublished manuscript.

de Jong, P. F., & van der Leij, A. (1999). Specific contributions of phonological abilities to early reading acquisition: Results from a Dutch latent variable longitudinal study. *Journal of Educational Psychology, 91*, 450–476.

de Jong, P. F., & van der Leij, A. (2002). Effects of phonological abilities and linguistic comprehension on the development of reading. *Scientific Studies of Reading, 6*, 51–77.

Ehri, L. C. (1998). Grapheme-phoneme knowledge is essential for learning to read words in English. In J. L. Metsala & L. C. Ehri (Eds.), *Word recognition in beginning literacy* (pp. 3–40). Mahwah, NJ: Lawrence Erlbaum Associates.

Ehri, L. C., & Saltmarsh, J. (1995). Beginning readers outperform older disabled readers in learning to read words by sight. *Reading and Writing: An Interdisciplinary Journal, 7*, 295–326.

Elbro, C. (1996). Early linguistic abilities and reading development: A review and a hypothesis. *Reading and Writing, 8*, 1–33.

Engle, R. W., Tuholski, S. W., Laughlin, J. E., & Conway, A. R. A. (1999). Working memory, short-term memory, and general fluid intelligence: A latent variable approach. *Journal of Experimental Psychology, 128*, 309–331.

Fowler, A. E. (1991). How early phonological development might set the stage for phoneme awareness. In S. A. Brady & D. P. Shankweiler (Eds.), *Phonological processes in literacy* (pp. 97–117). Hillsdale, NJ: Lawrence Erlbaum Associates.

Fürst, A. J., & Hitch, G. J. (2000). Separate roles for executive and phonological components of working memory in mental arithmetic. *Memory and Cognition, 28*, 774–782.

Gathercole, S. E. (1995). Is nonword repetition a test of phonological memory or long-term knowledge? It all depends on the nonwords. *Memory & Cognition, 23*, 83–94.

Gathercole, S. E., & Baddeley, A. D. (1990). The role of phonological memory in vocabulary acquisition: A study of young children learning new names. *British Journal of Psychology, 81*, 439–454.

Gathercole, S. E., Willis, C., & Baddeley, A. D. (1991). Differentiating phonological memory and awareness of rhyme: Reading and vocabulary development in children. *British Journal of Psychology, 82*, 387–406.

Geary, D. C. (1993). Mathematical disabilities: Cognitive, neuropsychological, and genetic components. *Psychological Bulletin, 114*, 345–362.

Goswami, U. (1993). Towards an interactive analogy model of reading development: Decoding vowel graphemes in beginning reading. *Journal of Experimental Child Psychology, 56*, 443–475.

Goswami, U. (2002). Phonology, reading development and dyslexia: A cross-linguistic perspective. *Annals of Dyslexia, 52*, 141–163.

Hall, J. W., Wilson, K. P., Humphreys, M. S., Tinzmann, M. B., & Bowyer, P. M. (1983). Phonemic similarity effects in good vs. poor readers. *Memory and Cognition, 11*, 520–527.

Hansen, J., & Bowey, J. A. (1994). Phonological analysis skills, verbal working memory, and reading ability in second-grade children. *Child Development, 65*, 938–950.

Hitch, G. J., & McAuley, E. (1991). Working memory in children with specific arithmetical learning difficulties. *British Journal of Psychology, 82*, 375–386.

Hulme, C., Maughan, S., & Brown, G. D. A. (1991). Memory for familiar and unfamiliar words: Evidence for a long-term memory contribution to short-term memory span. *Journal of Memory and Language, 30*, 685–701.

Hulme, C., Roodenrys, S., Brown, G., & Mercer, R. (1995). The role of long-term memory mechanisms in memory span. *British Journal of Psychology, 86*, 527–536.

Johnston, R. S. (1982). Phonological coding in dyslexic readers. *British Journal of Psychology, 73*, 455–460.

Johnston, R. S., Anderson, M., & Holligan, C. (1996). Knowledge of the alphabet and explicit awareness of phonemes in pre-readers: The nature of the relationship. *Reading and Writing, 8*, 217–234.

Kail, R., & Hall, L. K. (2001). Distinguishing short-term memory from working memory. *Memory-and-Cognition, 29*, 1–9.

Kane, M. J., & Engle, R. W. (2003). Working-memory capacity and the control of attention: the contributions of goal neglect, response competition, and task set to Stroop interference. *Journal of Experimental Psychology: General, 132*, 47–70.

Kyllonen, P. C., & Christal, R. E. (1990). Reasoning ability is (little more than) working memory capacity?! *Intelligence, 14*, 389–433.

Landerl, K., Wimmer, H., & Frith, U. (1997). The impact of orthographic consistency on dyslexia: A German-English comparison. *Cognition, 63*, 315–334.

Leather, C. V., & Henry, L. A. (1994). Working memory span and phonological awareness tasks as predictors of early reading ability. *Journal of Experimental Child Psychology, 58*, 88–111.

Lonigan, C. J., Burgess, S. R., & Anthony, J. L. (2000). Development of emergent literacy and early reading skills in preschool children: Evidence from a latent-variable longitudinal study. *Developmental Psychology, 36*, 596–613.

McDougall, S., Hulme, C., Ellis, A., & Monk, A. (1994). Learning to read: The role of short-term memory and phonological skills. *Journal of Experimental Psychology, 58*, 112–133.

McDougall, S. J. P., & Donohoe, R. (2002). Reading ability and memory span: Long-term contributions to span for good and poor readers. *Reading and Writing, 15*, 359–387.

McLean, J. F., & Hitch, G. J. (1999). Working memory impairments in children with specific arithmetic learning difficulties. *Journal of Experimental Child Psychology, 74*, 240–260.

Messbauer, V. C. S., & de Jong, P. F. (2003). Word, nonword, and visual paired associate learning in Dutch dyslexic children. *Journal of Experimental Child Psychology, 84*, 77–96.

Metsala, J. L., & Walley, A. C. (1998). Spoken vocabulary growth and the segmental restructuring of lexical representations: Precursors to phonemic awareness and early reading ability. In J. L. Metsala & L. C. Ehri (Eds.), *Word recognition in beginning literacy* (pp. 89–120). Mahwah, NJ: Lawrence Erlbaum Associates.

Miyake, A., Friedman, N. P., Emerson, M. J., Witzki, A. H., & Howerter, A. (2000). The unity and diversity of executive functions and their contributions to complex "frontal lobe" tasks: A latent variable analysis. *Cognitive Psychology, 41*, 49–100.

Muter, V., & Snowling, M. (1998). Concurrent and longitudinal predictors of reading: The role of metalinguistic and short-term memory skills. *Reading Research Quarterly, 33*, 320–337.

Pennington, B. F., & Lefly, D. L. (2001). Early reading development in children at family risk for dyslexia. *Child Development, 72*, 816–833.

Pennington, B. F., Van Orden, G., Kirson, D., & Haith (1991). What is the causal relation between verbal STM problems and dyslexia? In S. A. Brady & D. P. Shankweiler (Eds.), *Phonological processes in literacy* (pp. 173–186). Hillsdale, NJ: Lawrence Erlbaum Associates.

Perfetti, C. A. (1992). The representation problem in reading acquisition. In P. B. Gough, L. C. Ehri, & R. Treiman (Eds.), *Reading acquisition* (pp. 145–174). Hillsdale, NJ: Lawrence Erlbaum Associates.

Rack, J. P., & Olson R. K. (1993). Phonological deficits, IQ, and individual differences in reading-disability-genetic and environmental-influences. *Developmental Review 13*(3), 269–278.

Rohl, M., & Pratt, C. (1995). Phonological awareness, verbal working memory and the acquisition of literacy. *Reading and Writing, 7*, 327–360.

Roodenrys, S., & Hinton, M. (2002). Sublexical or lexical effects on serial recall for nonwords? *Journal of Experimental Psychology: LMC, 28*, 29–33.

Roodenrys, S., & Stokes, J. (2001). Serial recall and nonword repetition in reading disabled children. *Reading and Writing, 14*, 379–394.

Scarborough, H. S. (1998). Early identification of children at risk for reading disabilities: Phonological awareness and some other promising predictors. In B. K. Shapiro, P. J. Accardo, & A. J. Capute (Eds.), *Specific reading disability. A view of the spectrum* (pp. 75–119). Timonium, Maryland: York Press, Inc.

Shankweiler, D., Crain, S., Brady, S., & Macaruso, P. (1992). Identifying the causes of reading disability. In P. B. Gough, L. C. Ehri & R. Treiman (Eds.), *Reading acquisition* (pp. 275–305). Hillsdale, NJ: Lawrence Erlbaum Associates.

Shankweiler, D., Liberman, I. Y., Mark, L. S., Fowler, C. A., & Fischer, F. W. (1979). The speech code and learning to read. *Journal of Experimental Psychology: Human Learning and Memory, 5*, 531–545.

Share, D. L. (1995). Phonological recoding and self-teaching: Sine qua non of reading acquisition. *Cognition, 55*, 151–218.

Share, D. L. (1999). Phonological recoding and orthographic learning: A direct test of the self-teaching hypothesis. *Journal of Experimental Child Psychology, 72*, 95–129.

Share, D. L. (2004). Knowing letter names and learning letter sounds: A causal connection. *Journal of Experimental Child Psychology, 88*, 213–233.

Share, D. L., Jorm, A. F., MacClean, R., & Matthews, R. (1984). Sources of individual differences in reading acquisition. *Journal of Educational Psychology, 76*, 1309–1324.

Siegel, L. S. (1993). The development of reading. In H. W. Reese (Ed.), *Advances in Child Development and Behavior* (Vol. 24, pp. 63–97). San Diego: Academic Press.

Siegel, L. S., & Ryan, E. B. (1989). The development of working memory in normally achieving and subtypes of learning disabled children. *Child Development, 60*, 973–980.

Snow, C. E. (1991). The theoretical basis for relationships between language and literacy in development. *Journal of Research in Childhood Education, 6*, 5–10.

Snowling, M. J. (2000). *Dyslexia*. Oxford, England: Blackwell.

Snowling, M. J., Gallagher, A., & Frith, U. (2003). Family risk of dyslexia is continuous: Individual differences in the precursors of reading skills. *Child Development, 74*, 358–373.

Stanovich, K. E., Nathan, R. G., & Zolman, J. E. (1988). The developmental lag hypothesis in reading: Longitudinal and matched reading-level comparisons. *Child Development, 59*, 71–86.

Storch, S. A., & Whitehurst, G. J. (2002). Oral language and code-related precursors to reading: Evidence from a longitudinal structural model. *Developmental Psychology, 38*, 934–947.

Swanson, H. L. (1993). Working memory in learning disability subgroups. *Journal of Experimental Child Psychology, 56*, 87–114.

Swanson, H. L., & Ashbaker, M. H. (2000). Working memory, short-term memory, speech rate, word recognition and reading comprehension in learning disables readers: Does the executive system have a role? *Intelligence, 28*, 1–30.

Treiman, R., Mullenix, J., Bijeljac-Babic, R., & Richmond-Welty, E. D. (1995). The special role of rimes in the description, use, and acquisition of English orthography. *Journal of Experimental Psychology: General, 124*, 107–136.

Treiman, R., Tincoff, R., Rodriguez, K., Mouzaki, A., & Francis, D. J. (1998). The foundations of literacy: Learning the sounds of letters. *Child Development, 69*, 1524–1540.

Treiman, R., Weatherston, S., & Berch, D. (1994). The role of letter names in children's learning of phoneme-grapheme relations. *Applied Psycholinguistics, 15*, 97–122.

Turner, M. L., & Engle, R. W. (1989). Is working memory capacity task dependent? *Journal of Memory and Language, 28*, 127–154.

van Bon, W. H. J., & van der Pijl, J. M. L. (1997). Effects of word length and wordlikeness on pseudoword repetition by poor and normal readers. *Applied Psycholinguistics, 18*, 101–114.

van der Sluis, S., de Jong, P. F., & van der Leij, A. (2004). Inhibition and switching in children with learning deficits in arithmetic and reading. *Journal of Experimental Child Psychology, 87*, 239–266.

van der Sluis, S., van der Leij, A., & de Jong, P. F. (2005). Working memory in Dutch children with reading- and arithmetic-related LD. *Journal of Learning Disabilities, 38*(3), 207–221.

Wagner, R. K., & Torgesen, J. K. (1987). The nature of phonological processing and its causal role in the acquisition of reading skills. *Psychological Bulletin, 101*, 192–212.

Wagner, R. K., Torgesen, J. K., & Rashotte, C. A. (1994). Development of reading-related phonological processing abilities: New evidence of bidirectional causality from a latent variable longitudinal study. *Developmental Psychology, 30*, 73–87.

Wagner, R. K., Torgesen, J. K., Rashotte, C. A., Hecht, S. A., Barker, T. A., Burgess, S. R., et al. (1997). Changing relations between phonological processing abilities and word-level reading as children develop from beginning to skilled readers: A 5-year longitudinal study. *Developmental Psychology, 33*, 468–479.

Whitehurst, G. J., & Lonigan, C. J. (1998). Child development and emergent literacy. *Child Development, 69*, 848–872.

Willcutt, E. G., Pennington, B. F., Boada, R., Ogline, J. S., Tunick, R. A., Chhabildas, N. A., et al. (2001). A comparison of cognitive deficits in reading disability and attention-deficit/hyperactivity disorder. *Journal of Abnormal Psychology, 110*, 157–172.

CHAPTER

3

Children's Reading Comprehension: The Role of Working Memory in Normal and Impaired Development

KATE CAIN

Lancaster University

There is a strong relationship between children's working memory (WM) capacity and their ability to understand text: WM deficits are reliably found in children who do poorly on assessments of reading comprehension (e.g., Yuill, Oakhill, & Parkin, 1989), and a child's performance on a WM task is a good indicator of their reading comprehension level, even after factors such as their vocabulary knowledge and word reading ability have been taken into account (Cain, Oakhill, & Bryant, 2004; Seigneuric, Ehrlich, Oakhill, & Yuill, 2000). In this chapter, I evaluate the importance of WM to children's understanding of written text.

There are many stages involved in the comprehension of written text. First, the reader must decode the individual words on the page and access their meanings. The reader also needs to work out the syntactic structure and sense of each sentence. Once the meanings of words and sentences have been derived, the reader must engage in several additional processes to gain a full and accurate understanding of the overall content of the text. For example, the reader has to work out how the information expressed in the different sentences and phrases fits together, so they need to establish links between the different sentences (integration) and the meanings of pronouns such as "he" or "she" (anaphoric resolution). The reader may also access and incorporate general knowledge to fill in missing details (inference making) or use the surrounding text to work out the precise meaning of a particular word or phrase (use of context). In addition to these processes, skilled readers check their understanding of the text as they read, which can help them to identify, for example, whether they have worked out the correct referent for a pronoun or whether they need to make an inference. This latter process is referred to as comprehension monitoring.

In this chapter, I explore the nature of the relationship between WM and children's reading comprehension level by examining the contribution that WM makes to overall reading comprehension level and also to the following specific higher-level text processing skills: integration and inference, anaphoric processing, use of context, and comprehension monitoring. Studies that investigate both normal and impaired reading comprehension development are discussed.

WORKING MEMORY AND READING COMPREHENSION

The focus of this section is the relationship between WM capacity and reading comprehension in general. First, I consider what it means to comprehend and why memory resources are important for good reading comprehension. Then I review the evidence for a relationship between WM and reading comprehension in populations of children with normal reading development and those who experience difficulties with reading comprehension. Of interest here is the specificity of any relationship between WM and reading comprehension: Is there any evidence that WM capacity directly determines reading comprehension level, or is the relationship between the two mediated by a third variable? The studies considered explore the predictive power of WM in relation to other variables that we know are related to children's reading comprehension—namely, short-term memory (STM), word reading, and vocabulary knowledge.

Working Memory and Skilled Reading Comprehension

When reading a text, our aim as readers usually is to derive an overall interpretation of the text, rather than simply to retrieve the meanings of individual words or sentences.[1] This central purpose of reading is reflected in a factor common to all major theories of text comprehension—that comprehension involves the construction of a mental representation of the content of the text, often called a mental model or a situation model (Gernsbacher, 1990; Johnson-Laird, 1983; Kintsch, 1998).

---

[1] In particular circumstances our aim would be different—for example, if we were skim reading to find a particular name or to check a date.

Reading the individual words on the page involves recoding the written symbols into a phonological speech-based code. Phonological STM is, therefore, crucial to good reading comprehension because the reader must maintain the individual words of a sentence in memory to compute its syntactic structure. However, simply deriving the meanings of individual words and sentences is insufficient: To fully understand a text, the reader must build a coherent and integrated representation of the state of affairs described in the text, the mental model. The reader needs to integrate information from different sentences to establish local coherence and to incorporate background knowledge and ideas (retrieved from long-term memory, or LTM) to make sense of details that are only implicitly mentioned (Graesser, Singer, & Trabasso, 1994; Long & Chong, 2001). Consider the following (from Bishop, 1997):

> John was at the beach.
> He stepped on some broken glass.
> He had to go to the hospital.

To understand this text in a meaningful way, the reader must make links between successive sentences—for example, establishing that "he" in the second and third sentences refers to the protagonist "John" introduced in the first sentence. The reader also needs to draw on general knowledge to supplement the information provided literally by the wording. For example, the knowledge that we are usually barefoot on a beach enables the reader to infer that John cut his foot, hence the trip to the hospital.

The processes necessary to construct the mental model of even a very short text such as the one here require the reader to maintain the just-read wording in memory while concurrently processing the same or other information. This relevant information, either from the text itself or general knowledge, must be both available and accessible. WM is considered the workspace for this processing. It serves as a buffer for the most recently read propositions (or phrases) in a text, enabling the reader to integrate their meaning to establish local coherence between sentences, and holds information retrieved from LTM to facilitate its integration with the current mental model (Cooke, Halleran, & O'Brien, 1998; Daneman & Carpenter, 1980, 1983; Ericsson & Kintsch, 1995; Graesser et al., 1994).

The WM model proposed by Baddeley and Hitch (1974; Baddeley, 1986, 1996) has been influential in our understanding of the relationships between memory processes and reading comprehension. WM is conceptualized as a limited capacity system comprising three components: the central executive, the phonological loop, and the visuospatial sketchpad. The latter two components are dedicated to the temporary storage of verbal (the phonological loop) and visual-spatial (the visuo-spatial sketchpad) information. The central executive is attributed with coordinating the storage and processing of incoming information. There is considerable evidence that phonological

STM and overall verbal WM capacity are important for different aspects of reading (see Gathercole, 1998, for a review).

Phonological STM is usually measured by presenting spoken lists of words (word span) or digits (digit span), which have to be recalled in the order in which they were presented. The number of items in the list is increased until the maximum number of items that the individual can accurately recall is reached. For example, "*dog-cheek-plate,*" "*mug-chick-bed-tree,*" "*duck-man-bat-spoon-leg.*" The central executive acts as a coordinator, facilitating the integration of each new piece of information with the representation of the text's meaning constructed so far, the mental model. Typical measures of WM capacity assess this function of the central executive. These measures have been developed to have the same storage component as word span or digit span tasks but with an additional processing component. The reading span test developed by Daneman and Carpenter (1980, 1983) requires participants to read a set of unrelated sentences (processing component) and to recall the final word of each sentence at the end of the set (storage component). For example, "*I turned my memories over at random like pictures in a photograph album*" and "*The girl hesitated for a moment to taste the onions because her husband hated the smell*" recall "*album, smell*" (from Daneman & Carpenter, 1983). The listening span versions of this task involve spoken presentation of sentences that require either validity judgments (true, false) or final word completion of the sentence frames as the processing component. In this chapter I refer to tasks that assess the short-term storage of verbal information as measures of (phonological) *short-term memory* and tasks that involve simultaneous storage and processing of verbal information as measures of (verbal) *working memory*.

Assessments of phonological STM tap into the same storage system used for just-read text. Measures of verbal WM clearly draw on the same resources needed for integrating information between successive sentences in a text to construct the mental model and, therefore, comprehend a text well. There is a wealth of research demonstrating the distinction between these two aspects of memory. Measures of verbal WM, which tap concurrent storage and processing, are better predictors of undergraduates' performance on standardized assessments of reading comprehension ability than are measures of phonological STM, such as word span (Daneman & Carpenter, 1980). In addition, WM capacity is significantly correlated with a number of specific skills that are important for good text comprehension, such as the resolution of pronouns, memory for facts, and the inference of unknown word meanings from context (Daneman & Carpenter, 1980; Daneman & Green, 1986; Masson & Miller, 1983). A meta-analysis of 77 studies that investigated the relationship between language comprehension and WM confirmed the relationship between WM tasks that tapped the processing and storage of verbal information (words, sentences, numbers) and language comprehension (Daneman & Merikle, 1996).

Working Memory and Children's Reading Comprehension

Research with adults consistently finds that verbal WM is an important predictor of reading comprehension level and a better predictor of it than STM. The same is not necessarily true for children. Performance on measures of STM and verbal WM increase during early and middle childhood (see Gathercole, 1998, for a review) when reading comprehension skills are developing. Thus, we might expect the development of WM to limit overall reading comprehension level. However, several researchers have noted that children's basic reading and language skills also grow during this period. It has therefore been proposed that phonological STM, basic reading and language skills, or both underlie any WM limitations that are associated with children's comprehension level and specific reading comprehension problems. Thus, a very different relationship between WM and reading comprehension in children has been suggested, compared to the direct relationship found in adults. The different theoretical positions for the relationship between children's WM and reading comprehension are outlined next.

The Verbal Efficiency Hypothesis

The verbal efficiency hypothesis is an account of children's reading comprehension difficulties proposed by Perfetti (e.g., Perfetti, 1985, 1994). It seeks to explain reading comprehension problems by drawing on the relationship between word reading ability and reading comprehension. In children, word reading and reading comprehension are highly related; correlations fall within the range of 0.36 to 0.83, and word reading ability is a superior predictor of reading comprehension skill for children than for young adults (Gough, Hoover, & Peterson, 1996). Because young children's reading skills are still developing, their word reading is less fluent than that of older good readers. Slow and effortful word reading is also a characteristic of poor readers. The gist of the verbal efficiency hypothesis is that inefficient word reading by young children and poor readers might limit their ability to understand what they read.

Central to this hypothesis is the idea that WM is a limited capacity system, involving a trade-off between storage and processing. The processes involved in reading words and those involved in comprehending text compete for the same amount of processing capacity. Inefficient word reading will mean that a larger proportion of processing capacity is devoted to reading the words on the page, leaving little over for comprehension processes (such as working out the relationships between successive words, phrases, and sentences), which are needed to construct a coherent and meaningful representation of the sense of the text. The contents of STM are subject to decay. Therefore, slow word reading may mean that the information stored in STM will be lost before being fully processed or integrated with the current mental model. As a result, reading comprehension will suffer.

In its strongest form, the verbal efficiency hypothesis would predict that any relationship between reading comprehension and verbal WM will be mediated by word reading ability. There is some support for this view: Some children who are poor comprehenders have poor word reading skills and they take longer to name real words and pseudowords (e.g., *bope, flish, mamp*) than their skilled peers. Differences in naming speed between good and poor readers are specific to word reading: Good and poor readers do not differ in the time taken to name numerals and colors, items that do not require decoding (see Perfetti, 1985, for a review).

The Phonological Processing Limitation Hypothesis

Another processing-based account of comprehension difficulties is the phonological processing limitation hypothesis, proposed by Shankweiler and colleagues (see Shankweiler, 1989, for a review). This account links reading comprehension problems to deficits in phonological STM. As you might expect, some studies find that reading comprehension (as well as word reading ability) is correlated with phonological processing skills such as nonword repetition and phonemic awareness (e.g., Hatcher & Hulme, 1999; Stanovich, Nathan, & Vala-Rossi, 1986), particularly in populations of younger readers. This is because word reading ability and reading comprehension are highly correlated skills and phonological processing skills are well-established predictors of word reading ability.

The central idea of the phonological processing limitation hypothesis is that poor readers are unable to set up or sustain a sound-based representation of the text they are reading as a result of their phonological processing deficits. Consequently they experience difficulties in retaining this information in STM and, as a result, experience difficulties when processing language that makes heavy demands on verbal WM resources—for example, complex sentences, such as restrictive relative clauses (e.g., "The horse bit the pig that chased the sheep"). Thus, phonological STM deficits can lead to comprehension difficulties in young readers. In support of this hypothesis, children with word reading difficulties experience deficits in short-term recall of phonological information and comprehension of complex sentences, such as relative clauses (Shankweiler, 1989).

Impaired Semantic Knowledge

The other basic reading-related skill to be considered in relation to WM and reading comprehension is semantic knowledge. There is a strong relationship between the number of word meanings known by a child or adult and their reading comprehension level (Carroll, 1993). Clearly, text comprehension will be compromised if the reader does not know the meanings of sufficient key words in the text. However, semantic knowledge may be related to comprehension in another, indirect, way by supporting STM for verbal information.

In general, we find it easier to remember lists of words than of nonwords. Roodenrys, Hulme, and Brown (1993) explored this effect in children aged 5–6 and 9–11 years old. The older children's superior performance was not simply attributable to age-related differences in speech rate, which is known to affect short-term phonological memory. They suggested that the older children's representations of real words in LTM aided their storage in the recall task. In a similar way, recall of real words may be better than that of nonwords because the latter do not have a stored representation to be activated.

Building on this research, Nation and colleagues have proposed a semantic basis for comprehension difficulties. Their idea is that children with good reading comprehension skills have superior semantic knowledge to that of their skilled peers. Good comprehenders are better able to activate representations of words from LTM, which boosts their STM for verbal information (Nation, Adams, Bowyer-Crane, & Snowling, 1999). Similarly, Stothard and Hulme (1992) suggested that the relationship between WM and children's reading comprehension is mediated by verbal IQ (intelligence quotient).

Higher-Level Skill Deficits

In contrast to these positions, Jane Oakhill, our colleagues, and I have proposed that some children experience reading comprehension problems that are not related to any word reading, phonological processing, or vocabulary deficit. Instead, we have argued that reading comprehension problems can arise from deficits in higher-level comprehension-related skills such as integration and inference making, anaphoric processing, use of context, and comprehension monitoring (see Cain & Oakhill, 2004, for a review). These skills are involved in the construction of the representation of a text's meaning, which involves updating the mental representation of a text by incorporating newly read ideas with the sense so far and ensuring that the model is coherent. Both new and old information must be active for this processing to take place, indicating an important role for WM.

In our investigations into reading comprehension difficulties, we have been particularly interested in children who have a specific reading comprehension deficit: good word reading ability but impaired reading comprehension. These children have reading comprehension deficits despite age-appropriate word reading, sight vocabulary, and phonological processing skills (e.g., Cain, Oakhill, & Bryant, 2000a). This population also has WM impairments (Yuill, Oakhill, & Parkin, 1989). We have proposed that any WM deficits associated with this population's reading comprehension problems have not arisen from the lower-level word reading and vocabulary deficits suggested in the hypotheses outlined earlier because we match good and poor comprehenders on these measures (see Oakhill, Cain, & Yuill, 1998).[2]

Weak Inhibitory Processes

Another account that posits a direct link between WM and reading comprehension has been developed by de Beni and colleagues (de Beni & Palladino, 2000; de Beni, Palladino, Pazzaglia, & Cornoldi, 1998). They propose that individuals with weak WM are less efficient at regulating the level of activation of the contents of memory. Such regulation can involve maintaining activation of currently important information, reducing the activation of information that is no longer relevant, and preventing the entry of unnecessary or irrelevant information into WM. Because efficient maintenance, storage, and updating of information are crucial to the construction of a meaning-based representation of a text, de Beni and colleagues propose that such inhibitory deficits affect the ability to engage in processing that is crucial for good comprehension.

In support of this account, comparisons of children and adults with good and poor reading comprehension have found that they make qualitatively different types of error on standard listening or reading span measures of WM: Poor comprehenders are much more likely to incorrectly recall words from a previous trial (de Beni & Palladino 2000; de Beni et al., 1998). Thus, de Beni and colleagues are currently exploring a possible source of the WM deficits found in individuals with weak reading comprehension.

In summary, several different accounts have been put forward to explain the relationship between children's WM and their reading comprehension. Some propose an indirect relationship between the two, arguing that factors that affect memory efficiency, such as word reading skill, or those that affect short-term storage, such as phonological and semantic processing skills, are mediating factors. Others propose a direct relationship between the two, either simply that weak WM skills are apparent in the face of good word reading and vocabulary, or that inhibitory weaknesses are the source of the WM deficits that lead to poor reading comprehension. Evidence for these different positions is reviewed in the next two sections. First I consider developmental studies that have explored how well WM predicts reading comprehension level in relation to phonological STM, word reading, and semantic skills. Then I turn to research that has investigated the WM skills of children with reading comprehension difficulties.

---

[2]We do not contend that poor word reading and vocabulary skills do not lead to reading comprehension difficulties; simply, we are saying that some children experience reading comprehension deficits despite apparent fluency in these other language skills.

Developmental Studies of Working Memory and Reading Comprehension

Phonological Short-Term Memory and Phonological Processing

Several studies investigating children's reading comprehension have included measures of either phonological STM or phonological processing alongside measures of WM to determine the relative importance of each memory system to different age groups' reading skill. In general, these studies find that children's performance on tasks tapping phonological STM and WM are correlated and that both aspects of memory are related to reading comprehension.

de Jonge and de Jong (1996) assessed the verbal memory skills of children aged 9, 10, and 11 years. The children completed a battery of measures that assessed short-term storage of words and digits (STM) and simultaneous storage and processing of words and digits (WM). Reading comprehension scores were correlated with the measures of WM and one of the STM measures (digit span). The data were analyzed using confirmatory factor analysis to test the nature of the relationships between the different measures of memory and reading ability. The measures of STM and WM all loaded on to the same factor, indicating that they were tapping the same pool of skills. Reading comprehension loaded onto a separate factor. However, these two factors, memory processes and reading comprehension, were correlated. Engle, Carullo, and Collins (1991) also found sizeable correlations between measures of STM and WM in 9–11 year olds. Additionally, both aspects of memory were related to reading comprehension performance. However, consistent with the adult literature, Engle et al. found a much stronger relationship between verbal WM and specific comprehension skills than between STM and comprehension. For example, their WM measure correlated with performance on questions tapping pronoun reference, understanding of main ideas, and cause and effect in the reading comprehension texts, but the STM measure did not. This finding suggests a specific relationship between WM and the skills important for comprehending text.

The two studies described earlier found a strong association between a child's reading comprehension level and their WM capacity and also between their performance on STM and WM tasks. These studies do not rule out the possibility that the relationship between children's WM and their reading comprehension is mediated by their STM. To determine whether there is a direct link between WM and reading comprehension, we need to take into account the relationship between STM and WM. Studies that have controlled for this in their statistical analyses find that WM explains independent variance in children's reading comprehension.

Leather and Henry (1994) used a multiple regression design to determine the relative contribution of different skills to 7-year-olds' word reading,

reading comprehension, and mathematic ability. Of interest here are the analyses with reading comprehension as the criterion. These analyses demonstrated that STM only accounted for 5% of the variance in 7-year-olds' reading comprehension level but that WM explained an additional 33% of the variance in comprehension performance. A similar finding was reported by Swanson and Howell (2001) in a study of 9 and 14 year olds. WM and STM were both highly correlated with reading comprehension skill (0.68 and 0.57, respectively) as well as with each other (0.68). However, verbal WM explained an additional 9% of the variance in reading comprehension after the contribution made by STM and articulation rate had been taken into account.[3] Leather and Henry also included measures of phonological processing skill in their study. Performance on these tasks accounted for significant variance in reading comprehension skill, but WM explained additional unique variance. Gottardo, Stanovich, and Siegel (1996) found the same pattern of prediction with 8 year olds. Taken together, these studies suggest that WM predicts a child's reading comprehension level over and above STM.

Word Reading and Vocabulary Knowledge

The work reviewed thus far demonstrates a strong relationship between verbal WM and reading comprehension in 7–14 year olds that is independent of performance on measures of phonological STM. However, as mentioned earlier, two key predictors of young children's reading comprehension ability are their word reading accuracy and their vocabulary skills (Saarnio, Oka, & Paris, 1990). To determine the relative importance of verbal WM to children's reading comprehension ability, we need to see whether the relationship holds after performance on these basic skills has been controlled for, in the same way that the studies mentioned previously controlled for performance on STM tasks.

This was one of the aims of research conducted by Seigneuric et al. (2000). They gave 9 year olds four measures of verbal WM. Two tasks required the storage and manipulation of words, and two required the storage and manipulation of numbers. Performance on these tasks was significantly correlated to the children's reading comprehension level, vocabulary knowledge, and word reading ability. Further analyses revealed that WM explained performance on the reading comprehension task over and above a child's word reading and vocabulary knowledge.

Consistent with this finding are some results from a longitudinal study of children's reading comprehension conducted by Jane Oakhill, Peter Bryant, and me (Cain et al., 2004). We took several measures of reading-related skills when children were aged 8, 9, and 11 years old. These measures included word reading accuracy, verbal ability, written vocabulary

---

[3]A model with just verbal working memory and short-term memory is not reported.

knowledge, and receptive vocabulary knowledge, as well as measures of verbal WM capacity and reading comprehension. As you might expect, the basic reading-related and language skills (word reading, verbal ability, vocabulary) explained a sizeable proportion of the variance in reading comprehension at each time point: 26%, 43%, and 46%, when the children were aged 8, 9, and 11 years, respectively. However, at each time point, WM capacity explained unique variance in reading comprehension (between 5–7%) over and above these other measures.

Weak Inhibitory Processes

Recent work has explored the possibility of a common basis for poor performance on measures of reading comprehension and WM. One factor that might affect the attentional resources available in WM or the efficiency with which information is processed is an individual's ability to regulate the level of activation of the contents of memory. Such regulation can involve maintaining activation of currently important information and reducing the activation of information that is no longer relevant.

Adults and children with weak reading comprehension have deficient inhibitory mechanisms—for example, they are slower to suppress the irrelevant meanings of ambiguous words (Barnes, Faulkner, Wilkinson, & Dennis, 2004; Gernsbacher & Faust, 1991). In memory tasks, adults with weak reading comprehension are more likely to recall words that should have been forgotten, and therefore inhibited, than are good comprehenders (de Beni et al., 1998). Similarly, children with weak reading comprehension experience a greater number of intrusions in their recall on memory tasks and they are also more likely to remember material that is irrelevant to the main topic of a passage they have studied (de Beni & Palladino, 2000).

This body of work demonstrates that phonological STM and WM are both important predictors of children's reading comprehension across a wide age range. However, in a similar way to that for the adult literature, this research indicates that WM explains variance in reading comprehension that is independent of the relationship between reading comprehension and phonological STM and also reading comprehension, word reading ability, and vocabulary knowledge. One possibility is that weak inhibitory processes affect the regulation of the contents of WM, influencing performance on specific measures of WM and also reading comprehension in general.

Individual Differences in Reading Comprehension Skill and Working Memory

As mentioned earlier, poor word reading can adversely affect children's reading comprehension performance. Despite this, up to 10% of British school children have age-appropriate word reading skills but poor reading comprehension (Stothard & Hulme, 1996; Yuill & Oakhill, 1991). The extent

TABLE 3.1
The Mean Scores (and Standard Deviations) of Typical Groups

	Poor Comprehenders (N = 14)	Good Comprehenders (N = 12)	Comprehension-Age Match (N = 12)
Chronological age	7,7 (4.44)	7,7 (4.04)	6,6 (3.88)
Sight vocabulary	37.2 (4.00)	37.4 (3.00)	32.9 (2.91)
Word reading accuracy in context (age)	7,9 (5.17)	7,11 (5.73)	6,7 (4.98)
Reading comprehension (age)	6,7 (3.87)	8,1 (5.14)	6,8 (3.11)

Where appropriate, ages are given as years, months with standard deviations in months.

to which different research studies address reading comprehension difficulties, as opposed to general reading difficulties, is unclear because many studies use assessments of reading comprehension that do not provide separate measures of word reading and text comprehension or do not control for individual differences in word reading skill or single word comprehension (e.g., Nation et al., 1999; Smith, Macaruso, Shankweiler, & Crain, 1989). In this review I focus on studies of individual differences in reading comprehension skill that compare groups of good and poor comprehenders who are matched for basic word reading skill and vocabulary knowledge, so that we can consider the specific relationship between WM and reading comprehension. A number of research groups, have used this design extensively in our work (e.g., Cain & Oakhill, 1999; Ehrlich, Remond, & Tardieu, 1999; Oakhill, 1982, 1984; Stothard & Hulme, 1992). We carefully select groups of good and poor comprehenders matched for chronological age, word reading accuracy, and vocabulary knowledge. Typical characteristics of groups from my own research are shown in Table 3.1.

When matched for word reading ability and vocabulary knowledge, poor comprehenders' phonological STM is comparable with that of same-age good comprehenders. For example, Stothard and Hulme (1992) found no differences between good and poor comprehenders on a measure of digit span. Oakhill, Yuill, and Parkin (1986) also found no evidence of a relationship between comprehension deficits and impaired word span. Oakhill et al.'s word span task comprised lists of words that increased in the number of syllables (e.g., *spoon-leaf-swan-crown, hammer-mushroom-giraffe-monkey*). Both good and poor comprehenders were similarly affected by syllable length. Similarly, Cain et al. (2000a) found that good and poor comprehenders were equally susceptible to confusions in their recall of letter strings that rhymed (e.g., E, B, G, T), relative to their performance for letters that did not rhyme (e.g., H, K, L, Q). Together, these studies indicate that both good and poor comprehenders use phonological codes to maintain information in STM for recall.

In contrast to these findings, Nation et al. (1999) report a specific deficit in poor comprehenders' STM. In their study, good and poor comprehenders' recall of concrete nouns (e.g., *tooth*, *fruit*) was comparable, but the poor comprehenders recalled fewer abstract words (e.g., *luck*, *pride*) than did the good comprehenders. Nation and colleagues concluded that the poor comprehenders had impoverished semantic knowledge, which put them at a disadvantage when they had to maintain certain verbal stimuli, such as abstract words, in STM. However, the good and poor comprehenders in Nation et al.'s study were not matched for word knowledge (i.e., word reading accuracy or vocabulary). Thus, it is possible that they had poorer phonological representations of the abstract words because they had weaker word recognition and vocabulary skills, which could have led to the storage and recall difficulties. Further work is needed to determine whether semantic or phonological representations of words might account for memory problems in poor comprehenders who do not demonstrate an obvious word-level impairment.

Of interest then is whether children with specific reading comprehension difficulties experience WM deficits. Work conducted by Yuill et al. (1989) suggests that this is indeed the case. They developed a verbal WM task that involved the reading of digits rather than sentences. Therefore this task does not include the confounding element of sentence comprehension, a common criticism of reading and listening span tasks. In addition, the task does not require strong semantic support for the storage of the digits 1–9. In the digit reading WM task, children read out loud groups of three digits (processing component) through a viewing window (e.g., *1-5-4*; *3-2-7*). They are instructed to remember the final digit in each group (storage component) for later recall (e.g., *4*, *7*). Yuill et al. found that good and poor comprehenders performed comparably on the easiest level (two groups of digits). However, when the number of groups of digits increased (three and four) the poor comprehenders' performance was impaired. They concluded that the poor comprehenders experience specific WM deficits.

Stothard and Hulme (1992) gave a measure of verbal WM that involved sentence comprehension to good and poor comprehenders matched for vocabulary knowledge and word reading accuracy. Their listening span measure (based on the task developed by Daneman and Carpenter, 1980) required participants to listen to short sentences and make a true/false judgment after each one (the processing component)—for example, "*Butter goes on bread*" (true). The children had to remember the final word in each sentence (the storage component). In contrast to the findings of Yuill et al., Stothard and Hulme did not find a relationship between comprehension ability and WM. It is surprising that group differences were not apparent because the WM task that they used tapped (sentence) comprehension processes. However, all of the children found the task very hard, reducing its power to discriminate between groups. Two more recent studies have found differences between good and poor comprehenders on listening span tasks (de Beni & Palladino, 2000; Nation et al., 1999).

The evidence reviewed thus far largely supports the findings of the developmental studies: STM is not specifically related to reading comprehension skill over and above word reading and vocabulary skills. Research conducted by Swanson and Berninger (1995) supports this conclusion. They compared the STM and WM skills of four different reader groups: good and poor comprehenders with age-appropriate word reading ability and good and poor word readers with age-appropriate reading comprehension skill. They found that STM was related to word reading ability but not to reading comprehension, whereas WM was related to comprehension but not to word reading scores.

On balance, the evidence from the work conducted with poor comprehenders demonstrates that WM impairments are commonly found in children with reading comprehension difficulties. Although there is evidence that memory impairments can arise through word reading inefficiency; phonological processing difficulties; or, perhaps, poor semantic skills, there are also children whose WM limitations are not obviously the result of such impairments. Furthermore, WM appears to have a direct relationship with reading comprehension over and above STM, word reading ability, and vocabulary knowledge.

Summary

The review of studies investigating the relationship between children's reading comprehension and their memory skills demonstrates convergence between the results of work with unselected populations of children and those with specific comprehension difficulties. Phonological STM and WM are both predictors of children's reading comprehension across a wide age range. However, in a similar way to that found for the adult literature, there is evidence that WM explains unique variance in reading comprehension over and above a child's phonological STM and basic reading-related skills.

WORKING MEMORY AND CHILDREN'S SPECIFIC COMPREHENSION SKILLS

Thus far, I have considered the relationship between children's WM capacity and their reading comprehension in general. However, many different skills and abilities contribute to our understanding of a text. The focus of this section is the relationship between WM resources and higher-order skills that are involved in the integration of information across sentences and ideas in a text—namely, inference and integration, anaphor resolution, use of context, and comprehension monitoring.

These skills are all significantly correlated with reading comprehension skill (see Cain & Oakhill, 2004, for a review) and are crucial to the construction of the mental model of the text. Furthermore, it has been suggested that WM resources underpin the execution of these crucial comprehension-related skills (e.g., Seigneuric et al., 2000). In this section I will examine each skill in turn and consider why these skills tap our WM resources and how they are related to reading comprehension skill. I will also describe findings from a longitudinal study of children aged 7–10 years in which we explored the relationship between WM and a range of comprehension-related skills.

Inference and Integration

As discussed earlier, to fully understand a text we need to do more than simply derive the meanings of individual words and sentences. The reader needs to integrate information from different sentences to establish local coherence and to generate inferences to make sense of details that are only implicitly mentioned (Graesser et al., 1994; Long & Chong, 2001). There is now a substantial body of evidence that demonstrates a relationship between children's reading comprehension level and their inference and integration skills.

Early work by Oakhill compared good and poor comprehenders' ability to integrate information from different sentences (Oakhill, 1982) and to incorporate general knowledge with information in the text to generate inferences to fill in missing details (Oakhill, 1984). Poor comprehenders were impaired on both tasks. However, although this work demonstrates a relationship between inference-making ability and reading comprehension, the comparison between good and poor comprehenders does not enable us to distinguish between the two possible directions for that relationship. Proficiency in inference making might enable children to develop good reading comprehension skills; alternately good reading comprehension might enhance inference-making ability.

→ In work conducted in collaboration with Jane Oakhill, I sought to determine the more likely of these two possibilities (Cain & Oakhill, 1999). Three groups of children participated in this study: 7–8-year-old good and poor comprehenders, selected in the way described earlier, and a group of 6–7-year-old normally developing readers, who were matched to the poor comprehenders for reading comprehension level (the *comprehension-age* match group). The logic of the comprehension-age match group is similar to that of the *reading-age* match group (Bradley & Bryant, 1978). If the comprehension-age match group makes more inferences than the poor comprehenders, we can rule out the possibility that superior inference skill is the result of superior reading comprehension in general because the comprehension-age match group and poor comprehenders are matched for absolute level of reading comprehension. This result would identify

TABLE 3.2
Sample Inference Story and Questions (from Cain & Oakhill, 1999)

Debbie was going out for the afternoon with her friend Michael. By the time they got there they were very thirsty. Michael got a drink out of his duffel bag and they shared that. The orange juice was very refreshing. Debbie put on her swimsuit costume but the water was too cold to paddle in, so they made sand castles instead.

They played all afternoon and didn't notice how late it was. Then Debbie spotted the clock on the pier. If she was late for dinner her parents would be angry. They quickly packed up their things. Debbie changed and wrapped her swimsuit in her towel. She put the bundle in her backpack. Then they set off for home, pedaling as fast as they could. Debbie was very tired when she got home, but she was just in time for dinner.

Questions tapping facts in the text
1. Who did Debbie spend the afternoon with?
2. Where was the clock?

Questions tapping inter-sentence inferences
3. From where did Michael get the orange juice?
4. Where did Debbie put her towel when she packed up her things?

Questions tapping gap-filling inferences
5. Where did Debbie and Michael spend the afternoon?
6. How did Debbie and Michael travel home?

---

children's inferential skills as a likely cause of their reading comprehension ability (see Cain, Oakhill, & Bryant, 2000b, for a discussion of this methodology).

We compared the three groups' ability to generate inferences and to remember facts by asking them questions after they had read short narratives. An example of a narrative and associated questions is provided in Table 3.2. Both types of inference questions tap into WM resources. The inter-sentence inference questions require the reader to integrate information from two different sentences in the text, and the gap-filling questions require the integration of general knowledge with information given in the text to fill in missing details. The three groups did not differ in their ability to answer the questions tapping memory for facts in the text, but the poor comprehenders were poorer than the other groups on both types of inference questions; the difference between the poor comprehenders and comprehension-age match group was significant for the inter-sentence inference questions.

These results confirm previous findings that poor comprehenders have poor inference-making abilities and indicate that this deficit might be underlying their general problems with text comprehension. Their inference-making deficits are not attributable to poor memory for the text *per se*: Poor comprehenders make fewer inferences than skilled peers when the text is available (Cain & Oakhill, 1999; Oakhill, 1984) and their ability to remember facts from the stories is not necessarily unimpaired (Cain & Oakhill, 1999).

This study demonstrates that inference making is crucial to good text comprehension, so it is important to determine what underlies impaired inference-making ability. One possibility is that the poor comprehenders' weak WM skills prevent them from generating sufficient inferences and links between sentences, for the reasons given earlier. However, another possibility is simply that the poor comprehenders lack the general knowledge from which inferences can be drawn. My colleagues and I have explored the possibility that poor inference making is linked to general knowledge deficits (Cain, Oakhill, Barnes, & Bryant, 2001). In this study, good and poor comprehenders were first taught a set of facts about an imaginary planet until they achieved perfect recall. The children then read a story from which inferences could be drawn. To generate each inference, the reader had to integrate information from the story with information in the taught knowledge base. The crucial finding was that poor comprehenders generated fewer inferences than their skilled peers, even when memory of this taught knowledge base was controlled for.

These studies indicate that neither memory for the text itself nor knowledge deficits can fully account for children's difficulties with inference making. Research relating WM skills to poor comprehenders' inference-making ability is lacking. However, later in this chapter, I consider research that has investigated whether inference-making ability is dependent on WM capacity in an unselected population of children.

Anaphoric Processing

Anaphors are common linguistic devices that maintain cohesion between sentences and phrases in a text. An example of an anaphor is the pronoun *"he"* in the following: *"Chris was dirty after the football match, so he had a bath."* The pronoun *"he"* refers to *"Chris"* (the antecedent) in the preceding part of the text. A problem with establishing the meaning of anaphors (anaphor resolution) will adversely affect the ability to integrate information both within and between sentences, similar to difficulties with inference making. As a result, problems with anaphoric processing may lead to comprehension difficulties.

Several studies have found a relationship between children's reading comprehension skill and their performance on measures of anaphoric processing.[*] Relative to same-age peers, children with weak reading comprehension are poor at resolving the referents of pronouns—for example, *"Kate lent her coat to Sue because she was cold"* (Yuill & Oakhill, 1991, expt. 4.4). They are also poor at supplying the appropriate anaphor (she)—for example, *"Steven gave his umbrella to Penny in the park because _____ wanted to keep dry"* (Oakhill & Yuill, 1986).

In their pioneering study investigating WM and reading comprehension in adults, Daneman and Carpenter (1980) found that adults' WM capacity was related to their ability to resolve pronouns. In particular, adults with small WM capacity were more adversely affected by distance between the anaphor and its antecedent. In a similar fashion, when assessing the contribution that WM capacity makes to children's ability to resolve anaphors, the distance between the anaphor and antecedent has also been manipulated. The idea behind this is that the memory demands are less when an anaphor and its antecedent appear in adjacent sentences compared with when they are separated by one or two sentences of additional text. The results indicate that, in a similar manner to that for adults, WM affects children's ability to resolve anaphors.

In one study, Yuill and Oakhill (1988) compared 7–8 year olds' comprehension of different kinds of anaphors within a narrative text (rather than in individual sentences, as in the studies mentioned earlier). Within the story they manipulated the distance between each anaphor and its antecedent. One of the anaphor types that they included was ellipsis, where information has been omitted. For example, *"Alice had caught three fish. Bill hadn't caught any"* means that Bill hadn't caught any *fish*. Poor comprehenders were impaired at working out all types of anaphor used in the story. Furthermore, the poor comprehenders' difficulties with ellipsis were particularly pronounced when the anaphor and its referent were found in nonadjacent sentences in the story. These results suggest that WM capacity may have influenced their performance, at least for this type of anaphor.

A similar experiment with 9-year-old children adds support to this conclusion. Ehrlich and Remond (1999) also compared good and poor comprehenders' ability to resolve different types of anaphor and, again, manipulated the distance between anaphor and antecedent. Two different texts were used, which produced mixed results. For both texts, the poor comprehenders were less likely to resolve the anaphors. However, they were more greatly affected by the distance manipulation for only one of the texts. The other text revealed an unexpected pattern of results: For all children anaphors with far antecedents were easier to resolve than those with near antecedents. The texts were not matched for difficulty or number of protagonists, which may have led to the different patterns of performance. The important finding was that the poor comprehenders experienced difficulties with anaphor resolution.

These studies demonstrate that poor comprehenders experience difficulties with anaphoric processing: They are poor at resolving anaphors and supplying appropriate anaphors. A difficulty in establishing anaphoric reference will affect a reader's ability to integrate information between sentences and construct a coherent representation of the text's meaning. Clearly, further work is needed to determine the precise nature of the relationship between different types of anaphor and WM by not only manipulating the distance between anaphor and antecedent but by relating independent measures of WM to performance on these tasks.

TABLE 3.3

Example of Text Used in the Vocabulary Learning from Context Task (from Cain, Oakhill, & Elbro, 2003)

Introduction: Bill was always very careful when riding his bike but the other day he fell off. When he looked round he saw that the problem was a gromp.

Informative context: He phoned the council to complain. They sent a workman to mend the road and soon it was safe to ride along again.

Filler text: Bill only got a small cut on his knee, which did not hurt too much; no bones were broken. It was lucky that Bill had been wearing his crash hat. Otherwise he could have bumped his head when he fell off.

Note: In the far condition, the filler text appeared where marked by the asterisk (*). The text as presented to the children was continuous, not blocked as above, and the novel word was not underlined in the text that the children saw. The information printed in italics is included here for illustrative purposes only and was not included in the version presented to the child.

Acceptable responses: Something that he passed on his bike, a stone on the path (one point); a hole or a bump in the road (2 points).

Use of Context

Another language skill that might be related to WM capacity is vocabulary knowledge. As mentioned previously, vocabulary size is a good indicator of reading comprehension level in both children and adults (Carroll, 1993). Daneman (1988) has suggested that WM capacity mediates this relationship because inferring the meanings of unfamiliar words from context is an important means of expanding one's vocabulary. Certainly for adults, verbal WM capacity is related to adults' ability to infer the meanings of obscure words from narratives (Daneman & Green, 1986). There is also some evidence that WM capacity is related to children's performance on a similar task (Cull, cited in Daneman, 1988).

My colleagues and I have been exploring the relationship between WM capacity and children's vocabulary inference skills further. In a series of experiments, we presented good and poor comprehenders with short texts containing an unknown vocabulary item. Their task was to explain the meaning of the unknown word. An example text is provided in Table 3.3.

As you can see, the reason why Bill fell off his bike cannot be a problem concerning his bike or simply a stone on the pathway (as some poor comprehenders suggested). The informative context clearly points to a problem with the path that requires the attention of some council workmen. Thus, the reader is required to integrate these contextual clues with the fact that Bill fell off his bike and there was a problem to derive a meaning for the novel word. This integration requires that all relevant information is active in WM.

To investigate how WM might affect performance on this task, we manipulated the distance between the novel word and clues to its meaning. Other researchers have investigated memory load by varying whether the word to be learned appears before or after its useful context (e.g., Cull). However, such a manipulation not only varies the WM demands of the task; it also requires different processing strategies to be adopted in the two conditions. To study the specific effects of WM load, the relevant clues always appeared after the novel word in our experimental materials.

The first experiment revealed that 7–8-year-old poor comprehenders were impaired in their ability to work out the meanings of the novel words, particularly in the condition with the highest WM demands (far condition) (Cain, Oakhill, & Elbro, 2003). Further work replicated this finding with 9–10 year olds (Cain, Oakhill, & Lemmon, 2004). In this later study we also included independent assessments of WM (counting span, listening span) and phonological STM (forward digit span). Children's performance on the vocabulary inference task was related to their WM capacity in the far condition but not to their STM span or memory for facts in the text.

These studies indicate a link between WM and two language skills: reading comprehension and vocabulary acquisition. Comprehension of a text will rely to a certain extent on understanding the individual words. However, as I have already argued, text comprehension goes beyond retrieval of word meanings. Our experiments support Daneman's hypothesis that reading comprehension and vocabulary acquisition may both rely on a common processing mechanism. The implication is that children with reading comprehension deficits who also have weak WM skills might also experience slow vocabulary growth, particularly when they progress from reading books with controlled vocabularies as their word reading skills develop. Thus, vocabulary deficits that might not be evident in beginner readers might become apparent with age. Clearly, there is a need to study the relationship between WM and the ability to learn new vocabulary items from context over time.

Comprehension Monitoring

The ability to monitor our ongoing comprehension of a text as we read is an important skill. If we, the reader, detect that we have not fully understood a point, or find that the current idea unit does not fit with our understanding of other aspects of the text, we can take remedial steps, such as re-reading, to resolve the problem. Comprehension monitoring has been widely studied within a developmental framework. One way to measure a reader's ability to monitor their comprehension is to assess their ability to detect inconsistencies in text, such as scrambled sentences, contradictory sentences, or statements that conflict with external information (general knowledge). These error-detection tasks require the reader to evaluate their understanding of the text, although they do not necessarily require the reader to resolve the problem.

TABLE 3.4
Sample Comprehension Monitoring Text (from Cain,
Oakhill, & Bryant, 2004)

Last night Jill walked home through the woods.
She had just been to the movie theater with her friends.
*There was no moonlight, so Jill could hardly see her way.
She walked along the path.
*The moon was so bright that it lit the way.
Jill lives at the other side of the wood.
*Denotes lines containing inconsistent information

Performance on error-detection tasks improves with age (Baker, 1984; Markman, 1981), and it has been suggested that growth in this skill may be related to children's developing information processing capabilities such as their WM capacity (Ruffman, 1996; Vosniadou, Pearson, & Rogers, 1988). This is because readers can only detect an inconsistency if they are actively engaged in constructive processing, which requires them to build a model of the text's meaning and relate each new piece of information to that model, as it is read. An example of a text used in an inconsistency detection task is provided in Table 3.4. The reader can only detect the inconsistency if both the new and old information are active in WM.

Ehrlich has studied comprehension monitoring by investigating 12–13 year olds' and 14–15 year olds' ability to detect inconsistent anaphors in expository texts (Ehrlich, 1996). In the consistent texts, the anaphors were repetitions of an earlier noun phrase—for example, "*The protection of existing reserves. . . . This protection. . . .*" In the inconsistent version, the second (anaphoric) instance of *protection* was replaced by a noun phrase with a meaning that was contrary to its intended referent, for this example *wastage*. For both age groups, good comprehenders were more likely to detect the inconsistent anaphors than were poor comprehenders. Readers also answered questions after the texts to assess whether they had resolved the inconsistent anaphors. In the younger age group, good comprehenders appeared to resolve the inconsistencies through inference or revision of the text, when the inconsistency was not explicitly detected. In further experimental work with 10 year olds, Ehrlich and colleagues (Ehrlich, Remond, & Tardieu, 1999) found that good comprehenders spent more time reading sections of text containing inconsistent anaphors than did poor comprehenders. The good comprehenders were also more likely to look back to previous text when an inconsistent anaphor was encountered.

The research reviewed in the earlier section on anaphors showed that increasing the distance between the anaphor and its antecedent (and, therefore, the WM demands of the task) lead to increased difficulties in anaphor

TABLE 3.5
Inconsistency Detection Passage (from Oakhill, Hartt, & Samols 2005)

Moles are small brown animals and they live underground using networks of tunnels.
*Moles cannot see very well, but their hearing and sense of smell are good.
They sleep in underground nests lined with grass, leaves, and twigs.
Moles use their front feet for digging and their short fur allows them to move along their
    tunnels either forward or backward.
They mainly eat worms but they also eat insects and snails.
*Moles are easily able to find food for their young because their eyesight is so good.

---

*Denotes lines containing inconsistent information.

resolution. Similarly, in comprehension monitoring paradigms the distance between the two inconsistent pieces of information can be manipulated to vary the WM demands of the task. Oakhill, Hartt, and Samols (under review) used such a manipulation in their study of good and poor comprehenders' monitoring skill. Nine and 10 year olds read expository text containing inconsistent pairs of sentences, which were either in adjacent lines (low WM demands) or separated by filler text (high WM demands). An example is provided in Table 3.5.

Each child read two inconsistent passages in which the target information was in adjacent sentences and two in which the inconsistency was non-adjacent. The poor comprehenders performed worse in the far condition relative to the near condition, whereas the good comprehenders were not affected by the distance manipulation. WM capacity was measured using the digit reading and recall task described earlier (Yuill et al., 1989). The poor comprehenders' performance on the WM task was weak, and WM scores were significantly correlated with the ability to detect the inconsistencies in both the near and far conditions. These results indicate that WM impairments might underlie children's difficulties with comprehension monitoring.

This body of research indicates a strong link between WM capacity and children's ability to monitor their comprehension. Poor comprehenders are able to engage in monitoring processes and identify some, although not all, deliberate inconsistencies in texts. Thus, they do engage in some strategic processing and are not simply reading on a sentence-by-sentence basis. However, there is evidence that their performance is particularly impaired when the WM demands of the task are high—for example, when information must be compared across several sentences in a text. We now need to replicate this finding and relate independent measures of WM capacity to children's comprehension monitoring ability across a wider age range and with a greater range of problems and text genres. We also need to consider ways to support weak WM skills to aid children's ability to monitor their comprehension.

The Inter-Relations between Working Memory and Reading Comprehension Skills

The comprehension-related skills of inference and integration, use of context, anaphoric processing, and comprehension monitoring, described earlier, involve integration of information either within a text or between the text and general knowledge. Thus, we can determine good theoretical reasons to expect that a reader's WM capacity will place limits on their ability to engage in these processes. For example, to detect that an idea unit is inconsistent with previously read text, the reader must be actively constructing a mental model of the content of the text; inconsistent text will be detected when the reader tries to integrate this information with their model of the text so far. The research discussed has not directly investigated the contribution made by WM to performance on these tasks. In recent work, my colleagues and I have explored the extent to which WM underpins the execution of some of these comprehension-related skills.

There are two skills that I will focus on: inference and integration and comprehension monitoring, which were included in the longitudinal study of children's reading development described earlier (see Cain et al., 2004, for full details). At the outset, we selected a sample of 101 children in the year of their 8th birthday and assessed their performance on a wide battery of tasks. As well as inference and monitoring skills, we assessed their verbal IQ, word reading and reading comprehension, and WM capacity. WM was measured using two tasks described earlier: a listening span task in which children completed aurally presented sentences and remembered the completion word for later recall and the digit reading and recall task developed by Yuill et al. We used a sentence inconsistency detection task to assess comprehension monitoring when children were 8, 9, and 11 years of age. Integration within text was assessed when children were aged 8 years, using Oakhill's (1982) constructive integration task. Integration and inference was assessed when children were aged 9 and 11 years old using materials similar to those developed by Cain and Oakhill (1999).

At each time point (age 8, 9, and 11 years) WM explained unique variance in reading comprehension over and above vocabulary skills and word reading ability. In addition, the comprehension monitoring task (at each time point) and the inference task (at age 9 and 11 years only) were correlated with WM performance. These data support previous work that has shown strong links between WM capacity and comprehension-related skills.

We conducted a series of statistical analyses to determine the extent to which performance on our specific comprehension-related tasks and our standardized measure of reading comprehension were independent of, or mediated by, WM capacity. First we found that the variables likely to explain variance in reading comprehension—namely, word reading, sight vocabulary, receptive vocabulary, and verbal ability—explained a significant proportion (26–46%) of the variance in reading comprehension skill. After controlling for the influence of these skills on reading comprehension, we found that WM, inference and integration, and comprehension monitoring each predicted additional variance (5–10%) in reading comprehension at each time point. When we controlled for the relationship between WM and both inference and integration and comprehension monitoring we found that the inference and the comprehension monitoring tasks continued to explain significant variance in reading comprehension level, although the amount of variance explained was reduced. Therefore, although WM skill was consistently related to performance on these measures of comprehension-related skills, children's ability to engage in this type of processing was not wholly determined by their WM capacity.

Summary

There is now a sizeable body of work investigating the relationships between skills that are important to reading comprehension and WM in children. One of the consistent findings is that children with reading comprehension deficits are specifically impaired on comprehension-related skills that rely on WM resources. Readers frequently need to simultaneously store one piece of information while processing another to integrate the different pieces of information within a text and to integrate information in a text with prior knowledge. These studies have included children aged between 7 and 15 years, indicating an important role for these processing variables in the determination of reading comprehension from beginner through to fluent readers. Some of these studies suggest links between performance on these tasks and WM: Performance is significantly impaired when the WM demands of these tasks are high, and WM capacity is related to task performance. Work that has addressed the interrelations between WM and these comprehension skills demonstrates that WM capacity is an important predictor of reading comprehension level, over and above other basic reading and language skills. However, it also shows WM is not the sole determinant of performance on specific comprehension skills.

CONCLUSIONS

The aim of this chapter was to review the evidence that WM capacity is an important determinant of children's reading comprehension because it underpins many of the skills necessary to ensure good understanding of a text. The journey from print to meaning involves many stages. First, the reader must decode the words on the page and access their meanings. Then they need to compute the syntactic structures of individual sentences. Once they have completed these word- and sentence-level tasks, they need to establish links between the ideas in these different sentences to produce a coherent mental model of the content of the text. The work reviewed in the section "Working Memory and Children's Specific Comprehension Skills" demonstrated the importance of good WM resources in this process.

The proposal that WM capacity will limit reading comprehension is not particularly controversial. A common factor in the different theoretical positions concerning comprehension failure outlined in the first section is that WM deficits can lead to failures of comprehension because they prevent the reader from engaging in the integrative and constructive processing necessary to build a representation of meaning. Where these hypotheses differ is the source of the processing limitation and how fundamental this deficit is to reading comprehension difficulties. Do young readers and children with poor comprehension sometimes fail to understand text adequately because they have limited phonological processing ability, inefficient word reading skills, or impoverished knowledge of word meanings? If so, training in these basic skills should improve young readers' and poor comprehenders' WM skills as well as their reading comprehension level.

A different viewpoint, proposed by my colleagues and me (e.g., Oakhill et al., 1998) is that comprehension difficulties can be apparent in the absence of these lower-level deficits. Our work with poor comprehenders has produced no evidence that these children experience phonological processing deficits or word level deficits (Cain et al., 2000a; Yuill & Oakhill, 1991). In addition, our work and that of other researchers, such as Ehrlich and Swanson, has demonstrated that children who have reading comprehension difficulties despite good word reading or vocabulary have WM impairments and perform much more poorly when the processing demands of comprehension tasks are high. One possibility is that poor comprehenders experience WM problems because of weak inhibitory processes. In support of this position, poor comprehenders with good word reading skills not only experience difficulties in the inhibition of irrelevant information on WM tasks but on other comprehension as well (Barnes et al., 2004; de Beni & Palladino, 2000).

There have been few investigations relating concurrent measures of WM to reading comprehension level or to performance on specific comprehension-related skills. Furthermore, the lack of sufficient longitudinal and intervention studies means that we cannot make causal claims about the relationship between WM and the ability to produce causally linked and well-integrated text models. It may be that poor comprehenders' strategic processing is less effective than that of good comprehenders because of some fundamental difference in information-processing ability between the groups. Or, it may be that poor comprehenders know less about, or are less willing to use, strategies in comprehension.

The experimental evidence to date supports both positions. A number of investigations find that WM capacity is related to children's reading comprehension ability and specific reading comprehension skills. Other work, however, demonstrates that WM is not the sole determinant of children's reading comprehension ability. Furthermore, young readers and poor comprehenders benefit from instruction in strategic processing. For example, children's ability to monitor their comprehension improves when they are told about the nature of the errors in the text and if they are instructed in the use of mental imagery when reading (Paris, Wasik, & Turner, 1991). Children are also better able to monitor their comprehension when given an additional task that requires them to assess their understanding, such as constructing a pictorial storyboard of a text (Rubman & Waters, 2000). Inference-making skills can also be trained: Poor comprehenders make a greater number of inferences (assessed by responses to questions) when they are taught to look for clues when reading so as to establish specific locations and events that have been left implicit (Yuill & Joscelyne, 1988). This work suggests that providing information or supports for children as they are reading may benefit comprehension.

However, these training programs and comprehension aids do not specifically target WM resources. It is likely that they work by teaching children how to read strategically and process text constructively, rather than developing their WM skills. The educational and remediation implications are, therefore, very favorable. When both component skills and WM resources appear to be inadequate, instructing children in effective ways to process text may help to circumvent some of the impairments associated with limited WM capacity. It should also be noted that Tunmer (1989) has proposed that practice at representing and manipulating linguistic information may facilitate WM ability. Thus, the relationship between WM and reading comprehension may be reciprocal and it may be possible to strengthen WM capacity through practice in tasks that tap this resource.

Finally, it is important to remember that individual children may experience comprehension failures for different reasons. As work discussed earlier showed, some children experience poor comprehension because of problems at the phonological or word level of processing, whereas other children can be identified who do not show impairments in these lower-level skills. Work by Cornoldi, de Beni, and Pazzaglia (1996) suggests that the population of poor comprehenders with good word-level skills is also far from homogenous. They found different profiles of skill strength and deficit in a group of poor comprehenders with good word-level skills. For example, one child demonstrated metacognitive deficits but no WM deficits, whereas another demonstrated WM deficits but no metacognitive deficits—although the majority were impaired on some of the assessments of these two skills.

The work reviewed in this chapter demonstrates that young children and those with poor reading comprehension experience difficulties on a range of comprehension skills linked to the construction of adequate representations of a text's meaning. Different children may fail to construct coherent representations of text because of different underlying impairments, but limited processing resources will affect the ability to do so. Further research is needed to investigate the causal relations between reading comprehension level, comprehension-related skills, and WM resources and on ways to improve processing efficiency.

Summary Box

- Good text comprehension involves more than accessing the meanings of each word and deriving the sense of individual sentences. It also requires the construction of a meaning-based representation of the text, a mental model.
- To construct this mental model, the reader must engage in constructive and integrative processing, such as establishing links between the sentences in the text and also between the text and general knowledge.
- WM is considered to be the workspace for this processing to take place.
- It acts as a buffer for the most recently read propositions (or phrases) in a text, enabling the reader to integrate their meaning to establish local coherence. It also holds information retrieved from LTM.
- There is a strong relationship between children's WM capacity and their reading comprehension. WM capacity explains variance in young children's reading comprehension, and WM deficits are reliably found in children who do poorly on assessments of reading comprehension.
- Some poor comprehenders may experience difficulties on tasks that are heavily dependent on WM because their slow and effortful word reading, weak phonological STM, or poor semantic knowledge affect their ability to store and process information simultaneously.
- Other children have been identified who experience reading comprehension and WM deficits that appear to be independent of their word reading, vocabulary, or STM skills.
- Between the ages of 8 and 11 years, WM capacity explains variance in reading comprehension over and above that explained by the verbal ability, vocabulary knowledge, and word reading skill.
- Children with poor reading comprehension are impaired on a range of tasks that are dependent on working capacity, such as integration and inference, anaphoric processing, use of context, and comprehension monitoring.
- Despite the strong relationship between WM and reading comprehension, WM is not the sole determinant of children's reading comprehension level or their performance on specific comprehension-related skills.
- In addition to investigating ways to develop WM capacity, researchers and educators should consider using supports and teaching specific strategies that might alleviate some of the text processing difficulties experienced by children with weak WM.

Acknowledgments

I would like to thank Jane Oakhill for her contribution to the collaborative work discussed in this chapter and for her permission to use the materials in Table 3.5.

References

Baddeley, A. D. (1986). *Working Memory*. Oxford: Oxford University Press.

Baddeley, A. D. (1996). Exploring the central executive. *Quarterly Journal of Experimental Psychology: Human Experimental Psychology, 49A*, 5–28.

Baddeley, A. D., & Hitch, G. (1974). Working memory. In G. A. Bower (Ed.), *Recent Advances in Learning and Motivation (vol. 8)*, New York: Academic Press.

Baker, L. (1984). Spontaneous versus instructed use of multiple standards for evaluation comprehension: Effects of age, reading proficiency, and type of standard. *Journal of Experimental Child Psychology, 38*, 289–311.

Barnes, M. A., Faulkner, H., Wilkinson, M., & Dennis, M. (2004). Meaning construction and integration in children with hydrocephalus. *Brain and Language, 89*, 47–56.

Bishop, D. V. M. (1997). *Uncommon Understanding: Development and Disorders of Language Comprehension in Children*. Hove: Psychology Press.

Bradley, L., & Bryant, P. E. (1978). Difficulties in auditory organization as a possible cause of reading backwardness. *Nature, 271*, 746–747.

Cain, K., & Oakhill, J. V. (1999). Inference making and its relation to comprehension failure. *Reading and Writing, 11*, 489–503.

Cain, K., & Oakhill, J. (2004). Reading comprehension difficulties. In T. Nunes & P. Bryant (Eds.), *Handbook of Children's Literacy* (pp. 313–338). Dordrecht: Kluwer Academic Publishers.

Cain, K., Oakhill, J., & Bryant, P. E. (2004). Children's reading comprehension ability: Concurrent prediction by working memory, verbal ability, and component skills. *Journal of Educational Psychology, 96*, 31–42.

Cain, K., Oakhill, J. V., & Bryant, P. E. (2000a). Phonological skills and comprehension failure: A test of the phonological processing deficit hypothesis. *Reading and Writing, 13*, 31–56.

Cain, K., Oakhill, J. V., & Bryant, P. E. (2000b). Investigating the causes of reading comprehension failure: The comprehension-age match design. *Reading and Writing, 12*, 31–40.

Cain, K., Oakhill, J. V., & Elbro, C. (2003). The ability to learn new word meanings from context by school-age children with and without language comprehension difficulties. *Journal of Child Language, 30*, 681–694.

Cain, K., Oakhill, J., & Lemmon, K. (2004). Individual differences in the inference of word meanings from context: the influence of reading comprehension, vocabulary knowledge, and memory capacity. *Journal of Educational Psychology, 96*, 671–681.

Cain, K., Oakhill, J. V., Barnes, M. A., & Bryant, P. E. (2001). Comprehension skill, inference making ability and their relation to knowledge. *Memory and Cognition, 29*, 850–859.

Carroll, J. B. (1993). *Human Cognitive Abilities: A Survey of Factor-Analytic Studies*. New York: Cambridge University Press.

Cooke, A. E., Halleran, J. G., & O'Brien, E. J. (1998). What is readily available during reading? A memory-based view. *Discourse Processes, 26*, 109–129.

Cornoldi, C., de Beni, R., & Pazzaglia, F. (1996). Profiles of reading comprehension difficulties: An analysis of single cases. In C. Cornoldi and J. Oakhill (Eds.), *Reading Comprehension Difficulties: Processes and Interventions* (pp. 113–136). Mahwah, NJ: Lawrence Erlbaum Associates.

Daneman, M. (1988). Word knowledge and reading skill. In M. Daneman, G., MacKinnon, and T. G. Waller (Eds.), *Reading Research: Advances in Theory and Practice, vol. 6* (pp. 145–175). San Diego: Academic Press.

Daneman, M., & Carpenter, P. A. (1980). Individual differences in working memory and reading. *Journal of Verbal Learning and Verbal Behavior*, *19*, 450–466.

Daneman, M., & Carpenter, P. A. (1983). Individual differences in integrating information between and within sentences. *Journal of Experimental Psychology: Learning, Memory and Cognition*, *9*, 561–584.

Daneman, M., & Green, I. (1986). Individual differences in comprehending and producing words in context. *Journal of Memory and Language*, *25*, 1–18.

Daneman, M., & Merikle, P. M. (1996). Working memory and language comprehension: A meta-analysis. *Psychonomic Bulletin and Review*, *3*, 422–433.

de Beni, R., & Palladino, P. (2000). Intrusion errors in working memory tasks: Are they related to reading comprehension ability. *Learning and Individual Differences*, *12*, 131–143.

de Beni, R., Palladino, P., Pazzaglia, F., Cornoldi, C. (1998). Increases in intrusion errors and working memory deficit of poor comprehenders. *Quarterly Journal of Experimental Psychology: Human Experimental Psychology*, *51A*, 305–320.

de Jonge, P., & de Jong, P. F. (1996). Working memory, intelligence, and reading ability in children. *Personality and Individual Differences*, *21*, 1007–1020.

Ehrlich, M. F. (1996). Metacognitive monitoring in the processing of anaphoric devices in skilled and less-skilled comprehenders. In C. Cornoldi and J. V. Oakhill (Eds.), *Reading Comprehension Difficulties: Processes and Remediation* (pp. 221–249). Mahwah, N.J.: Lawrence Erlbaum Associates.

Ehrlich, M. F., & Remond, M. (1997). Skilled and less skilled comprehenders: French children's processing of anaphoric devices in written texts. *British Journal of Developmental Psychology*, *15*, 291–309.

Ehrlich, M. F., Remond M., & Tardieu, H. (1999). Processing of anaphoric devices in young skilled and less skilled comprehenders: Differences in metacognitive monitoring. *Reading and Writing*, *11*, 29–63.

Engle, R. W., Carullo, J. J., & Collins, K. W. (1991). Individual differences in working memory for comprehension and following directions. *Journal of Educational Research*, *84*, 253–262.

Ericsson, K. A., & Kintsch, W. (1995). Long-term working memory. *Psychological Review*, *102*, 211–245.

Gathercole, S. E. (1998). The development of memory. *Journal of Child Psychology and Psychiatry*, *39*, 3–27.

Gernsbacher, M. A. (1990). *Language Comprehension as Structure Building*. Hillsdale, NJ: Lawrence Erlbaum Associates.

Gernsbacher, M. A., & Faust, M. (1991). The mechanism of suppression: A component of general comprehension skill. *Journal of Experimental Psychology: Learning, Memory and Cognition*, *17*, 245–262.

Gough, P. B., Hoover, W. A., & Peterson, C. L. (1996). Some observations on a simple view of reading. In C. Cornoldi & J. V. Oakhill (Eds.), *Reading Comprehension Difficulties: Processes and Remediation*. Mahwah, NJ: Lawrence Erlbaum Associates.

Gottardo, A., Stanovich, K. E., & Siegel, L. S. (1996). The relationships between phonological sensitivity, syntactic processing, and verbal working memory in the reading performance of third-grade children. *Journal of Experimental Child Psychology*, *63*, 563–582.

Graesser, A. C., Singer, M., & Trabasso, T. (1994). Constructing inferences during narrative text comprehension. *Psychological Review*, *101*, 371–395.

Hatcher, P. J., & Hulme, C. (1999). Phonemes, rhymes, and intelligence as predictors of children's responsiveness to remedial reading instruction: Evidence from a longitudinal intervention study. *Journal of Experimental Child Psychology*, *72*, 130–153.

Johnson-Laird, P. N. (1983). *Mental Models*. Cambridge: Cambridge University Press.

Kintsch, W. (1998). *Comprehension: A Paradigm for Cognition*. New York: Cambridge University Press.

Leather, C. V., & Henry, L. A. (1994). Working memory span and phonological awareness tasks as predictors of early reading ability. *Journal of Experimental Child Psychology*, *58*, 88–111.

Long, D. L., & Chong, J. L. (2001). Comprehension skill and global coherence: A paradoxical picture of poor comprehenders' abilities. *Journal of Experimental Psychology: Learning, Memory, & Cognition, 27*, 1424–1429.

Markman, E. M. (1981). Realizing that you don't understand: Elementary school children's awareness of inconsistencies. *Child Development, 50*, 643–655.

Masson, M. E. J., & Miller, J. A. (1983). Working memory and individual differences in comprehension and memory of text. *Journal of Educational Psychology, 75*, 314–318.

Nation, K., Adams, J. W., Bowyer-Crane, C. A., & Snowling, M. J. (1999). Working memory deficits in poor comprehenders reflect underlying language impairments. *Journal of Experimental Child Psychology, 73*, 139–158.

Oakhill, J. V. (1982). Constructive processes in skilled and less-skilled comprehenders. *British Journal of Psychology, 73*, 13–20.

Oakhill, J. V. (1984). Inferential and memory skills in children's comprehension of stories. *British Journal of Educational Psychology, 54*, 31–39.

Oakhill, J. V., & Yuill, N. M. (1986). Pronoun resolution in skilled and less good comprehenders: Effects of memory load and inferential complexity. *Language and Speech, 29*, 25–37.

Oakhill, J., Cain, K., & Bryant, P. E. (2003). The dissociation of word reading and text comprehension: evidence from component skills. *Language and Cognitive Processes, 18*, 443–468.

Oakhill, J. V., Cain, K., & Yuill, N. (1998). Individual differences in young children's comprehension skill: Toward an integrated model. In C. Hulme & R. M. Joshi (Eds.), *Reading and Spelling: Development and Disorders*. Mahwah, NJ: Lawrence Erlbaum Associates.

Oakhill, J., Hartt, J., & Samols, D. (2005). Levels of comprehension monitoring and working memory in good and poor comprehenders. *Reading and Writing, 18*, 657–686.

Oakhill, J. V., Yuill, N. M., & Parkin, A. (1986). On the nature of the difference between skilled and less-skilled comprehenders. *Journal of Research in Reading, 9*, 80–91.

Paris, S. G., Wasik, B. A., & Turner, J. C. (1991). The development of strategic readers. In R. Barr, M. L., Kamil, P. B. Mosenthal, & P. D. Pearson (Eds.), *Handbook of Reading Research, Vol. II*) (pp. 609–640). New York: Longman.

Perfetti, C. A. (1985). *Reading Ability*. Oxford: Oxford University Press.

Perfetti, C. A. (1994). Psycholinguistics and reading ability. In M. A. Gernsbacher (Ed.), *Handbook of Psycholinguistics* (pp. 849–894). San Diego: Academic Press.

Roodenrys, S., Hulme, C., & Brown, G. (1993). The development of short-term memory span: Separable effects of speech rate and long-term memory. *Journal of Experimental Child Psychology, 56*, 431–442.

Rubman, C. N., & Waters, H. S. (2000). A, B Seeing: The role of constructive processes in children's comprehension monitoring. *Journal of Educational Psychology, 92*, 503–514.

Ruffman, T. (1996). Reassessing children's comprehension-monitoring skills. In C. Cornoldi and J. V. Oakhill (Eds.), *Reading Comprehension Difficulties: Processes and Intervention* (pp. 33–67). Mahwah, NJ: Lawrence Erlbaum Associates.

Saarnio, D. A., Oka, E. R., & Paris, S. G. (1990). Developmental predictors of children's reading comprehension. In T. H. Carr and B. A. Levy (Eds.), *Reading and its Development: Component Skills Approaches* (pp. 57–79). New York: Academic Press.

Seigneuric, A., Ehrlich, M.-F., Oakhill, J. V., & Yuill, N. M. (2000). Working memory resources and children's reading comprehension. *Reading and Writing, 13*, 81–103.

Shankweiler, D. (1989). How problems of comprehension are related to difficulties in decoding. In D. Shankweiler & I. Y. Liberman (Eds.), *Phonology and Reading Disability: Solving the Reading Puzzle* (pp. 35–68). Ann Arbor: University of Michigan Press.

Smith, S. T., Macaruso, P., Shankweiler, D., & Crain, S. (1989). Syntactic comprehension in young poor readers. *Applied Psycholinguistics, 10*, 429–454.

Stanovich, K. E., Nathan, R. G., & Vala-Rossi, M. (1986). Developmental changes in the cognitive correlates of reading ability and the developmental lag hypothesis. *Reading Research Quarterly, 21*, 267–283.

Stothard, S. E., & Hulme, C. (1992). Reading comprehension difficulties in children: The role of language comprehension and working memory skills. *Reading and Writing*, *4*, 245–256.

Stothard, S. E., & Hulme, C. (1996). A comparison of phonological skills in children with reading comprehension difficulties and children with word reading difficulties. *Journal of Child Psychology and Child Psychiatry*, *36*, 399–408.

Swanson, H. L., & Howell, M. (2001). Working memory, short-term memory, and speech rate as predictors of children's reading performance at different ages. *Journal of Educational Psychology*, *93*, 720–734.

Swanson, H. L., & Berninger, V. (1995). The role of working memory in skilled and less-skilled readers' comprehension. *Intelligence*, *21*, 83–108.

Tunmer, W. E. (1989). The role of language-related factors in reading disability. In D. Shankweiler, & I. Y. Liberman (Eds.), *Phonology and Reading Disability: Solving the Reading Puzzle* (pp. 91–131). Ann Arbor: University of Michigan Press.

Vosniadou, S., Pearson, P. D., & Rogers, T. (1988). What causes children's failures to detect inconsistencies in text? Representation versus comparison difficulties. *Journal of Educational Psychology*, *80*, 27–39.

Yuill, N., & Joscelyne, T. (1988). Effect of organizational cues and strategies on good and poor comprehenders' story understanding. *Journal of Educational Psychology*, *80*, 152–158.

Yuill, N., & Oakhill, J. (1988). Understanding of anaphoric relations in skilled and less skilled comprehenders. *British Journal of Psychology*, *79*, 173–186.

Yuill, N., & Oakhill, J. (1991). *Children's Problems in Text Comprehension: An Experimental Investigation*. Cambridge: Cambridge University Press.

Yuill, N. M., Oakhill, J. V., & Parkin, A. J. (1989). Working memory, comprehension ability and the resolution of text anomaly. *British Journal of Psychology*, *80*, 351–361.

CHAPTER 4

Working Memory, Executive Functioning, and Children's Mathematics

REBECCA BULL

University of Aberdeen

KIMBERLY ANDREWS ESPY

University of Nebraska—Lincoln

Approximately 3–6% of school-age children are estimated to have mathematics difficulties (Badian, 1983; Gross-Tsur, Manor, & Shalev, 1996; Kosc, 1974, Lewis, Hitch, & Walker, 1994). There are many more children in regular school classrooms who struggle with mathematics but whose performance is not considered sufficiently poor to be classified as meriting a specific disability in mathematics. Specific mathematic learning disability (MLD) is defined in psychiatric and educational venues as a large discrepancy between mathematics ability compared to reading and general intellectual ability, although the size of the discrepancy required varies. To further complicate matters, mathematic difficulties are associated with other developmental disorders, in particular nonverbal learning disabilities (Rourke, 1993; Rourke & Conway, 1997). It is surprising that the cognitive underpinnings of mathematic abilities have not been well described in typically developing children, those with neurodevelopmental disorders, or those with MLD. The purpose of this chapter is to examine the role of working memory (WM) and the central executive (CE), originally described by the Baddeley and Hitch (1974) model, in children's mathematic competence.

Mathematics is a complex domain, and a whole host of cognitive skills contribute to performance. In young children, mathematics competence is described by proficient counting, whereas in a college student, mathematics competence is marked by solving complex trigonometric problems and integrating equations. Not surprisingly, different cognitive abilities likely contribute to mathematics performance across development. Because of the greater complexity of algebra and geometry, developmental models are lacking. In contrast, more progress has been made in understanding the development of children's basic arithmetic skills (see in particular the work of Siegler, 1988; Siegler & Shrager, 1984). As such, many studies choose to focus on the procedural difficulties and related cognitive limitations shown by children when solving basic arithmetic problems. Several investigators have suggested that basic arithmetic and number skills form the building blocks for acquisition of more complex mathematic skills (e.g., Geary & Burlingham-Dubree, 1989) based on the strong relationship of arithmetic accuracy and response times to general mathematic proficiency. Therefore, evidence across the developmental age range will be presented to identify age-related communalities and differences.

One issue that complicates the study of the cognitive underpinnings of mathematics proficiency is how mathematic abilities are assessed. Regardless of whether preschool, school-age, or adolescent students are studied, mathematic proficiencies can be measured by traditional, individually administered standardized achievement tests—for example, mathematic subtests from the Wide Range Achievement Test (WRAT-R; Woodcock & Johnson, 1989) and the Wechsler Intelligence Scales (WPPSI; Wechsler, 1990; WISC, Wechsler, 1977), individually administered problem-based assessments (Test of Everyday Mathematics Ability, TEMA), or group-administered curriculum assessments carried out by schools (e.g., California, Iowa Math, curriculum key stage assessments, and Performance Indicators in Primary School). There may be important differences in the identified cognitive substrates dependent on the measurement method. Therefore, diverse evidence relating WM and various mathematic skills, measured by different methods, are presented here.

WORKING MEMORY MODEL

Cognitive studies of mathematic achievement and disorder provide a valuable insight into the deficits that might underlie difficulties in learning mathematics. Many of these studies have used the WM model of Baddeley and Hitch (1974, see also Baddeley, 1986, 1996, 2000 for recent developments of the WM model) as a framework within which to study a range of cognitive skills. Although there are many models of WM, executive control, or both (Miyake & Shah, 1999), most researchers now agree that the process of mental arithmetic calculation involves WM to a substantial degree. Baddeley and Hitch (1974) proposed a multi-modal model with WM consisting of three subcomponents: the central executive (CE), the phonological loop (PL), and the visuo-spatial sketchpad (VSSP). The two "slave" systems, the PL and the VSSP, are specialized for processing language-based and visuo-spatial information, respectively. The CE is responsible for controlling the two slave systems, allocating attentional resources between them, and mediating the relation between WM short-term storage and retrieval from long-term memory (LTM; Baddeley, 1999).

Baddeley suggests that the PL itself can be divided into two separate subcomponents: a passive phonological store and an active phonological rehearsal mechanism. Information held in the phonological store is subject to decay, unless it can be refreshed by subvocal rehearsal, a process akin to repeating under one's breath the information one is trying to retain. Subvocal rehearsal, then, can be disrupted by secondary tasks that also use the verbal resources of the PL. This characteristic of the PL has been used ingeniously by several researchers to study PL processes, using the secondary or dual-task methodology. For example, the use of articulatory suppression (repeating a word such as "the") as an active phonological secondary task disrupts performance of a primary verbal task, such as digit recall.

The second slave system of WM, the VSSP, is less well specified. Until recently the VSSP has been treated as a single component, responsible for the processing of visual and spatial information. Logie and his associates (e.g., Logie, 1986, 1995; Logie & Marchetti, 1991; Pearson, 2001) have been instrumental in deepening our understanding of the nature of the VSSP. The VSSP also has been studied by examining selective interference through dual-task methods. Quinn and McConnell (1999, 2000) have demonstrated that secondary visual tasks (e.g., dynamic visual noise) interfere more with performance on the primary visual task than do secondary spatial tasks. The converse also is true—that is, secondary spatial tasks (e.g., spatial tapping) have a greater negative effect on performance on the primary spatial task than do secondary visual tasks (Logie, 1995; Meiser & Klauer, 1999). However, the attentional/executive demands of visuo-spatial WM tasks are still the matter of much debate (Hamilton, Coates, & Heffernan, 2003).

The CE, despite being arguably the most important of the three components of WM, is certainly the least well defined. Although most researchers consider the CE to be multi-functional and complex, there remains considerable debate, both about the precise nature of its functions and whether there is indeed unity or diversity of the functions. The CE is thought to be of limited capacity, but it controls the allocation of resources between the PL and the VSSP. Miyake, Friedman, Rettinger, Shah, and Hegarty (2001) suggest that the VSSP has a much closer relationship with the CE than the PL, claiming that the VSSP can place much heavier demands on the CE. In view of this dubiety, it has been difficult to ascertain the most appropriate tasks for measuring its supposed functions. Most experimental tasks attempt to obtain a measure of the participants' abilities to combine concurrent processing and storage by using such measures as listening span

(Daneman & Carpenter, 1980) or counting span (Case, Kurland, & Goldberg, 1982).

This chapter begins with a brief discussion of research examining the slave systems of WM and their role in children's arithmetic, followed by a more detailed examination of the recent research investigating the potential role of the functions subserved by the CE.

ARITHMETIC AND THE SLAVE SYSTEMS

Hunter (1957) saw mental calculation as "a succession of stages," each part of a calculation being carried out and stored until the next part of the calculation is completed before processing the products of the two stages. Hitch (1978) suggested that the performance of mental arithmetic required some form of "working storage" but did not speculate about its precise nature at that point. More recent studies with adults, however, have found strong evidence of a major role for the language-based PL in exact arithmetic calculation. Logie, Gilhooly, and Wynn (1994) asked participants to add two-digit numbers while simultaneously performing other tasks known to selectively disrupt the three components of WM. This dual-task technique is used to demonstrate how, when a task is of a certain nature (e.g., phonological, visuo-spatial, or executive), the posited limited resources of the component of WM involved can be engaged. If the loading is sufficient, and if the task being performed is dependent on that aspect of WM, performance of the primary task, secondary task, or both will be disrupted. Logie et al. used articulatory suppression as an active phonological secondary task. Loading the PL in this way prevents subvocal rehearsal and, consequently, information in the phonological store will be subject to decay. They found that performance of the concurrent secondary verbal task had a significant effect on arithmetic performance. Performance of the secondary task was also disrupted by a concurrent arithmetic task. Using a different methodology, where the phonological similarity of the digits is manipulated, Noel, Desert, Aubrun, and Seron (2001) found that adults' performance on arithmetic problems deteriorated significantly where the digits used were phonologically similar, suggesting that PL resources are used in the temporary storage of addends. Similarly, Hecht (2002) observed that where adults have to rely on counting strategies for solving even simple arithmetic problems, phonological and CE resources are necessary for the efficient execution of that strategy. Therefore, from studies of adults' arithmetic performance, there is robust evidence that the PL plays a critically important role, potentially because of the need to hold the operands in some form of short-term storage.

Studies investigating the role of the VSSP in adult arithmetic are much less common. Heathcote (1994), in a study of adult arithmetic performance, found that multi-digit addends are simultaneously stored in both phonological and visual-spatial memory, evidenced by the disruption of calculation performance by a secondary visuo-spatial task, particularly on complex addition problems requiring carrying. Heathcote concluded that, whereas the PL holds the initial problem and running totals, the VSSP is a "mental blackboard or workbench" (p. 237), responsible for the spatial aspects of the problem such as number place and carrying. Hayes (1973) described visual imagery as an alternative to the external cues usually generated by paper and pencil. Others also have suggested that the use of mental number lines and spatial arrangements can support mental calculation (e.g., Dehaene, 1992; Seron, Pesenti, Noel, Deloche, & Cornet, 1992) and that visual-spatial skills are particularly important in certain types of mathematics problems, such as geometry (Hartje, 1987).

Although these results have afforded some insight into the roles of the slave systems of WM in performance on mental arithmetic problems by adults, the picture with children, especially those younger than age 7 years, is even less clear. We do know that children use a range of strategies for solving arithmetic problems and that some of these strategies (even when used by adults) load heavily on WM resources (Hecht, 2002). At the basic level, children use fingers or other concrete referents to aid them in the counting process. From these simple strategies, children progress to auditory counting using the sum procedure (counting all numbers in the problem) to the min procedure (count-on the smallest number). Finally, children can retrieve arithmetic facts directly from LTM (see Siegler, 1999). Geary, Brown, and Samaranayake (1991) argued that for a representation of an answer to a specific arithmetic problem to become established in LTM, both the numbers presented in the problem and the answer must be simultaneously active in WM. Numerous studies now have shown that children who perform poorly in mathematics use immature counting strategies, take more time to solve calculation problems, commit more computational and memory-retrieval errors, and fail to shift from procedural-based problem solving (e.g., counting) to memory-based problem solving (e.g., fact retrieval, Bull & Johnston, 1997; Bull, Johnston, & Roy, 1999; Geary, 1990; Geary & Brown, 1991; Geary et al., 1991; Geary, Bow-Thomas, & Yao, 1992; Geary, Hamson, & Hoard, 2000; Jordan & Montani, 1997; Ostad, 1997). Some of these difficulties have been attributed to a lack of understanding of basic counting concepts, especially appreciating counting rules and knowledge of Arabic numbers (Geary et al. 1992; Geary, Hoard, & Hamson, 1999; Geary et al., 2000).

However, WM resources are also known to influence the development of mathematic proficiency. Geary et al. (1991) found a numeric memory span advantage of approximately one digit for normally achieving children, and shorter memory span was related to more frequent computation errors. Because memory span is related to how quickly items can be retrieved from LTM and then articulated and rehearsed in the PL, it has been proposed that those children with mathematic difficulties count more slowly than normally achieving children when using counting strategies to solve arithmetic problems (Geary et al., 1991; Hitch & McAuley, 1991). In children who use slow and inefficient counting methods, information may be lost from WM, and hence no representation (or a representation of an incorrect answer) is created in LTM. Thus, in a roundabout way, slower counting speed may be a manifestation of the observed fact-retrieval problems of children with mathematic difficulties.

It is interesting that this link between capacity of the PL (as measured by short-term memory (STM) span tasks such as digit and word span) and arithmetic has been called into question. In a number of studies, no association was found, or the association was not robust after statistically controlling for the influence of other cognitive skills. For example, Bull and Johnston (1997) found that if general speed of processing (measured by symbol matching and motor speed) was included in the model, there was no relation between STM and arithmetic. Furthermore, in a number of studies, children with mathematic difficulties show deficits on WM span tasks, particularly where the information has to be manipulated in some way before recall (e.g., Digits Backwards) and hence more likely under the control of the CE, rather than indicating a deficit in STM capacity *per se* (Passolunghi, Cornoldi, & De Liberto, 1999; Swanson, 1994). Therefore, the role of the CE, with functions such as attentional control and the updating of information in WM, may be of greater importance in supporting arithmetic proficiency in children, in comparison to adults.

Furthermore, because children only begin to spontaneously subvocally rehearse at about the age of 7 years (Baddeley, Gathercole, & Papagno, 1998), younger children would have significant difficulty maintaining information in the PL. If such rehearsal is age limited and if arithmetic performance is dependent on the storage of information in the PL, how can the finding be explained that even very young children (as young as 3 or 4 years) are able to complete sums (albeit very simple ones)? According to this developmental limitation, any verbally coded information, such as the addends of a sum, could not be rehearsed and, therefore, will be subject to rapid decay, preventing accurate computation. This inability to rehearse subvocally in the face of some computational ability necessarily implies that a component of WM other than the PL must be involved, at least in young children. Because direct retrieval of arithmetic facts is improbable in children this young, it is unlikely that CE functions relating to the retrieval of information from LTM are involved heavily. However, other CE skills, such as the ability to attend to the appropriate aspects of information and switch between procedures, may be important if the child is using a reconstructive strategy. Moreover, the VSSP may be one critical component involved in young children's arithmetic, a fact overlooked in many early studies examining young children's skills in this domain.

Children's use of phonological versus visual-spatial encoding of information was examined in a study of immediate serial recall of line drawings

(Palmer, 2000). Children were asked to recall previously presented pictures chosen for either their visual or phonological similarity. The pictures were also labeled verbally or were unlabeled at presentation. Whereas older children benefited from labeling of pictures at presentation, younger children did not, suggesting that younger children could not make use of verbal codes stored in the PL. Furthermore, younger children tended to show visual similarity effects—that is, more difficulty recalling items that are visually similar (e.g., dog and goat) compared to older children. In contrast, recall in older children was more consistent with phonological similarity effects—that is, a difficulty recalling items that are alike in their phonological sound (e.g., room and spoon). Palmer concluded that young children progress from a period of purely visuo-spatial strategy use at around 4 years of age; through a stage of dual (visuo-spatial and verbal) strategy use; to an adultlike, mainly verbal, strategy usage at the age of about 8 or 9 years, although this progression has not been investigated longitudinally. The transitional period of dual coding, Palmer suggests, is a critical time during which the CE is maturing (e.g., Baddeley, 1996), supporting flexible switching of strategies and recoding of visually presented material into a phonological form and vice versa.

The development of the cognitive processes that support retention of information in WM has rarely been directly studied in children during the performance of simple mental arithmetic. Davis and Bamford (1995) examined children's (aged 4–5 years) use of visual imagery in arithmetic performance, examining the solution of both simple problems (e.g., $1 + 1$, $2 - 1$) and more difficult problems (e.g., $6 + 2$, $8 - 1$). Children were presented with arithmetic problems that had contextual support—that is, concrete representations (in the form of small toys) for each number involved in the calculation—or had no visible concrete support, instead referring to hypothetical toys. Some of the children also were prompted to use an imagery strategy—that is, imagining a mental picture of the concrete representations. Davis and Bamford found that concrete contextual support led to the production of more correct answers. Furthermore, the children prompted in the use of the imagery strategy performed at an even higher level of accuracy. Therefore, it would appear that visual imagery does provide a useful resource in solving simple arithmetic problems, at least for young children. A number of studies also note that visual-spatial skills are an important contributor to mathematic ability (Casey, Nuttall, & Pezaris, 1997; Geary, Saults, Liu, & Hoard, 2000).

McKenzie, Bull, and Gray (2003) examined the cognitive mechanisms involved in children's mental arithmetic performance at age 6 and 8 years. By differentially disrupting phonological and visuo-spatial WM in younger and older children, they hoped to demonstrate different profiles of interference on arithmetic performance in the two age groups in comparison with a baseline arithmetic score. If younger children rely more on visuo-spatial strategies to perform simple arithmetic calculations (thereby supported by the VSSP), while older children depend more on verbal strategies

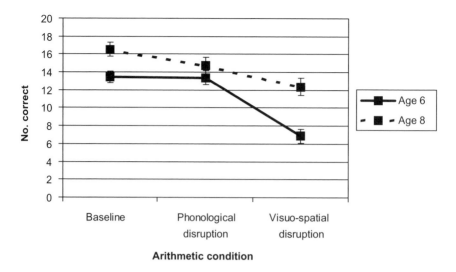

FIGURE 4.1

Arithmetic performance of 6- and 8-year-old children under baseline conditions and with disruption to either the phonological loop or the visual-spatial sketchpad.

in calculation (supported by the PL), then, taken with Palmer's (2000) findings, the shift in strategy use from visual-spatial to verbal slave systems might not necessarily be task dependent; instead, it might reflect a general developmental phenomena that would apply more broadly to a range of tasks that require the storage and manipulation of information in WM. The PL and VSSP slave systems were disrupted by using two passive interference tasks: irrelevant speech and dynamic visual noise (DVN; McConnell & Quinn, 2000), respectively. The results are shown in Figure 4.1. As predicted, DVN disrupted younger children's arithmetic performance, suggesting that 6-year-old children rely on the VSSP to support simple arithmetic calculations. Listening to irrelevant speech, however, did not disrupt arithmetic performance in younger children, in comparison to baseline performance. For older children, the results differed somewhat. Both DVN and listening to irrelevant speech interfered with arithmetic performance, suggesting that the older, 8-year-old children may rely on both the PL and VSSP to support calculation. Consistent with Palmer's (2000) speculation, the cognitive mechanisms recruited by children during arithmetic tasks appears to differ with age.

These results suggest that more attention should be given to the role of visual-spatial WM in children's developing mathematic competencies. Clearly, such cognitive resources are being used to aid arithmetic performance and seem to be of critical importance to younger children, supporting Geary's et al. (1993) suggestion that spatial factors are more important for early mathematics abilities that are engaged less automatically or are in a rapid phase of acquisition. DVN can be selective in the nature of visuo-spatial functioning that it disrupts, with some authors concluding that DVN disrupts visual imagery or the vividness of visual images but not the actual storage of images within visual STM (Andrade, Kemps, Werniers, May, & Szmalec, 2002; Baddeley & Andrade, 2000). If DVN preferentially impairs visualization but not storage in children as well, then McKenzie et al.'s results suggest that young children are using the VSSP as a "workspace" where visual representations can be actively manipulated (an active visual buffer), rather than just as temporary storage of the information in a passive visual cache (see Pearson, 2001, and Pearson, Logie, & Gilhooly, 1999 for a description of the distinction between the active visual buffer and the passive visual cache). The distinction between a visual buffer versus cache and the precise contributions of the visual-spatial and executive components to visual-spatial WM task performance is being investigated in adults by Hamilton and his colleagues (Hamilton et al., 2003), and the ability to make use of both phonological and visual-spatial slave system resources should be fruitful targets of future investigations examining arithmetic and mathematic skills across development.

THE CENTRAL EXECUTIVE

Even at the early stages of examining the role of the PL in arithmetic proficiency, it was acknowledged that this relationship may be important because children with mathematic difficulties are less skilled in allocating their attention and in monitoring the problem-solving process—that is, in using the CE (Geary et al., 1991). Furthermore, results from studies are consistent with substantial overlap between performance on VSSP and CE measures, perhaps in part because many tasks used to measure the visual and spatial elements of the VSSP are also found to make demands on the attentional resources of the CE. For example, verbal fluency, used to measure CE (e.g., Phillips, 1997) has been found to interfere considerably with performance on both visual and spatial span tasks in both children and adults (Hamilton et al., 2003). Therefore, the demonstrated link between either the PL or VSSP and arithmetic proficiency in children may be mediated by some kind of CE processing.

The consideration of CE functioning in relation to children's abilities has become relatively common in recent years. CE function has been investigated in numerous populations, including those with learning disabilities, language and comprehension problems, autism spectrum disorders, attention deficit/hyperactivity disorder (ADHD), and behavioral problems (e.g., Adams, Bourke, & Willis, 1998; Cornoldi, Barbieri, Gaiani, & Zocchi, 1999; Hughes, 1998; Lorsbach, Wilson, & Reimer, 1996; Ozonoff & Jensen, 1999; Russell, Jarrold, & Henry, 1996; Swanson, 1993, 1999; Swanson, Ashbaker,

& Lee, 1996). In school-age children and adolescents, mathematic skills also are related, at least in part, to CE functioning (Bull & Scerif, 2001; Cirino, Morris, & Morris, 2002; Gathercole & Pickering, 2000a; McLean & Hitch, 1999). In adults, CE functions have been implicated in both simple and complex mental addition (e.g., Hecht, 1999, 2002; Logie et al., 1994; de Rammelaere, Stuyven, & Vandierandonck, 2001), subtraction (e.g., Geary, Frensch, & Wiley, 1993), multiplication (e.g., Seitz & Schumann-Hengsteler, 2000); they also have been indirectly implicated in division (LeFevre & Morris, 1999). More generally—that is, independent of mathematic proficiency—CE functions are involved in retrieval of information from LTM (Baddeley, 1996), planning (Duncan, 1986), inhibition of dominant actions (Diamond, 1989), dual-task performance (Baddeley, Bressi, Della Sala, Logie, & Spinnler, 1991), and switching of strategies (Duff & Logie, 2000).

One of the few studies to consider the role of WM in direct relation to children's classroom performance is that of Gathercole and Pickering (2000a), who studied early-elementary–aged children's mathematics performance on the National Curriculum assessments. The Working Memory Test Battery for Children (WMTB-C; Pickering & Gathercole, 2001) was administered to a large cohort of 6- and 7-year-old children, with the aim of identifying those children performing below nationally expected levels. The results revealed a close link between performance on national curriculum assessments and WM skills. CE functioning, as measured by WM span tasks (i.e., counting, listening, and backward digit span) was found to be poorer for children performing below expected achievement levels compared with those performing at expected levels. These results are consistent with earlier findings by Geary et al. (1999) who reported that children with mathematic difficulties have more limited CE function, as indicated by poorer performance on a backward digit span task. Gathercole and Pickering argued that the importance of executive functioning is apparent informally if one considers the types of processing that occur day-to-day in the classroom, where the child continually must process new information and integrate it with information that has been retrieved from LTM or is being held in WM. Therefore, children with a restricted capacity to engage in such mental activities will fail to make adequate progress within school, although this argument speaks more generally to the role of CE skills in school achievement, not necessarily mathematics specifically.

In other studies, basic mathematic proficiency has been assessed through standardized, individually administered paper and pencil tests. Bull et al. (1999) found that 7-year-old children with poorer mathematic and arithmetic abilities also performed more poorly on a measure of CE functioning—the Wisconsin Card Sorting Test (WCST; Heaton, Chelune, Talley, Kay, & Curtiss, 1993). This test examines the ability to use feedback to determine criteria for sorting the cards and the ability to flexibly switch between criteria (e.g., shape, color, and number). It is interesting that children's difficulty on the WCST was restricted to perseverative errors; children of lower mathematic ability made more errors consistent with the previous conceptual set when the new set was active—that is, they found it more difficult to flexibly switch their sorting to a new criteria (e.g., sorting by shape) once one particular routine had become established (e.g., sorting by color). Rourke (1993) has reported similar findings, in the analysis of the types of errors made by children with specific mathematic learning disabilities, where one prominent error type was difficulty switching between psychological sets (e.g., from addition to subtraction problems). Bull et al. (1999) interpreted their results as suggesting a problem with CE functioning, specifically with inhibition of a prepotent response. Finally, in a sample of 122 9-year-old children who scored below the 25% percentile of a standardized mathematic test, time to complete an auditory, written-visual, and color Trail Making Test were also related to arithmetic performance (McLean & Hitch 1999). The authors concluded that both spatial WM span and switching between retrieval plans using the CE contributed to mathematic proficiency.

In a number of studies, the role of WM and CE functioning in solution of arithmetic word problems has been examined. CE attentional control skills are thought to be involved in arithmetic word problem solving because of the significant requirement for text comprehension, where incoming information must be integrated with the previous information maintained in WM for problem solution, and requires that the solver build a mental representation of that problem in WM (see Chapter 3 of this volume for further information on text comprehension and WM). Furthermore, the incoming problem information must be examined for its relevance and then selected or inhibited according to its importance for the solution of that problem. Swanson et al. (1993) measured WM span using a variant of the reading span task and found a significant positive correlation to the number of word problems that children solved.

However, a number of authors claim that differences in WM span may not be related to the quantity of information that can be held in memory but rather to the efficiency of inhibition of irrelevant, or no-longer-relevant, information from WM. Passolunghi et al. (1999) compared memory performance of children (aged approximately 9.5 years) who were either good or poor at problem solving, defined by their performance on short written word arithmetic problems. Good problem solvers had a significantly higher listening span and remembered significantly fewer non-final sentence words (i.e., irrelevant words) than poor problem solvers. Therefore, although both groups recalled overall similar numbers of words, good problem solvers were better able to inhibit irrelevant words and recall the last target word from each sentence, whereas the poor problem solvers struggled to inhibit the nonfinal words. Passolunghi and Siegel (2001) also found that children who were poor problem solvers demonstrated lower WM spans for material across a number of domains, not just for numeric information, as was found earlier (Siegel & Ryan, 1989), and these children who were less proficient had more difficulty inhibiting the no-longer-relevant or irrelevant information. Similar results have been reported in school-aged children with ADHD. Marzocchi, Lucangeli, De Meo, Fini, and Cornoldi (2002) administered word problems that contained no irrelevant information, irrelevant numeric information, or irrelevant verbal information. They hypothesized that any detrimental effects of the presence of the irrelevant information would occur during the procedural aspects of the computation, such as when choosing the appropriate procedures, because all pieces of relevant information need to be properly integrated using the CE resources of WM. Because the actual calculations presumably require simple fact retrieval without information integration, the irrelevant information was not presumed to affect calculation accuracy. Children with ADHD did indeed make more errors when the problems contained either irrelevant numeric information or irrelevant verbal information, with many of these errors in the procedural choice rather than in calculation accuracy.

The Nature of the Central Executive

Whether the CE plays a role in children's arithmetic is not in question. What is debated is how we should conceptualize the CE theoretically. This issue has implications for how the CE is assessed as well as on how it supports other cognitive abilities, such as children's mathematic proficiency. Although many researchers would agree that the CE does not have a unitary function (e.g., Miyake et al., 2000, Welsh & Pennington, 1988), there remains considerable controversy regarding the specific constructs that are "executive" *per se*. Consistent with fractionated executive function models (e.g., Miyake et al., 2000), multiple CE functions are identified by factor analytic techniques; however, the components or factors are not usually completely independent; they share some common variance. Studies that have used factor analytic techniques to account for shared variance between test performance (e.g., principal components analysis, exploratory and confirmatory factor analysis) routinely identify WM and inhibition CE constructs (e.g., Espy, Kaufmann, and Glisky, 1999; Hughes, 1998; Miyake et al., 2000; Pennington, 1997) and commonly a flexibility or shifting CE construct (e.g., Espy et al., 1999; Hughes, 1998; e.g., Pennington, 1997; Welsh, Pennington, & Groisser, 1991). One advantage of these factor analytic procedures is that individual test level data are reduced empirically to meaningful, shared CE constructs, which may better characterize their contribution to emergent mathematic abilities. One limitation of the studies already described (and many others in the field) is that the functions ascribed to the CE are often vague or isolated and are not tied to cognitive theory to better characterize and understand how CE difficulties might arise and what they might mean for mathematic proficiency. Often, only one genre of WM task is used (such as span tasks *or* measures of inhibition *or* measures of shifting ability), or only complex, global measures of CE function are selected that clearly require multiple cognitive abilities for performance (e.g., WCST, Tower tasks). Therefore, it is difficult to pinpoint the specificity or generality of the identified difficulties in CE function that relate directly to mathematic skills.

More recently, a number of researchers have aimed to focus more specifically on different components of CE functioning and their potential role in the development of children's arithmetic and mathematic skills. Based on theoretical, fractionated accounts of CE functioning, the main focus of attention has been on inhibition, shifting, and updating of information in WM. From this perspective, inhibition may be needed to override information or routines that have been automatically activated from LTM and can be measured by tasks such as random generation where the participant is required to generate a random list of letters, trying to inhibit known sequences such as ABC, CIA, and so on (e.g., Baddeley, Emslie, Kolodny, & Duncan, 1998), and the Stroop task, where participants must inhibit the automatic tendency to read a word to instead name the color of the ink in which the word is written (Stroop, 1935). However, inhibition also may be required to override a particular way of responding that may have been established within a task (e.g., stop sorting by color and start sorting by shape). Again, difficulties arise here in differentiating inhibition from shifting abilities; later in the chapter, this type of inhibitory process will be referred to as "conscious inhibition." Shifting ability is generally measured by complex tasks such as the WCST (Heaton et al., 1993) or the Dimensional Change Card Sort Task (Frye, Zelazo, & Palfai, 1995). On these more complex tasks, there is much more interplay between processes for successful performance, including evaluation of the current strategy according to feedback provided, as well as on-line maintenance of the relevant dimension. This broad recruitment of different processes is supported by neuroimaging studies suggesting that a number of cortical areas are active during WCST performance (Berman et al., 1995) as well as other tasks of executive function (Collette et al., 1999). Despite these neuroimaging findings, cognitively, Miyake et al. (2000) found that WCST performance was predicted best by the ability to shift between strategies (measured by, for example, global–local, number–letter tasks) rather than by updating in WM (e.g., tone monitoring and letter memory tasks) or inhibition (e.g., antisaccade and stop-signal tasks).

Another CE feature is the capacity for the temporary activation of LTM, whereby the CE encodes and retrieves information both from the PL and VSSP slave systems and from temporarily activated components of episodic LTM. This skill is measured through tasks such as Daneman and Carpenter's (1980) reading span task and the counting span task of Case et al. (1982), as used in the studies by Gathercole and Pickering (2000a, b). These tasks require the simultaneous processing and storage of information and do appear to allow the use of elaborate strategies to aid performance. Indeed, Towse and Hitch (1995) and Towse, Hitch, and Hutton (1998) account for individual differences on such tasks not in terms of resource sharing but in terms of task switching between the processing and maintenance aspects of the tasks, a dichotomy also supported by neuroimaging findings (Rypma, Berger, & D'Esposito, 2002).

Complicating the use of these tasks to assess CE function is the fact that the overlap and interplay among these functions is large and deciding on the best methods to assess these skills is difficult. Consequently, many investigators resort to selecting specific tests in research batteries to measure salient CE functions on the basis of face validity alone. Because of the interrelated nature of CE function constructs, measures that are included to tap a single CE function inevitably demand multiple CE abilities for proficient performance. For example, other information is invariably inhibited (e.g., Diamond, 1985) to maintain information in WM for upcoming responding. To flexibly shift responses in the light of conflicting rules requires maintaining the rule in mind and inhibiting prepotent, previous responses. Such interrelations make it difficult to assess the unique contributions of differing CE functions to outcomes, such as mathematic proficiency.

Using confirmatory factor analysis, Miyake et al. (2000) found that three target functions—namely, inhibition, shifting between mental sets and strategies, and updating of information in WM—were distinguishable, although not independent. Miyake et al. went on to suggest that unity among CE functions may be accounted for by inhibition because all functions of the CE involve some inhibitory processes to properly guide and regulate cognition—for example, ignoring previous incoming information in a WM task, changing to a new mental set, and so on. Therefore, equating tests (e.g., WCST) to constructs (shifting) on the basis of face validity alone, rather than by using underlying measurement characteristics, can easily lead to erroneous conclusions because of the correlated nature of CE functions.

In an attempt to understand more fully the role of CE functions in mathematics ability, Bull and Scerif (2001) administered a battery of CE measures to 7-year-old children who were under achieving and normally achieving in mathematics. Tasks were selected to map onto the main CE functions proposed by Miyake et al. (2000), including the WCST as an index of shifting ability, a number Stroop task to measure inhibition, and counting span to assess memory updating. Regression analyses revealed that all CE measures predicted unique variance in mathematics proficiency. Specifically, even after the variance associated with other CE measures was controlled statistically in the model, CE measures of inhibition, shifting, and WM updating all accounted for additional, unique variance in mathematics ability.

Early Development of the Central Executive and Mathematic Skills

In very young children—preschoolers and early kindergartners—it is even less clear whether CE functions are related to emergent mathematic abilities. Although some investigators have argued that simple mathematic skills are evident in infancy (e.g., Wynn, 1992), there is a marked emergence of informal mathematic skills (abilities that are not learned through formal instruction) during the preschool period. Gelman and Gallistel (1978), for example, have argued that preschool children possess a fundamental understanding of mathematic principles about counting, such as stable order, one-to-one correspondence, and cardinality, although young children may not fully understand the implications of these principles in various enumeration contexts (e.g., Geary, 1994; Sophian, 1996). There are significant changes in counting skills and arithmetic problem solving (e.g., Baroody, 1992; Sophian, 1996) and in spatial and geometric abilities (e.g., Newcombe & Huttenlocher, 2000) during the preschool years, which provide the foundation for later mathematic knowledge and procedural competencies gained through formal schooling in the primary grades and beyond (Geary, 1994; Ginsburg, 1989; Rittle-Johnson & Siegler, 1998).

During this same preschool period, there is a rapid development in the functions subserved by the CE, such as inhibitory, memory updating, and flexible shifting skills (e.g., Diamond et al., 1997, Espy, 1997, Espy et al., 1999, Jacques & Zelazo, 2001). Therefore, examining the relations between CE functions and emergent arithmetic skills in young children may provide insight into the shared ontogenetic organization of these abilities. One limitation that has hampered such endeavors in young children is the lack of available instruments to assess CE functions because most standardized, general cognitive tools designed for preschool children do not adequately assess such abilities. Tasks adapted from developmental and cognitive neuroscience investigations offer one fruitful method by which to investigate CE functions (e.g., Diamond, 1985; Espy et al., 1999; Espy et al., 1999). Such tasks are advantageous because their relation to prefrontal cortical function has been established, at least in well-controlled studies with nonhuman animals or using similar neuroimaging paradigms with adult humans, and have demonstrated sensitivity in young children with various clinical disorders (Diamond et al., 1997; Espy, Kaufmann, & Glisky, 1999; Espy, Kaufmann, Glisky, & McDiarmid, 2001; Espy, McDiarmid, Senn, Cwik, & Hamby, 2002). Such developmental cognitive neuroscience tasks (e.g., Diamond, 1985; Espy et al., 1999; Welsh & Pennington, 1988) provide the potential to tap differing functions of the CE that may have unique relations to emerging mathematics abilities in this very young age range.

Espy, McDiarmid, Cwik, Stalets, Hamby, and Senn (2004) aimed to determine whether CE functions established empirically were related to emergent mathematic proficiency in preschool children. Two groups of children participated in this study: typically developing and preterm children at low neurobiologic risk, aged between 2 and 5 years. Although the two groups did not differ significantly in performance characteristics such as estimated IQ, children born preterm are known to be at risk for arithmetic impairments (Hack, Klein, & Taylor, 1995; Hunt, Cooper, & Tooley, 1988). Therefore, these children served to provide a more variable range of mathematic ability. Additionally, there is emerging evidence of specific impairments in CE functions in children born preterm during the preschool period (e.g., Espy et al., 2002), in school age (Taylor et al., 1995), and into adolescence (Taylor et al., 2000). How such specific CE dysfunction in children born preterm contributes to more global outcomes, such as mathematic proficiency, remains unclear.

CE functions, namely working memory, inhibitory control, and shifting, were determined empirically by conducting principal components analysis on the individual test-level data to identify meaningful CE components using the shared variance across individual tests. In turn, these CE components were related using hierarchical regression analyses to emergent mathematic proficiency in preschool children, measured by the Applied Problems subtest from the Woodcock-Johnson-Revised Test of Academic Achievement (Woodcock & Johnson, 1989). Inhibitory control, and to a lesser extent WM, contributed substantively to mathematic performance in these very young children. Specifically, the magnitude of the contribution of inhibitory control to early mathematic skills was large, even when the effects of child age, estimated child verbal intelligence, and maternal education level were controlled statistically. Furthermore, inhibitory control predicted emergent mathematics skills in preschoolers even when the influences of WM and shifting were removed, still accounting for 12% of mathematics skill variability. These findings provide a developmental link to similar relations between executive function and mathematic performance previously reported in school-age children (e.g., Bull & Scerif, 2001; Gathercole & Pickering, 2000; McLean & Hitch, 1999). Given the differences in age range, methods used, and design between this study and others, the consistency of the relationship between executive functions and mathematic performance is persuasive.

The WM component also accounted for significant variance in early mathematic proficiency, when the influences of child age, estimated child verbal intelligence, and maternal education level were controlled, but not when the other CE functions were removed. In this age range, WM skills were correlated substantially with inhibitory control ($r = 0.50$, $p < 0.0001$), limiting the amount of unique variance in emergent mathematic skills that could be accounted for by WM. It is interesting that shifting or mental flexibility did not contribute substantively to mathematics skills in very young children. These findings are in contrast to those reported for older, school-age children (Bull & Scerif, 2001; McLean & Hitch, 1999). Mental flexibility may have contributed more to mathematics proficiency in school-age children, given the necessity for the older child to flexibly apply different mathematic procedures (e.g., borrowing, carrying) to obtain correct mathematic solutions. More complex mental flexibility skills also may be later developing and thus may be less related to mathematic abilities in very young children.

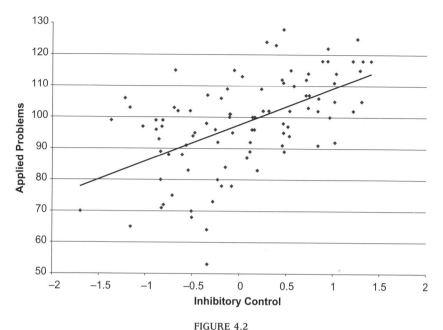

FIGURE 4.2

Woodcock-Johnson-R Applied Problems standard score as a function of inhibitory control z-score in preschool children.

Children born preterm did score lower on the WM component in comparison to the typically developing children, consistent with a growing literature identifying weaknesses in WM in this population (e.g., Espy et al., 2004, Luciana et al., 1999; Ross et al., 1992). Despite the observed performance difference, the nature of the relation between inhibitory control (in Figure 4.2) or WM and early mathematic abilities did not differ between typically developing preschoolers and those born preterm at low risk for neurodevelopmental sequelae. Both groups of preschool children, then, appear to utilize the CE functions, inhibitory control, and WM, in a comparable fashion to solve simple mathematic problems. Because of the attenuated relationship between WM and early mathematic proficiency in preschool children, compared with what has been reported elsewhere for school-age children, the deficits in WM reported for preschool children born preterm may not have much impact on functional outcomes such as mathematics in this age range.

Finally, preliminary results are presented from a longitudinal study conducted by Bull, Espy, & Wiebel (in prep). Given that CE functions predict mathematic achievement in older children, and appear to be related to mathematics proficiency even in very young preschool children (Espy et al., 2004), can CE functions measured in preschoolers be used to identify those children who go on to develop specific difficulties in mathematics?

Furthermore, given that basic number skills assessed early in development are good indicators of those children at risk for later mathematic difficulties (Geary et al., 1999, 2000), would assessment of CE functions provide additional utility in identification, beyond that of basic number skills? In this study, CE functions were derived empirically through parsing of shared task variance with exploratory factor analysis. Similar to Espy et al. (2004), three factors were identified, which Bull et al. chose to refer to as "working memory updating," "automatic inhibition," and "conscious inhibition" (i.e., as would be required when a particular format of responding has been learned within a task and then had to be consciously inhibited).

Starting in 2000, 140 preschool children (mean age of 4.5 years) were administered the CE test battery and basic number knowledge was also assessed, including number recognition and writing (Arabic to verbal translation and vice versa), magnitude understanding, and basic knowledge of counting principles. Mathematic proficiency was measured by individually administered classroom assessments, namely the Performance Indicators in Primary School (PIPS; Tymms, 1999). The PIPS is conducted on entry to the first year of primary school (age 4–5), then again at the end of the first (age 5–6), third (age 7–8), fifth (age 9–10), and the seventh year (11 years). Currently data are available for the first 2 of these testing periods. Children also completed the arithmetic subtest of the WPPSI during their preschool year. Initial analyses examined the contribution of each CE component in predicting mathematics performance and the unique contribution to predicting mathematics ability after the other CE components had been taken into account statistically. Finally, the independent and unique contributions of the CE components were examined, after removing the variance in mathematics accounted for by basic number skills. Results are summarized in Table 4.1.

The top panel of the table indicates the contribution made by each component of executive functioning in predicting children's mathematics. WM updating and conscious inhibition account for large amounts of variance in mathematics ability when entered as the only predictor in the model. However, when the variance associated with other CE functions has been controlled statistically (as shown in the second panel), only the WM component predicted unique variance in mathematics ability at both the early and later curriculum assessments.

Basic number skills accounted for a substantial amount of the variance in mathematics ability, particularly on the first PIPS assessment when the children were just entering primary school (as shown in the third panel of the table). The skills assessed at this first stage include basic number recognition, shape recognition, counting, and so on, resulting in considerable overlap with the basic number skills assessed in the preschool battery. Despite this large degree of overlap, the WM updating component was related to additional variance in mathematics proficiency on the PIPS, even after these basic number skills have been removed statistically.

TABLE 4.1
Preschool Executive Function and Basic Number Skills as Predictors of Mathematic Ability at Different Ages

	WPPSI Arithmetic (Age 4)	PIPS Age 4–5	PIPS Age 5–6
Independent Contribution of EFs			
WM updating	22.8***	36.3***	25.5***
Automatic inhibition	11*	8.8	5.8
Conscious inhibition	25.5***	20.5**	21.5***
Unique Contributions of EFs			
WM updating	8.8*	15.9**	9.6*
Automatic inhibition	7^m	0.4	4.4
Conscious inhibition	7.9^m	2.3	4.7
Independent Contributions of EFs Over and Above Variance Accounted for by Basic Number Skills			
Basic number skills	32.3***	56.7***	34.3***
WM updating	5.1	7.1**	5.6^m
Automatic inhibition	4	0.3	3.4
Conscious inhibition	8*	1.9	5.8^m
Unique Contribution of EFs Over and Above Variance Accounted for by Basic Number Skills and Other EF Skills			
WM updating	5.8	6.7*	3.3
Automatic inhibition	5.3	3.4	2.5
Conscious inhibition	6.8^m	1.6	3.1

EF, executive functioning. Figures represent percentage of additional variance accounted for. ***$p < .001$, **$p < .01$, *$p < .05$, m = marginal significance ($p < .10$).

However, a word of caution is needed here. Different measures of mathematics proficiencies likely would yield a different pattern of results. The PIPS is an individually administered tool, designed to assess curricular progress. In terms of understanding the role of cognitive skills, such as CE functions in everyday outcome, using achievement measures that are more closely tied to performance in the classroom has real advantages in terms of greater ecologic validity. However, the nature of the assessment— that is, individually administered versus group, standard based versus proficiency—might affect the nature of the cognitive abilities that support performance. These issues clearly merit careful thought and further study. Overall, these preliminary findings demonstrate that CE functions, in particular, WM updating, are related to mathematics proficiency and are important beyond basic number skills. Assessments that include both CE functions and basic number skills might be useful to identify at an early age those children who eventually evidence a specific mathematic disability. It will be interesting to see how CE functions assessed in very young preschool children relate to PIPS scores at age 7 years. At this age, the mathematic problems are more complex than those at the first stage of PIPS testing. The attention skills of inhibition and shifting may be a more prominent predictor of proficiency at this age, consistent with previous findings in school-age children (e.g., Bull & Scerif, 2001; McLean & Hitch, 1999; Gathercole & Pickering, 2000a).

Although we have tried to focus on the communality in findings, clearly some results are contradictory, particularly between those in preschool versus school age children, and those within an age range that use different types of mathematics assessments, for example, Espy et al. (2004) versus Bull et al. (in prep). It is likely that at least some of these differences result from the tools used to assess CE functions across studies and ages. In Espy et al., many of the tasks used to assess inhibitory control required inhibition or suppression of a prepotent motor response—for example, pushing a button when a target animal is presented, but not pressing the response key when the animal's sound is paired with the incorrect animal picture; maintaining a still posture despite distractions; inhibiting reaching for an enticing gift; and inhibiting searching at a previously rewarded location. In contrast, Bull et al. used inhibitory tasks that demanded a stronger "cognitive" inhibitory component, such as the Stroop Interference, and its preschool variant, the Day/Night Stroop (Gerstadt, Hong, & Diamond, 1994). Relations between the more primitive, "motorically" based inhibitory control and the more "cognitive" inhibition are not clear. Although Ruff and Rothbart (1996) conceptualize the motoric inhibitory control as a developmental precursor to the cognitive inhibition, such relations have not been demonstrated empirically. Until such relations are clarified with longitudinal designs, the ontogenetic relation between inhibitory control and the development of mathematic competency cannot be elucidated fully.

Similarly, the role of shifting (also referred to as cognitive flexibility or conscious inhibition) differs across studies. In preschool children, shifting was unrelated to mathematics performance in both Espy et al. and Bull et al. Measuring cognitive flexibility in preschool children has proved to be challenging because reversal task performance may discriminate only those with severe disturbances in flexibly shifting between response sets, such as children diagnosed with severe disorders (MçEvoy, Rogers, & Pennington, 1993). Other measures that focus on concept formation may prove to be more useful in this regard (e.g., Smidts, Jacobs, & Anderson, 2004; (Jacques & Zelazo, 2001). Furthermore, as noted by Espy et al. and in line with findings from school-age children (Bull et al., 1999; Bull & Scerif, 2001; McLean & Hitch, 1999), the ability to shift flexibly, or consciously inhibit certain procedures or information, may be more critical for performance on more complex mathematic problem solving that is not assessed until later in elementary school. Mathematics problems for preschool children involve counting and simple regrouping, that, at least on the surface, do not demand as much WM updating to achieve adequate proficiency as problems that involve carrying and borrowing, which are more typical in early elementary school grades. In fact, most of the early items from the WJ-R Applied Problems subtest can be solved with knowledge of small quantity numbers (National Institute of Child Health and Human Development, 2002), and early items on the PIPS assessment only assess very basic number skills and counting. It is not surprising that more proficient performance on these simple problems may require more basic inhibitory control or maintenance in a short-term storage system, perhaps with the CE performing the role of coordinating representations of the information being held in the slave systems. Using multiple measures of mathematic abilities and assessing mathematic proficiencies longitudinally is clearly critical in determining how CE functions are related to the dynamic development of mathematics skills.

One important strength of the approach used by both Espy et al. and Bull et al. is the empirical derivation of the CE components. Three components were extracted in each study, labeled as Working Memory, Inhibitory Control (automatic inhibition), and Mental Flexibility (shifting, conscious inhibition), consistent with other studies in older children (e.g., Kelly, 2000; Lehto, Juujarvi, Kooistra, & Pulkkinen, 2003; H.S. Levin, et al., 1996; Pennington, 1997; Welsh, et al., 1991). Although these observed measurement patterns were derived empirically, the labels applied are a matter of individual preference and judgment. The labels were applied on the basis of previous findings and historical context; however, other labels from other frameworks might also easily describe the derived factors. However, an important limitation of this approach is that the observed loading pattern is test specific— that is, a different loading pattern may be evident if different tests, or even different variables scored from the same test, had been included in the statistical models. What is needed are systematic studies that use measurement model approaches to better characterize CE function organization in children (e.g., confirmatory factor analysis), similar to that initiated by Miyake et al. (2000) in college students, because structural equation modeling approaches can more accurately represent the relations among observed test performance and latent constructs. Only by understanding CE organization in different age ranges will it be possible to better describe the resultant relations to other functional outcomes, such as mathematics proficiency.

The relation between executive function and mathematic proficiency suggests an important role of prefrontal systems in this age range, consistent with findings from imaging studies in adults and children relating various mathematics skills and frontal lobe function (Fullbright et al. 2000; Gruber, Indefrey, Steinmetz, & Kleinschmidt, 2001; Levin et al., 1996; Menon, Riveria, White, Glover, Reiss, 2000; Miles & Stelmack, 1994; Prabhakaran, Rypma, & Gabrieli, 2001; Zago et al., 2001). However, without direct measurement of brain function and concurrent behavioral assessment in this age range, the specific areas that contribute to emergent mathematic proficiency in children are unknown. Because of the technical limitations of the use of functional imaging methods with young children, high-density sensor array event-related potential methods may be a more suitable tool by which to examine such relations.

More generally, the use of developmental and cognitive neuroscience paradigms in the assessment of CE functions offers the opportunity to better assess more discrete neuropsychological skills that are related to functional outcomes, such as emergent mathematic proficiency. Such methods are particularly appealing because relations of test performance to specific brain areas may be stronger than more traditional general ability (e.g., intelligence) measures. Although the neuropsychological structure in young children is likely to be less differentiated than in older children, these methods are useful in highlighting CE performance discrepancies that relate to functional academic outcome. Even in modern investigations that focus on direct brain measurement with highly specialized and technical methods, the careful description of behavior–behavior relations across the developmental context (Fletcher & Taylor, 1984) is still of central relevance today if we are going to try and pin down the exact nature of the CE functions that underlie poor mathematics skill development.

WHAT ARE THE IMPLICATIONS FOR EDUCATION?

When solving an arithmetic or mathematic problem, it is clear that WM may be involved at a number of stages. Solving virtually any arithmetic or mathematic problem will require the solver to hold information in memory, through the use of verbal or visual-spatial codes that use the slave systems. Studies examining the slave systems revealed that children make differential use of visual-spatial and verbal codes at different points throughout development, which may have important implications for the methods of presenting and teaching mathematic skills to children.

The ability to hold, manipulate, and update information in WM has been found to be of crucial importance for the mathematic performance of children of all ages. Difficulty updating information in memory may occur if the child is unable to efficiently retrieve information from LTM to support that being held in short-term storage. Furthermore, the child may have to select and integrate the relevant and critical information, abilities that are likely to be dependent on inhibition and short-term maintenance and manipulation of information. Particularly where tasks contain even small amounts of irrelevant information, children may have difficulty not in selecting the appropriate information, but in inhibiting the inappropriate information that is not relevant to the context at hand. WM may then be overloaded, resulting in difficulty completing the procedural aspects of the task. Finally, shifting ability, or mental flexibility, has been found to play an important role in the mathematics performance of older children, where more complex mathematic tasks such as multi-digit addition and multiplication may require the child to shift between procedures and interim solutions, or even shift between multiplying and adding if decomposition strategies are being used. Similarly, shifting also may be required for carrying operations in complex arithmetic. Therefore, mathematic skills require not only basic storage functions involving the WM slave systems, but also the attentional control functions of the CE.

In the classroom, there might be ways in which the memory load, or the need to recruit CE resources, can be reduced to improve children's performance and learning. Use of external representations reduces load on WM during activities such as learning and problem solving. Frequent revision will mean that concepts needed to provide meaning to new information will be readily available in LTM. Hence, retrieval will be more efficient and the processing load placed on LTM will be lower. Presenting information in a more logical sequence also may make information processing more efficient. Children who may rely more on VSSP as a workspace for calculation may be aided by adjusting the mode of presentation from verbal to visual (Riding, Grimley, Dahraei, & Banner, 2003). It may also be possible to devise strategies for increasing the inhibition of irrelevant information. For example, children could be made more aware of the types of irrelevant information that may interfere with problem solving. Alternatively, children could be taught to underline relevant information, cancel out the irrelevant information, and differentially rehearse the two types of information (Marzocchi, et al., 2002).

Can CE function skills be improved with training? Dowsett and Livesey (2000) found that repeated exposure to tasks facilitating the acquisition of increasingly complex rule structures (such as card sorting tasks) resulted in improved inhibitory control in children as young as 3 years of age. They argued that experience with such tasks increased the acquisition of complex rules by placing demands on CE functions, including response control (of actions and attention), representational flexibility, maintenance of information in WM, and proficiency at error detection. What we do not know is whether any gains made through CE training generalize to other contexts or have a secondary benefit on those skills that we know depend to a large extent on CE functions, such as mathematics.

Do WM assessments at school entry provide accurate prospective indicators of failure to reach normal levels of attainment at later points in the educational process? Compared to assessments of basic concepts (e.g., early number skills), which might be heavily influenced by cultural factors and the quantity and quality of environmental support, WM assessments would be likely to be novel to all children. Hence, such additional assessments may be a useful supplement to existing evaluation using knowledge-based methods for identification of at-risk children (Gathercole & Pickering, 2000a). Certainly, the findings from Bull et al. (in prep) and Espy et al. (2004) provide indirect support for utility of such assessments at a young age. The next obvious step is to use advances in our theoretical and practical understanding of WM and the educational, curricular knowledge and teacher expertise to devise large-scale screening and pilot intervention studies to determine the true utility of such approaches in identifying children at risk for difficulties in mathematic achievement. Because of the protracted development of WM abilities and the changing nature of the mathematic skills that need to be acquired by children at different ages, longitudinal studies will need to be constructed carefully to more fully address this issue.

Summary Box

- Cognitive limitations in childhood do lead to difficulties in learning basic arithmetic and mathematic skills, and we need to pinpoint these cognitive limitations if we are to help children in their learning.
- Mathematic skills are supported by verbal and visual-spatial STM resources, the reliance on which may vary depending on age and experience.
- Children of poorer mathematics ability find it more difficult to inhibit irrelevant information and stay focused on the task at hand.
- Children of poorer mathematics ability find it more difficult to update information in WM and to flexibly switch from one established strategy to another.
- The nature of executive abilities remains to be fully defined and operationalized, particularly for young children.
- Different executive abilities relate to mathematics achievement at different ages and at varying levels of mathematics complexity.
- Executive abilities relate to mathematics differently in typically and atypically developing populations.
- Using a combination of subject specific tasks and general WM tasks, it may be possible to identify children at risk of developing mathematic difficulties.
- A deeper understanding of the cognitive limitations will help us to develop teaching strategies to overcome or circumvent these difficulties.

References

Adams, A. M., Bourke, L., & Willis, C. (1998, September). *Working memory: Implications for individual differences in language development*. Poster presented at the British Psychological Society Developmental Section Annual Conference. Lancaster, England.

Andrade, J., Kemps, E., Werniers, Y., May, J., & Szmalec, A. (2002). Insensitivity of visual short-term memory to irrelevant visual information. *Quarterly Journal of Experimental Psychology*, *55A*, 753–774.

Baddeley, A. D. (1986). *Working Memory*. Oxford: Oxford University Press.

Baddeley, A. D. (1996). Exploring the central executive. *Quarterly Journal of Experimental Psychology, 49A*, 5–28.

Baddeley, A. D. (1999). *Essentials of Human Memory*. Hove: Psychology Press.

Baddeley, A. D. (2000). The episodic buffer: a new component of working memory? *Trends in Cognitive Science, 4*, 417–423.

Baddeley, A. D., & Andrade, J. (2000). Working memory and the vividness of imagery. *Journal of Experimental Psychology: General, 129*, 126–145.

Baddeley, A. D., Bressi, S., Della Sala, S., Logie, R., & Spinnler, H. (1991). The decline of working memory in Alzheimer's disease: A longitudinal study. *Brain, 114*, 2521–2542.

Baddeley, A. D., Emslie, H., Kolodny, J., & Duncan, J. (1998). Random generation and the executive control of working memory. *Quarterly Journal of Experimental Psychology, 51A*, 819–852.

Baddeley, A. D., & Hitch, G. J. (1974). Working memory. In G. A. Bower (Ed.), *Recent advances in learning and motivation* (Vol. 8, pp. 47–90). New York: Academic Press.

• Baddeley, A. D., Gathercole, S., & Papagno, C. (1998). The phonological loop as a language learning device. *Psychological Review, 105*, 158–173.

Badian, N. A. (1983). Dyscalculia and nonverbal disorders of learning. In H. R. Myklebust (Ed.) *Progress in Learning Disabilities*. New York: Stratton.

Baroody, A. J. (1992). The development of preschoolers' counting skills and principles. In J. Bideau, C. Meljac, & J. Fischer (Eds.), *Pathways to number* (pp. 99–126). Hillsdale, NJ: Erlbaum.

Berman, K. F., Ostrem, J. L., Randolph, C., Gold, J., Goldberg, T. E., Coppola, R., et al. (1995). Physiological activation of a cortical network during performance on the Wisconsin Card Sorting test: A positron emission tomography study. *Neuropsychologica, 33*, 1027–1046.

Bull, R., Espy, K. A., & Wiebe, S. (in prep). Executive function skills as longitudinal predictors of children's mathematics ability.

Bull, R., & Johnston, R. S. (1997). Children's arithmetical difficulties: Contributions from processing speed, item identification, and short-term memory. *Journal of Experimental Child Psychology, 65*, 1–24.

Bull, R., Johnston, R. S., & Roy, J. A. (1999). Exploring the roles of the visual-spatial sketch pad and central executive in children's arithmetical skills: Views from cognition and developmental neuropsychology. *Developmental Neuropsychology, 15*(3), 421–442.

Bull, R., & Scerif, G. (2001). Executive functioning as a predictor of children's mathematics ability: Inhibition, switching, and working memory. *Developmental Neuropsychology, 19*, 273–293.

Case, R., Kurland, D. M., & Goldberg, J. (1982). Operational efficiency and the growth of short-term memory span. *Journal of Experimental Child Psychology, 33*(3), 386–404.

Casey, M. B., Nuttall, R., & Pezaris, E. (1997). Mediators of gender difference in mathematics college entrance scores: A comparison of spatial skills with internalized beliefs and anxieties. *Developmental Psychology, 33*, 669–680.

Cirino, P. T., Morris, M. K., & Morris, R. D. (2002). Neuropsychological concomitants of calculation skills in college students referred for learning difficulties. *Developmental Neuropsychology, 21*, 201–218.

Collette, F., Salmon, E., Van der Linden, M., Chicherio, C., Belleville, S., Degueldre, C., et al. (1999). Regional brain activity during tasks devoted to the central executive of working memory. *Cognitive Brain Research, 7*, 411–417.

Cornoldi, C., Barbieri, A., Gaiani, C., & Zocchi, S. (1999). Strategic memory deficits in attention deficit disorder with hyperactivity participants (ADHD): The role of executive processes. *Developmental Neuropsychology, 15*, 53–71.

Daneman, M., & Carpenter, P. A. (1980). Individual differences in working memory and reading. *Journal of Verbal Learning and Verbal Behaviour, 19*, 450–466.

Davis, A., & Bamford, G. (1995). The effect of imagery on young children's ability to solve simple arithmetic. *Education Section Review, 19*, 61–68.

Dehaene, S. (1992). Varieties of numerical abilities. *Cognition*, *44*, 1–42.

de Rammelaere, S., Stuyven, E., & Vandierendonck, A. (2001). Verifying simple arithmetic sums and products: Are the phonological loop and the central executive involved? *Memory & Cognition*, *29*, 267–273.

Diamond, A. (1989). *The development and neural bases of higher mental functions*. New York: New York Academy of Science.

Diamond, A. (1985). Development of the ability to use recall to guide action, as indicated by infants' performance on AB. *Child Development*, *56*, 868–883.

Diamond, A., Prevor, M. B., Callender, G., & Druin, D. P. (1997). Prefrontal cortex cognitive deficits in children treated early and continuously for PKU. *Monographs of the Society for Research in Child Development*, *62*, 1–205.

Dowsett, S. M., & Livesey, D. J. (2000). The development of inhibitory control in preschool children: Effects of "executive skills" training. *Developmental Psychobiology*, *36*, 161–174.

Duncan, J. (1986). Disorganization of behaviour after frontal lobe damage. *Cognitive Neuropsychology*, *3*, 271–290.

Duff, S. C. & Logie, R. H. (2000). Processing and storage in working memory span. *Quarterly Journal of Experimental Psychology*, *54A*, 31–48.

Espy, K. A. (1997). The shape school: Assessing executive function in preschool children. *Developmental Neuropsychology*, *13*, 495–499.

Espy, K. A., Kaufmann, P. M., & Glisky, M. L. (1999). Neuropsychological function in toddlers exposed to cocaine in utero: A preliminary study. *Developmental Neuropsychology*, *15*, 447–460.

Espy, K. A., Kaufmann, P. M., Glisky, M. L., & McDiarmid, M. D. (2001). New procedures to assess executive functions in preschool children. *The Clinical Neuropsychologist*, *15*, 46–58.

Espy, K. A., Kaufmann, P. M., McDiarmid, M. D., & Glisky, M. L. (1999). Executive functioning in preschool children: Performance on A-not-B and other delayed response format tasks. *Brain and Cognition*, *41*, 178–199.

Espy, K. A., McDiarmid, M. D., Cwik, M. F., Stalets, M. M., Hamby, A., & Senn, T. E. (2004). The contribution of executive functions to emergent mathematics skills in preschool children. *Developmental Neuropsychology*, *26*, 465–486.

Espy, K. A., Stalets, M. M., McDiarmid, M. D., Senn, T. E., Cwik, M. F., & Hamby, A. F. (2002). Executive functions in preschool children born preterm: Applications of cognitive neuroscience paradigms. *Child Neuropsychology*, *8*, 83–92.

Fletcher, J. M., & Taylor, H. G. (1984). Neuropsychological approaches to children: Towards a developmental neuropsychology. *Journal of Clinical Neuropsychology*, *6*, 39–56.

Frye, D., Zelazo, P. D., & Palfai, T. (1995). Theory of mind and rule-based reasoning. *Cognitive Development*, *10*, 483–527.

Fullbright, R. K., Molfese, D. L., Stevens, A. A., Skudlarski, P., Lacadie, C. M., & Gore, J. C. (2000). Cerebral activation during multiplication: A functional MR imaging study of number processing. *American Journal of Neuroradiology*, *21*, 1048–1054.

Gathercole, S. E., & Pickering, S. J. (2000a). Working memory deficits in children with low achievements in the national curriculum at 7 years of age. *British Journal of Educational Psychology*, *70*, 177–194.

Gathercole, S. E. & Pickering, S. J. (2000b). Assessment of working memory in six- and seven-year-old children. *Journal of Educational Psychology*, *92*, 377–390.

Geary, D. C. (1990). A componential analysis of an early learning deficit in mathematics. *Journal of Experimental Child Psychology*, *49*, 363–383.

Geary, D. C. (1994). *Children's Mathematical Development*. Washington, DC: American Psychological Association.

Geary, D. C., Bow-Thomas, C. C., & Yao, Y. (1992). Counting knowledge and skill in cognitive addition: A comparison of normal and mathematically disabled children. *Journal of Experimental Child Psychology*, *54*, 372–391.

Geary, D. C., & Brown, S. C. (1991). Cognitive addition: Strategy choice and speed of processing differences in gifted, normal, and mathematically disabled children. *Developmental Psychology, 27*, 398–406.

Geary, D. C., Brown, S. C., & Samaranayake, V. A. (1991). Cognitive addition: A short longitudinal study of strategy choice and speed-of-processing differences in normal and mathematically disabled children. *Developmental Psychology, 27*, 787–797.

Geary, D. C., & Burlingham-Dubree, M. (1989). External validation of the strategy choice model for addition. *Journal of Experimental Child Psychology, 47*, 175–192.

Geary, D. C., Frensch, P. A., & Wiley, J. G. (1993). Simple and complex mental subtraction: Strategy choice and speed-of-processing differences in younger and older adults. *Psychology and Aging, 8*, 242–256.

Geary, D. C., Hamson, C. O., & Hoard, M. K. (2000). Numerical and arithmetical cognition: A longitudinal study of process and concept deficits in children with learning disability. *Journal of Experimental Child Psychology, 77*, 236–263.

Geary, D. C., Hoard, M. K., & Hamson, C. O. (1999). Numerical and arithmetical cognition: Patterns of functions and deficits in children at risk for a mathematical disability. *Journal of Experimental Child Psychology, 74*, 213–239.

Geary, D. C., Saults, S. J., Liu, F., & Hoard, M. K. (2000). Sex differences in spatial cognition, computational fluency, and arithmetical reasoning. *Journal of Experimental Child Psychology, 77*, 337–353.

Gelman, R., & Gallistel, C. R. (1978). *The Child's Understanding of Number*. Washington, DC: American Psychological Association.

Gerstadt, C. L., Hong, Y. J., & Diamond, A. (1994). The relationship between cognition and action: Performance of children 31/2–7 years on a Stroop-like day-night test. *Cognition, 53*, 129–153.

Ginsburg, H. P. (1989). *Children's Arithmetic, 2nd Ed.* Cambridge, MA: Harvard University Press.

Gross-Tsur, V., Manor, O., & Shalev, R. S. (1996). Developmental dyscalculia: Prevalence and demographic features. *Developmental Medicine and Child Neurology, 38*, 25–33.

Gruber, O., Indefrey, P., Steinmetz, H., & Kleinschmidt, A. (2001). Dissociating neural correlates of cognitive components in mental calculation. *Cerebral Cortex, 11*(4), 350–359.

Hack, M., Klein, N. K., & Taylor, H. G. (1995). Long-term developmental outcomes of low birth weight infants. *The Future of Children, 5*, 176–196.

Hamilton, C. J., Coates, R. O., & Heffernan, T. (2003). What develops in visuo-spatial working memory development? *European Journal of Cognitive Psychology, 15*, 43–69.

Hartje, W. (1987). The effect of spatial disorders on arithmetical skills. In G. Deloche & X. Seron (Eds.), *Mathematical disabilities: A cognitive neuropsychological perspective.* (pp. 121–135). Hillside, NJ: Lawrence Erlbaum Associates.

Hayes, J. R. (1973). On the function of visual imagery in elementary mathematics. In W. G. Chase (Ed.), *Visual information processing* (pp. 177–214). New York: Academic.

Heathcote, D. (1994). The role of visuo-spatial working memory in the mental addition of multi-digit addends. *Current Psychology of Cognition, 13*, 207–245.

Heaton, R. K., Chelune, G. J., Talley, J. L., Kay, G. G., & Curtiss, G. (1993). *Wisconsin Card Sorting Test manual.* Odessa, FL: Psychological Assessment Resources.

Hecht, S. (1999). Individual solution processes while solving addition and multiplication math facts in adults. *Memory and Cognition, 27*, 1097–1107.

Hecht, S. A. (2002). Counting on working memory in simple arithmetic when counting is used for problem solving. *Memory and Cognition, 30*, 447–455.

Hitch, G. J. (1978). The role of short-term working memory in mental arithmetic. *Cognitive Psychology, 10*, 302–323.

Hitch, G. J., & McAuley, E. (1991). Working memory in children with specific arithmetical learning difficulties. *British Journal of Psychology, 82*, 375–386.

Hughes, C. (1998). Executive function in preschoolers: Links with theory of mind and verbal ability. *British Journal of Developmental Psychology, 16*, 233–253.

Hunt, J. V., Cooper, B. A. B., & Tooley, W. H. (1988). Very low birth-weight infants at 8 and 11 years of age. Role of neonatal illness and family status. *Pediatrics, 82,* 596–603.

♦ Hunter, I. M. L. (1957). *Memory: Facts and fallacies.* Baltimore: Penguin.

Jacques, S., & Zelazo, P. D. (2001). The Flexible Item Selection Task (FIST): A measure of executive function in preschoolers. *Developmental Neuropsychology, 20,* 573–591.

Jordan, N. C., & Montani, T. O. (1997). Cognitive arithmetic and problem solving: A comparison of children with specific and general mathematics difficulties. *Journal of Learning Disabilities, 30,* 624–634.

Kelly, T. P. (2000). The development of executive function in school-aged children. *Clinical Neuropsychological Assessment, 1,* 38–55.

Kosc, L. (1974). Developmental dyscalculia. *Journal of Learning Disabilities, 7,* 164–177.

LeFevre, J. & Morris, J. (1999). More on the relation between division and multiplication in simple arithmetic: Evidence for mediation of division solutions via multiplication. *Memory and Cognition, 27,* 803–812.

Lehto, J. E., Juujarvi, P., Kooistra, L., & Pulkkinen, L. (2003). Dimensions of executive functioning: Evidence from children. *British Journal of Developmental Psychology, 21,* 59–80.

Levin, H., Fletcher, J., Kufera, J., Harward, H., Lilly, M., Mendelsohn, D., et al. (1996). Dimensions of cognition measured by the Tower of London and other cognitive tasks in head-injured children and adolescents. *Developmental Neuropsychology, 12,* 17–34.

Levin, H. S., Scheller, J., Grafman, J., Martinkowski, K., Winslow, M., & Mirvis, S. (1996). Dyscalculia and dyslexia after right hemisphere injury in infancy. *Archives of Neurology, 53*(1), 88–96.

Lewis, C., Hitch, G. J., & Walker, P. (1994). The prevalence of specific arithmetic difficulties and specific reading difficulties in 9- to 10-year-old boys and girls. *Journal of Child Psychology and Psychiatry, 35,* 283–292.

Logie, R. H. (1986). Visuo-spatial processing in working memory. *Quarterly Journal of Experimental Psychology, 38A,* 229–247.

Logie, R. H. (1995). *Visuo-spatial working memory.* Hove: UK. Lawrence Erlbaum Associates.

Logie, R. H., Gilhooly, K. J., & Wynn, V. (1994). Counting on working memory in arithmetic problem solving. *Memory and Cognition, 22,* 395–410.

Logie, R. H., & Marchetti, C. (1991). Visuo-spatial working memory: Visual, spatial or central executive? In Logie R. H., Denis M. (Eds.), *Mental Images in Human Cognition,* pp 105–115. Amsterdam: Elsevier Science Publishers BV.

Lorsbach, T. C., Wilson, S., & Reimer, J. F. (1996). Memory for relevant and irrelevant information: Evidence for deficient inhibitory processes in language/learning disabled children. *Contemporary Educational Psychology, 21,* 447–466.

Luciana, M., Lindeke, L., Georgieff, M., Mills, M., & Nelson, C. A. (1999). Neurobehavioral evidence for working memory deficits in school-aged children with histories of prematurity. *Developmental Medicine and Child Neurology, 41,* 521–533.

Marzocchi, G. M., Lucangeli, D., De Meo, T., Fini, F., & Cornoldi, C. (2002). The disturbing effect of irrelevant information on arithmetic problem solving in inattentive children. *Developmental Neuropsychology, 21,* 73–92.

McConnell, J., & Quinn, J. G. (2000). Interference in visual working memory. *Quarterly Journal of Experimental Psychology, 53A,* 53–67.

McEvoy, R. E., Rogers, S. J., & Pennington, B. F. (1993). Executive function and social communication deficits in young autistic children. *Journal of Child Psychology and Psychiatry, 34,* 563–578.

● McKenzie, B., Bull, R., & Gray, C. (2003). The effects of phonological and visual-spatial interference on children's arithmetic performance. *Educational and Child Psychology, 20,* 93–108.

McLean, J. F., & Hitch, G. J. (1999). Working memory impairments in children with specific arithmetic learning difficulties. *Journal of Experimental Child Psychology, 74,* 240–260.

Meiser, T., & Klauer, K. C. (1999). Working memory and changing-state hypothesis. *Journal of Experimental Psychology: Learning, Memory, and Cognition, 25,* 1272–1299.

Menon, V., Riveria, S. M., White, C. D., Glover, G. H., & Reiss, A. L. (2000). Dissociating pre-frontal and parietal cortex activation during arithmetic processing. *Physical Review Letters*, 85(3), 520–524.

Miles, J., & Stelmack, R. M. (1994). Learning disability subtypes and the effects of auditory and visual priming on visual event-related potentials to words. *Journal of Clinical & Experimental Neuropsychology*, 16(1), 43–64.

Miyake, A., Friedman, N. P., Emerson, M. J., Witzki, A. H., Howerter, A., & Wager, T. D. (2000). The unity and diversity of executive functions and their contributions to complex frontal lobe tasks: A latent variable analysis. *Cognitive Psychology*, 41, 49–100.

Miyake, A., Friedman, N. P., Rettinger, D. A., Shah, P., & Hegarty, M. (2001). How are visuo-spatial working memory, executive functioning, and spatial abilities related? A latent variable analysis. *Journal of Experimental Psychology: General*, 130, 621–640.

Miyake, A., & Shah, P. (1999). *Models of working memory: Mechanisms of active maintenance and executive control*. Cambridge, UK: Cambridge University Press.

National Institute of Child Health and Human Development. (2002). Workshop, *Early Childhood Education and School Readiness*. October, Baltimore.

Newcombe, N., & Huttenlocher, J. (2000). *Making Space: The development of spatial representation and reasoning*. Cambridge, MA: MIT Press.

Noel, M. P., Desert, M., Aubrun, A., & Seron, X. (2001). Involvement of short-term memory in complex mental calculation. *Memory and Cognition*, 29, 34–42.

Ostad, S. A. (1997). Developmental differences in addition strategies: a comparison of mathematically disabled and mathematically normal children. *British Journal of Educational Psychology*, 67, 345–357.

Ozonoff, S., & Jensen, J. (1999). Brief report: Specific executive function profiles in three neurodevelopmental disorders. *Journal of Autism and Developmental Disorders*, 29, 171–177.

• Palmer, S. (2000). Working memory: A developmental study of phonological recoding. *Memory*, 8, 179–193.

Passolunghi, M. C., Cornoldi, C., & De Liberto, S. (1999). Working memory and intrusions of irrelevant information in a group of specific poor problem solvers. *Memory and Cognition*, 27(5), 779–790.

Passolunghi, M. C., & Siegel, L. S. (2001). Short-term memory, working memory, and inhibitory control in children with difficulties in arithmetic problem solving. *Journal of Experimental Child Psychology*, 80, 44–57.

Pearson, D. G. (2001). Imagery and the visuo-spatial sketch pad. In J. Andrade (Ed.), *Working memory in perspective* (pp. 33–59). Hove, UK: Psychology Press.

Pearson, D. G., Logie, R. H., & Gilhooly, K. J. (1999). Verbal representations and spatial manipulation during mental synthesis. *European Journal of Cognitive Psychology*, 11, 295–314.

Pennington, B. F. (1997). Dimensions of executive functions in normal and abnormal development. In N. A. Krasnegor, G. R. Lyon, & P. S. Goldman-Rakic (Eds.), *Development of the prefrontal cortex* (pp. 265–281). Baltimore: Paul H. Brookes Publishing Co., Inc.

Phillips, L. (1997). Do "frontal tests" measure executive function? Issues of assessment and evidence from fluency tests. In P. M. A. Rabbitt (Ed.), *Methodology of Frontal and Executive Functions*. Hove: LEA.

Pickering, S., & Gathercole, S. (2001). *Working Memory Test Battery for Children (WMTB-C)*. London: Psychological Corporation.

Prabhakaran, V., Rypma, B., & Gabrieli, J. D. E. (2001). Neural substrates of mathematical reasoning: A functional magnetic resonance imaging study of neocortical activation during performance of the necessary arithmetic operations test. *Neuropsychology*, 15(1), 115–127.

Quinn, J. G., & McConnell, J. (1999). Manipulation of interference in the passive visual store. *European Journal of Psychology*, 11, 373–389.

Quinn, J. G., & McConnell, J. (2000). Interference in visual working memory. *Quarterly Journal of Experimental Psychology*, 53A, 53–67.

Riding, R., Grimley, M., Dahraei, H., & Banner, G. (2003). Cognitive style, working memory and learning behavior and attainment in school subjects. *British Journal of Educational Psychology*, *73*, 149–169.

Rittle-Johnson, B. & Siegler, R. S. (1998). The relationship between conceptual and procedural knowledge in learning mathematics: A review. In C. Donlan (Ed.), *The Development of Mathematical Skills* (pp. 75–110). East Sussex, UK: Psychology Press.

Ross, G., Tesman, J., Auld, P. A. M., & Nass, R. (1992). Effects of subependymal and mild intraventricular lesions on visual attention and memory in preterm infants. *Developmental Psychology*, *28*, 1067–1074.

Rourke, B. P. (1993). Arithmetic disabilities, specific and otherwise: A neuropsychological perspective. *Journal of Learning Disabilities*, *26*, 214–226.

Rourke, B. P., & Conway, J. A. (1997). Disabilities of arithmetic and mathematical reasoning: Perspectives from neurology and neuropsychology. *Journal of Learning Disabilities*, *30*, 34–46.

Ruff, H. A., & Rothbart, M. K. (1996). *Attention in early development: Themes and variations*. New York: Oxford University Press.

Russell, J., Jarrold, C., & Henry, L. (1996). Working memory in children with autism and with moderate learning difficulties. *Journal of Child Psychology and Psychiatry*, *37*, 673–686.

Rypma, B., Berger, J. S., & D'Esposito, M. (2002). The influence of working memory demand and subject performance on prefrontal activity. *Journal of Cognitive Neuroscience*, *14*, 721–731.

Seitz, K. & Schumann-Hengsteler, R. (2000), Mental multiplication and working memory. *European Journal of Cognitive Psychology*, *12*, 552–570.

Seron, X., Pesenti, M., Noel, M., Deloche, G. & Cornet, J. (1992). Images of numbers, or "When 98 is upper left and 6 sky blue." *Cognition*, *44*, 159–196.

Siegel, L. S., & Ryan, E. B. (1989). The development of working memory in normally achieving and subtypes of learning disabled children. *Child Development*, *60*, 973–980.

Siegler, R. S. (1988). Strategy choice procedures and the development of multiplication skill. *Journal of Experimental Psychology: General*, *117*, 258–275.

Siegler, R. S. & Shrager, J. (1984). Strategy choice in addition and subtraction: How do children know what to do? In C. Sophian (Ed.), *Origins of Cognitive Skill*. Hillside, NJ: Erlbaum.

Siegler, R. S. (1999). Strategic development. *Trends in Cognitive Sciences*, *3*, 430–435.

Smidts, D. P., Jacobs, R., & Anderson, V. (2004). The object classification test for children (OCTC): A measure of concept generation and mental flexibility in early childhood. *Developmental Neuropsychology*, *26*, 385–401.

Sophian, C. (1996). *Children's Numbers*. Boulder, CO: Westview Press.

Stroop, J. R. (1935). Studies of interference in serial verbal reactions. *Journal of Experimental Psychology*, *18*, 643–662.

Swanson, H. L. (1993). Working memory in learning disability subgroups. *Journal of Experimental Child Psychology*, *56*, 87–114.

Swanson, H. L. (1999). Reading comprehension and working memory in learning-disabled readers: Is the phonological loop more important than the executive system? *Journal of Experimental Child Psychology*, *72*, 1–31.

Swanson, H. L., Ashbaker, M. H., & Lee, C. (1996). Learning disabled readers working memory as a function of processing demands. *Journal of Experimental Child Psychology*, *61*, 242–275.

Swanson, H. L., Cooney, J. B., & Brock, S. (1993). The influence of working memory and classification ability on children's word problem solution. *Journal of Experimental Child Psychology*, *55*, 373–395.

Taylor, H. G., Hack, M., Klein, N. K., & Schatschneider, C. (1995). Achievement in children with birth weights less than 750 grams with normal cognitive abilities: Evidence for specific learning disabilities. *Journal of Pediatric Psychology*, *20*, 703–719.

Taylor, H. G., Klein, N. K., Minich, N. M., & Hack, M. (2000). Middle-school-age outcomes in children with very low birthweight. *Child Development*, *71*, 1495–1511.

Towse, J. N., & Hitch, G. J. (1995). Is there a relationship between task demands and storage space in tests of working memory capacity? *Quarterly Journal of Experimental Psychology, 48A*, 108–124.

Towse, J. N., Hitch, G. J., & Hutton, U. (1998). A reevaluation of working memory capacity in children. *Journal of Memory and Language, 39*, 195–217.

Tymms, P. (1999). *Baseline Assessment and Monitoring in Primary Schools: Achievement, Attitudes, and Value-Added Indicators.* London: David Fulton Publishers.

Wechsler, D. (1977). *Wechsler Intelligence Scale for Children—Revised.* Windsor: NFER-Nelson

Wechsler, D. H. (1990). *Wechsler Preschool and Primary Scale of Intelligence—Revised.* Kent: The Psychological Corporation

Welsh, M. C., & Pennington, B. F. (1988). Assessing frontal lobe functioning in children: Views from developmental psychology. *Developmental Neuropsychology, 4*(3), 199–230.

Welsh, M. C., Pennington, B. F., & Groisser, D. B. (1991). A normative-developmental study of executive function: A window on prefrontal function in children. *Developmental Neuropsychology, 7*(2), 131–149.

Wilson, K. M., & Swanson, H. L. (2001). Are mathematics disabilities due to a domain-general or domain-specific working memory deficit? *Journal of Learning Disabilities, 34*, 237–248.

Woodcock, R. W., & Johnson, M. B. (1989). *Woodcock-Johnson Psycho-Educational Battery-Revised.* Allen, TX: DLM Teaching Resources.

Wynn, K. (1992). Addition and subtraction by human infants. *Nature, 358* (6389), 749–750.

Zago, L., Pesenti, M., Mellet, E., Crivello, F., Mazoyer, B., & Tzourio-Mazoyer, N. (2001). Neural correlates of simple and complex mental calculation. *Neuroimage, 13*(2), 314–327.

Working Memory and Dynamic Testing in Children with Learning Disabilities

H. LEE SWANSON

University of California Riverside

This chapter reviews some of our work on working memory (WM), learning disabilities (LD), and dynamic testing. We find (e.g., Swanson, 2003; Swanson & Ashbaker, 2000; Swanson & Siegel, 2001a, 2001b), as do several others (Bull, Johnston, & Roy, 1999; Chiappe, Hasher, & Siegel, 2000; De Beni, Palladino, Pazzaglia, & Cornoldi, 1998; de Jong, 1998; Passolunghi, Cornoldi, & De Liberto, 1999; Siegel & Ryan, 1989), that children with normal intelligence and LD suffer severe WM deficits. These WM deficits have been found to be related to the poor performance on measures of reading, arithmetic, writing, and problem solving in children with LD (see Swanson & Siegel, 2001a, b, for a comprehensive review). Several important questions have emanated from this work. For example, can WM performance be improved in children with LD? Are their WM deficits stable or easily influenced by simple strategies? Can the WM deficits of children with LD be distinguished from other children who are also having difficulty in reading or math? Are the WM deficits of children with LD isolated only to verbal tasks, or are they also related to visual-spatial tasks? To answer these questions, testing procedures need to be developed to determine the persistence and extent of these deficits.

In this chapter, we focus on our use of dynamic testing measures to better understand the processing difficulties of children with LD. We briefly review our work on developing a WM measure that follows dynamic assessment (DA) procedures and how this work helps us identify children with LD.

Working Memory and Education
125

Before discussing some of our research in these areas, however, we will briefly define the terms *working memory, learning disabilities,* and *dynamic assessment.*

WHAT ARE WORKING MEMORY, LEARNING DISABILITIES, AND DYNAMIC ASSESSMENT?

Working Memory

WM is defined as a processing resource of limited capacity, involved in the preservation of information while simultaneously processing the same or other information (e.g., Baddeley & Logie, 1999; Engle, Tuholski, Laughlin, & Conway, 1999). To illustrate what we mean by this consider the following example of a WM task we use to test children, adapted from an earlier study by Daneman and Carpenter (1980). The examiner reads sentences arranged into sets of two, three, four, or five. To a child an example of a sentence at the three-sentence level might include the following:

1. We waited in line for a *ticket.*
2. Sally thinks we should give the bird its *food.*
3. My mother said she would write a *letter.*

After the presentation of sentences in a set, the child is asked a question by the examiner ("Where did we wait?") and then the child is asked to recall the last words in each sentence. Thus, the WM task engages the child in at least two activities after initial encoding: 1) response to a question, or questions, about the material or related material to be retrieved, and 2) the retrieval of item information of increasing difficulty. The first part of the task is a distracter of the initial encoding of items, whereas the second part tests storage.

We assume that tasks that measure WM assess an individual's ability to maintain task-relevant information in an active state and to regulate controlled processing (e.g., Miyake, 2001). For example, individuals performing WM tasks must remember some task elements and ignore, or inhibit, other elements as they complete task-relevant operations. In addition, WM tasks require some inference, transformation, or monitoring of relevant and irrelevant information (e.g., Gathercole & Pickering, 2000; Hitch & Towse, 1995; Miyake, 2001). By contrast, *short-term memory* measures differ from WM tasks because they usually involve situations that do not vary initial encoding—that is, participants are not instructed to infer, transform, or vary processing requirements. In measures of short-term memory participants are simply asked to recall a sequence of items in the order in which they were presented.

Learning Disabilities

Children with LD are defined as those individuals who have normal intelligence but suffer deficits in the area of reading, mathematics, or both. These academic deficits are *not* the result of inadequate opportunity to learn, general intelligence, or physical or emotional disorders; they result from basic disorders in specific psychological processes, and these specific processing deficits are a reflection of neurological, constitutional, or biological factors. Several definitions refer to LD as reflecting a heterogenous group of individuals with an intrinsic disorder that is manifested by specific difficulties in the acquisition and use of listening, speaking, reading, writing, reasoning, or mathematic abilities. In our work, however, we operationally defined participants with LD as those children who have general IQ (intelligence quotient) scores on standardized tests of higher than 85 and who have reading scores or math scores on standardized tests of less than the 25th percentile.

Dynamic Assessment

Procedures that attempt to modify test performance via examiner assistance in an effort to understand learning potential are called *dynamic assessment* (DA) (e.g., see Grigorenko & Sternberg, 1998; Swanson & Lussier, 2001). Although DA is a term used to characterize several distinct approaches (see Grigorenko & Sternberg, 1998; Swanson & Lussier, 2001, for a review), it includes two critical features that are designed to do the following (Embretson, 1987, 1992):

- Determine the learner's potential for change when given assistance.
- Provide a prospective measure of performance change independent of assistance.

Unlike traditional testing procedures, score changes as a result of examiner intervention are not viewed as threatening task validity. In fact, some authors argue that they increase construct validity (e.g., Carlson & Wiedl, 1979; Swanson, 1992). Thus, our studies have viewed that one possible alternative, or supplement, to traditional assessment of LD is to measure a child's gain in performance when given examiner assistance on WM measures. We argue that because WM tasks are highly correlated with achievement measures (e.g., Daneman & Merikle, 1996), these measure provide a foundation for understanding LD (see Swanson & Siegel, 2001b, for an extensive review). These testing procedures are also helpful in understanding life span development in WM (Swanson, 1999b). We assume that "potential" for learning new information (or accessing previously presented information) is measured in terms of the distance, difference between, or change from unassisted performance to a performance level with assistance. In our studies, we use a systematic series of probes (i.e., hints or cues) to understand children's WM performance when they are provided with assistance. These procedures will be discussed later in the chapter.

PUTTING THE INFORMATION TOGETHER

How can DA help us understand LD? One possibility relates to better discriminating among various groups of children who are having difficulty learning in the classroom. Accurate assessment procedures need to be developed that separate children with LD from other poor learners. Unfortunately, the identification of LD has been clouded by current practices that focus on uncovering a significant discrepancy between achievement in a particular academic domain (e.g., reading) and general psychometric intellectual ability (see Hoskyn & Swanson, 2000, for a review of this literature). These procedures have questionable validity, and other approaches must be formalized.

Although DA has been suggested as an alternative to traditional assessment, no published standardized data are available to the author's knowledge. In fact, DA has been criticized because of its highly clinical nature and poor reliability (e.g., Grigorenko & Sternberg, 1998; Swanson & Lussier, 2001). Moreover, interactive testing procedures have not been operationalized in terms of test-related interventions characteristic of a psychologist's testing situation. For example, a school psychologist usually samples a student's processing ability during short testing sessions, not over an extended period of days or sessions. In response to these concerns, we have developed a standardized test that assesses general information-processing ability with and without examiner assistance.

Prior to discussing our research on WM, LD, and DA, it would be helpful to provide some detail about our WM tasks and probing procedures. The test battery we have developed we have labeled as the S-CPT (Swanson, 1995). The tasks in the battery are simple to administer and can be readily incorporated into any individual testing procedures. Consistent with a number of studies, these WM tasks require the maintenance of some information during the processing of other information. In addition, the processing of information can be assessed by asking children simple questions about the to-be-remembered material, whereas storage can be assessed by how well they accurately retrieve information. It is important to note, however, that in our tasks the difficulty of the processing question remains constant within task conditions, thereby allowing the source of individual differences to reflect increases in *storage demands*. Further, the questions focus on the discrimination of items (old and new information) rather than deeper levels of processing, such as computing mathematic problems, found in other WM measures (e.g., Towse, Hitch, & Hutton, 1998). We will briefly review 11 tasks or subtests we have standardized, the type of scores we use, and related research using these measures.

Subtests

Task 1—Rhyming.   The purpose of this task is to assess the participant's recall of acoustically similar words. The participant listens to sets of words that rhyme. Each successive word in the set is presented every 2 seconds. Nine word sets range from 2 to 14 monosyllabic words. (This task will be described in more detail later.)

Task 2—Visual Matrix.   The purpose of this task is to assess the child's ability to remember visual sequences within a matrix. The child is asked to study a series of dots in a matrix for 5 seconds. After removing the matrix, the child is shown a blank matrix (with no dots) and asked a discrimination question (i.e., "Were there any dots in the first column?"). Then the child is asked to draw the dots in the correct boxes on the blank matrix. The task difficulty ranges from a matrix of 4 squares and 2 dots to a matrix of 45 squares and 12 dots. The dependent measure is the number of matrices recalled correctly (range of 0–11).

Task 3—Auditory Digit Sequence.   The purpose of this task is to assess the child's ability to remember numeric information embedded in a short sentence. Prior to stimulus presentation, the child is shown a figure depicting four strategies for recalling numeric information. These strategies are pictorial representations of rehearsal, chunking, associating, and elaborating of information. (A verbal description of strategies, prior to administration of targeted items, is the same format used for Tasks 4, 7, 8, 10, and 11). After all strategies have been explained, children are then presented numbers in a sentence context. A sample sentence (Item 3) is as follows: "Now suppose somebody wanted to have you take them to the supermarket at *8 6 5 1* Elm Street. . . ." They are then presented a process question: "What is the name of the street?" They are then told that they will have to recall the numbers in the sentence in order shortly *after* they select from (point to) a pictorial array the strategy that best approximates how he or she will attempt to remember the information. No further information about the strategies shown in the picture is provided to the child. The range of recall difficulty is 3–14 digits, and the dependent measure is the number of sets correctly recalled (range of 0–9).

Task 4—Mapping and Directions.   The purpose of this task is to determine whether the child can remember a sequence of directions on a map that is void of labels. The examiner presents the child with a street map with lines connected to a number of dots that illustrate the direction a bike would go to get out of the city. The dots represent stoplights, and the lines represent the direction the bicycle should go. The map is removed after 10 seconds. The child is asked a process question and is asked to point to the strategy (picture) they think they will use to remember the street directions. Finally, they are asked to draw on another map the street directions (lines) and stop lights (dots). The process question is as follows: "Were there any dots in the first street (column)?" Using the same pictorial format as Task 3, strategies are pictorial representations of elemental, global, sectional, or backward processing of patterns. The range of difficulty includes dots that range in number from 4 to 19. The dependent measure is the number of maps drawn correctly (range of 0–9).

Task 5—Story Retelling.   The purpose of this task is to assess the child's ability to remember a series of episodes presented in a paragraph. The examiner reads a paragraph, asks a process question, and then asks the child to recall all the events that have occurred. The paragraph is a 12-sentence story, and each sentence includes two idea units and 8–11 words. The paragraph is related to the famous battle of the Armada where a small fleet of English ships beats the Spanish fleet. For the process question, the child is asked, "Who won the battle, the large or small ships"? The dependent measure is the number of sentences recalled correctly in order (range of 0–11). For a sentence to be recalled correctly it must include two idea units and occur in the correct order.

Task 6—Picture Sequence.   The purpose of this task is to assess the child's ability to remember a sequence of shapes of increasing spatial complexity. Pictures of shapes are presented on a series of cards, a process question is presented, cards are gathered and shuffled, and then the child is instructed to arrange those cards in the correct sequence. The process question is as follows: "Is this card (Distractor Card) or this card (card selected from another set) the one I presented?" The dependent measure is the number of sets of cards correctly reproduced. The set size varies from 3 to 15, and scores vary from 0 to 9.

Task 7—Phrase Sequence.   The purpose of this task is to determine the child's ability to remember isolated phrases. An increasing number of phrases are presented. After each presentation, a process question is asked, and the child is informed that he or she will have to remember this information shortly after selecting the best strategy to help him or her remember the material. The strategies are pictorial representations of elaborating, indexing, associating, and chaining information. A sample sequence of phrases (Set 3) is as follows: "A flowing river, a slow bear, a growing boy, a gripping tire." A sample process question is as follows: "Are the words about a bear or boat?" The range of difficulty is 2–12 phrases. The dependent measure is the number of sets recalled correctly (range of 0–9).

Task 8—Spatial-Organization.   The purpose of this task is to determine the child's ability to remember the spatial organization of cards that have pictures of various shapes. These cards are ordered in a top-down fashion. The presentation of this task includes 5 steps: 1) a description of each strategy is provided; 2) the examiner presents the sequenced cards in their correct organization and allows the child 30 seconds to study the layout; 3) the examiner gathers up the cards, shuffles them, then asks a process question; 4) the examiner asks the child to select a strategy that he or she will use to remember the cards; and 5) the child is directed to reproduce each series of cards in the order in which they were given. For the process question, prior to the child placing the cards in the correct rows and order, the examiner takes out the first card (Row 1) and last card (Row 8) and asks "Which card came first?" Following the same format as Task 3, the strategies to be selected are pictorial representations focusing on imagery, pattern similarity, pattern dissimilarity, and visual sequencing. The dependent measure is the number of rows recalled correctly (range of 0–8).

Task 9—Semantic Association.   The purpose of this task is to determine the child's ability to organize words into abstract categories. The child is presented a set of words (approximately one every second), asked a process question, and asked to recall the words that go together. Sample instructions are as follows:

> I am going to say words. Some of the words go together. For example, if I say the words "car—baseball—truck—football," you would say "car and truck" first because they go together and then you would say "baseball and football" because they go together. This is because a car and truck are something you ride in and baseball and football are sports. Now remember when I give you the words mixed up, I want you to change the order of the words and tell me the words that go together. I will ask you a question about the words and then you tell me the words that go together.

The range of difficulty for the sets is from 2 words within a category to 8 categories with 3 words within each category. The score range is 0–8 sets.

Task 10—Semantic Categorization.   The purpose of this task is to determine the child's ability to remember words within categories. One word is presented every 2 seconds, and the child is told that she or he will have to remember this information shortly after telling the examiner how he or she will attempt to remember the material. The child is asked to recall the category name *first* and then any word that went with that category. Prior to recall of the words, however, the child is asked a process question and then asked to select a strategy that will facilitate the recall of the words. A sample item is as follows: "*job*, teacher, fireman, policeman, *season*, summer, winter, fall." A sample process question is as follows: "Which word, 'soldier' or 'summer,' was presented? The four pictorial examples of strategies include the following: top-down superordinate organization, inter-item discrimination, inter-item associations, and subjective organization. The range of difficulty for the sets is from 2 words within a category to 8 categories with 3 words within each category. The score range is 0–8 sets.

Task 11—Nonverbal Sequencing.   The purpose of this task is to determine the child's ability to sequence a series of cards with pictures of nonsense shapes. The child is presented a series of cards in which the organization is not provided by the examiner. The child is allowed to organize the cards into any rows that he or she would like with the stipulation that a certain number of cards be included in each row. The first row must have 1 card, the second row must have 2 cards, the third row must have 4 cards, the fourth row must have 6 cards, and the fifth and sixth row must have 8 cards. The child is given 2 minutes to place the cards in rows. After the rows have been established and the child has studied them for 30 seconds, the cards are gathered up and the child is asked a process question. The process question states: "Is this card (card in the first row) or this card (distractor card randomly chosen) the one you put into the first row?" The child is then asked to select the picture that best represents how she or he is planning to remember this sequence. The four strategies depicted in the illustration include an image of hierarchical association, subordinate association, global sorting, and bottom-up sequencing. The examiner then collects the cards, inserts two distractor cards, shuffles the cards, and asks the child to reproduce the cards by each row. The range of difficulty is the recall of 1 card per row to 8 cards per row. The dependent measure is number of cards placed correctly in each row (range of 0–6).

The 11 subtests are described in detail elsewhere (Swanson, 1992, 1994, 1996) and were therefore described only briefly in this chapter. One means of classifying these subtests relates to *how information is forgotten*. For example, suppose an individual is to retell a story and forgets to include some critical episode in the story just heard. This may be because the story that was listened to required little conscious control on the student's part or because the student attempted to overlearn information and failed to attend to the action-event sequence. This same story, of course, could be forgotten in a different way if a student knew he or she could reflect on the story and develop a plan of action for retrieving the story at a later point in time. The first kind of memory difficulty reflects a *retrospective* memory failure and is reflected by subtests 1, 2, 5, 6, and 9. These memory tests require that the participant recall a series of items immediately after their presentation. The second type of error relates to, for lack of a better term, *prospective* memory and is reflected in subtests 3, 4, 7, 8, 10, and 11. This type of memory error focuses on the type of strategies used by the student to prepare for the eventual recall of information. The S-CPT accomplishes this by first presenting the student pictorial representations of strategies that may be helpful for retrieving items. After students have been presented these strategies, stimulus items to be recalled are administered. Prior to retrieval, students are asked a question about items and are asked to select the strategy in a picture they think will help them retrieve the stimulus items.

   Another division of the subtests includes those that require primarily *verbal* processing (i.e., listening and verbal recall, subtests 1, 3, 5, 7, 9, and

10) and those that require *visual-spatial* processing (i.e., the manipulation of pictures or shapes, subtests 2, 4, 6, 8, and 11).

Probing

A complete description and example of probing (DA) is provided in Swanson (1992). One important feature of this approach is that guidance is provided to the examinee after she or he fails a particular item in each subtest. This guidance takes the form of probes—hints or cues given to the child to aid their response on the task. The hints are ordered in terms of explicitness, with the general hints given first and more explicit hints given later. Hints are administered based on the type of error made (i.e., whether the error is related to recency, primacy, or middle item), and probing procedures continue until all targeted items cannot be recalled. The "bow-shaped curve," commonly found in episodic memory studies, provides the basis for ordering a series of hints from implicit to explicit information.

For example, consider the Rhyming Task (subtest 1) and sample instructions. The examiner says, "I'm going to say some words, then ask you a question about the words, and then I would like you to say the words in order for me. For example, I would like you to remember 'mat, cat,' but first I would like you to answer a question about those words. Which word did I say—'cat' or 'rat'?" (pause for the child's response). "That's right. 'Cat' was the word I said. Now can you tell me all the words that I said in order (mat, cat)? Now let's try some other words." The examiner says each word in each set with approximately a 1-second interval between word presentations. After the words have been presented in each set, the child is asked a question about the words in the set, and then he or she is asked to recall the words in order.

If a child fails a discrimination question, testing is stopped for that test. If the child passes the discrimination question but omits, inserts, or incorrectly orders the words, a series of probes are presented. Sample probing instructions are as follows: "You missed recalling some of the words in order. I think you know the order of those words but may be confused. Let me try giving you some hints. It will help to remember if you divide words that come at the beginning, words in the middle, and words at the end of the list. Now let me give you some hints to help you remember the words I presented to you."

Probe 1. "The last word(s) in the sequence was (were) _____. Now can you tell me all the words in order?"

Probe 2. "The first word(s) in the sequence is (are) _____. Now can you tell me all the words in order?"

Probe 3. "The middle words in the sequence are _____. Now can you tell me all the words in order?"

Probe 4. "All words in order are _____. Now tell me all the words in order."

If less than four probes are needed, the examiner presents the next most difficult set within the subtest.

Three additional examples of the probing procedure are as follows:

1. Suppose the child was presented the words car-/star-/bar-/far and the child responds "car-bar-far." The child obviously left out a word in the middle, so the examiner would provide a hint related to the middle words (Probe 3 in this case). If Probe 3 did not provide the correct answer, the examiner would then present Probe 4.
2. If the child's response was "car-star-par," then an error has occurred at the end and middle of the list. In this case, the child would start at Probe 1 (hints related to the last word) and move through Probes 2–4. Probe 2 is presented (probe related to the beginning of the list) although that word was initially in the correct order.
3. If the child initially said "bar-far" in their response, then an error has occurred at the beginning of the list. In this case, the hints would start with Probe 2 and, based on the child's response, move through Probes 3–4. Probing continues until the child provides the correct response. Probing ceases when the child can no longer provide the correct response.

The *maintenance condition* is implemented after the other tasks described here are administered. The child is presented again the longest set of words that were recalled successfully (gain score), but this time the longest set is presented without the help of probes. The instructions are as follows: "These words that I'm going to say for you now I presented earlier. I want to see if the words are now easier for you to remember."

Which Score to Use?

An unresolved issue in DA concerns the nature of scores necessary to measure processing potential (referred to as *cognitive modifiability* in the DA literature; see Embretson, 1992; Swanson & Lussier, 2001). For example, Campione and Brown (1987) measure modifiability as the number of hints required to solve a problem that has been failed (also see Brown & Ferrara, 1999; Campione, 1989). The fewer the hints, the more modifiable the child's processing. Embretson (1987) has suggested, however, that this score "merely provides a better estimate of initial processing ability" (see p. 149). She suggests that a more appropriate measure is to bring scores to an asymptotic level (under the probing conditions) and then obtain a second measure on the task performance after the probes have been removed. The basic rationale for this measure is to eliminate performance differences as a result of different processing strategies or unfamiliarity with the laboratory procedures (Embretson, 1992). Another measure of cognitive modifiability is a simple difference score (gain score minus initial score). Such a score, however, is subject to regression toward the mean. In short, there is as yet no agreed-on measure of cognitive modifiability.

To address these issues, seven composite scores are provided in the S-CPT. First, the initial score estimates the student's WM ability. This score can be interpreted in much the same fashion as an IQ score. The second measure, the gain score or asymptotic level, is defined as the highest WM score that is obtainable under probing conditions. A third measure, probe score (referred to in the test as instructional efficiency), is determined as the number of prompts necessary to achieve the asymptotic level in WM. Because processing efficiency (probe scores) is a major diagnostic element in graduated prompting, it would be expected that children with higher responsiveness to probes would be more adaptable to novel or intense learning situations than those with lower probe scores. For example, a child with a low probe score, as well as low initial, gain, and maintenance WM scores, may require more intense intervention than a child with a high probe score.

A fourth measure, maintenance score, is the stability of the asymptotic level without the support of probes or hints. A fifth measure captures the difference between the gain and initial scores. This *processing difference* score measures the difference between the actual performance level and the level of potential performance as determined under guided assistance. Vygotsky (1935, 1978) considered this in-between state "the zone of proximal development." A sixth score captures *processing stability*. This score is determined by subtracting the initial score from the maintenance score. A high stability score suggests that some internalization of previous guided instruction has occurred.

A final score, *strategy efficiency*, relates to those subtests that required subjects to select a picture of someone using a strategy that best reflects how they plan to remember. This score reflects the student's procedural knowledge prior to DA.

Psychometric Qualities

Standardization

Normative data were first gathered from 1988 to 1994 on the 11 WM tasks. A second renorming is now in progress (started in 2001), and we have tested an additional 1500 children and adults in the standardization. The first version of the S-CPT was originally administered to 1611 children and adults (age range 4.5–78.6 years) in 10 American states (Arizona, California, Colorado, Florida, Indiana, Kansas, Massachusetts, New Mexico, Washington, and Wyoming) and two Canadian provinces (British Columbia and Ontario). Based on the total sample, the composite characteristics were as follows: 1) gender: 45% female and 55% male; 2) handicapping condition: 90%

nonhandicapped and 10% special education (of this 10%, 90% were diagnosed LD, 2% mildly retarded, 1% mildly hearing impaired, and 7% behaviorally disordered); 3) ethnicity: 72% Anglo, 13% Hispanic, 5% Asian, 9%
Black, and 1% other; and 4) community: 75% urban and 25% rural. Based
on schools attended, parent's occupational level, or residence of classifiable
cases, social economic status of the sample was estimated as follows: 35%
low income and 65% middle to high income. Of the sample's principal language, 89% spoke English principally, whereas the remaining 11% were
bilingual (second languages represented were Spanish, Chinese, French, or
Navajo).

Total testing time was approximately 120 minutes per student for the 11
tasks and 50 minutes for the abbreviated form (6 tasks). Students were
administered tasks in which initial, probe, gain, and maintenance scores
were determined. For the complete test, maintenance performance on subtests 1–5 was tested *after* the administration of subtest 5, and maintenance
performance on the remaining subtests was tested after the administration
of subtest 11. For the abbreviated test, maintenance was assessed after the
administration of 6 subtests.

Validity

Evidence was presented in several articles (Swanson, 1992, 1995c, 1996,
2003) and the manual (1995b) as to the technical properties of the S-CPT.
In summary, the results suggest that the two-factor solution obtained for the
full and abbreviated test was a reasonable interpretation for initial scores.
Swanson (1992, 1995b, 1995c) presents the factor structure of the S-CPT.
During the preliminary factor analytic investigations, separate factor solutions were found for elementary (K–6), secondary (grades 7–12), and adult
(CA >19–35; >36) samples, indicating the items tended to cluster on the
same factors. Currently we have tested a factor model in which two first-
order factors reflect visual-spatial WM and verbal WM and a second order
factor reflects the shared variance (executive processing) between the first-
order factors. A series of confirmatory factor analyses suggested that a
second order model provides a good fit and is consistent with a WM model
outlined by Baddeley (1986).

In general, across initial, gain, and maintenance testing conditions, the
Rhyming Word, Phrase Sequence, Semantic Association, and Semantic Categorization tests loaded highly on a single first-order factor. This factor was
interpreted as measuring verbal WM. A second factor includes high loadings on the Visual Matrix, Map/Directions, and the Nonverbal sequencing
subtests and reflects visual-spatial WM. Maximum-likelihood estimates were
obtained for the factorial model on standard scores for the initial testing
condition for the complete and abbreviated test. Two studies by Swanson
(1992, 1996) also suggested that the S-CPT was significantly correlated with

a seminal measure of WM (Sentence Span; Daneman & Carpenter, 1980), suggesting strong construct-related validity.

Table 5.1 provides a summary of some correlations between the S-CPT and various psychometric measures. These criterion-related measures were obtained during the first standardization of the S-CPT. As shown across Table 5.1, the correlations indicate that the composite scores of initial, gain, and maintenance of the S-CPT are more sensitive to academic, intellectual, and processing tests than the supplemental scores (i.e., differences, instructional efficiency, stability, and strategy efficiency). The S-CPT *initial* scores are correlated with intelligence (r's range from 0.80 with K-ABC, from 0.38 to 0.88 with Weschler tests; from 0.30 with the Slosson Intelligence Test; 0.60 with the Raven Progressive Matrices Test, from 0.57 with the PPVT-R) and achievement (r's range from 0.53 to 0.57 on Wide Range Achievement Test; 0.50 to 0.66 on Peabody Individual Achievement Test; 0.47 to 0.63 on TOWL-2). In contrast, supplemental measures (Instructional-Efficiency, Stability, and Processing Difference Scores) yield low correlations to intelligence and achievement.

This divergent validity for the supplemental measures is important if one assumes that some components of processing potential may be weakly correlated with performance on traditional standardized measures. An expected finding was that the Strategy Efficiency Index was related to metacognition (i.e., an individual awareness of knowledge and processing abilities) but not performance on various psychometric measures. The weak correlations between strategy efficiency and achievement may occur because knowledge of strategies may not "direct" performance on traditional psychometric measures.

Reliability

Evidence also suggests that the S-CPT has high internal reliability with, of course, higher reliabilities reported for composite than subtest scores. The S-CPT involves a test–teach–test format, which yields three testing conditions: initial, gain, and maintenance. Thus, probing procedures will produce varying amounts of improvement in retest scores. Because it is assumed that initial scores are malleable, it follows that different reliability besides test–retest is necessary. The Cronbach Alpha Procedure, with the effects of age partialed out in the analysis, was used to determine reliability. The total Alpha score (sum of scores across subtests for initial, gain, and maintenance) for the S-CPT is highly reliable ($r = 0.98$). The Cronbach Alpha for Composite and Component scores with the influence of age partialed out range from 0.82 to 0.95, with 64% (16 of 25) of the reliabilities at 0.90 or greater. Reliability with the effects of age partialed out for supplemental scores were 0.83 for instructional efficiency (number of probes to establish gain score), 0.82 for processing difference, 0.86 for strategy efficiency (strategy choices), and

TABLE 5.1

Correlation between Composite Scores from the S-CPT and Various Psychometric Measures, Partialed for Age

	Initial	Gain	Maintenance	Processing	Differences	Instructional Efficiency Stability	Instructional Strategy Efficiency
I. Achievement							
1. Wide Range Achievement Test (N = 768, Age Range 6–75 Years)							
Reading	0.53	0.54	0.54	0.27	0.07	0.23	0.10
Achievement	0.62	0.60	0.60	0.26	0.001	0.22	0.19
Spelling	0.57	0.54	0.54	0.33	0.05	0.15	0.18
2. Peabody Individual Achievement Test (N = 168, Age Range 6–18 Years)							
Mathematics	0.66	0.69	0.66	0.41	0.16	0.29	0.13
Reading Recognition	0.58	0.63	0.57	0.44	0.25	0.27	0.12
Reading Comprehension	0.61	0.62	0.60	0.39	0.21	0.30	0.05
Spelling	0.55	0.54	0.49	0.32	0.16	0.18	0.04
Information	0.56	0.50	0.51	0.24	0.12	0.22	0.14
3. Test of Written Language-2 (N = 39, Age Range 8–18 Years)							
Vocabulary	0.63	0.60	0.48	0.14	0.17	-0.18	0.12
Spelling	0.59	0.71	0.59	0.36	0.37	0.11	0.13
Style	0.58	0.70	0.56	0.38	0.31	0.06	0.18
Logical Sentences	0.49	0.56	0.44	0.24	0.25	0.25	0.11
Sentence Combination	0.56	0.62	0.49	0.26	0.27	-0.04	0.12
Contextual Vocabulary	0.47	0.53	0.39	0.24	0.15	-0.05	0.18
Thematic Maturity	0.59	0.64	0.61	0.32	0.30	0.21	0.43
Total Composite Score	0.47	0.62	0.51	0.39	0.32	0.13	0.42
4. Stanford Diagnostic Mathematics Test (Learning-Disabled Sample, N = 30, Age Range 9–13 Years)							
Number System	0.49	0.50	0.48	0.33	0.13	0.23	-0.30
Computation	0.56	0.70	0.54	0.66	0.42	0.25	-0.02
Application	0.65	0.65	0.67	0.47	0.19	0.45	-0.33

5. Stanford Diagnostic Reading Test (Learning-Disabled Sample, N = 30, Age Range 9–13 Years)							
Reading Comprehension	0.62	0.56	0.63	0.33	0.20	0.38	-0.08
Vocabulary	0.53	0.30	0.46	-0.07	-0.12	0.16	0.08
Sound Discrimination	0.73	0.54	0.68	0.08	0.02	0.18	-0.25
Blending	-0.30	-0.25	-0.20	-0.12	-0.07	-0.04	-0.17
Rate of Reading	0.12	0.22	0.18	0.25	-0.01	0.18	-0.15
6. Iowa Test of Basic Skills (N = 45, Age Range 12–14 Years Based on Retrospective Subtests)	0.52	0.52	0.58	0.13	0.18	0.18	—
II. Intelligence Test							
1. Raven Progressive Matrices (N = 30, Age Range 12–17 Years)	0.64	0.63	0.65	0.26	-0.02	0.36	-0.15
2. WISC-R (Clinic Sample) (N = 30, Age Range 6–13 Years)							
Verbal	0.62	0.52	0.64	0.19	0.04	0.55	0.04
Performance	0.88	0.78	0.81	0.49	0.28	0.64	0.37
3. WAIS-R (N = 28, Age Range 16–42 Year)							
Verbal	0.38	0.55	0.34	0.54	0.39	0.18	-0.07
Performance	0.49	0.35	0.58	0.12	-0.46	0.54	0.01
5. WISC-R (LD Sample N = 27, Age Range 6–13 Years)							
VIQ	0.52	0.49	0.54	0.25	0.08	0.35	0.14
PIQ	0.43	0.44	0.38	0.30	0.22	0.04	0.11
6. K-ABC Subtest (N = 119, High-Risk Sample, Age Range 5–12 Years)							
Sequential Processing	0.48	0.50	0.43	0.20	0.14	-0.02	0.15
Scale	0.52	0.51	0.52	0.17	0.08	0.09	0.16
Hand Movements	0.44	0.42	0.39	0.16	0.15	0.02	-0.02
Number Recall	0.33	0.37	0.30	0.30	0.35	0.11	0.07
Word Order	0.33	0.39	0.33	0.29	0.17	0.13	-0.01
Simultaneous Processing	0.47	0.43	0.44	0.18	0.13	0.11	0.03

Table 5.1—*Continued*

	Initial	Gain	Maintenance	Processing	Differences	Instructional Efficiency Stability	Instructional Strategy Efficiency
Scale	0.48	0.52	0.52	0.34	0.20	0.26	0.10
Gestalt Closure	0.39	0.41	0.39	0.24	0.17	0.16	0.08
Triangle							
Matrix Analogies							
Spatial Memory							
Photo Series							
IV. Process Measures							
Detroit Test of Learning Aptitude (N = 152, Age Range 5–25 Years)							
Sentence Imitation	0.32	0.41	0.34	0.22	0.25	0.03	0.06
Word Sequence	0.40	0.47	0.44	0.26	0.28	0.12	0.07
Design Reproduction	0.28	0.48	0.39	0.43	0.28	0.22	0.001
Object Sequence	0.12	0.28	0.27	0.28	0.30	0.21	−0.23
Symbolic Relations	0.11	0.24	0.23	0.27	0.32	0.22	−0.11
Peabody Picture Vocabulary Test (N = 141, CA 12–17 Years)	0.57	0.58	0.54	0.38	0.33	0.23	0.26
Metacognitive Questionnaire (N = 60, Age Range 12–14 Years)							
Diverse sample in reading skills only includes retrospective subtests	0.57	0.52	0.54	0.03	−0.02	0.14	—

0.82 for the stability index. Subtest reliabilities, as a function of initial, gain, and maintenance conditions, were also calculated. Of the coefficients 60% (16 of 33) for individual subtests are 0.80 or greater. Thus, reliability is much higher for composite than isolated subtest scores. Subtest scores range from 0.72 to 0.92 across initial, gain, and maintenance conditions.

Related Research

We will now review two earlier studies that investigated the validity of our measures. The first study addressed the question: *Does the DA of WM better predict achievement of children with LD than a traditional IQ measure?*

The question of interest is whether LD children's performance on WM tasks of, as reflected on the S-CPT, provides any unique prediction to achievement beyond what is already contributed by IQ. It was also of interest to determine if WM measures that reflect assisted processing performance are better predictors of achievement than initial or unassisted WM performance on the same processing measures. It was assumed that assisted WM performance better reflects processing potential than unassisted performance and would therefore contribute significant variance to academic achievement. If this were the case, then measures of performance gain would provide better estimates of academic performance than initial performance measures.

To this end, one study (Swanson, 1995a) compared the criterion-related validity of the initial and DA scores from the S-CPT with that of the Wechsler Intelligence Test for Children (WISC-R). Sixty-one children (24 females and 37 males) of varying reading ability participated in Study 1. To ensure a wide range of achievement performance, the present sample included children with poor reading skills (standard scores <92), skilled readers (scores between 95 and 115), and highly skilled readers (score >115) based on the reading subtest of the Wide Range Achievement Test (Jastak & Jastak, 1984). The only other stipulation in sample selection was that children show a higher standard score for the gain (dynamic) than initial testing condition. It was assumed that if a valid test is to be made of the assumption that gain performance contributes unique variance to academic achievement, then the sample should reflect improved standard scores for the gain when compared to the initial testing condition. Children were tested in school districts surrounding a large urban area in the northwest United States. All participants were selected from middle-class to upper-middle-class schools. Ethnicity for the sample was Anglo-European. The mean chronological age for the sample was 10.63. All children were individually administered the Wechsler Intelligence Test, reading and mathematics subtests from the WRAT, and the S-CPT.

A hierarchical regression was computed on the criterion measures of reading and mathematics. For predictor variables, WISC-R Full scale, Initial, Gain and Maintenance composite scores were used to predict reading and mathematics performance. The results indicated that gain scores were better predictors of achievement in the current sample than WISC scores. Further, gain scores were the only variable that significantly contributed unique variance to mathematics performance (26% of the variance).

What does this study suggest about classification of children suspected of LD? First, when contrasted with a traditional measure of intelligence (WISC), the results suggest that the dynamic testing of WM, via the S-CPT, contributes significant variance in predicting reading and math achievement. Although the usefulness of intelligence scores has been questioned in the past in terms of their value in predicting reading (Hoskyn & Swanson, 2000; Stanovich & Siegel, 1994), the present study does suggest that DA measures contribute important variance. Second, the results suggest that reading and math performance can be better predicted from scores on the S-CPT than the WISC. Finally, scores that reflect processing potential (gain) are better predictors of achievement than initial WM scores and WISC scores, suggesting that criterion-related validity is enhanced under dynamic testing conditions. In general, the results support the validity of using DA measures in predicting achievement. This finding was also replicated in a more recent study (Swanson & Howard, 2005).

We now address a second question: *Do DA procedures help in the accurate classification of LD?*

Dynamic testing may produce changes in some children's ability group classification because it is assumed that many psychological entities are not static. Given this assumption, it is important to describe what can be generalized from our studies on the S-CPT related to the classification of LD. Although we have tested various handicapping conditions among children (Swanson & Gansle, 1994; Swanson & Howard, 2005), this discussion will focus on students with LD.

Swanson (1995a, Exp. 2) compared school-identified LD and skilled readers on an array of subtests from the S-CPT administered under nonassisted (static) and assisted (dynamic) testing conditions. One hundred and fifty-five school-identified LD readers (83 females, 72 males) and 351 skilled readers (176 females, 175 males) participated in this study. Consistent with the recent literature, children with LD met a minimum level or basal level (>85) on standardized IQ tests and performed below a standard score of 85 on a word recognition measure. For readers with LD, ethnicity was 57% Anglo-European, 8% Black, 31% Hispanic, and 4% other. For skilled readers, ethnicity was 71% Anglo-European, 5% Black, 21% Hispanic, and 3% other. Chronological age was 10.55 for poor readers and 10.66 for skilled readers. All children were selected from public and private schools surrounding large urban areas.

No significant differences were found between ability groups in terms of chronological age or gender, but clear differences did emerge between groups in terms of ethnic representation. All ethnic groups spoke English as their primary language. The high ethnic representation in the poor reading (LD) sample reflects the geographic region of sample selection (Southern California).

In short, the sample of children reflected the diversity of children classified with LD found in the majority of American schools (i.e., IQ scores in the average to low-average range, but achievement scores significantly below average). Full-scale or composite mean IQ scores were 98.14 for children with LD and 104.85 for skilled readers. As expected, all S-CPT scores are significantly higher for skilled readers when compared to LD readers. To determine which measure best predicted reading ability group classification, the six composite scores (e.g., initial, gain, maintenance, probe, processing difference, and stability score) from the S-CPT were entered into a hierarchical regression analysis. The analysis indicated that gain Scores best predicted ability group classification. However, it is was clear by examining the large standard deviation in S-CPT performance that tremendous heterogeneity existed within each reading group.

To address this problem, subgroups were empirically derived via a cluster analysis. A nearest centroid sorting procedure created *four* subgroups within each sample. Variables used to cluster the groups were arithmetic, gain scores, and responsiveness to instruction (probe scores) performance. Arithmetic was used as a clustering variable because it has served as a major variable in the subtype classification (Siegel & Ryan, 1989). Gain scores were used because these scores best predicted reading classification, and probe scores were used because they reflect responsiveness to hints.

Four subgroups captured the school-identified LD samples. Subgroup 1 (*poor learners*) showed minimal discrepancy between S-CPT and achievement scores. This group performed poorly on all classification variables. Most importantly, their mean potential score (gain score) was at the same level as their reading and math scores. This group was defined as slow learners. Subgroup 2 showed no important discrepancies between mathematics performance and S-CPT scores, but clear discrepancies existed related to reading. This subgroup's achievement scores were characteristic of children with dyslexia identified in the literature (e.g., Siegel & Ryan, 1989). Coupled with their average performance in math but below average performance in reading, this group was defined as *dyslexic* or *children with specific LD in reading*.

Consider one child in this cluster. His verbal and visual-spatial standard scores under dynamic testing were as follows:

	Verbal WM	Spatial WM	Total WM
Initial	85	110	98
Gain	81	114	97
Maintenance	85	109	98

Thus, as the reader can tell, the child's WM scores remained fairly stable between initial and dynamic testing conditions. Subgroup 3 showed a large discrepancy between achievement and gain and maintenance scores when compared to the discrepancy between achievement and initial scores. This group also had the highest gain and probe scores when compared to the other subgroups in the school-identified LD samples. These children were operationally defined as *instructionally deficient* because of their high responsiveness to probes when compared to other subgroups as well as their above-average scores on the S-CPT (based on the standardization sample).

Subgroup 4 showed a large discrepancy (similar in range to subgroup 2 and 3) in S-CPT scores and achievement in both reading and mathematics. However, their gain and probe scores were in the low-average range. This subgroup was defined as having *LD in reading and mathematics*.

Thus, based on the cluster analysis, approximately 17% of the sample's (i.e., subgroup 3's) WM performance was easily modified and therefore reflects instructionally deficient children, whereas 9% of the poor reading sample (subgroup 1) was best classified as slow learners. More importantly, subgroup 2 and 4's discrepancies between potential (gain scores) and achievement scores were clearly distinguishable from slow learners (i.e., no significant discrepancy emerged in this sample).

No significant differences were found between subgroups related to gender. However, clear differences emerged between subgroups in terms of ethnicity. A high representation of minority children was found in the instructionally deficient group (subgroup 3) in the LD sample. This is a critical finding because some children of minority group representation are placed inappropriately in classrooms for students with LD. Further, a large proportion of the minority children readily respond to examiner assistance, thereby providing a better estimate of their information-processing performance. In essence, a high representation of children was apparently incorrectly labeled as LD.

In summary, we find that dynamic testing does improve WM performance of children with LD. However, such improvement does not allow them to catch up to average achievers matched on chronological age and intelligence. Thus, their WM performance remains stable (below average) across WM conditions. The S-CPT was able to identify children who fit an *a priori* definition of LD. This definition focuses on the *stability* of WM performance from the initial to gain conditions. Assuming that LD reflects a neurological base to WM deficiencies, we would not expect that such children would perform in the normal range on such measures under DA conditions—that is, although their performance may be modified, performance remains below average across WM conditions. The results indicated that processing ability was below average for three subgroups (dyslexic, slow learners, disabled reading/math) in the school-identified LD sample. However, one subgroup (instructionally deficient) exhibited high or above-average modifiability in processing performance. This finding is important because some children school classified as LD were comparable to normal-achieving children in general information-processing ability and therefore were *incorrectly* classified—that is, children who are instructionally or teaching deficient are incorrectly labeled as LD.

A Cross-Sectional Study

A final study I would like to review details our attempts to show that DA procedures help us uncover some processing difficulties experienced by children with LD. Although the other two studies addressed issues of validity, this study attempted to determine potential sources of processing difficulties in LD participants. This study (Swanson, 2003) compared children with LD specifically in the area of reading and children who are average achievers in reading. One of the key issues involved in identifying the sources of WM differences between LD and skilled readers is whether differences in WM are related to their processing efficiency (e.g., strategy use), capacity, or both. A theory frequently cited in the literature is that age-related differences in WM for normal-achieving children are related to processing efficiency (see Case, 1995, for a review). The assumption of these studies is that, although overall capacity may not increase with age, the strategic allocation of capacity is sensitive to variations in age. However, several studies in the developmental literature have attributed age-related changes in WM to capacity (e.g., Cowan, 1995; however, see Towse, Hitch, & Hutton, 1998, for a competing view).

We report here one of the few studies that have addressed the issue of whether the sources of age-related WM deficits in LD readers are a function of limitations in processing efficiency or capacity. This study (Swanson, 2003) compared LD and skilled readers' WM performance across four age groups (7, 10, 13, and 20) for phonological, visual-spatial, and semantic information. One hundred and twenty-six (126) skilled readers and 100 LD readers participated in this study (N = 226). The study presented WM tasks under 3 conditions discussed earlier. These conditions included the following: 1) presentation of WM tasks without cues to assess initial performance (initial condition), 2) presentation of graduated cues to help participants access forgotten information from the initial condition and to continue the use of cues until span scores can no longer be improved (referred to as the gain or asymptotic condition), and 3) presentation of the highest span level achieved for the gain condition after a brief interlude but without the support of cues (referred to as the maintenance condition). Thus, a key component in 2 of these conditions (gain and maintenance) was our use of DA procedures. Probes or cues were used to provide systematic feedback (corrective hints) related to poorly retrieved information. In addition to these three conditions, we administered 3 of our measures that required the recall of phonological (Rhyming Task), semantic (Semantic Association Task), and visual-spatial information (Visual-Matrix Task).

What Was Our Rationale for These Procedures?

Given that the reader has some sense of the task administration, our rationale for the procedures was as follows. It was reasoned that individual differences in WM performance under initial conditions reflect idiosyncratic processing as well as individual differences in accessing items in storage. To obtain an assessment of individual differences in item accessibility, cues were presented to help participants reinstate the memory trace or retrieve forgotten items. This condition, referred to as the gain condition, allows participants to use as many probes as necessary to access previously forgotten information. Because the number of probes used to retrieve information provides an assessment of the status of information in memory, we reasoned that a finding of reading group differences on the gain condition supports the inference that a failure to activate new information in storage is an important determinant of WM development in LD readers. The major limitation in interpreting gain performance, however, is that there is *no* basis for inferring constraints on storage capacity. Thus, it was necessary in this study to reinstate the highest level achieved successfully under gain conditions but without probes (referred to as the *maintenance* condition).

The sources of age-related WM differences between LD and skilled readers under the aforementioned conditions were assessed in three ways. First, LD and skilled readers in various age groups were compared on measures of processing efficiency and storage. We calculated processing efficiency as the difference in span scores between maintenance and initial conditions divided by the number of probes necessary to reinstate the memory trace. A low score on this measure reflected more efficient processing of information than a high score. We argued that the validity of this measure rests heavily on three assumptions. The first is that processing efficiency is partially a function of the maintenance of information in storage and the number of probes necessary to reinstate the memory trace. We assumed that the accessing of previously stored information in WM performance with a minimum number of probes is more efficient than relying on several probes. The second is that individuals vary in the number of probes necessary to activate a complete set of items recently presented but temporarily forgotten. This is because the extent of the information available in memory places upper limits on an individual's performance (e.g., Anderson, Reder, & Lebiere, 1996; Kane & Engle, 2000; Rosen & Engle, 1997)—that is, if the information has not been stored, it is logically unavailable for retrieval and therefore probes are ineffective. The final assumption is that if WM deficits in LD readers are partly the result of less efficient processing, then the number of probes relied on to access information should be greater in LD readers than skilled readers.

However, functional storage capacity was investigated by focusing on whether LD readers were less accurate than skilled readers in maintaining information. We assumed that storage capacity is related to the preservation of information during conditions that place high demands on processing (c.f., Salthouse, 1992). On the assumption that 1) storage in WM involves the preservation of information during processing and 2) LD readers experience greater constraints in the storage component of WM than skilled readers, then LD readers would be less accurate at maintaining information than skilled readers when experimental procedures control for processing difficulty (see Conway & Engle, 1996, for a related discussion of this paradigm)—that is, if processing difficulty rather than storage drives WM differences between LD and skilled readers, then equating the two groups on the difficulty of the task should eliminate reading group differences. However, if span differences between LD and skilled readers are related to storage, then equating them on the difficulty of the span task should not affect the relationship.

To equate processing difficulty across participants, we first determined each participant's highest span level under gain (probed) conditions. Therefore, we identified each participant's asymptotic performance with external support. After a brief interlude (approximately 10 minutes), we then readministered the same task at the highest span level established under the gain condition but this time without probes. We assumed that the readministration of WM tasks at the participant's highest span level under nonprobed conditions (referred to as the maintenance condition) placed more demands on the maintenance (storage) of information than probed (gain) conditions because external support was removed. We further assumed that if 1) the information to be stored between the probed and nonprobed conditions was exactly the same and 2) the information presented in the nonprobed (maintenance) condition was previously recalled under probed (gain) conditions, then a failure to recall information under nonprobed conditions would reflect demands on storage (see Cowan, 2001, for a review of various models to infer storage). We argue that if LD readers have a weaker storage system (i.e., are less likely to maintain information) than skilled readers, then they will experience a greater loss of previously accessed information (via the gain condition). Thus, the reductions or costs in the preservation of information from the gain to maintenance condition would be greater in LD readers than in skilled readers.

Second, to determine whether increases in the information retrieved reflected the involvement of a general or specific system, we determined whether a linear relationship exists between reading groups as a function of age across WM tasks and conditions, via a model outlined by Hale (1990) and Kail (1993). According to Hale and Kail, the relative contribution of a global system (e.g., central executive system) is revealed by the relative performance of one group to the other across a broad array of tasks and conditions. A general system hypothesis assumes that all information-processing components develop in concert (e.g., similar rates; Hale, 1990). It is also assumed that the absolute quantity of processing resources increases with cognitive maturity (e.g., age). Thus, if a domain-general system underlies WM performance, then overall performance should be predicted without regard to the nature of the WM task because all components are equally affected by development (cf. Hale, 1990, p. 654). In accordance with this model, we expected that if LD readers' WM performance is a linear function of a general system, then their performance could be accurately predicted from the performance of skilled readers. In contrast, a nonlinear function implies that residual differences between reading groups are attributable to isolated processes (e.g., verbal versus visual-spatial WM systems).

Finally, we determined whether WM performance is a consequence of reading skill. Turner and Engle (1989) (also see Cantor & Engle, 1993; Engle, Cantor, & Carullo, 1992; Kane & Engle, 2000) suggested that people are poor readers because they have a small "general" WM capacity and that this capacity is "independent" of reading. Poor readers are viewed as having a weaker WM than skilled readers, not as a direct consequence of their poor reading skills, but because they have less WM capacity available for performing a reading and nonreading task. As stated by Turner and Engle, "working memory may be a unitary individual characteristic, independent of the nature of the task in which the individual makes use of it" (p. 150). We tested this assumption in a hierarchical regression model that partials out the linear trend of reading scores from WM performance. If reading group differences in WM across various conditions hold across age, then one may assume that a domain-general WM system is in operation. However, a domain-specific process model would be supported if reading differences in WM tasks are eliminated once the domain (e.g., reading) is partialed from the analysis.

What Did the Testing Procedures Tell Us?

Given these details, we now consider our findings. In general, we find that children with LD suffer WM problems related to demands on capacity. Their WM problems were unrelated to the type of material processed. Five specific findings emerged in support of this view.

1. The general pattern across the three WM tasks and three memory conditions was 1) adults (20 year olds) performed better than children and 2) skilled readers performed better than LD readers. These findings were qualified, however, by the interactions. The interaction showed that performance differences between skilled and LD readers were greater on the gain and maintenance conditions than in the initial condition.
2. Processing efficiency scores were statistically comparable between LD and skilled reading groups. Efficiency scores were calculated as follows: (maintenance-initial span scores)/number of probes.
3. Performance demands (costs) were greater for LD readers than for skilled readers. These demands were not domain specific because they did not interact with the type of WM task (phonological, visual-spatial, and semantic). We adapted a formula from dual-task studies (see Baddeley, Della Sala, Papagno, & Spinnler, 1997; MU score) to assess the performance costs on the maintenance conditions. Performance costs were calculated using a formula that included the

gain span score minus the maintenance span score divided by the gain score plus the maintenance score (gain − maintenance/gain + maintenance).

4. Poor WM performance in LD readers was not isolated to peripheral storage (phonological, visual-spatial, semantic) but to a domain-general system.

5. Processes not specific to reading separate the ability groups. We partialed from the criterion variables (WM for the initial, gain, and maintenance conditions) the linear trend of reading standard scores, mathematics standard scores, and chronological age, thus removing the variance in the criterion measure (WM) associated with achievement and age. The important findings were that skilled readers were superior to LD readers on conditions that enhanced the retrieval of new information (gain scores) and the maintenance of old information (maintenance scores) when reading, mathematics, and age were partialed from the results.

In summary, our most recent findings show that WM performance of readers with LD is depressed across verbal and visual-spatial tasks and across a number of testing conditions. Further, the results suggest that their poor performance is not merely an artifact of their reading ability; WM problems remain even when their reading performance is taken into consideration statistically.

WHAT HAS OUR RESEARCH ON WORKING MEMORY AND LEARNING DISABILITIES TOLD US TO DATE?

DA procedures have allowed us to conclude that WM deficits are fundamental problems for children with LD (Swanson, 2000; Swanson & Siegel, 2001). Although WM is obviously not the only skill that contributes to their academic difficulties, WM does play a significant role in accounting for performance on reading and mathematics measures. Depending on the academic task, age, and type of disability, general and specific WM systems are involved in their disabilities. We find that in situations that place high demands on controlled attentional processing (such as monitoring limited resources, suppressing conflicting information, updating information); children with LD are at a clear disadvantage when compared with their chronological-aged counterparts. Our research has shown that these deficits are sustained when articulation speed (Swanson & Ashbaker, 2000), phonological processing (Swanson & Sachse-Lee, 2001a), verbal short-term memory (e.g., Swanson, Ashbaker, & Lee, 1996), and reading (Swanson, 1999b) are partialed from the analysis. This impaired capability for controlled processing appears to manifest itself across visual-spatial and verbal WM tasks and therefore reflects a domain-general deficit or executive processing deficit.

CONCLUSIONS AND NEW DIRECTIONS

We have attempted to translate our research on WM into an assessment tool to help practitioners in the assessment of LD. We find evidence that the performance of children with LD on various WM tasks can be improved with dynamic testing (e.g., Swanson, 1992). We also find that in some cases WM measures administered under DA conditions do a better job of predicting achievement than traditional IQ measures used in the schools. Unfortunately, however, we find that these levels of improvement in WM in children with LD are still substantially below that of their average-achieving counterparts. We have not, at this point, related our measures of DA to instruction. It is important to note that there are no data, to the author's knowledge, that suggest that a certain profile on DA measures would warrant a certain type of instructional approach. It seems unlikely, however, that children completely unresponsive to probes would be responsive to methods and materials that emphasize active or constructed learning strategies (e.g., reciprocal teaching, learning strategies) or highly interactive teacher/student approaches. Such children would most likely benefit from procedures that place minimal demands on constructing strategies. Such approaches would emphasize relevant conceptual knowledge (via drill and practice), motivation, and programmed (e.g., computer-mediated) instruction (see Swanson & Hoskyn, 1998, for a review).

Given these caveats, the dynamic assessment of WM using the S-CPT may inform the teacher about instruction in at least 5 ways:

1. Effectiveness of simple feedback on children's WM performance.
2. Children's general knowledge of strategies (procedural knowledge).
3. Degree to which changes in WM performance are maintained after probes are removed.
4. Children's flexibility to simple intervention.
5. Children's preference (responsiveness) for verbal or visual-spatial information.

No doubt other measures of processing must be developed to capture the subtle processing strengths and weaknesses between children with LD and their normal-achieving counterparts.

We have turned some of our attention away from our focus on achievement (crystallized intelligence) to understanding the role of WM in the fluid intelligence of children with LD. How is it that children with LD, given their poor WM and achievement, have normal intelligence? Can DA help us in separating out WM processes related to achievement and those related to fluid intelligence? These are particularly difficult questions to answer because performance on WM tasks in normal-achieving samples has been strongly correlated with fluid intelligence (e.g., Conway, Cowan, Bunting, Therriault, Minkoff, 2002; Engle et al., 1999; Kyllonen & Christal, 1990; however, see Ackerman, Beier, & Boyle, 2002). Kyllonen and Christal (1990), for example, reported a correlation between latent variables for reasoning and WM at approximately 0.80. Executive processing is seen as a key component linking these two tasks. Thus, it is rather unexpected that children with LD will have difficulty on tasks (especially those related to executive processing) ostensibly related to normal intelligence.

We are exploring three explanations as to why this may occur. Answers to these questions may provide a valuable link between instruction and our attempt to accommodate individual differences in WM. First, the relationship between executive processing and fluid intelligence may be indirect in samples with LD; only weak to moderate relations exist between WM and fluid intelligence in LD samples. Swanson and Alexander (1997) found that the magnitude of the correlations between executive processing and fluid intelligence (Raven Progressive Matrices Test) varied between 0.04 to 0.34 in LD readers and –0.05 to 0.46 in normal readers (see Table 4, Swanson & Alexander, 1997). We take this as evidence that fluid intelligence, although clearly drawing on the executive system, is not an exclusive manifestation of such a system.

Second, our work on problem solving shows that children with LD may use different routes or processes to problem solve, although their solution accuracy is comparable to CA-matched peers (Swanson, 1988, 1993a). For example, Swanson (Swanson, 1988, 1993) found students with LD successfully set up a series of subgoals for task solution. Further, their problem-solving performance was statistically comparable to their CA-matched peers on a number of fluid measures of intelligence (Picture Arrangement subtest on the WISC-R, Swanson, 1988; Tower of Hanoi, Combinatorial, and Pendulum Task, Swanson, 1993a). However, the studies also found that individuals with LD in some cases relied on different cognitive routes than skilled readers in problem solving. For example, on measures of fluid intelligence, problem solving was augmented by "emphasizing problem representation (defining the problem, identifying relevant information or facts given about the problem) rather than procedural knowledge or processes used to identify algorithms" (Swanson, 1993a, p. 864). Thus, there is evidence suggesting that performance by individuals with LD on fluid measures of intelligence may involve compensatory processing. This compensation can partially overcome problems in attention allocation (we use the word "partially" because we do not know the threshold where compensatory process are no longer effective) that in turn may allow them to perform in the normal range. However, we recognize very little research has focused on the compensatory processes that underlie the links between intelligence and executive processing.

Finally, individuals with LD may achieve normal intelligence because the information they experience in their environment does not always place high demands on their *WM*. As our standardized test of WM (S-CPT; Swanson, 1995b) shows, for example, the majority of individuals with LD score at the 21st percentile on WM measures (scaled scores across 11 subtests hovered around 8, or a standard score of 88; see Swanson, 1995b, p. 167), suggesting they have very weak but adequate WM ability to process information and then store it over the long term. Of course, individuals with LD may rely heavily on existing knowledge in long-term memory to help them in the processing of information. With the accumulation of long-term memory links and connections, there is some control over the processing demands of new information. Such control over processing demands may reduce potential links between fluid intelligence and WM, but it may also provide an important potential mechanism for education mediation.

In summary, we conclude that our focus on WM has allowed us to pinpoint some of the information-processing difficulties that underlie LD. In practical terms, our research using DA measures shows that children with LD may have difficulties maintaining and holding information. This may manifest itself in a number of practical ways. For example, these children may have difficulties keeping a person's address in mind while listening to instructions about how to get there, listening to a sequence of events in a story while trying to understand what the story means, locating a sequence of landmarks on a map while determining the correct route, or listening to specific word features among several in one ear and suppressing the same features in the other ear. All these tasks have the quality of interference (a competing memory trace that draws away from the targeted memory trace) and monitoring (decisions related to the allocation of attention to the stimulus that is under consideration together with the active consideration of several other stimuli whose current status is essential for successfully completing the task). Further research in this area may allow us to help such children to cope with the complex demands of their everyday lives.

Summary Box

- WM tasks engage participants in at least two activities after initial encoding: processing and storage.
- Participants with LD are those children who have general IQ scores on standardized tests higher than 85 and who have reading scores or math scores on standardized tests below the 25th percentile.
- Procedures that attempt to modify test performance via examiner assistance in an effort to understand learning potential are called dynamic assessment (DA).
- Interactive testing procedures have not been operationalized in terms of test-related interventions characteristic of a psychologist's testing situation.
- The S-CPT has adequate reliability and validity data and may inform practitioners in various ways:

○ Effectiveness of simple feedback on children's performance.
○ Children's general knowledge of strategies (procedural knowledge).
○ Degree to which changes in WM performance are maintained after hints are removed.
○ Children's flexibility to simple intervention.
○ Children's preference (responsiveness) for verbal or visual-spatial information.

• Dynamic testing does improve the WM performance of children with LD. However, such improvement does not allow them to catch up to average achievers matched on chronological age and intelligence.
• In some samples, reading and math performance may be better predicted by WM scores derived from DA procedures (e.g., S-CPT) than traditional measures of intelligence (WISC-III).

References

Ackerman, P. L., Beier, M. E., & Boyle, M. O. (2002). Individual differences in WM within a nomological network of cognitive and perceptual speed abilities. *Journal of Experimental Psychology: General, 131*, 567–589.

Anderson, J. R., Reder, L. M., & Lebiere, C. (1996). Working memory: Activation limitations on retrieval. *Cognitive Psychology, 30*, 221–256.

Baddeley, A. D. (1986). *Working memory*. London: Oxford University Press.

Baddeley, A., Della Sala, S., Papagno, C., & Spinnler, W. (1997). Dual-task performance in dysexecutive and nondysexecutive patients with a frontal lesion. *Neuropsychology, 11*, 187–194.

Baddeley, A., & Logie, R. H. (1999). Working memory: The multiple-component model. In A. Miyake & P. Shah (Eds.), *Models of Working Memory: Mechanisms of Active Maintenance and Executive Control* (pp. 28–61). New York: Cambridge University Press.

Bull, R., Johnston, R. S., & Roy, J. A. (1999). Exploring the roles of the visual-spatial sketchpad and central executive in children's arithmetical skills: Views from cognition and developmental neuropsychology. *Developmental Neuropsychology, 15*, 421–442.

Cantor, J., & Engle, R. W. (1993). Working memory capacity as long-term memory activation: An individual-differences approach. *Journal of Experimental Psychology: Learning, Memory, and Cognition, 19*, 1101–1114.

Campione, J. C. (1989). Assisted assessment: taxonomy of approaches and an outline of strengths and weaknesses. *Journal of Learning Disabilities, 22*, 151–165.

Campione, J. C., & Brown, A. L. (1987). Linking dynamic testing with school achievement. In C. S. Lidz (Ed.), *Dynamic Testing* (pp. 82–115). New York: Guilford Press.

Cantor, J., & Engle, R. W. (1993). Working memory capacity as long-term memory activation: An individual-differences approach. *Journal of Experimental Psychology: Learning, Memory, and Cognition, 19*, 1101–1114.

Case, R. (1995). Capacity-based explanations of working memory growth: A brief history and reevaluation. In F. E. Weinert & W. Schneider (Eds.), *Memory Performance and Competencies: Issues in Growth and Development* (pp. 23–44). Mahwah, NJ: Lawrence Erlbaum and Associates.

Carlson, J. S., & Wiedl, K. H. (1979). Toward a differential testing approach: Testing the limits employing the Raven matrices. *Intelligence, 3*, 323–344.

Chiappe, P., Hasher, L., & Siegel, L. S. (2000). Working memory, inhibitory control, and reading disability. *Memory & Cognition, 28*, 8–17.

Conway, R. A., & Engle, R. W. (1996). Individual differences in working memory capacity: More evidence for a general capacity theory. *Memory, 4,* 577–590.

Conway, R. A., Cowan, N., Bunting, M. F., Therriault, D. J., & Minkoff, S. R. B. (2002). A latent variable analysis of working memory capacity, short-term memory capacity, processing speed, and general fluid intelligence. *Intelligence, 30,* 163–183.

Cowan, N. (1995). *Attention and memory: An integrated framework.* Oxford, England: Oxford University Press.

Cowan, N. (2001). The magical number 4 in short-term memory: A reconsideration of mental storage capacity. *Behavioral and Brain Sciences, 24,* 87–185.

Daneman, M., & Carpenter, P. A. (1980). Individual differences in working memory and reading. *Journal of Verbal Learning and Verbal Behavior, 19,* 450–466.

Daneman, M., & Merikle, P. M. (1996). Working memory and language comprehension: A meta-analysis. *Psychonomic Bulletin & Review, 3,* 433–442.

De Beni, R., Palladino, P., Pazzaglia, F., & Cornoldi, C. (1998). Increases in intrusion errors and working memory deficit of poor comprehenders. *Quarterly Journal of Experimental Psychology: Human Experimental Psychology, 51,* 305–320.

de Jong, P. (1998). Working memory deficits of reading disabled children. *Journal of Experimental Child Psychology, 70,* 75–95.

Embretson, S. E. (1987). Toward development of a psychometric approach. In C. Lidz (Ed.), *Dynamic assessment: Foundations and fundamentals* (pp. 141–172). New York: Guilford.

Embretson, S. E. (1992). Measuring and validating cognitive modifiability as an ability: A study in the spatial domain. *Journal of Educational Measurement, 29,* 25–50.

Engle, R. W., Cantor, J., & Carullo, J. J. (1992). Individual differences in working memory and comprehension: A test of four hypotheses. *Journal of Experimental Psychology: Learning, Memory and Cognition, 18,* 972–992.

Engle, R. W., Tuholski, S. W., Laughlin, J. E., & Conway, A. R. (1999). Working memory, short-term memory, and general fluid intelligence: A latent-variable approach. *Journal of Experimental Psychology: General, 128,* 309–331.

Gathercole, S. E., & Pickering, S. J. (2000). Assessment of working memory in six- and seven-year-old children. *Journal of Educational Psychology, 92,* 377–390.

Grigorenko, E. L., & Sternberg, R. J. (1998). Dynamic testing. *Psychological Bulletin, 124,* 75–111.

Hale, S. (1990). A global developmental trend in cognitive processing speed. *Child Development, 61,* 653–663.

Hitch, G. J., & Towse, J. N. (1995). Working memory: What develops? In F. E. Weinert & W. Schneider (Eds.), *Memory performance and competencies: Issues in Growth and Development* (pp. 3–21). Mahwah, NJ: Lawrence Erlbaum Associates.

Hoskyn, M., & Swanson, H. L. (2000). Cognitive processing of low achievers and children with reading disabilities: A selective meta-analytic review of the published literature. *The School Psychology Review, 29,* 102–119.

Jastak, J. J., & Jastak, S. (1984). *Manual: The Wide Range Achievement Tests.* Wilmington, DE: Jastak Associates.

Kail, R. (1993). The role of global mechanisms in developmental change in speed of processing. In M. Howe & R. Pasnak (Eds.), *Emerging Themes in Cognitive Development Vol. 1* (pp. 97–116). New York: Springer-Verlag.

Kane, M. J., & Engle, R. W. (2000). Working memory capacity, proactive interference, and divided attention: Limits on long-term memory retrieval. *Journal of Experimental Psychology: Learning, Memory, and Cognition, 26,* 336–358.

Kyllonen, P. C., & Christal, R. E. (1990). Reasoning ability is (little more than) working-memory capacity? *Intelligence, 14,* 389–433.

Miyake, A. (2001). Individual differences in working memory: Introduction to special edition. *Journal of Experimental Psychology: General, 130,* 163–168.

Miyake, A., Friedman, N. P., Emerson, M. J., Witzki, A. H., & Howerter, A. (2000). The unity and diversity of executive functions and their contributions to complex "frontal lobe" tasks: A latent variable analysis. *Cognitive Psychology, 41,* 49–100.

Miyake, A., & Shah, P. (1999). Toward unified theories of working memory. Emerging general consensus, unresolved theoretical issues, and future research directions. In A. Miyake & P. Shah (Eds.), *Models of Working Memory: Mechanisms of Active Maintenance and Executive Control* (pp. 442–481). New York: Cambridge University Press.

Palladino, P., Cornoldi, C., De Beni, R., & Pazzaglia, F. (2001). Working memory and updating processes in reading comprehension. *Memory & Cognition, 29*, 344–354.

Passolunghi, M. C., & Siegel, L. S. (2001). Short-term memory, working memory, and inhibitory control in children with difficulties in arithmetic problem solving. *Journal of Experimental Child Psychology, 80*, 44–57.

Passolunghi, M. C., Cornoldi, C., & De Liberto, S. (1999). Working memory and intrusions of irrelevant information in a group of specific poor problem solvers. *Memory & Cognition, 27*, 779–790.

Rosen, V. M., & Engle, R. W. (1997). The role of working memory capacity in retrieval. *Journal of Experimental Psychology: General, 126*, 211–227.

Salthouse, T. A. (1992). Working memory mediation of adult age differences in integrative reasoning. *Memory & Cognition, 20*, 413–423.

Siegel, L. S. (1994). Working memory and reading: A life-span perspective. *International Journal of Behavioral Development, 17*, 109–124.

Siegel, L. S., & Ryan, E. B. (1989). The development of working memory in normally achieving and subtypes of learning disabled. *Child Development, 60*, 973–980.

Stanovich, K. E., & Siegel, L. (1994). Phenotypic performances profile of children with reading disabilities: A regression-based test of the phonological-core variable-difference model. *Journal of Educational Psychology, 86*, 24–53.

Swanson, H. L. (1988). Learning disabled children's problem solving: An information processing analysis of intellectual performance. *Intelligence, 12*, 261–278.

Swanson, H. L. (1992). Generality and modifiability of working memory among skilled and less skilled readers. *Journal of Educational Psychology, 84*, 473–488.

Swanson, H. L. (1993a). An information processing analysis of learning disabled children's problem solving. *American Education Research Journal, 30*, 861–893.

Swanson, H. L. (1993b). Working memory in learning disability subgroups. *Journal of Experimental Child Psychology, 56*, 87–114.

Swanson, H. L. (1994). Short-term memory and working memory: Do both contribute to our understanding of academic achievement in children and adults with learning disabilities? *Journal of Learning Disabilities, 27*, 34–50.

Swanson, H. L. (1995a). Effects of dynamic testing on the classification of learning disabilities: The predictive and discriminant validity of the S-CPT. *Journal of Psychoeducational Assessment, 13*, 204–229.

Swanson, H. L. (1995b). *S-Cognitive processing test.* Austin, TX: PRO-ED.

Swanson, H. L. (1995c). Using the Cognitive Processing Test to assess ability: Development of a dynamic measure. *School Psychology Review, 24*, 672–693.

Swanson, H. L. (1996). Individual and age-related differences in children's working memory. *Memory & Cognition, 24*, 70–82.

Swanson, H. L. (1999a). Reading comprehension and working memory in skilled readers: Is the phonological loop more important than the executive system? *Journal of Experimental Child Psychology, 72*, 1–31.

Swanson, H. L. (1999b). What develops in working memory? A life span perspective. *Developmental Psychology, 35*, 986–1000.

Swanson, H. L. (2000). Are working memory deficits in readers with learning disabilities hard to change? *Journal of Learning Disabilities, 33*, 551–566.

Swanson, H. L. (2003). Age-related differences in learning disabled and skilled readers' working memory. *Journal of Experimental Child Psychology, 85*, 1–31.

Swanson, H. L., & Alexander, J. (1997). Cognitive processes that predict reading in learning disabled readers: Revisiting the specificity hypothesis. *Journal of Educational Psychology, 89*, 128–158.

Swanson, H. L., & Ashbaker, M. H. (2000). Working memory, short-term memory, speech rate, word recognition and reading comprehension in learning disabled readers: Does the executive system have a role? *Intelligence, 28*, 1–30.

Swanson, H. L., Ashbaker, M. H., & Lee, C. (1996). Learning-disabled readers' working memory as a function of processing demands. *Journal of Experimental Child Psychology, 61*, 242–275.

Swanson, H. L., & Gansle, K. (1994). Specificity and modifiability of working memory in exceptional children: The role of dynamic assessment. In T. E. Scruggs & M. Mastropieri (Eds.), *Advances In Learning and Behavioral Disabilities (Vol. 8)* (pp. 65–104). Greenwich, CT: JAI Press.

Swanson, H. L., & Hoskyn, M. (1998). Experimental intervention research on students with learning disabilities: A Meta-analysis of treatment outcomes. *Review of Educational Research, 68*, 277–321.

Swanson, H. L., & Howard, C. (2005). Children with reading disabilities: Does dynamic assessment help in the classification? *Learning Disability Quarterly, 28*, 17–34.

Swanson, H. L., & Lussier, C. (2001). A selective synthesis of the experimental literature on dynamic assessment. *Review of Educational Research, 71*, 321–363.

Swanson, H. L., & Siegel, L. (2001a). Elaborating on working memory and learning disabilities: A reply to commentators. *Issues in Education: Contributions from Educational Psychology, 7*, 107–129.

Swanson, H. L., & Siegel, L. (2001b). Learning disabilities as a working memory deficit. *Issues in Education: contributions from Educational Psychology, 7*, 1–48.

Swanson, H. L., & Sachse-Lee, C. (2001a). A subgroup analysis of working memory in children with reading disabilities: Domain general or domain specific deficiency? *Journal of Learning Disabilities, 34*, 249–263.

Swanson, H. L., & Sachse-Lee, C. (2001b). Mathematical problem solving and working memory in children with learning disabilities: Both executive and phonological processes are important. *Journal of Experimental Child Psychology, 79*, 294–321.

Towse, J. N., Hitch, G., & Hutton, U. (1998). A reevaluation of working memory capacity in children. *Journal of Memory and Language, 39*, 195–217.

Turner, M. L., & Engle, R. W. (1989). Is working-memory capacity task dependent? *Journal of Memory and Language, 28*, 27–154.

Vygotsky, L. S. (1978). Interaction between learning and development. In M. Cole, V. John-Steiner, S. Scribner, & E. Souberman (Eds.), *Mind in society: The development of higher psychological processes* (pp. 79–91). Cambridge, MA: Harvard University Press (original work published 1935).

Wilson, K., & Swanson, H. L. (2001). Are mathematics disabilities due to a domain-general or domain-specific working memory deficit? *Journal of Learning Disabilities, 34*, 237–248.

Deconstructing Working Memory in Developmental Disorders of Attention

KIM CORNISH

McGill University

JOHN WILDING

Royal Holloway College, University of London

CATHY GRANT

University of Birmingham

The central executive (CE) of working memory (WM) has been connected directly with attentional control through Baddeley's suggestion that the CE can be conceptualized as equivalent to the *supervisory attentional system* proposed by Norman and Shallice (1980). Norman and Shallice suggested that there is a basic system in which incoming information from different sources competes for processing space, with the strongest competitor winning. However, this relatively automatic type of selection can be over-ridden by a supervisory attentional system that selects by other criteria such as prior instructions or preferences. Therefore, impairments in WM are likely to affect attentional control.

The aim of this chapter is to explore weaknesses in attention and their relations to WM. Studies that investigate selective attention, switching of attention, and maintenance of attention in typically developing children and children with poor attentional control will be discussed. We will suggest that there is no clear distinction between many aspects of attention and the functioning of WM, in particular the CE system of WM, and we argue that children with poor attentional control have an impairment of some aspects of WM function. Depending on the precise nature of the WM impairment, different aspects of attentional control may be impaired; hence different support and remediation may be required in different cases.

THE NATURE OF ATTENTION AND ATTENTIONAL DISORDER

Attention is an imprecisely defined concept in cognitive psychology, comprising a number of different cognitive skills. Detailed studies by Posner and Peterson (1990), Posner et al. (Posner, Walker, Friedrich, & Rafal, 1984), and Mirsky (1996) have suggested that different aspects of attention are associated with different areas of the brain. Consequently, several different disorders of attention may be distinguishable.

However, the definition of developmental disorders of attention remains controversial and entirely based on relatively simplistic ratings of broad behavioral criteria. The definition of attention deficit disorder in the American Psychiatric Association's *Diagnostic and Statistical Manual of Mental Disorders* (DSM III, 1980; DSM IIIR, 1987; DSM IV, 1994) has changed with every new edition as a result of a controversy over whether more than one subcategory, or only one broad disorder, is identifiable. It is widely agreed that the key features are poor control and organization of behavior (attention), hyperactivity, and impulsivity. Currently, DSM IV distinguishes three different syndromes defined by disorders of attention only, of hyperactivity only, or of both in combination, but the World Health Organization's *International Classification of Diseases* (10th Edition, 1992) recognizes only the combined type, which is also the most commonly diagnosed and is conventionally labeled as ADHD (or AD/HD) for "attention deficit/ hyperactivity disorder." The symptoms must not be attributable to other causes, must be persistent, and must be present in both home and school contexts. However, the severity of these symptoms is vaguely defined and diagnosis is often made by a psychiatrist after a relatively brief encounter with the child (diagnosis is some 20 times more common in the United States than in the United Kingdom, which does not induce great confidence in the objectivity of the system). There is no clear agreement on whether a qualitative difference from the normal population is involved (as a result, for example, of malfunction of one or more specific processes) or whether the differences represent the extreme of a normal variation in the population.

There are few systematic studies using a theoretically instructed range of tasks designed to identify the key features of the disorder, develop hypotheses on the causes of these features, and then test them. It is often unclear exactly what many of the tests that have been used are actually measuring because the same tasks have been used by different researchers to test attention, memory, and executive function (Morris, 1996).

A number of theories have been offered regarding the underlying cause of attentional impairment, all of which propose a single explanation for all potential impairments. Currently, the most influential is Barkley's (1997) "behavioral inhibition" theory, an elaborate model embracing a wide range of behavior but dependent on an ill-defined mechanism that operates apparently from outside and independent of the cognitive system. Another view is Sonuga-Barke and colleagues' idea (Sonuga-Barke, E. J. S., Taylor, E., Sembi, S., & Smith, J., 1992; Sonuga-Barke, E. J. S., Williams, E., Hall, M., & Saxton, T., 1996) that children with attention deficit disorder are intolerant of delay, whereas Van der Meere (1996) suggests that there is a weakness in the arousal modulating system. These views all agree in rejecting an explanation in terms of some simple deficit of "attention" in a narrow sense and are part of the growing consensus that the source of the disorder lies in some weakness in higher processes of executive functioning.

OUR STUDIES OF THE NATURE OF ATTENTION AND ATTENTIONAL DISORDER

Our studies have looked at different groups with poor attention, as indicated by ratings, general observation, or previous studies. Initially we report a study comparing children rated by teachers as being in the bottom 25% on a scale of attentional ability with those rated as being in the upper 50% of the population. Hence this study was not restricted to extreme cases at either end of a postulated continuum (such as would attract clinical diagnosis at the lower end), and this ensured that any task successfully discriminating between these two groups needed to be reasonably sensitive. A follow-up study further refined the conclusions drawn.

Subsequently we investigated a group of young males with fragile X syndrome (FXS), a genetic disorder widely reported to produce deficits in attention. This group was compared with a group of young males with Down syndrome (DS) and with otherwise normal groups with poor attention, matched on mental age (MA) and chronological age (CA), to discover whether the impairment in the FXS group was similar to that in the normal poor attention groups or qualitatively different. Following this, another study examined much younger children with FXS. In this chapter we report the results from all these studies, discuss the differences observed in the nature of the impairments in different groups, and attempt to interpret the findings in terms of WM processes. Finally, we discuss the implications for educational procedures.

Study 1: Comparing Mainstream Schoolchildren with Good and Poor Attention

In the first study undertaken (Wilding, Munir, & Cornish, 2001), two groups of young males took part (mean age 10 years 1 month, with 50 participants

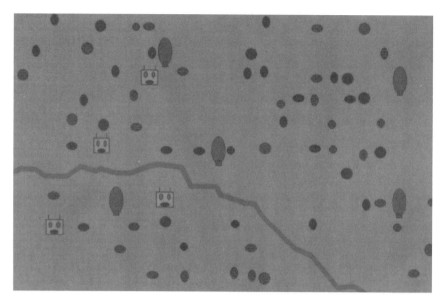

FIGURE 6.1
The display in the visual search task, after detection of four targets.

per group). One group was in the bottom 25% of the population in attentional ability, as defined on the ACTeRs (ADD-H Comprehensive Teacher/ Parent Rating Scales) rating scale completed by teachers (Ullman, Sleator, & Sprague, 1984), and the other group was in the upper 50%. Verbal MA was calculated from the British Picture Vocabulary Scale (Dunn, Dunn, Whetton, & Pintillie, 1982), and nonverbal MA was calculated from the Matrix Analogies Test (Naglieri, 1985). A large number of tasks was given designed to measure a variety of aspects of attention and WM function, with a view to identifying the critical differences between the groups (see Wilding et al., 2001, for a full list). However, only one of the attention tasks is discussed here. This was the VISEARCH task, designed by Wilding as a test of selective attention that would engage the interest of young children and enable a great deal of information to be acquired in a short time. It is a computerized search task. The children see on the computer screen a display on a green background with a river and some stylized trees, plus "holes" of four different shapes (vertical ellipses measuring 5 × 3 mm, horizontal ellipses, small circles 3 mm in diameter, and large circles 5 mm in diameter) either black or speckled brown in color (Figure 6.1). There are 25 targets randomly positioned among 100 holes in all. The children are told that monsters are hiding in some of the holes, and their task is to find the king of the monsters by clicking on holes with the computer mouse and making the monsters pop out. Unknown to the children, the king only ever appears on the twentieth click or if 50 clicks are made without achieving 20 correct responses.

There are two versions of the single target search task, one searching in holes that are black ellipses on end and the other searching in holes that are brown ellipses on their side. The number of correct responses, false alarms (clicks on nontargets of various sorts such as repetitions, shape confusions, background), time taken, distance traveled, and number of mouse movements are all recorded. The alternating target visual search task requires the child to click first on a black ellipse on its end, then on a brown ellipse on its side, and so on (15 targets of each type are present). In the original paper (Wilding et al., 2001), the visual search measure that discriminated best between the two attention groups was the distance traveled during the search in the alternating search task, which was assumed to measure efficiency of search. However, subsequent calculations by Wilding (2003) found that, if the distance resulting from errors was removed from this measure, it ceased to discriminate between the groups, so the original finding was in fact a reflection of the number of errors made. The number of errors is now regarded as the superior measure, and in this chapter we discuss our findings with respect to the number of errors made in the more difficult version of the task—the alternating target visual search.

Five WM tasks were administered to the two groups. One task required the repetition of spoken nonwords (i.e., invented, pronounceable letter strings, such as "meck"), and another required the recall of a series of digits. Both of these tasks were designed to measure phonological loop function. Visuo-spatial sketchpad function was measured by a task involving the recall of the location of objects, whereas CE function was assessed using recall of a series of digits in reverse order and story recall.

Relations between Working Memory Measures and Attention

According to the WM model, three separate components should be distinguishable from the tasks used to test WM, and according to our argument listed previously, the attention measure should be most closely related to the scores on the tasks measuring CE function. However, all these tasks are likely to implicate general verbal and nonverbal intelligence, so, to avoid spurious correlations resulting from the common contribution of general intelligence to all scores, the contribution of intelligence was removed before carrying out any correlations. (In statistical terms each measure was regressed in turn on the two intelligence measures and the residual score was calculated, and these residual scores were then used in future calculations.)

Table 6.1 reports the correlations between all six variables; a criterion probability level of $p < 0.01$ was adopted. The attention measure correlated most highly with story recall and backward digit span, supporting our claim that it reflects CE function. Apart from this finding, the pattern was not strongly supportive of the WM model because spatial memory was correlated strongly both with measures of phonological loop function and with the attention measure. Principal components analysis (a statistical method

TABLE 6.1
Correlations between the Five Measures of Working Memory Function and the Measure
of Attention in the Normal Groups

	Forward Digit Span	Spatial Memory	Backward Digit Span	Story Recall	Error in Alternating Visual Search
Nonword repetition	0.36^b	0.59^b	0.14	0.13	−0.22
Forward digit span		0.42^b	0.49^b	0.28^a	−0.21
Spatial memory			0.19	0.11	$−0.27^a$
Backward digit span				0.35^b	$−0.35^b$
Story recall					$−0.31^a$

[a]Differences significant at the 0.01 level.
[b]Differences significant at the 0.001 level.

designed to discover whether the different scores can be grouped together to reflect a smaller number of underlying processes) yielded two imprecise components, one of which accounted for 51% of the variance and consisted of the short-term memory (STM) tasks (nonword recall, forward and backward digit span, and spatial memory, all with loadings of more than 0.5) and the other of which accounted for 17% of the variance and consisted mainly of CE tasks (attention, story, backward digit span, but also forward digit span, all with loadings of more than 0.5). (Forward digit span would also seem to require some contribution from the control system, so its presence in this context is not wholly unexpected.)

Despite failing to support clearly the classic WM model, these results do support our interpretation of attentional ability as involving CE function because the measure of errors in the alternating visual search task was closely related to other measures generally believed to reflect CE function.

Group Differences in Working Memory and Attention

Table 6.2 reports the mean score in each group for the five measures of WM and the attention measure, together with the significant differences between the groups. (The attention error measure is usually highly skewed because of a few very high scores, and a logarithmic transformation has been adopted in all analyses to reduce this.) The WM measures produced consistent differences between the groups by analysis of covariance with verbal and nonverbal MA as the covariates (this method ensures that statistically significant differences between the attention groups are independent of any MA differences between groups that may be present). The error measure from the alternating visual search task also differed significantly between the poor and good attention groups, as defined by the teacher ratings ($F(1,96) = 24.64$, $p < 0.001$), as did the same measure from the single target visual search ($F(1,96) = 20.42$, $p < 0.001$).

TABLE 6.2
Mean Scores of the Good and Poor Attention Groups on Five Measures of Working Memory Function and One Measure of Attention

	Good Attention	Poor Attention	Difference
Nonword repetition	39.20 (0.97)	38.74 (1.08)	
Forward digit span	9.50 (2.31)	7.60 (2.29)	a
Spatial memory	16.96 (1.87)	14.82 (2.66)	b
Backward digit span	7.30 (1.87)	5.46 (1.43)	b
Story recall	15.28 (5.69)	10.28 (5.82)	a
Error in alternating visual search	3.10 (3.30)	8.80 (6.40)	b
Errors in difficult single target visual search	12.17 (9.30)	23.58 (9.58)	b

[a]Significant at the 0.01 level.
[b]Significant at the 0.001 level.

In summary, Study 1 demonstrated that attentional ability as measured by accuracy in the visual search tasks was related to measures reflecting CE function. Moreover, children who were rated by teachers as having poor attention also performed worse on measures of WM than children who were rated as having good attention.

Study 2: A Further Study of Attention in Mainstream Schoolchildren

Wilding (2003) raised the important question of whether the differences in errors on the alternating visual search task could be ascribed to weakness in a specific CE function of switching attention or some more general weakness. Noting that it was the more difficult version of the search task that discriminated best between the groups, he introduced another variation in difficulty, adding a large number of nontargets that were highly similar to the target. The number of errors in this variation of the task yielded even better discrimination between the groups than the errors in the alternating search task (see Table 6.2). In this later study, the groups did not differ significantly on the easier single target search task, but they differed significantly on both the difficult single target search and the alternating search. However, in neither case was the increased difference solely a result of the number of errors associated directly with the key manipulation (i.e., errors on the similar foils in the former case and failures to switch targets in the latter). Other types of error, such as shape confusions, also increased and increased more in the poor attention group, suggesting that coping with the more difficult tasks caused a more general breakdown in efficiency in participants with weak attentional control. One possibility is that a weakness in inhibition leads to a failure to prevent responses to stimuli with some of the features of the target. This would primarily affect responses to similar foils (when present, as in the new variation of the task) or the incorrect alternative in the alternating search task. These errors could in turn weaken the internal definition of the correct target and induce other types of error. We will return later to the argument for this conclusion and its implications.

Study 3: Identifying Working Memory Deficits in Attention Deficit/Hyperactivity Disorder Subtypes

ADHD is a major public health problem because of its high prevalence and its consequences for affected children, their families, and society. As indicated earlier, ADHD is defined by a set of symptoms including increased motor activity, impulsivity, and poor attention, representing the extremes of normal behaviors. It is now well established that genetic factors play a significant role in the pathogenesis of ADHD as indicated by family, twin, and adoption studies. In recent years the majority of researchers have focused on identifying susceptibility genes in clinical samples of ADHD (see Asherson & Curran, 2001, for a review). There is now growing support for viewing ADHD as a continuum and the possibility that the genes responsible for the clinical disorder of ADHD may also be responsible for individual differences in attention and activity levels in the normal child population. Hence, it may be more appropriate to think of ADHD as an extreme form of a genetically influenced trait distributed on a continuum in the population. Positive findings of an association between the dopamine DAT1 480 bp allele (allele 10) with clinical ADHD (combined type) have been reported (e.g., Cook et al., 1995; Daly, Hawi, Fitzgerald, & Gill, 1999), although there have also been some negative reports of an association (e.g., Holmes et al., 2000; Maher, Marazita, Ferrell, & Vanyukov, 2002). Meanwhile, it has been suggested that the association and linkage of ADHD and DAT1 is strongest for the combined subtype (ADHD-C) and weakest for the inattentive-only subtype (ADHD-I) (Waldman et al., 1998).

These findings, although exciting, require careful interpretation given that they are based on clinic samples and in view of the arbitrary nature of DSM-IV cut-offs as a basis for genetic research criteria. In an attempt to address these concerns, Cornish and colleagues (funded by the Sir Jules Thorn Charitable Trust) have completed a 2-year population-based study of primary schoolchildren in Nottinghamshire (United Kingdom) to explore the feasibility of identifying the association between polymorphisms in the dopamine transporter DAT1 gene with ADHD symptom scores. We predicted that the separate dimensions (inattentive subtype, ADHD-combined subtype) would not only show differential associations with genetic markers but also have differing cognitive correlates. Specifically, we predicted that the inattentive subtype would be characterized by a primary deficit in WM compared to the ADHD-combined subtype, which would be characterized by a primary deficit in response inhibition.

All Nottinghamshire primary schools (more than 400 schools) were initially contacted and invited to participate in this first stage of the study.

Teachers rated primary schoolchildren on attention and hyperactivity scales (Swanson, McStephen, Hay, & Levy, 2001). In total, 1811 completed questionnaires were returned. From these we recruited the top 10% (good attenders; N = 68) and the bottom 10% (poor attenders; N = 58) of our sample. In a further analysis we divided these 2 groups into 6 subgroups comprising the following: inattentive only (group 1; N = 15); overactive only (group 2; N = 22); combined inattentive and overactive (group 3; N = 21); good attention (group 4; N = 15); good activity (group 5; N = 27); and combined attentive and good activity (group 6; N = 26). The number of high-risk alleles was recorded on DAT1—either 9/10 (heterozygous) or 10/10 (homozygous). The children were also tested on measures of WM, attention, and inhibition. WM was tested using the Working Memory Test Battery for Children (WMTB-C; Pickering & Gathercole, 2001). This measures phonological memory (e.g., being able to recall a series of digits, such as "four, two, eight"), visuo-spatial memory (e.g., being able to remember the route out of a maze), and CE (e.g., being able to recall a series of digits in backward order). (See Chapter 9 of this volume for a detailed description of this battery.) Attention and inhibition were measured using the Test of Everyday Attention for Children (TEAcH) (Manly, Robertson, Anderson, & Nimmo-Smith, 1999). The attention measures comprised selective/focused attention (maintaining attentional focus; e.g., the ability to search for specific targets amongst lots of distracters), sustained attention (maintaining attention to a task over a long period; e.g., counting the number of "scoring" sounds on a tape), and divided attention (focusing on more than one task at a time; e.g., counting "scoring" sounds while performing a visual search task). The inhibition measures required participants to inhibit or delay responding to target stimuli. The computerized visual search task described earlier was also used.

Analysis of covariance with IQ (intelligence quotient; as measured by the Weschler Abbreviated Scale of Intelligence, or WASI) as the covariate showed a number of very interesting findings.

Good "Attenders" versus Poor "Attenders"

On the WM measures, after IQ differences had been removed through the covariance analysis, group differences emerged only on tasks that explicitly tapped the CE and were in the expected direction, with poor attenders performing worse than good attenders. In contrast, performance was comparable between groups on tasks that tapped phonological memory and spatial memory. See Table 6.3 for the mean standardized scores. The pattern of these findings is different from that of Study 1, in which the good and poor attention groups still differed on digit span and spatial memory but not nonword recall, even after IQ differences had been removed. The reason for this discrepancy is unclear at present, but both studies found differences between groups on the CE tasks, supporting the view that attentional ability

TABLE 6.3
Mean Standardized Scores for the Good and Poor Attenders
on the Subtests and Component Scores of the WMTB-C

	Good Attention	Poor Attention
Digit recall	110.56 (19.07)	93.97 (19.48)
Word matching	107.66 (18.98)	91.64 (18.53)
Word recall	108.06 (15.27)	95.03 (18.37)
Nonword recall	115.85 (15.34)	103.72 (21.68)
Corsi blocks	95.63 (15.40)	82.60 (18.51)
Mazes	104.87 (12.83)	89.98 (15.85)
Visual patterns	98.59 (11.60)	86.61 (15.29)
Listening span	106.29 (14.70)	82.40 (17.93)[a]
Counting span	103.21 (14.36)	82.29 (17.69)
Backward digit recall	105.15 (17.26)	81.04 (15.05)[a]
Total for Each Component		
Phonological loop	114.21 (17.78)	94.40 (21.06)
Visuo-spatial scratch pad	99.59 (13.72)	82.64 (17.11)
Central executive	104.50 (16.10)	73.81 (20.39)[a]

[a]Difference significant after removing IQ effect and correction
for multiple testing.

involves CE operations. It is interesting that when IQ differences were not removed before comparing the attention groups, group differences were present on all WM measures (phonological loop, visuo-spatial sketchpad, and CE) in Study 3, suggesting that IQ accounts for some differences in performance but not all. Not unexpectedly given our earlier findings, group differences (with good attenders performing better than poor attenders) also emerged for all measures of attention and inhibition.

The genetic findings, however, were far less robust. In part, we replicated and extended previous work that has indicated an association between ADHD symptoms and the DAT1 allele. Of the 62 participants who carried two copies of the high-risk 10 allele, 56% were poor attenders compared to 43% of good attenders (chi-squared = 5.27, $p = 0.03$). However, we found only a selective impact of the DAT1 gene on WM performance, and where differences emerged the obtained interactions between genetic measure and group were confined to measures of phonological memory, specifically tasks that involved word matching and word recall. Having a double copy of the 10 repeat allele was detrimental to the performance of the poor attenders but appeared to enhance performance in the good attenders.

Attention Deficit/Hyperactivity Disorder Subtypes

As noted earlier, group differences emerged only on tasks that tapped the CE, attention, and inhibition. There were no other group differences. However, closer inspection of the data revealed a potentially interesting pattern of performance with the "overactive-only" subtype performing better overall than the "inattentive-only" subtype and the ADHD-combined subtype. Contrary to our predictions, these latter two groups performed at a comparable level across the majority of measures, suggesting that the relevant difference was attention, already demonstrated in the previous analysis.

Examination of the genetic findings indicated that marginally more children with the ADHD-combined subtype (13.1%) compared with children in the inattentive-only subtype (11.2%) and the overactive-only subtype (8.4%) carried two copies of the high-risk 10 allele. However, this is hardly convincing evidence for a differential association between DAT1 and ADHD subtypes. There was also no evidence of a significant differential impact of the DAT1 gene on any of the WM tasks across ADHD subtypes. This suggests that if there is an association between ADHD, variability in the DAT1 gene, and WM, then it is weak and is perhaps related more to a general attention deficit than to a specific subtype.

Overall, the negativity of these findings does not lend support to an association between DAT1 and specific ADHD subtypes, nor between DAT1 and differential WM performance across subtypes. However, these findings should be interpreted with caution; it is difficult to be certain to what extent our negative findings reflect a lack of statistical power given the relatively small sample size within each subtype. The pattern is clearer when differences on the attention dimension only are considered. Here group differences emerged on a wide range of CE tasks and remained present even when IQ was a covariate. In addition, there was some suggestion of an interesting association between DAT1, poor attention, and some measures of phonological memory.

Results from the computerized visual search task were as follows. Analysis of covariance with CA and IQ as covariates showed that the attention groups differed in error rates in both the single target search task and the alternating search task. The difference on the single target task was only marginally significant, but the difference on the alternating search task was significant at the 0.01 level. No differences were found associated with the DAT1 genetic measures. Thus this study confirms the earlier findings that good and poor attention groups differ in the number of errors, particularly in the alternating visual search task, and provides additional findings that genetic differences, which have been associated with attention ability by some authors, showed no evidence whatsoever of a relation to performance on the search task. However, there was a weak relation between status on DAT1 and attention group, suggesting that there is some connection between genetic status and overall attention, which must depend on factors other than the abilities tapped in the search tasks.

In summary, Study 3 further demonstrated that children who were rated by teachers as having poor attention performed worse on measures of CE function and visual search than children who were rated as having good attention. These findings held even after IQ differences had been removed.

However, no convincing evidence emerged for a relationship between genetic status and either CE function or visual search performance. A weak relationship was present between overall ratings of attentional ability and genetic status, but it is as yet unclear which aspects of behavior produce this relation.

Study 4: Fragile X Syndrome and Other Neurodevelopmental Disorders

The results of Wilding et al. (2001) on attention in normal groups led to the conclusion that children with poor attention have a weakness in CE function that impairs ability to cope with tasks incorporating the need to follow some form of complex rule to achieve successful responses. More specifically, it was suggested that inhibition of responses to foils with features that are related to those defining the target is impaired. The authors used the five WM tasks and the visual search task used in Study 1 with a group of boys who were learning disabled and had FXS or DS (Munir et al., 2000a, b; Wilding, Cornish, & Munir, 2002).

Fragile X Syndrome

FXS is a neurodevelopmental disorder that has received considerable attention in recent years. The condition represents the most common form of inherited mental retardation after DS; its prevalence approaches 1 per 5000 worldwide. It is an X-linked condition, and in nearly all cases the disorder is the result of an anomaly in the translated region of the FMRI gene on the X chromosome. Because of X-linkage, the majority of affected males will present with a more severe behavioral and cognitive profile than affected females, whose phenotype is buffered by an additional X chromosome. However, because our studies involved only males, we restrict ourselves here to an outline of what is known about the cognitive functioning of males with FXS. Characteristic features include a low IQ (<70), stereotyped motor behavior such as hand flapping, and shyness including poor eye contact and social interaction (e.g., Reiss & Freund, 1990; Turk & Cornish, 1998). Perseveration in speech, rapid rhythm, and echoing of others' speech is also frequently reported (see Hagerman & Hagerman, 2002, for a review).

At the behavioral level, the most striking and consistent primary behavioral problem identified in *young* children with FXS is attention and hyperactivity problems, which include a behavioral triad of severe and persistent *inattention*, *overactivity*, and *impulsiveness* (e.g., Baumgardner, Reiss, Freund, & Abrams, 1995; Turk, 1998). The triad of symptoms leads to many children with FXS, especially boys, being clinically diagnosed with ADHD. At the cognitive level, accumulating evidence points to particular weaknesses in STM for complex, sequential information (e.g., Freund & Reiss, 1991; Hodapp et al., 1992; Jakala et al., 1997; Schapiro et al., 1995); visuoconstructive and visuo-spatial skills (Cornish, Munir, & Cross, 1998; 1999; Freund & Reiss, 1991; Mazzocco, Pennington, & Hagerman, 1993); planning and verbal fluency (Mazzocco et al., 1993, 1994); and perseverative, repetitive, impulsive speech (Ferrier, Bashir, Meryash, Johnston, & Wolff, 1991; Sudhalter, Cohen, Silverman, & Wolf-Schein, 1990). In contrast, performance on tasks that required STM for simple, meaningful information (Schapiro et al., 1995), visuo-perceptual integration (gestalt processing) (Cornish et al., 1999; Hodapp et al., 1992), face and emotion recognition (Simon & Finucane, 1996; Turk & Cornish, 1998), and syntax (Sudhalter, Scarborough, & Cohen, 1991; Sudhalter, Maranion, & Brook, 1992) are not as severely impaired, with performance equivalent to developmental age, but not CA, control children.

The constellation of strengths and difficulties in FXS raises an important issue, namely that the pattern of findings suggests that the profile cannot simply be viewed in terms of a catalog of spared and impaired cognitive functions, nor can the phenotype be described in terms of simple dichotomies (such as good verbal abilities versus poor spatial abilities, or poor sequential processing versus good simultaneous processing). If this were the case, then we would see skills that tap cognitive strengths performed at a comparable level to those of age-matched, typically developing children. In most studies, as highlighted in the previously explained profile, a cognitive "strength" is likely to involve a developmental age equivalent performance rather than a CA performance. Instead, the profile, at least by middle to late childhood, appears to point to executive difficulties, with those skills that tap attentional control through WM most impaired. Such weaknesses would tend to produce widespread difficulties in the development of intellectual function, perhaps differing between individuals, rather than a single pattern of specific function loss. Affected individuals would be likely to fall progressively behind their normally functioning peers on cognitive achievements, as has been reported to be the case (e.g., Fisch et al., 1996, 1999). To delineate the WM and attentional deficit in FXS, a series of studies was undertaken using the tasks previously used with normal children.

Down Syndrome

DS is the most common genetic cause of mental retardation, with a prevalence of 1 per 800 worldwide (Hayes & Batshaw, 1993). In most cases, the syndrome originates from errors during meiosis giving rise to three, rather than two, copies of chromosome 21. Some children with DS may only have triplication of part of chromosome 21 instead of the whole chromosome (partial trisomy 21), whereas other cases will represent mosaicism or result from translocation of an extra piece of the long arm of chromosome 21. Characteristic features of males with DS include a low IQ (<70) and, counterbalancing the stereotypes of bright disposition and positive affect, elevated levels of stereotypy, stubbornness, perseveration, and excess speech (e.g., Coe et al., 1999; Pueschel, Bernier, & Pezzullo, 1991).

At the behavioral level, children with DS also display high levels of attention and hyperactivity problems (Coe et al., 1999; Clark and Wilson, 2003; Wilding & Cornish, 2003) alongside oppositional (noncompliance) behaviors, conduct problems, and social withdrawal (Dykens, 1998; Gath & Gumley, 1986). At the cognitive level, several studies indicate problems in STM for verbal information compared to STM for visuo-spatial information, suggestive of a specific impairment of the phonological loop in DS (for a review see Jarrold & Baddeley, 2001; also Jarrold, Baddeley, & Phillips, 2002; Jarrold, Baddeley, & Hewes, 1999). However, in a 2003 study using a broad range of WM measures, no significant differences were reported between children with DS and typically developing control children (Pennington, Moon, Edgin, Stedron, & Nadel, 2003). In contrast, certain spatial skills, most notably those that tap drawing ability, are a relative strength in children with DS (Silverstein, Legutki, Friedman, & Takayama, 1982) compared to weaknesses on tasks that tap visuo-construction abilities and visuo-perceptual integration (Cornish et al., 1999).

Testing for Developmental Disabilities

Studies of developmental disabilities need to ask both whether the disabilities take the form of simply delayed development, so that the disabled group is equivalent to a group of typically developing but chronologically younger children, or whether the disabled group differs in other respects from typically developing children of the same developmental level. This issue is conventionally addressed by including one comparison group of typically developing children matched on CA and another matched on MA (who will necessarily be chronologically younger). However, it should be pointed out that this procedure is not perfect because normally developing children and children who are learning disabled usually achieve the same overall score on the test by different routes. The participants who are learning disabled will be inferior on tasks requiring fluid intelligence—that is, the ability to cope with novel demands requiring executive control, planning, and so on—but can compensate for this on tasks requiring acquired knowledge as a result of their greater age (crystallized intelligence). Hence, it is always likely that learning disabled groups matched on MA to a typically developing group will perform worse on any novel task that is not highly dependent on experience.

As well as comparing a learning disabled group with typically developing comparison groups, it is also desirable to investigate whether any impairments are similar to those of other such groups with a different cause for their disability to discover whether a particular impairment is unique to the specific disability under investigation. Consequently it is important to include at least one group with a different disability.

TABLE 6.4
Correlations between the Five Measures of Working Memory Function and the Measure
of Attention in the Fragile X Syndrome and Down Syndrome Groups

	Forward Digit Span	Spatial Memory	Backward Digit Span	Story Recall	Error in Alternating Visual Search
Nonword repetition	0.34	0.53^b	0.57^b	−0.11	−0.35
Forward digit span		0.47^a	0.76^b	0.26	-0.60^b
Spatial memory			0.69^b	0.19	-0.63^b
Backward digit span				0.17	-0.78^b
Story recall					-0.44^a

[a]Significant at the 0.01 level.
[b]Significant at the 0.001 level.

In Study 4, the focus was on attentional ability and WM function because the existing findings on FXS suggested a weakness in the former. We were particularly concerned to reveal the detailed nature of any attentional malfunction and whether it was similar to that exhibited by normal children with poor attention. Therefore, we used only comparison groups with poor rated attention (bottom 25% of the population as described earlier), one group matched with the FXS group on CA and the other on MA.[1] To investigate differences between FXS and another type of learning disability, a group of boys with Down syndrome was included matched on MA and attentional ability to the boys with FXS. Table 6.4 gives the CA and MA for each group.

Results: Relations between Attention and Working Memory Function

As with the typically developing children discussed previously, correlations were calculated for the combined learning disabled groups between the best attentional measure—that is, the number of errors on the alternating visual search—and the five measures of working memory function (nonword repetition, digit span forward, recall of spatial position, digit span backward, and story recall) to discover the separability of WM components and the relationship of the attention measure to CE function. As before, the criterion probability was set at $p < 0.01$, all measures were first regressed on MA, and residuals were calculated before carrying out the correlational calculations to remove spurious correlations resulting from the common factor of general ability.

---

[1]These control groups were the ones used in the Working Memory study (Munir et al., 2000a). In the study of attention (Munir et al., 2000b), two MA matched groups with good and poor attention were used. For present purposes the attention results have been recalculated using the same control groups as in the Working Memory study.

TABLE 6.5

Mean Scores of the Fragile X Syndrome (FXS), Down Syndrome (DS), and Mental Age (MA), and Chronological Age (CA) Matched Control Groups with Poor Attention on Five Measures of Working Memory Function (differences given were significant at the 0.01 level)

	FXS	DS	MA Poor Attention	CA Poor Attention	
CA (months)	131 (27)	134 (30)	91 (19)	133 (26)	
MA (months)	81 (19)	73 (18)	84 (16)	122 (14)	
Nonword repetition	27.08 (7.34)	34.88 (4.58)	38.44 (1.04)	39.04 (1.00)	FXS < DS, MA, CA
Forward digit span	3.92 (1.47)	4.28 (1.40)	8.20 (2.02)	8.20 (2.35)	FXS, DS < MA, CA
Spatial memory	3.64 (2.45)	8.24 (5.22)	13.32 (1.46)	16.32 (2.76)	FXS < DS < MA, CA
Backward digit span	2.12 (0.88)	3.56 (0.77)	5.04 (1.27)	5.88 (1.48)	FXS < DS < MA, CA
Story recall	6.88 (4.08)	3.80 (1.32)	8.16 (6.48)	12.40 (4.21)	FXS, DS, MA < CA

Table 6.4 gives the correlations and shows that, apart from story recall, the measures were substantially, and in most cases significantly, related to each other. The attention measure, however, was the only measure significantly related to story recall and it was also significantly related to all other measures (although the correlation with nonword repetition did not quite achieve significance). The highest correlation for this measure was with backward digit span. The other WM measures, other than story recall, were all interrelated. Once again, therefore, there was no clear separation of the supposedly separate WM components, but the attention measure related strongly to CE function.

Group Differences

Table 6.5 presents the means and a summary of the group differences on the WM tasks. On these tasks (Munir et al., 2000a), analysis of covariance with verbal MA as the covariate (nonverbal MA was at floor in all members of the learning disabled groups) showed that the FXS group performed worse than both the control groups on all but story recall and worse than the DS group on all but story recall and forward digit span. As expected, although matched on MA with the poor attention group, FXS generally failed to match this group on performance, especially on the presumably less familiar tasks. Also, although matched on MA with the DS group, their performance was generally worse than that of the latter group.

The DS group was worse than both control groups on forward digit span, backward digit span, and spatial recall. They differed from the CA matched group attention group (but not MA matched group) on story recall, and they differed from neither control group on nonword recognition.

These results do not support any view that some specific component of WM is impaired in FXS. All tasks, except story recall, showed impaired performance in FXS compared with poor attention controls, and performance was also impaired in this group compared with DS on all tasks except story recall and forward digit span. Previous results for DS performance on WM tasks have suggested a marked impairment in functioning of the phonological loop, although the precise cause for this is still uncertain, and a relative strength in functioning of the visuo-spatial sketchpad (Jarrold et al., 1999; Laws, 2002). Pennington et al. (2003) have argued that children with DS are impaired on all tasks that involve the hippocampal memory system and unimpaired on tasks requiring frontal lobe involvement. The current results do not completely support this view. Although forward digit span was impaired compared with the control groups, nonword repetition was not, and spatial recall was also impaired. The latter has commonly been tested by the Corsi blocks span test, whereas the current study used recall of the position of pictures, which may have engaged verbal encoding in the normal groups, favoring them against DS, in which verbal ability is impaired. In a careful test of visuo-spatial functioning in DS, Laws (2002) found that memory for colors with strong verbal associations was inferior in children with DS compared with controls, but when colors without strong verbal associations were used, performance in normally developing children declined and performance in children with DS did not. It would seem, therefore, that the precise pattern of results varies somewhat with the tasks used to measure components of WM and that further clarification is still needed.

Munir et al. (2000a) carried out more detailed analyses in an attempt to clarify the nature of the strengths and weaknesses over all these tasks in the FXS group and concluded that this group showed better performance when they had some prior experience or familiarity with a memory task (story recall) and showed poorer performance when the task required memory but the material was unfamiliar or relatively meaningless (digit span and nonword recall). In the latter case, planning and similar functions would be necessary to address the tasks.

A similar pattern of performance to that observed across groups with the WM tasks was apparent in the attention tasks, with FXS producing fewer correct responses and more errors than all the other groups and DS worse than both comparison groups. Numbers of correct responses and errors in both single and alternating search tasks are presented in Table 6.6. Analyses of covariance confirmed that in single target search the FXS group and DS group did not differ significantly on either number of correct responses or number of errors and both were worse than the two control groups, which did not differ significantly. In the alternating search task, the FXS group performed worse than the DS group, who performed worse than the two control

TABLE 6.6
Means for Each Group of Hits, Total Errors, Repetition, and Other Errors in the Single Target Visual Search Task and Hits, Total Errors, Repetition Errors, Perseverative Errors, and Other Errors in the Alternating Visual Search Task (differences given were significant at the 0.01 level)

	FXS	DS	MA Poor Attention[2]	CA Poor Attention	
Single Target Search					
Hits (max. 20)	14.18	16.83	19.48	20.00	FXS = DS, MA, CA
	(6.16)	(4.05)	(0.92)	(0)	FXS < MA = CA
All errors	36.72	28.50	11.84	6.15	FXS = DS > MA = CA
	(10.70)	(9.30)	(7.36)	(4.91)	
All repetitions	36.72	21.71	4.03	0.13	FXS > DS
	(10.70)	(13.16)	(2.61)	(0.31)	FXS, DS > MA= CA
All other errors	0	6.79	7.81	6.02	FXS < DS = MA = CA
		(11.25)	(4.72)	(4.77)	
Alternating Target Search					
Hits (max. 20)	7.56	10.56	19.48	19.91	FXS < DS < MA = CA
	(3.71)	(2.24)	(1.47)	(0.42)	
All errors	42.44	39.44	14.76	8.70	FXS = DS > MA = CA
	(3.71)	(2.24)	(11.95)	(8.73)	
All repetitions	17.75	23.44	2.86	0.04	FXS = DS > MA = CA
	(9.69)	(11.07)	(3.48)	(0.21)	
All perseverations	24.69	9.44	3.38	1.04	FXS > DS , MA, CA
	(11.72)	(5.61)	(3.80)	(2.06)	DS > CA
All other errors	0 (0)	6.56	8.52	7.61	FXS < MA FXS = DS
		(13.07)	(7.78)	(7.51)	

FXS, Fragile X syndrome; DS, Down syndrome; MA, mental age; CA, chronological age.
[2]Several values in this group differ from those given in Wilding et al. (2001) as a result of correction of some errors, but the conclusions remain unchanged.

groups. The two control groups did not differ significantly in their performance on the task.

None of these findings provides any immediate insight into the nature of the impairment of the children with FXS or the differences between them and the DS group. Although the FXS group tended to perform at a lower level than the DS group, there was no suggestion of qualitative differences in the pattern of performance, and, whereas both groups performed worse than the group matched on MA and attention, there was no indication as to whether their performance was similar but worse or different in some way.

More detailed examination of error types, however, provided a significant advance in our understanding. The normally developing children and the learning disabled groups, particularly the FXS group, produced substantially different patterns of error types. Taking the single target visual search first, the FXS group *never* clicked on a target of the wrong shape or color. Whereas about half the errors in normally developing children were shape confusions, FXS errors consisted entirely of repetitions on targets already located.

These occurred although the original target shape had been hidden by the appearance of a bright red "monster" face when it was clicked on. Such repetitions might take the form of an immediate repetition following a successful hit on the target or one or more repeat repetitions following this initial one. Sometimes returns occurred to already located targets after other intervening responses, and further repetitions might also occur following such returns. These different types of repetition were examined separately, but group differences were consistent across all three types, so we consider here only the combined totals. Means are shown in Table 6.6 and demonstrate the high proportions of errors that were accounted for by repetitions in this group. Repetitions following errors could not be investigated in the single target visual search because all errors were repeats on targets in the FXS group. However, in the alternating search task, there were errors of other types in the FXS group, and examination of these revealed that the same tendency was present to repeat responses on errors as on correct responses, although the initial click produced no feedback indicating success in the former case.

Children with DS displayed similar repetition behavior to the FXS group, but to a lesser degree, and made relatively few responses to patterns of the wrong shape or color, so in this group too the highest proportion of errors were repetitions of some sort, unlike the control groups.

Clearly both groups' poor performance on this task (low numbers of hits as a result of making 50 responses without locating 20 targets and a high number of errors) was the result entirely (or almost entirely in the DS group) of their failure to move on and search for a new target after a successful response, combined with a tendency to return to already located targets or to continue clicking on a target that produced no success. We argued that the most plausible explanation for this weakness was a failure to inhibit a response just (or recently) emitted in order to move on to a new response, an essential process in most behavior. However, we consider possible alternative explanations after further evidence from the alternating search task is presented.

In the alternating search task the same tendency to repeat responses was apparent in both the learning disabled groups. These two groups did not differ significantly from each other and produced significantly more repetitions per hit than the two comparison groups, which also did not differ from each other; both scored at or near to zero on this measure. This version of the task provided another possibility of looking at inhibition failure. Switching between target types after each response requires inhibition of the previously correct attentional focus. Failure of such inhibition would produce perseverations—that is, continued responding to the same target type. Such perseverations could occur on one incorrect target after a hit, or perseverative responses might be made to a succession of different targets of the wrong type. Separate examination of the number of times a first response occurred to targets of the same type (initial perseverations) and the number of repeats on a perseverative target showed the same pattern of differences between groups, so only total perseverations are reported here. Table 6.6 gives the mean numbers of perseverative responses for each group. The FXS group produced significantly more perseverations (i.e., failed more often to switch target) than the DS group, which did not differ significantly from the comparison groups.

Weakness in inhibition has been suggested as a possible explanation for these findings. However, there are some possible alternative explanations to consider. The tendency for repetition on errors could be explained as the result of an assumption that the response had been inaccurate or ineffective (because nothing happened as a result) and could arise from an attempt to repeat the response more accurately. However, this explanation cannot hold for repetitions on correct responses, still less for returns to previously located targets. These returns also cannot be explained by failure to remember which targets had already been located because these were all marked with a bright red monster face. Likewise, although repetitions could be the result of impulsive responding or failure to register the feedback indicating a correct response or poor motor control, no such explanation is valid for returns or initial perseverations because both these types of error required moving to a new location. Perseverations could be explained in terms of forgetting which type of target had just been located or failure to fully grasp the concept of alternation, and such explanations require further testing. However, the total picture of increased repetitions, returns, and perseverations in the FXS group is most economically explained by weakness in inhibitory control of sequential responding. There was a strong positive correlation between repetitions per hit and returns per hit and a low positive correlation between repetitions per hit and perseverations per hit in the learning disabled groups, suggesting a common origin for these different types of error (and a high and significant positive correlation occurred between these error types in the control groups, although the absolute numbers of these errors were very low in these cases, so no great weight should perhaps be placed on this finding).

Thus a fundamental problem of FXS, and to a lesser extent DS, appears to be a weakness in switching attention (or response) that could be ascribed to a weakness in inhibitory functions. Switching and inhibition of prepotent responses (such as well-learned responses to a particular stimulus) are widely regarded as key processes in executive function (EF) and necessary to adapt to new situations. So, once again we have suggestive evidence that weaknesses in aspects of EF are crucial components of attentional problems. This conclusion has already been suggested in respect of the study of typically developing children with good and poor attention, but the evidence on error types in FXS and DS is more specific and implies a difference in either the degree or nature of the weakness in these groups compared with normal groups of poor rated attentional ability. We return to this issue after describing a further study with much younger children with FXS and a group of children of similar age with Williams syndrome.

In summary, Study 4 demonstrated that attentional ability as measured by the alternating visual search task correlates most strongly with measures reflecting CE function in children with FXS and DS. The group comparisons do not support the view that some specific component of WM is impaired in FXS, with the FXS group performing worse than the other groups across the majority of the tasks. On the attention tasks, although the FXS group tended to perform at a lower level than the DS group, there was no qualitative difference in the pattern of performance between these two groups. Both groups' poor performance on this task was the result of repetitive and perseverative errors.

Study 5: Attention in Young Children with Fragile X Syndrome and Williams Syndrome

Williams Syndrome

Williams syndrome (WS) is a relatively rare neurodevelopmental disorder with a prevalence of approximately 1 in 20,000 worldwide (Donnai & Karmiloff-Smith, 2000). In most cases, the syndrome is caused by a submicroscopic deletion on chromosome 7q11.23. Although a number of genes have now been identified in the deleted region, there is no clear consensus as to their cognitive function. Characteristic features of WS include mild to moderate mental retardation and a specific personality profile. Interest in WS stems from the very uneven cognitive profile displayed in the phenotypic outcome, with relative strengths in phonological STM, language, and face processing (e.g., Wang & Bellugi, 1994) accompanied by severe difficulties in number and visuo-spatial processing (Wang & Bellugi, 1994; Bertrand, Mervis, & Eisenberg, 1997; Farran & Jarrold, 2003). It is interesting that evidence points to a selective deficit in spatial cognition with levels of performance not consistent across all spatial tasks (Farran & Jarrold, 2003). Atypical visual processing has also been shown by electrophysiologic and behavioral evidence (Grice et al., 2001; Deruelle, Mancini, Livet, Casse, & de-Schonen, 1999).

Scerif et al. (Scerif, Cornish, Wilding, Driver, & Karmiloff-Smith, 2004) carried out Study 5 using a simplified version of the visual search task. The targets were 10 black circles (24 mm in diameter) on a pale green background, and 8 correct responses were required before the king of the monsters appeared. The display might consist entirely of targets (baseline condition) or include 6 or 24 foils. Foils were smaller black circles, and the difference in size between targets and foils was either high (foil diameter 12 mm) or low (18 mm). After checking that the children could distinguish the targets and foils and understood the task, they first performed on the

TABLE 6.7
Repetitions per Hit and Total Number of Size Confusions in Children with FXS and WS,
Together with MA and CA Matched Controls

	FXS	WS	MA Control	CA Control
Repetitions per hit	0.89	0.32	0.13	0.04
Number of size confusions	2.23	4.81	1.13	0.63

FXS, Fragile X syndrome; WS, Williams syndrome; MA, mental age; CA, chronological age.

baseline condition with no foils and then on the 4 experimental conditions in random order, formed by the combination of 6 or 24 foils and high or low discriminability of targets from foils. Instead of clicking on targets with a computer mouse, the children pointed directly at targets on a touch screen.

Eight boys with FXS took part, with an age range of 34–50 months, mean 43.5 months, and mean MA as assessed by the Bayley Scale of Development II (Bayley, 1993) of 29.1 months (range 23–36 months); and eight children with WS (4 boys and 4 girls, age range 37–50 months, mean 45.8 months, mean MA 27.9 months, range 24–37 months) took part, with a comparison group individually matched to the FXS group on MA and another comparison group matched on CA.

Once again we focus on differences between the groups in the number and nature of the errors. Results are shown in Table 6.7. The children with FXS and WS made significantly more errors than the comparison groups, but the FXS and WS groups did not differ from each other in the total number of errors. Errors were subdivided into repetitions, touches on distractors, and other types (which were not considered further). Children with WS touched foils significantly more than the other groups and, unlike the comparison groups, did this more often when foils and targets were more similar. Children with FXS made significantly more repetitions than all other groups. When baseline performance was used as a covariate, thus equating all groups on nonattentional differences such as motor control and understanding of the task, all these results were confirmed except one. The difference between children with FXS and WS in the number of returns to previously located targets disappeared because the difference was present in the baseline condition with no foils present because of the occurrence of such repetitions in the FXS group even in this condition. This suggests that the problem of selecting the next target in the more complex display is not a crucial factor in inducing repetitions in FXS.

These results confirmed the previous findings that children with FXS tend to repeat successful responses (no analysis of repetitions on errors was attempted in this study) and showed that this tendency is present from an early age and that it occurred even when all the stimuli present were targets, so it is not associated specifically with selection processes. The study has also shown that WS affects a different ability, namely discrimination of visual targets from nontargets, at least on the basis of size. This type of error has some similarity to the increase in responses to closely similar foils found in typically developing children with poor attention and described previously (Wilding, 2003). It was suggested that this might arise from a weakness in ability to inhibit responses to stimuli similar to the targets and hence might also involve EF. However, the term "executive function" is poorly defined and can be used to encompass a wide range of putative processes, so this conclusion must be tentative. Some previous studies have suggested executive dysfunction in WS, and the present evidence could support this, but the degree or nature of the weakness is clearly different from that observed in FXS.

In summary, Study 5 demonstrated that infants with FXS and WS performed worse than normal controls on a simplified visual search task. However, examination of the error types indicates that the poor performance of the FXS group is related to repetitive responding, whereas the poor performance of the WS group is related to difficulties in discriminating visual targets.

CONCLUSIONS ON ATTENTION, WORKING MEMORY, AND INHIBITION

Simply invoking "inhibition" in a vague and general sense to explain all the different types of weakness that have been described in this group of studies is clearly only an initial step toward understanding. Are we to account for the different patterns of error between FXS and poor attention groups and between FXS and WS in terms of some qualitative difference in the nature of the postulated neurologic impairment or in the degree of impairment of the same system? Typically developing children with poor attention show a weakness in inhibiting responses to inputs similar to the target (as do children with WS) and also in switching in the alternating search task; they also show increases in errors in general in the more difficult tasks. Children with FXS, and to a lesser extent children with DS, show poor ability to inhibit repetitions of responses, whether signaled as correct or receiving no such feedback, and also show a greater difficulty in switching response in the alternating task than even the poor attention normally developing children. These different problems would seem to implicate at least three different forms of inhibition:

1. Inhibition of the response just made (defined in these cases by a click at a specific location, although presumably the nature of the response might be the relevant attribute in other cases).
2. Inhibition of response to inputs similar to the defined target.
3. Inhibition of a response that is inappropriate in terms of a rule about the correct sequence of responding.

These different types of response seem to vary from relatively automatic processes (a system that has just been active inhibits itself from immediate repetition); through processes of inhibition between competing inputs or responses, which depend on activating cross connections through instructions from a control system on the nature of the targets and nontargets; and through inhibition that has to be manipulated on-line according to a more complex rule about the required sequence of actions. It is likely that, when inhibition requires more involvement of a control system, it will become more vulnerable to impairment. Hence even mild impairments would affect operations of switching attention, whereas less mild impairments would affect ability to exclude irrelevant inputs. However, inhibition of repetitions would only fail when the impairment is severe because such inhibition is relatively automatic and self-sufficient. Thus we find typically developing children with poor attention affected on switching tasks requiring supervisory control of attention but producing almost no repetitions, whereas the more impaired learning disabled groups, particularly the FXS group, fail on even the simplest of inhibitory demands. The DS and WS groups occupy an intermediate position on this putative scale of impairment. The children with FXS were not, of course, tested on the search task with closely similar targets and foils; because they made no visual confusions, this would be a particularly interesting test of these suggestions—they ought to be impaired in this ability because it is postulated to be more demanding than avoiding repetitions. However, this may be difficult to test because the reason for the absence of visual confusions in our study may be related to the huge preponderance of repetitions on the few hits achieved, which soon produced 50 responses and termination of the task, giving very few opportunities for visual confusions to occur. It might, however, be possible to test this suggestion using the simpler version of the search task.

It will be noted that these proposals depart from the simplicity of explaining our findings in terms of a single basic process by invoking higher order systems that structure and control the postulated basic process. This suggestion resembles the system proposed by Norman and Shallice (1980) and described briefly in the first section of this chapter. The explanation has therefore come full circle from rather general proposals about CE malfunction, via an attempt to specify the nature of this malfunction more precisely, to invoking again more general ideas about CE control processes that supervise the lower order components.

EDUCATIONAL IMPLICATIONS OF THE FINDINGS

We turn now to consider how impairments, such as those we have identified in the different groups, will affect their ability to learn and to deal with the demands of the learning environments to which they are likely to be exposed. It would be desirable to have some inventories detailing the type of activity and learning materials that proved most difficult and easiest for the children with these different impairments and then to relate these observations to the more theoretical analysis we have been developing about the nature of the different disabilities. It should in due course become possible to derive hypotheses about why certain tasks prove difficult, or are not affected, and to devise methods of instruction that circumvent the key problems. However, at present such data are not available, and we will have to speculate about the types of input and information structures that are likely to be most vulnerable.

Attention Weakness

We have suggested that children with poor attention have few problems with tasks that are simple and straightforward in their specification, with the relevant features of the input clearly discriminated and the required action uncomplicated. The children with attention weakness (ADHD) did, however, perform worse than their contemporaries with good attentional ability once the task became difficult, either because some irrelevant inputs possessed features similar to those of the relevant input (the foils similar to the targets in our task) or because the relevant features changed continually as action progressed. Ability to inhibit responses to irrelevant stimuli was impaired in these situations, but further studies will be needed to establish exactly which types of difficulty are critical, whether it is basic inhibitory processes that are impaired or higher control systems that switch the inhibitory links on and off. For the present, we need to identify, in the educational process, analogies that are likely to occur to these sources of difficulty so as to ameliorate their likely effects. The WM tasks in Study 1 also showed that the poor attention group was worse than the good attention group on all the tests of WM except nonword repetition, implying impairment of spatial memory and possibly of the phonological loop as well as the CE. (It is presumed to be likely that poor CE function will affect the operation of the subsystems; consequently we may only be observing the consequences of poor functioning of the latter key component of WM.)

Weaknesses such as those we have described could affect educational progress in two main ways. First, functioning in the normal classroom situation will be affected because this situation provides an environment with all the features that adversely affect the child with poor attention. The teacher is normally the required focus of attention, but many competing inputs are present with similar attributes (faces, speech, etc.). Shifting of focus is frequently required (e.g., from speech to pictures or blackboard to book), and information has to be stored temporarily, then retrieved for use again, as when a series of instructions is given. Second, specific learning tasks may require just those types of operation that function badly in the child with poor attention. Language learning requires retention of sequences, as does reading. In the latter task, pronunciation rules in English are conditional on context. Learning arithmetic also requires much handling of sequences, beginning with the initial steps of learning to count.

In children with this type of impairment, the general classroom factors are likely to be the most influential, causing switches of attention when these are maladaptive and failures to switch when switching is required. Fortunately these adverse factors can to some extent be manipulated. Competing inputs, especially attractive ones or those likely to intrude when unwanted, need to be minimized as far as possible. Instructions on sequences of steps to be taken should be broken down into smaller units, and changes of focus need to be signaled clearly.

Neurodevelopmental Disorders

The last decade has seen unparalleled changes in the field of neurodevelopmental disorders. These changes have taken place simultaneously in several fields including molecular genetics, developmental neuroscience, and neuropsychiatry. Significant advances in each of these disciplines have increased our knowledge of the genetic causes and the neurobiological underpinning of many neurodevelopmental disorders. These changes have important consequences for understanding the specific cognitive and behavioral outcomes of children with genetically based disorders such as FXS, DS, and WS. The findings highlight important similarities across syndromes especially in terms of attention problems and hyperactivity. All three of the syndromes cited in this chapter clearly present with ADHD symptoms. However, research has also indicated important differences between the phenotypes of these syndromes. For example, in the case of FXS, we have suggested that affected children suffer from all the problems common to children with ADHD, plus additional ones as a result of the more severe nature of their inhibitory weakness. So, even relatively simple or well-practiced sequences of actions are hard for them to deal with, as shown in our single target search task, and in other behaviors noted earlier such as speed repetition, echoing the speech of others and hand flopping. We have argued from our own data that there is impairment in the basic inhibitory system that normally restrains repetition of responses to enable sequences of behavior to be programmed. Verbal ability, however, is generally quite good in these children, as shown in several earlier findings and in our own data, by their relatively good memory for a story. It seems that the language system itself is reasonably efficient but that specific aspects of speech production or responding to the speech of others are affected by their difficulty in controlling input and output sequences.

Study 5 demonstrated that the weakness in inhibiting response repetition was present from an early age. This weakness will affect the development of many skills needed as building blocks for further progress, and this is reflected in the widening gap in IQ, which has been noted between children with FXS and normally developing children as age increases. This profile differs somewhat from that presented in children with DS who demonstrate less impairment on most of the tasks used, but it may be more impaired when the task incorporates a large verbal element or opportunity for verbal mediation, as would be expected from their known verbal weaknesses. Study 5 showed that children with WS presented a very different profile of errors from children with FXS in the visual search task, confusing targets with foils that were visually similar but making few repetition errors. This result confirms earlier reports of a perceptual weakness in this group.

Similar problems apply in the classroom to those identified previously in the case of children with poor attention. There will, however, be a much greater need to break tasks into small units that are well demarcated to facilitate progress from one step to another and to signal changes in task demands very clearly. Furthermore, as our knowledge of the differences between these syndromes increases, we should increasingly be able to identify which tasks have special problems for each syndrome and move away from treating developmental disorders as a homogeneous group, all to be dealt with through similar remedial procedures. Dealing with novel tasks is a major problem for FXS presumably because of difficulty in setting up control plans in the CE, and such tasks must be reduced to their simplest components and practiced thoroughly to achieve familiarity. Tasks requiring sequential control of behavior are likely to be particularly difficult, and it is suggestive that children with FXS are particularly poor at arithmetic, where the fundamental task of learning to count requires precise sequential responding. Retention of learned information does not appear to be a major problem because familiarity with a task can be achieved and greatly aids performance. Tasks depending on various aspects of language will be more problematic for children with DS, whereas children with WS clearly have some problem of visual perception that requires clearer identification. Thus, the "one size fits all" process of remedial education will increasingly need to be sensitively adapted to the particular needs of the individual child.

Summary Box

- Attention is imprecisely defined and involves several different skills, so a variety of aspects may be impaired. However, current theories tend to focus on a single cause of impairment, particularly impaired CE function.
- Comparisons of groups rated by teachers as having good or poor attention have shown differences in all aspects of WM function and in a visual search task testing selective attention and switching of attention. The attentional measures were related to measures of CE function in WM.

- Boys with FXS, a specific genetic disorder affecting a range of cognitive abilities, including attention, have demonstrated a strong tendency to repeat responses when carrying out visual search. This suggests a weakness in inhibitory processes. A similar but weaker tendency was present in children with DS.
- However, children with WS, another genetic disorder, demonstrated poor discrimination of targets and nontargets in visual search.
- Hence visual searching by different groups has revealed weaknesses in 1) inhibiting repetition of a response just made (FXS and DS), 2) inhibiting responses to foils similar in appearance to the target stimulus (WS, normal children with poor attention), and 3) switching attention from one type of target to another (FXS, DS, normally developing children with poor attention).
- The differences between different groups may reflect qualitative differences in the impairment, or variation in the degree of impairment in inhibitory systems, varying from minor impairment affecting mainly difficult tasks such as switching attention and involving CE function, to major impairment that affects even relatively automatic inhibitory systems necessary to control sequential responding.
- Careful analysis of different genetic syndromes reveals different characteristic weaknesses in performance. As knowledge increases, it should become possible to develop more effective remediation tailored to the weakness present in particular syndromes.

Acknowledgments

The research presented in this chapter was funded in part by the Sir Jules Thorn Charitable Trust awarded to Kim Cornish. The authors would also like to thank Amira Rahman, McGill University, for her useful and insightful comments during the preparation of this chapter.

References

American Psychological Association. (1980). *Diagnostic and statistical manual of mental disorders* (3rd Edition). Washington, DC: American Psychiatric Publishing, Inc.

American Psychological Association. (1987). *Diagnostic and statistical manual of mental disorders* (3rd Edition Revised). Washington, DC: American Psychiatric Publishing, Inc.

American Psychological Association. (1994). *Diagnostic and statistical manual of mental disorders* (4th Edition). Washington, DC: American Psychiatric Publishing, Inc.

Asherson, P. J., & Curran, S. (2001). Approaches to gene mapping in complex disorders and their application in child psychiatry and psychology. *British Journal of Psychiatry, 179*, 122–128.

Barkley, R. A. (1997). Behavioural inhibition, sustained attention and executive functions: Constructing a unifying theory of ADHD. *Psychological Bulletin, 121*, 65–94.

Baumgardner, T. L., Reiss, A. L., Freund, L. S., & Abrams, M. T. (1995). Specification of the neurobehavioral phenotype in males with fragile X syndrome. *Pediatrics, 95*, 744–752.

Bayley, N. (1993). *Bayley Scale of Infant Development* (2nd ed.). San Antonio: The Psychological Corporation.

Bertrand, J., Mervis, C. B., & Eisenberg, J. D. (1997). Drawing by children with Williams syndrome: A developmental perspective. *Developmental Neuropsychology, 13*, 41–67.

Clark D., & Wilson G. N. (2003). Behavioral assessment of children with Down syndrome using the Reiss psychopathology scale. *American Journal of Medical Genetics, 118A*(3), 210–216.

Coe, D. A., Matson, J. L., Russell, D. W., Slifer, K. J., Capone, G. T., Baglio, C., et al. (1999). Behavior problems of children with Down syndrome and life events. *Journal of Autism and Developmental Disorders, 29*, 149–156.

Cook, E. H. Jr., Stein, M. A., Krasowski, M. D., Cox, N. J., Olkon, D. M., Kieffer, J. E., et al. (1995). Association of attention-deficit disorder and the dopamine transporter gene. *American Journal of Human Genetics, 56*, 993–998.

Cornish, K. M., Munir, F., & Cross, G. (1998). The nature of the spatial deficit in young females with fragile X syndrome: A neuropsychological and molecular perspective. *Neuropsychologia, 36*, 1239–1246.

Cornish, K. M., Munir, F., & Cross, G. (1999). Spatial cognition in male with Fragile-X syndrome: Evidence for a neuropsychological phenotype. *Cortex, 35*, 263–271.

Daly, G., Hawi, Z., Fitzgerald, M., & Gill, M. (1999). Mapping susceptibility loci in attention deficit hyperactivity disorder: Preferential transmission of parental alleles at DAT1, DBH and DRD5 to affected children. *Molecular Psychiatry, 4*, 192–196.

Deruelle, C., Mancini, J., Livet, M. O., Casse, P. C., & de-Schonen, S. (1999). Configural and local processing of faces in children with Williams syndrome. *Brain and Cognition. 41*, 276–298.

Donnai, D., & Karmiloff-Smith, A. (2000). Williams syndrome: from genotype through to the cognitive phenotype. *American Journal of Medical Genetics, 97*(2), 164–171.

Dunn, L., Dunn, P., Whetton, C., & Pintillie, D. (1982). *British Picture Vocabulary Scale*. Windsor: NFER.

Dykens, E. M. (1998). Maladaptive behavior and dual diagnosis in persons with genetic syndromes. In J. A. Burack, R. M., Hodapp, & E. Zigler (Eds.), *Handbook of mental retardation and development.* (pp. 542–562). New York: Cambridge University Press.

Farran, E. K., & Jarrold C. (2003). Visuospatial cognition in Williams syndrome: Reviewing and accounting for the strengths and weaknesses in performance. *Developmental Neuropsychology, 23*(1–2), 173–200.

Ferrier, L. J., Bashir, A. S., Meryash, D. L., Johnston, J., & Wolff, P. (1991). Conversational skills of individuals with fragile-X syndrome: A comparison with autism and Down syndrome. *Developmental Medicine and Child Neurology, 33*, 776–778.

Fisch, G. S., Carpenter, N., Holden, J. J., Howard-Peebles, P. N., Maddalena, A., Borghgraef, M., et al. (1999). Longitudinal changes in cognitive and adaptive behaviour in fragile X females: a prospective multicenter analysis. *American Journal of Medical Genetics, 83*(4), 308–312.

Fisch, G. S., Simensen, R., Tarleton, J., Chalifoux, M., Holden, J. J., Carpenter, N., et al. (1996). Longitudinal study of cognitive abilities and adaptive behaviour levels in fragile X males: a prospective multicenter analysis. *American Journal of Medical Genetics, 64*(2), 356–361.

Freund, L. S., & Reiss A. L. (1991). Cognitive profiles associated with the fra(X) syndrome in males and females. *American Journal of Medical Genetics, 38*, 542–547.

Gath, A., & Gumley, D. (1986). Behaviour problems in retarded children with special reference to Down's syndrome. *British Journal of Psychiatry, 149*, 156–161.

Grice, S. J., Spratling, M. W., Karmiloff-Smith, A., Halit, H., Csibra, G., de Haan, M., et al. (2001). Disordered visual processing and oscillatory brain activity in autism and Williams syndrome. *Neuroreport. 28, 12*(12), 2697–2700.

Hagerman, R. J., & Hagerman, P. J. (2002). *Fragile X Syndrome: Diagnosis, Treatment and Research*, 3rd edition. Baltimore: The Johns Hopkins University Press.

Hayes, A., & Batshaw, M. L. (1993). Down syndrome. *Pediatrics Clinics of North America, 40*(3), 523–535.

Hodapp, R. M., Leckman, J. F., Dykens, E. M., Sparrow, S., Zelinsky, D. G., & Ort, S. I. (1992). K-ABC profiles of children with fragile X syndrome, Down syndrome and non-specific mental retardation. *American Journal on Mental Retardation, 97,* 39–46.

Holmes, J., Payton, A., Barrett, J. H., Hever, T., Fitzpatrick H., Trumper, A. L., et al. (2000). A family-based and case-control association study of the dopamine D4 receptor gene and dopamine transporter gene in attention deficit hyperactivity disorder. *Molecular Psychiatry,* 5(5), 523–530.

Jakala, P., Hanninen, T., Ryynanen, M., Laakso, M., Partanen, K., Mannermaa, A., et al. (1997). Fragile-X: neuropsychological test performance, CGG triplet repeat lengths, and hippocampal volumes. *Journal of Clinical Investigation, 100*(2), 331–338.

Jarrold, C., & Baddeley, A. D. (2001). Short-term memory in Down syndrome: applying the working memory model. *Downs Syndrome, Research and Practice,* 7(1), 17–23.

Jarrold, C., Baddeley, A. D., & Hewes, A. K. (1999). Genetically dissociated components of working memory: evidence from Down's and Williams syndrome. *Neuropsychologia, 37,* 637–651.

Jarrold, C., Baddeley, A. D., & Phillips, C. E. (2002). Verbal short-term memory in Down syndrome: a problem of memory, audition, or speech? *Journal of Speech, Language, and Hearing Research,* 45(3), 531–544.

Laws, G. (2002). Working memory in children and adolescents with Down syndrome: evidence from a color memory experiment. *Journal of Child Psychology and Psychiatry, 43,* 353–364.

Maher, B. S., Marazita, M. L., Ferrell, R. E., & Vanyukov, M. M. (2002). Dopamine system genes and attention deficit hyperactivity disorder: A meta-analysis. *Psychiatric Genetics, 12*(4), 207–215.

Manly, T., Robertson, I. H., Anderson, V., & Nimmo-Smith, I. (1999). *Test of Everyday Attention for Children.* Bury St Edmunds: Thames Valley Test Company.

Mazzocco, M. M., Pennington, B. F., & Hagerman, R. J. (1993). The neurocognitive phenotype of female carriers of fragile X: additional evidence for specificity. *Journal of Developmental and Behavioral Pediatrics, 14,* 328–335.

Mazzocco, M. M., Pennington, B. F., & Hagerman, R. J. (1994). Social cognition skills among females with fragile X. *Journal of Autism and Developmental Disorders, 24,* 473–485.

Mirsky, A. F. (1996). Disorders of attention: A neuropsychological approach. In G. R. Lyon and N. A. Krasnegor, (Eds.), *Attention, Memory and Executive Function* (pp. 71–95). Baltimore: Brookes.

Miyake, A., Friedman, N. P., Emerson, M. J., Witzki, A. H., & Howerker, A. (2000). The unity and diversity of executive functions and their contribution in complex frontal lobe tasks: a latent variable analysis. *Cognitive Psychology, 38,* 1261–1270.

Morris, R. D. (1996). Relationships and distinctions among the concepts of attention, memory and executive function. In G. R. Lyon and N. A. Krasnegor, (Eds.), *Attention, Memory and Executive Function* (pp. 11–16). Baltimore: Brookes.

Munir, F., Cornish, K. M., & Wilding, J. (2000a). Nature of the working memory deficit in Fragile-X syndrome. *Brain and Cognition, 44,* 387–401.

Munir, F., Cornish, K. M., & Wilding, J. (2000b). A neuropsychological profile of attention deficits in young males with fragile X syndrome. *Neuropsychologia, 38,* 1261–1270.

Naglieri, J. A. (1985). *Matrix analogies test—short form.* New York: The Psychological Corporation, Harcourt, Brace Jovanovich.

Norman, D., & Shallice, T. (1980). *Attention to action: Willed and automatic control of behaviour.* University of California at San Diego, CHIP Report 99.

Pennington, B. F., Moon, J., Edgin, J., Stedron J., & Nadel, L. (2003). The neuropsychology of Down syndrome: Evidence for Hippocampal dysfunction. *Child Development, 74,* 75–93.

Pickering, S., & Gathercole, S. (2001). *Working Memory Test Battery for Children.* London: The Psychological Corporation.

Posner, M. I., & Peterson, S. E. (1990). The attention system of the human brain. *Annual Review of Neuroscience, 13,* 25–42.

Posner, M. I., Walker, J. A., Friedrich, F. J., & Rafal, R. D. (1984). Effects of parietal injury on covert orienting of attention. *Journal of Neuroscience, 4,* 1863–1874.

Pueschel, S. M., Bernier, J. C., & Pezzullo, J. C. (1991). Behavioural observations in children with Down's syndrome. *Journal of Mental Deficiency Research, 35,* 502–511.

Reiss A. L., & Freund, L. (1990). Fragile X syndrome. *Biological Psychiatry, 27,* 223–240.

Scerif, G., Cornish, K. M., Wilding, J., Driver, J., & Karmiloff-Smith, A. (2004). Visual search in typically developing toddlers and toddlers with Fragile X or Williams syndrome. *Developmental Science, 7,* 116–130.

Schapiro, M. B., Murphy, D. G., Hagerman, R. J., Azari, N. P., Alexander, G. E., Miezejeski, C. M., et al. (1995). Adult fragile X syndrome: neuropsychology, brain anatomy, and metabolism. *American Journal Medical Genetics, 60*(6), 480–493.

Silverstein, A. B., Legutki, G., Friedman, S. L., & Takayama, D. L. (1982). Performance of Down syndrome individuals on the Stanford-Binet Intelligence Scale. *American Journal Mental Deficiency, 86*(5), 548–551.

Simon, E. W., & Finucane, B. M. (1996). Facial emotion identification in males with fragile X syndrome. *American Journal of Medical Genetics, 67,* 77–80.

Sonuga-Barke, E. J. S., Taylor, E., Sembi, S., & Smith, J. (1992). Hyperactivity and delay aversion—I. The effect of delay on choice. *Journal of Child Psychology and Psychiatry, 33,* 387–398.

Sonuga-Barke, E. J. S., Williams, E., Hall, M., & Saxton, T. (1996). Hyperactivity and delay aversion. III. The effects on cognitive style of impossible delay after errors. *Journal of Child Psychology and Psychiatry and Allied Disciplines, 37,* 189–194.

Sudhalter, V., Cohen, I. L., Silverman, W., & Wolf-Schein, E. G. (1990). Conversational analyses of males with fragile X, Down syndrome, and autism: comparison of the emergence of deviant language. *American Journal of Mental Retardation, 94*(4), 431–441.

Sudhalter, V., Scarborough, H. S., & Cohen, I. L. (1991). Syntactic delay and pragmatic deviance in the language of fragile X males. *American Journal of Medical Genetics, 38*(2–3), 493–497.

Sudhalter, V., Maranion, M., & Brook, P. (1992). Expressive semantic deficit in the productive language of males with fragile X syndrome. *American Journal of Medical Genetics, 43,* 65–71.

Swanson, J., McStephen, M., Hay, D., & Levy, F. (2001). *The potential of the SWAN rating scale in genetic analysis of ADHD.* Poster at the international Society for Research in Child and Adolescent Psychiatry. 10th Scientific Meeting, Vancouver, June 2001.

Turk, J. (1998). Fragile X syndrome and attentional deficits. *Journal of Applied Research in Intellectual-Disabilities, 11*(3), 175–191.

Turk, J., & Cornish, K. (1998). Face recognition and emotion perception in boys with fragile-X syndrome. *Journal of Intellectual Disability Research, 42*(6), 490–499.

Ullman, R. K., Sleator, E. K., & Sprague, R. L. (1984). A new rating scale for diagnosis and monitoring of ADD children. *Psychopharmacology Bulletin, 20,* 160–164.

Van der Meere, J. J. (1996). The role of attention. In S. Sandberg (Ed.), *Hyperactivity disorders in childhood* (pp.111–148). Cambridge: Cambridge University Press.

Waldman, I. D., Rowe, D. C., Abramowitz, S. T., Kozel, S. T., Mohr, J. H., Sherman, S. L., et al. (1998). Association and linkage of the dopamine transporter gene and attention-deficit hyperactivity disorder in children: heterogeneity owing to diagnostic subtype and severity. *American Journal of Human Genetics, 63,* 1767–1776.

Wang, P. P., & Bellugi, U. (1994). Evidence from two genetic syndromes for a dissociation between verbal and visual-spatial short-term memory. *Journal of Clinical Experimental Neuropsychology, 16,* 317–322.

Wilding, J. (2003). Attentional difficulties in children: weakness in executive function or problems in coping with difficult tasks? *British Journal of Psychology, 94,* 427–436.

Wilding, J., & Cornish, K. M. (2003). Efficiency of working memory and attention in children and young adults with Down syndrome. In J. A. Mallard (Ed.), *Focus on Down Syndrome Research* (pp. 147–162). New York: Nova Science.

Wilding, J., Munir, F., & Cornish, K. M. (2001). The nature of attentional differences between groups of children differentiated by teacher ratings of attention and hyperactivity. *British Journal of Psychology*, *92*, 357–371.

Wilding, J., Cornish, K. M., & Munir, F. (2002). Further delineation of the executive deficit in males with fragile-X syndrome. *Neuropsychologia*, *40*, 1343–1349.

World Health Organization (1992). *International classification of diseases* (10th ed.). Geneva: World Health Organization.

Working Memory and Deafness: Implications for Cognitive Development and Functioning

MADELEINE KEEHNER

Curtin University of Technology

JOANNA ATKINSON

University College London

Traditional conceptualizations of working memory (WM) make a number of well-founded assumptions about cognitive phenomena. Visuo-spatial and verbal processes are viewed as separable, and a sound-based phonological code is believed to underlie the processing of language. For deaf individuals, however, the typical assumptions may not apply. Linguistic inputs for deaf children can differ dramatically from the norm, both in modality (as in signed languages) and in quality (as for deaf children exposed exclusively to aural–oral language). Such factors affect the development of the cognitive architecture and WM functioning in both verbal and visuo-spatial domains. This chapter reviews evidence pertaining to WM in deaf children and explores potential implications arising from the unique characteristics of the deaf experience.

DEFINING DEAFNESS

The construct of deafness can be framed in different ways. Both audiological and cultural definitions exist, but these can give rise to differing expectations. While audiological criteria emphasize limited functioning, cultural definitions highlight differences, rather than deficits.

Audiological criteria for deafness assess the degree of hearing loss or impairment in units known as dBHL (decibel hearing level). In the United Kingdom, profound deafness is associated with hearing impairments of more than 95 dB in the better ear. Lesser degrees of impairment are graded as mild (25–39 dB), moderate (40–69 dB), and severe (70–94 dB),[1] whereas children with hearing losses up to 25 dB across all frequencies are considered normally hearing. According to the National Deaf Children's Society (NDCS), approximately 25,000 children in the United Kingdom have permanent, moderate to profound deafness, a level of hearing impairment that is severe enough to create significant barriers to learning.

In some contexts, most notably educational settings, a child's deafness is defined not only by degree of hearing impairment, but also by factors such as family circumstances and oral–aural language capabilities. In separating differing degrees of deafness, the weight given to oral language skills can even prevail over audiological data. As Marschark (1993) points out, "two children with identical hearing impairment might be differentially identified as 'deaf' and 'hard of hearing' solely because one has parents who can afford the cost of extensive speech therapy" (p. 13).[2]

A nonaudiological criterion also underlies the label *culturally Deaf*.[3] In the United Kingdom, this term usually applies to individuals who use British Sign Language (BSL) and consider themselves members of the Deaf community. Traditionally, Deaf culture and sign language are transmitted transgenerationally within Deaf families. However, individuals from hearing families may also identify with and join the Deaf community and in so doing become culturally Deaf. Any member of the Deaf community who uses sign language as their primary form of communication may thus be considered culturally Deaf because this definition rests more on self-defined membership of a community or group, with shared cultural values, than on a strict measure of hearing impairment.

For the present purposes, a useful definition may be the one provided by the NDCS (2002): "children identified as having special educational needs due to their deafness" (p. 2). Prelingual deafness, occurring from birth or before age 5 years, has unique implications for cognitive development, especially in the domain of language. This chapter therefore focuses primarily

---

[1]Precise boundaries between grades of deafness differ somewhat between the United Kingdom and the United States, and an additional category of moderately severe (56–70 dB) is used in the United States.

[2]The term "hard of hearing" sometimes has been used to differentiate a subgroup of children who are profoundly deaf but who have more fully developed oral language capabilities; however, this distinction has become viewed as potentially unhelpful and is now avoided by many working in the field.

[3]The term Deaf, spelled with an uppercase "d," usually denotes a culturally defined notion of deafness, rather than one based on audiological criteria. Self-defined members of the Deaf community in the United Kingdom are generally native or primary users of BSL, although their level of deafness and age of onset may vary.

on the special case of prelingually deaf children, whose educational needs differ substantially from those of children who are later deafened.

FACTORS AFFECTING WORKING MEMORY DEVELOPMENT IN DEAF CHILDREN

Our understanding of the relationship between WM and deafness is complicated by the fact that deafness is not a unitary construct. As Stokoe (2001) has succinctly put it, "People who cannot hear are not all the same" (p. 6). While the developmental progress of some individuals parallels hearing children, others face substantive difficulties in acquiring cognitive, linguistic, and social skills. Given that the deaf experience differs dramatically from one child to another, many researchers argue strongly for an individual differences approach to studying the development of deaf children (Stokoe, 2001).

WM processes are uniquely diverse within this population. As Lichtenstein (1998) has noted, deaf children represent information in a number of different ways. Studies of short-term memory have uncovered a variety of preferences for maintaining linguistic material, including visual codes (Conrad & Rush, 1965), fingerspelling codes (Locke & Locke, 1971), sign codes (Bellugi, Klima, & Siple, 1975), and speech-based phonological codes (Conrad, 1972). An important challenge for research, therefore, is to better understand the factors that lead to different patterns of WM functioning among this population.

As in hearing children, many variables interact to affect cognitive functioning in deaf children. The range of individual circumstances that exists in the deaf population, however, is perhaps even greater than in the hearing population. Not only does the precise form of one child's hearing impairment differ from the next, but etiologies also vary widely. Deafness frequently cooccurs with other disabilities and in some cases may be caused by underlying organic neuropathology that can give rise to additional developmental effects. As a result, it can be difficult to separate the consequences of hearing impairment *per se* from those resulting from other, correlated phenomena. Stokoe (2001) suggests that one key factor determining individual differences is the milieu in which a child is raised. In his words, "the difference in outcome has less to do with being deaf than with what others do about it" (p. 6).

A number of factors have been implicated in the development of WM in deaf children. Among the most important of these are degree of hearing impairment and age of onset, family environment (deaf or hearing), primary language mode (speech or sign), and schooling (predominantly oral, total communication, or bilingual). These variables do not stand in isolation; they interact to create a set of conditions that are unique for every individual. Clearly, many other important factors, such as those linked to social and emotional development, also affect cognitive functioning, but they are beyond the scope of this chapter (for a review of these issues, see Marschark, 1993, Chapters 3 and 4).

A child's level of hearing impairment (mild, moderate, severe, profound) and the age at which he or she becomes deaf (prelingually or postlingually) have obvious implications for the development of phonological WM. Children who have less severe hearing impairment (and thus greater access to phonological input), or who become deafened after developing some spoken language, are likely to have greater phonological awareness than children who are profoundly prelingually deaf (Conrad, 1972; Lichtenstein, 1998). However, a lack of phonological awareness does not preclude language acquisition if the child has access to a language mode that is perceptually accessible, such as sign language.

During the early years, the family provides the primary language environment. In the vast majority of cases (estimated at around 9 out of 10), deaf children are born to hearing parents and are raised in families where speech is the predominant or only communication form. For these children, normal immersion in a natural language is severely impeded, and effective communication with family members can be difficult. A small minority of deaf children, however, are born into families where signing is the predominant form of communication. For these individuals, sign is acquired naturally, and language development follows a path akin to that for spoken language, with recognizable milestones analogous to those seen in hearing children (Morgan, Herman, & Woll, 2002; Newman, Bavelier, Corina, Jezzard, & Neville, 2002; Siple, 1997).

Some hearing parents have begun to explore signed languages as a means of communicating with their children. Although their levels of fluency are not equivalent to native language users, initiatives such as bilingual preschool or home-school liaison can provide additional fluent input and help to support a normal language acquisition trajectory in sign.

A number of writers have argued in favor of exposing deaf children to sign language from an early age, to facilitate language development generally and to realize the broader cognitive and social benefits of effective communication skills. It has been argued that "a sign language environment for deaf children is as important to their cognitive development as a spoken language environment is for hearing children" (Stokoe, 2001, p. 6). Certainly there is empirical evidence to suggest that early exposure to sign language benefits later linguistic abilities, including those for spoken language (Mayberry, Lock, & Kamzi, 2002; Morford & Mayberry, 2000) and English literacy skills (Strong & Prinz, 1997).

Later in childhood, school becomes an important part of a child's language environment. A central, and highly controversial, debate in deaf education concerns the relative merits of oral versus bilingual (sign language and English) educational approaches. While many favor an emphasis on the development of oral language skills, others argue that exposure to sign language is more productive for cognitive development in the long term. Supporters of bilingual education argue that competence in a first language, such as sign, is essential as a basis for teaching English because deaf children cannot access spoken language phonologically. "The child should have access to the *easiest* language to learn at the earliest time and this should be the means of interaction and communication. . . . what this model does is to ensure that the child arrives at school at least with a high level of competence in sign language and therefore, a vehicle for learning and interaction." (Kyle, 1994, p. 136). Although there are different models of bilingual education, most focus on fostering sign as a strong first language and then teaching English as a second language, usually with greater emphasis on the written form.

A major obstacle for proponents of bilingual education is the widespread view that exposure to sign language will handicap the development of spoken language. "There remains a fear that if the child does not speak early and exclusively, then the processes of speech will never develop" (Kyle, 1994, p. 138). Prevailing beliefs such as these may have prevented it from becoming the norm, but writers such as Hamers and Blanc (1989) argue that bilingual schooling can enhance the academic achievement of deaf children, as it has been claimed to do for other minority children.

The debate over which language mode(s) should be used in deaf schooling remains unresolved and will continue to be a source of controversy. Nevertheless, a deaf child's language environment has important implications for WM. As we shall see, exposure to sign language has significant consequences for cognitive functioning, both within and beyond the verbal domain.

WORKING MEMORY AND SIGN LANGUAGE

For centuries sign languages have been fundamental to the communication of deaf people. Records dating from before the 4th century AD describe informal sign systems, which evolved within families or small communities containing a number of deaf persons. Entries in the *Talmud,* the Hebrew book of Jewish law, indicate that these communication methods were even sanctioned by the wider community for religious and official purposes (cited in Miles, 1988). Wherever a number of deaf people coexist, local signing systems have been observed to spontaneously occur (e.g., Feldman, Goldin-Meadow, & Gleitman, 1978).

Despite their ancient origins, relatively little was known about signed languages until recent times, and the general consensus among linguists was that they did not possess the formal properties of natural language. Speech is clearly the most common mode of human communication, and for centuries the universal features of language have been considered synonymous with the physical characteristics of the vocal–auditory domain (Klima &

Bellugi, 1979). As a result, the study of psycholinguistic phenomena has mainly focused on the mechanisms underpinning *spoken* language and on modality-specific functions made possible by internal representations that reflect the phonological properties of speech.

It was not until the 1960s, when William C. Stokoe produced his seminal work on the linguistics of American Sign Language (ASL), that a general acceptance of signed communication began to emerge (Stokoe, 1960, 1978). Stokoe was largely responsible for a dawning realization within mainstream linguistics that sign language is much more than a series of "pictures in the air" and that this form of communication is indeed a true language. Since this time, studies with both brain-damaged and normally-functioning individuals have confirmed that the same language-relevant neural substrates that underpin *spoken* language also support *sign* language (Atkinson, Marshall, Thacker, & Woll, 2002; Bavelier et al., 1997; Corina, 1997, 1998; Corina, Poizner, Feinberg, Dowd & O'Grady, 1992; Hickok, Bellugi, & Klima, 1996; Neville et al., 1997; Poizner, Klima, & Bellugi, 1987; Soderfeldt, Ronnberg, & Risberg, 1994). Such parallels suggest that sign and speech are functionally equivalent, a conclusion that is theoretically crucial, not only from a linguistic or cultural standpoint, but also for ensuing implications for underlying cognitive mechanisms.

However, a question remains over whether the cognitive processes associated with verbal WM are relevant to signed languages. WM researchers have traditionally defined verbal material as speech-based input or phonologically recodeable visual items such as print (Baddeley, 1986) or lipread stimuli (Campbell & Dodd, 1980; Gardiner, Gathercole, & Gregg, 1983). The very term *phonological* implies a form based on the sounds (phonemes) of speech.

As Wilson and Emmorey (1997b) point out, signed languages provide a challenge to this traditional division. These languages do not take a vocal–auditory form, but instead use the *corporal–visual* channel to represent and communicate concepts symbolically (Sutton-Spence & Woll, 1999). Sign and speech exist within entirely separate sensory domains and use different articulatory apparatus. A central issue in the sign language literature, therefore, concerns the question of how signs are represented in WM and what types of cognitive resources support their processing. This raises an important theoretical question: Do parallel cognitive mechanisms, analogous to those for speech, support reception and production in sign?

Anecdotally, a number of reported phenomena support the idea of an "inner voice of the hands" (Klima & Bellugi, 1979). As Klima and Bellugi (1979, p. 89) have noted, "Deaf parents tell us that their children sign to themselves in their sleep; we have observed deaf toddlers signing to themselves and their toy animals before bedtime when they thought they were alone. We have seen hands 'muttering' to themselves. . . . Deaf people tell us they dream in signs, plan conversations in signs, imagine the perfect retort in signs."

The evidence has become more than anecdotal. Experimental paradigms from the WM approach have provided compelling evidence of internal representations that preserve the physical properties of signs, analogous to the phonological coding of speech. To grasp the implications of these findings, it is necessary to understand something of the structure of sign language.

The Sublexical Structure Of Signs

Although it clearly differs from spoken language in a number of ways, sign language has certain key features in common with speech that make internal representation possible. Like words, signs are comprised of a relatively small number of constituent physical elements, or formational parameters. These sublexical components are analogous to the phonemes of speech, and like speech sounds, they can be combined in rule-governed ways to form meaningful whole units (Wilson & Emmorey, 1997b). These phoneme-like building blocks, or cheremes (Stokoe, 1978), have been broadly grouped into three major types of formational parameters: hand configuration or handshape, place of articulation or spatial location, and movement[4] (Klima & Bellugi, 1979). Each of these different aspects contributes to the construction of a sign, and, as with words, two signs may differ in just one formational parameter. For example, in BSL the signs TELL and ASK are identical in location and movement, but they differ in the handshape used (Figure 7.1, upper). Similarly, in some regions the BSL signs NAME and AFTERNOON have the same movement and handshape but have different locations (Figure 7.1, lower). In each case, a single component is sufficient to distinguish the meaning of two signs, in the same way that the English words *pin* and *bin* can be differentiated by a change to just one phonemic element.

Just as different spoken languages have different phonologies, each sign language has its own *cherology,* a distinctive set of permissible sublexical units, and implicit rules by which these can be legally combined. For example, in an analysis of Chinese Sign Language (CSL), Klima and Bellugi (1979) identified a large number of representative CSL forms that do not exist in ASL. In many cases, these items were perceived by ASL signers as impossible constructions. The signs were judged as inadmissible because of their use of ASL-illegal phonemes (such as handshapes, locations, or movements that do not exist in ASL) or the use of ASL-illegal combinations of formational parameters (such as two handshapes contacting in a way that is inadmissible in ASL). Such language-specific patterning of sublexical units is analogous to the surface differences found between spoken languages.

Research into the structure of spoken language has established that the phonemes of speech can be broken down into distinguishing features such as voicing (the presence or absence of vocal cord vibrations) or place (the parts of the mouth active in production). These atomic constituents, or

[4]Some analyses also include an additional parameter of palm orientation.

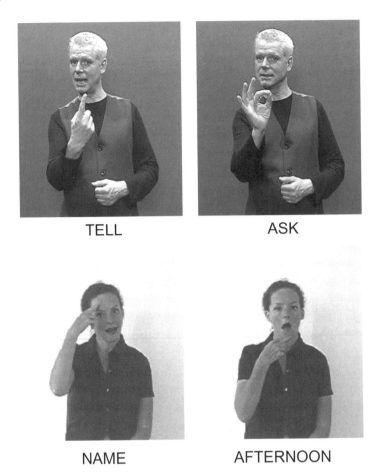

TELL   ASK

NAME   AFTERNOON

FIGURE 7.1
Pairs of British Sign Language (BSL) signs differing in a single formational
parameter: *upper figure*) TELL and ASK (same locations and movements,
different handshapes); *lower figure*) NAME and AFTERNOON (same
movements and handshapes, different locations).

featural primes, are perceived by listeners as separable, independent features, and some are more crucial than others for perceptual discrimination
between phonemes (Miller & Nicely, 1955). Sign language researchers have
found analogous patterns for signers' perceptions of the primes constitut-
ing signs. Using a paradigm adapted for visual presentation, Lane, Boyes-
Braem, and Bellugi (1979) identified 11 separate classes of ASL handshape,
distinguishable by the presence or absence of 20 featural primes (such as
the configuration of the fingers or the orientation of the palm), which in
varying combinations can produce all legal ASL handshapes. To validate

their model, Lane et al. (1979) analyzed recall errors from Bellugi et al. (1975). Of the handshape substitutions resulting in recall errors for ASL signs, 90% differed by just 1 featural prime. The model correctly predicted the occurrence of WM phenomena such as phonological (or cherological) errors during acquisition, maintenance, and recall of signed stimuli. Such findings suggest that fundamental parallels, resulting from shared linguistic characteristics, exist for the processing of words and signs.

Working Memory for Signs

As with the phonemes of speech, the manual components of sign language are crucial for its representation in WM. Shand and Klima (1981) argue that, like speech, sign is a *primary language code*. Unlike text, which is routinely recoded into a phonological form, sign, like speech, does not need to be recoded because the one-to-one relationship between perception and production permits direct rehearsal (Wilson & Emmorey, 1997b). In support of this idea, research with deaf signers has produced evidence of a number of sign-based WM phenomena that are remarkably analogous to those found with speech inputs.

One source of evidence for parallel cognitive mechanisms is so-called "slips of the hand" (Klima & Bellugi, 1979). These production errors are caused by unintended reorderings of sublexical elements in ways that are analogous to "slips of the tongue", such as spoonerisms. These error patterns are predictable and nonrandom, consistently preserving the combinatorial constraints of the language. The misorderings observed in these output errors confirm the psychological independence of separable sublexical units, both at the phonological level and at the more atomic level of featural primes. Similarly, creative uses of the language, such as punning and producing novel forms, use permissible substitutions of sublexical features (Klima & Bellugi, 1979). Using paradigms adapted from verbal WM experiments, researchers have uncovered evidence of a mechanism for the internal representation of signs. Experimental data suggest that this is a dual-component system, comprising both a phonological store and an articulatory rehearsal mechanism, mirroring the hypothesized structure of the phonological loop.

Evidence for a phonological store that preserves the cherological or physical features of signs comes from a number of sources. For example, Shand and Klima (1981) found evidence of a nonacoustic suffix effect in signers, suggesting that a cherological trace held within some kind of storage mechanism can be disrupted by new input when there is overlap in the sensory or physical features of the stored material and the suffix. This finding is analogous to the disruptive effects of acoustic suffixes on phonological material, a phenomenon commonly used to argue for the existence of a memory code based on the sensory properties of speech (Baddeley & Hull, 1979; Campbell & Dodd, 1980).

Sign analogs of phonological errors have also been shown. Klima and Bellugi (1979) found that the intrusion errors made by deaf native signers in immediate recall of ASL signs were unrelated to either the phonological or orthographic forms of corresponding English words. Rather, recall errors were highly visually or kinesthetically similar to the target item, preserving all but one of the major formational parameters. These effects are analogous to phonological errors made by hearing participants when presented with spoken words and suggest a storage code based on sign phonology or cherology.

A similarity effect has been found for signs sharing the same handshape (Poizner, Bellugi, & Tweney, 1981; Wilson & Emmorey, 1997a). Strings of formationally similar signs are more difficult to recall, causing confusion errors in immediate memory tasks. Such confusability suggests that WM preserves the physical features of signs, just as it preserves the phonological properties of speech sounds.

A number of findings suggest the existence of an articulatory rehearsal mechanism permitting the "submanual" rehearsal of signs. Wilson and Emmorey (1997b) describe this function as "a relatively automatic quasi-motoric process for refreshing information in working memory" (p. 123). In support of this idea, Wilson and Emmorey (1998) showed that recall scores for long signs (items that take more time to articulate) are lower than recall scores for short signs, and this difference reflects the articulatory duration of signed ASL items, not their English equivalents. The sign-length effect is analogous to the word-length effect and, like this speech-based phenomenon, suggests an articulatory rehearsal process with a finite capacity—that is, longer signs take up relatively more of the rehearsal mechanism's capacity, so fewer items can be maintained. This hypothesis is also indirectly supported by the finding that immediate memory span for signed items is smaller than that for spoken items, reflecting the longer articulatory duration of signs relative to words (Hanson, 1982; Klima & Bellugi, 1979; Krakow & Hanson, 1985).

Additional evidence for a rehearsal mechanism is provided by the sign suppression effect. Irrelevant hand movements performed during WM tasks have been shown to impair recall of signs in deaf native signers (Wilson & Emmorey, 1997a). This phenomenon is analogous to the disruptive effects of articulatory suppression, which is assumed to impair the recall of phonological material by disrupting internal rehearsal processes. For signers, concurrent hand movements appear to similarly disrupt the internal rehearsal of signs.

The patterns of interactions found between WM phenomena in sign language research are intriguingly similar to those observed for speech. For example, the sign-length effect disappears under concurrent sign suppression (Wilson & Emmorey, 1998), indicating that this phenomenon originates within an articulatory rehearsal process, which, like that underpinning speech rehearsal, is blocked by concurrent articulation. The sign similarity effect, however, is not affected by concurrent sign suppression, implying the existence of a phonological or cherological memory trace, which is separate from the articulatory rehearsal process (Wilson & Emmorey, 1997a). Short-term storage of signs thus appears to be based on cherological features, and signs, like speech, can gain automatic access to this store even when the recoding process is blocked. In contrast, with nameable pictures (which require recoding prior to loading into a cherological store), concurrent sign suppression (which disrupts the articulatory mechanism required for recoding) abolishes the similarity effect (Wilson & Emmorey, 1997a). Thus, in signers, simultaneous articulation blocks the recoding of nonverbal material into a sign-based form, just as articulatory suppression prevents hearing participants from recoding nonverbal material into a phonological form.

In summary, there is much evidence to suggest that deaf native signers have access to a short-term memory system permitting the representation of sign language and that this system operates in a way that is analogous to the phonological loop. As with speech-based verbal WM, the system appears to have two parts: "(1) a buffer that retains information using the phonological structure of the language, and (2) a rehearsal process based on representations for movement of the articulators used in language production" (Wilson & Emmorey, 1997a, p. 319).

Overall, the body of evidence suggests that early exposure to sign language significantly influences the development of WM, giving rise to cognitive adaptations that permit the internal representation of signs. These internal representations preserve the physical properties of sign movements and produce sign-based analogs of phonological processes. At first glance, such findings might appear to conflict with current conceptualizations of WM. However, if the phonological loop component uses an articulatory code, it is conceivable that the same cognitive architecture could serve both signed and spoken languages. In line with this possibility, imaging studies have shown that "inner signing" of sentences (analogous to subvocal articulation) engages frontal brain areas traditionally associated with the phonological loop (McGuire et al., 1997). If correct, this hypothesis suggests a somewhat unorthodox view of the phonological loop as a general mechanism that is not limited by modality.

The effects of sign language experience are not limited to verbal functions. In the following section, we examine consequences of sign language experience that extend into the visuo-spatial domain of WM.

VISUO-SPATIAL WORKING MEMORY IN DEAF CHILDREN

A commonly held assumption is that the loss of one sensory modality leads to compensation in the remaining intact senses, giving rise to superior visual processing in deaf individuals. This "sensory compensation" hypothesis was popular even among the scientific community until relatively recently. Although a number of researchers have suggested that deaf people might develop enhanced visual functions to compensate for lack of auditory input (Blair, 1957), empirical studies have failed to provide reliable evidence for the existence of superior visual memory in this population (Parasnis, Samar, Bettger, & Sathe, 1996; Tharpe, Ashmead, & Rothpletz, 2002).

Nevertheless, research has shown that visuo-spatial processes do differ in systematic ways between deaf *signers* and hearing individuals. However, this appears to be the result, not of deafness *per se,* but of experience with sign language. The processing of signed, as compared to spoken, language makes unique demands on visuo-spatial cognition because many of the processes involved in everyday sign discourse map onto the known properties of visuo-spatial WM. As a consequence, native exposure to sign language produces unique adaptations to visuo-spatial WM functioning. To appreciate why this should be, it is necessary to understand the integral role of space in sign language.

Space in Sign Language

Sign movements are produced within a three-dimensional area located in front of the signer's body, extending to the waist, the top of the head, and the lateral reach of the forearms with elbows close to the torso. All sign languages make use of this *signing space.* Information about real-world topographical space can be communicated by mapping real spatial relations within signing space (Emmorey, Corina, & Bellugi, 1995). Classifier[5] signs can be used to represent objects within scenes, and these can be manipulated to show the real-world locations, orientations, and movements of objects. As Emmorey (1996) points out, this function is unique to signed languages: "The use of space to directly represent spatial relations stands in marked contrast to spoken languages, in which spatial information must be recovered from an acoustic signal that does not map onto the information content in a one-to-one correspondence" (p. 175).

Signing space can also be used to specify abstract syntactical relationships. Referents can be arbitrarily assigned to positions that indicate the grammatical relationships between them. A common example of this is the pronomial use of space. There are no signs to indicate constructs such as *he* or *she,* so when describing an event involving a number of people, a signer must first identify the relevant individuals using a lexical noun and assign each one to a specific locus within signing space. Each spatial location is unique to a specific referent and remains stable over the duration of

---

[5]A classifier is a handshape that indicates a generic class of objects. For example, in BSL, different classifier handshapes are used to represent vehicles, furniture, animals, and people. These can be placed in signing space to indicate the positions, orientations, and relations of their real-world referents.

the discourse, allowing the signer to refer to a referent periodically by pointing to its hypothetical location. Both signer and addressee must generate and maintain these imagined locations in signing space, a process that is somewhat analogous to image generation (Kosslyn, Cave, Provost, & vonGierke, 1988). Studies have shown superior performance in native signers on tasks requiring the active generation of mental images, and it seems plausible that the repeated operation of this type of process during sign discourse might account for enhancements to these visuo-spatial functions (Emmorey, Kosslyn, & Bellugi, 1993).

Neurophysiological research has shown just how inseparable space and language are in signed communication. Unique right-hemisphere activations have been found during the processing of signed languages, suggesting that space is processed concomitantly with linguistic features and has an integral role within the message (Bavelier et al., 1997; Corina, 1998; Hickok et al., 1996; Soderfeldt et al., 1994). It is possible that such right-hemisphere activation is simply an artefact of reception in the visuo-spatial modality, engaging low-level processing by visuo-spatial areas, analogous to activation of the visual cortex in hearing people viewing unvoiced speech. However, research indicates that after a stroke, signers with right-hemisphere brain damage acquire subtle impairments to linguistic processing of prepositional and classifier structures as well as grammar that is specified on the face (Atkinson, Campbell, Marshall, Thacker, & Woll, 2003; Marshall, Atkinson, Thacker, & Woll, 2004).

Atkinson et al. (2004) argue that impairment of visuo-spatial cognition indirectly affects the processing of a relatively small subset of sign language structures that require higher order visuo-spatial processing. Interestingly, they found that signers with right-hemisphere damage were able to process neutral, unspecified classifiers, but when the classifiers were manipulated to represent real-world topographical relationships between objects they were markedly impaired. This finding suggests that classifiers are processed lexically by the left hemisphere, unless they possess true visuo-spatial properties, in which case the right hemisphere is called into play. Thus, although the right hemisphere does not have a primary role in the linguistic analysis of signs, it acts in concert with the left hemisphere when an interface between visuo-spatial and linguistic processing occurs.

Consequences of Sign Language Experience for Visuo-Spatial Working Memory

A number of studies have shown that deaf native signers outperform non-signers on WM tasks involving dynamic spatial information. Deaf signing children have enhanced memory for spatial locations, orientation, and movement, as shown by their superiority to hearing age-matched controls on the Corsi spatial span task (Wilson, Bettger, Niculae, & Klima, 1997). Deaf signing children are also better than hearing children at analyzing and recalling dynamic point light displays, such as Japanese Kanji figures (Poizner, Fok, & Bellugi, 1989). Deaf signers have been shown to outperform nonsigners on identifying the direction of movement in peripheral vision (Neville & Lawson, 1987), rapidly shifting visual attention from one spatial location to another (Parasnis & Samar, 1985), and scanning visual stimuli (Rettenbach & Diller, 1999). Taken together, these findings indicate that native experience with sign language produces significant enhancements to a number of visuo-spatial functions.

In face-to-face sign discourse, two individuals are usually positioned roughly opposite each other, such that each views the other's signing space as 180 degrees rotated. In BSL and other sign languages, topographical descriptions are routinely produced from the signer's own perspective, rather than from the perspective of the addressee. This presumably requires the addressee to perform something akin to a spatial transformation (e.g., a mental rotation of the space or an imagined shift of perspective), so that they can comprehend the spatial relations as if from the signer's perspective (Emmorey, Klima, & Hickok, 1998). Experimental data show that cognitive functions involving these types of spatial transformations are enhanced in native signers. Relative to hearing nonsigners, they are better at detecting mirror-image reversals (Emmorey et al., 1993) and are superior on tasks that involve 180-degree rotation in the horizontal plane (Emmorey et al., 1998). It is arguable whether signers perform these tasks via a mental rotation-type spatial transformation or (where the stimuli are sign movements) by invoking a submotor articulatory code, processing observed movements as if they themselves had produced them. Nonetheless, their facility for these types of functions stands in sharp contrast to the nonsigning population.

Another key difference between signed and spoken languages arises from the fundamentally simultaneous nature of the visuo-spatial modality (Penney, 1989). Unlike speech, which uses temporally sequenced strings of sounds, different components of signs can be produced concurrently. In sign language, grammatical constructions occur in parallel within space, rather than unfolding sequentially in time, so location and spatial organization fulfills the syntactic functions achieved in spoken language by serial word order. In relation to this, studies have demonstrated superior memory in deaf signers for simultaneously presented, as opposed to sequentially presented, stimuli. Todman and colleagues showed that deaf children outperformed hearing children on short-term memory for complex visual figures, *except when the stimuli were presented serially or demanded serial recall* (Todman & Cowdy, 1993; Todman & Seedhouse, 1994). Wilson et al. (1997) found that deaf signing children, although poorer on forward span tasks, outperformed hearing children on backward-recall tasks. Essentially, they showed no cost of reversal, performing equally well regardless of whether the material had to be recalled in forward or backward order. Such findings clearly have important implications for the use of serial recall paradigms for measuring short-term memory function, and we shall return to this issue later.

In sign language, semantic information is not only embedded within the four formational parameters, it is also conveyed by shoulder and head position, facial expression, and eye gaze. Meaning is transmitted not only in the movements of the hands, but also of the face. Facial expression can signal linguistic purpose—for example, to indicate that a question is being asked—while a shift in eye gaze to a specific location can signal allusion to a referent imaginally positioned within signing space. A number of studies have shown superior WM for faces in signers. Arnold and Murray (1998) found that recall of faces was better among deaf signers than among hearing signers, who were in turn better than hearing nonsigners. Likewise, enhanced discrimination of faces has been shown among ASL users (Bettger, Emmorey, McCullough, & Bellugi, 1997; McCullough & Emmorey, 1997). Much of the data indicate an increased sensitivity to facial features with communicative importance (especially the eyes and mouth, which are the areas used in signing), rather than enhanced global face processing. No increased recognition memory has been found for overall configuration of faces, only for the detection and discrimination of local features that perform grammatical functions. Once again, this cognitive advantage appears to be constrained by the demands of sign language.

Hearing native signers (hearing people with deaf parents, who are exposed to sign language from birth) have shown many of these enhanced visuo-spatial abilities, whereas deaf nonsigners have been found to perform at the same levels as hearing nonsigners on many of these tasks (Emmorey et al., 1993). This implies that it is experience with a visuo-spatial language, not lack of auditory input, that is responsible for these differences.

In summary, native experience with sign language enhances certain visuo-spatial WM functions. This conclusion has obvious implications for teaching and learning preferences among deaf signing children. Even in deaf children who do not sign, however, a greater reliance on visuo-spatial processing has been shown (Hermelin & O'Connor, 1973; O'Connor & Hermelin, 1972). This preference for the visuo-spatial modality, with its inherent sensory properties, is likely to favor representations that use simultaneous, spatially organized information over sequential or serial presentation. We return to this theme later in the chapter.

PHONOLOGICAL WORKING MEMORY IN DEAF CHILDREN

While verbal-sequential representations are viewed as fundamental to the operation of short-term memory in hearing people (Baddeley, 1986; Conrad & Hull, 1964), the unique nature of the deaf experience means that this assumption may not hold true for deaf people. Whereas hearing children rely primarily on phonological coding for serial recall, deaf children may recruit alternative strategies, such as visuo-spatial coding, to perform tasks traditionally associated with verbal WM.

Historically, researchers assumed that deafness *per se* gave rise to inferior short-term memory abilities across the board (Moores, 1996). Much of the support for this idea came from early memory research, with shorter serial recall spans reported for deaf participants in both speech and sign (Blair, 1957). Such findings were frequently used as support for oral education methods because it was noted that deaf children raised orally had longer memory spans for digits than deaf children raised in nonoral environments. Given what we now know about the efficacy of phonological coding for serial recall tasks, and the fact that signs have longer articulation times than words (leading to correspondingly lower memory spans under sign-based coding), this finding is not altogether surprising.

Somewhat later, researchers began to realize that not all deaf children represent information using the same underlying memory code. One early research program that was highly influential in establishing the diversity of WM processes in this population was a series of studies conducted by Conrad and colleagues with British deaf schoolchildren. Conrad's research examined the memory codes used by deaf students when processing written information. Using error analyses from immediate written recall of consonant sequences, he identified two major subgroups of deaf readers: one that relied primarily on phonological coding (preserving the phoneme–grapheme correspondences in written material) and another group of "nonarticulators", conceptualized by Conrad as using a primarily "visual code" (Conrad, 1970). Conrad's findings provided the important insight that the memory codes used by deaf children are not uniform and that understanding the type of code used by an individual child is crucial to finding appropriate methods to support learning and comprehension.

Further research into the phonological codes used by deaf children revealed that these were articulatory, rather than auditory, in nature. Experiments by Campbell and Dodd (1980) with hearing people showed that even silent, lipread lists left a trace in immediate memory, analogous to an "echo." The lack of sound in the input precluded the possibility of this being a strictly auditory phenomenon. Studies with deaf people revealed the same "echo" from lipread material (which did not exist with written material), once again suggesting an articulatory, rather than auditory, phenomenon (Dodd, Hobson, Brasher, & Campbell, 1983). In relation to this, a number of researchers have hypothesized that lipreading skill enhances the development of phonological coding by allowing deaf children to perceive the correspondence between lip patterns for similar sounds (Dodd & Hermelin, 1977). The articulatory nature of this code is further supported by the relationship between oral production skills and phonological indicators. Deaf people with good speech skills have demonstrated phenomena commonly associated with phonological coding, such as longer digit spans

(Lichtenstein, 1988), and sensitivity to regularity in letter strings (Hanson, 1986).

Findings such as these led to a reconceptualization of WM abilities in deaf children. Researchers concluded that memory span was not predicted by deafness *per se* but by the type of underlying memory code used on a given task. For example, Lichtenstein (1998) reported a positive correlation between memory span and number of errors on phonetically similar lists, a phenomenon that implies the use of a phonological code. Thus, in serial recall paradigms, children who use verbal-sequential coding outperform children who use an alternative (nonspeech–based) memory code. As Marschark and Mayer (1998) point out, although speech and sign are equally able to provide a natural communication mode for children (whether deaf or hearing), and both permit normal cognitive and linguistic development, differences in spoken language abilities affect memory span. The inherent advantage of using a phonological strategy on traditional tests of short-term memory, and other tests of cognitive abilities that implicitly tap sequential memory, may lead to underestimation of the abilities of children who use alternative strategies. The resulting assumption of inferior, rather than different, functioning is likely to have important implications for educational and assessment practice.

Another important issue is the prevalence of bilingual or mixed memory codes among this population. Findings from Lichtenstein (1998), Hamilton and Holzman (1989), and Kyle (1981) indicate that some deaf individuals use both sign- and speech-based coding in WM tasks. Research suggests that which code is used depends primarily on the demands of the task in question. One interesting theoretical question is whether these different memory codes have separable processing systems in WM. Early studies suggested that sign coding relied on visuo-spatial processes (Blair, 1957), but more recent research suggests an articulatory system that operates in a manner akin to the phonological loop component of WM (see "Working Memory for Signs" in this chapter). A number of studies have shown that memory span in deaf people is adversely affected by both oral *and* manual suppression tasks (MacSweeney, Campbell, & Donlan, 1996; Marschark, 1996). Furthermore, when the difference in articulation times between signed and spoken digits is controlled for, the difference in memory capacity for speech and sign diminishes (Wilson & Emmorey, 1997b). It is possible, therefore, that a single system is responsible for handling both types of memory code (speech and sign), in which case the phonological loop may not be modality limited but may consist of a common architecture that can support articulatory processes in both languages.

Whatever the underlying mechanisms, it is important to remember that speech-based codes permit more efficient serial span performance in both deaf and hearing participants. Although most deaf people use both sign and English codes to some extent, their uses vary across different situations, and this provides an interesting challenge for WM research.

Phonological Awareness and Reading Skills in Deaf Children

One area in which phonological coding is thought to have a major impact is literacy. Research with deaf children has repeatedly confirmed significant difficulties with reading (see Marschark, 1993, for a review), and the teaching of literacy skills is an ongoing challenge for educators of the deaf. Yet there is considerable individual variation, with some deaf children achieving well above the average, suggesting that such differences are not inevitable. A significant challenge for research is to disentangle the complex array of variables that affect literacy skills in deaf children.

Much of the evidence points to a strong relationship between phonological coding and reading skills. Hanson and Lichtenstein (1990) found a positive correlation between the ability to read well and the use of primarily speech-based codes in memory tasks (an indicator of phonological coding). Arnold and Kopsel (1996) showed that, for orally trained deaf children, reading ability was significantly correlated with lipreading skills.

Harris and Beech (1998) note that it is important to distinguish between *implicit* phonological awareness and *explicit* phonological awareness, or *phonemic* awareness. Implicit phonological awareness exists among prereaders and includes skills such as making similarity judgments about rhyming sounds and initial sounds in words, also known as *rime and onset*. Studies have shown that young children who are good at making such judgments at the syllabic or subsyllabic level make good progress in reading (at least in orthographically nonregular languages such as English; Lundberg, Frost, & Peterson, 1988). By contrast, explicit phonological awareness or phonemic awareness is the ability to recognize and manipulate phonemes within words. This skill is acquired through the process of learning to read.

As Harris and Beech (1998) point out, most studies of phonological coding have looked at deaf children who are already able to read. To explore the precursors of reading ability, they examined the relationship between implicit phonological awareness in prereaders and their progress in the first year of reading instruction. They used a pictorial test of rime and onset to measure implicit phonological awareness in deaf and hearing children. As expected, the hearing children scored higher as a group on this measure, but both groups showed a positive correlation between implicit phonological awareness and reading gain in the first year. Implicit phonological awareness was also correlated with oral ability (defined as clarity of articulation) among the deaf children. These findings indicate that pre-existing differences in such skills among young deaf children may be important predictors of early reading progress.[6]

---

[6]This finding may be partly driven by the generally audiocentric approaches used to teach reading, which focus on grapheme–phoneme correspondence. It is possible that alternative methods for teaching reading might show different predictors among deaf children.

Studies indicate that, for children who are deaf, the role of phonological coding in reading changes over time, with a shift toward phonemic awareness arising, as expected, from the process of learning to read. However, there is evidence that this developmental step occurs more readily in individuals with good speech production skills.

A number of studies have explored these processes using lexical decision tasks, in which a child has to decide whether a visually presented letter string is a real word or a fictitious pseudo-word. Younger deaf children undertaking these tasks are not affected by phenomena such as regularity (whether a letter string follows the implicit rules that characterize word construction in a given language) or pseudohomophones (items that sound like real words but are actually nonwords; Beech & Harris, 1997; Harris & Beech, 1995; Merrills, Underwood, & Wood, 1994). The fact that younger deaf children are unaffected by such phenomena suggests that they are not using phonological coding in reading—that is, their internal representation of the material does not preserve phoneme–grapheme correspondences. This finding concurs with the view that early deaf readers do not yet have phonemic awareness (although they may have *implicit* phonological awareness) and suggests that they are using nonphonological strategies to decode text. Ironically, as Merrills et al. (1994) point out, such direct, visually mediated orthographic processes are the same kinds of mechanisms that *skilled* hearing readers use to access the meanings of words. However, as they also acknowledge, in deaf children these mechanisms are "slower and less accurate than those of their hearing counterparts" (p. 365).

By contrast, older deaf children do show evidence of phonemic awareness during reading, suggesting that this facility can develop with age and experience. Dodd (1980) found evidence of regularity effects in deaf 14 year olds, suggesting that they were recoding the items phonologically (although the effect was still less marked than in age-matched hearing children). Similarly, Campbell (1992) found phonological similarity effects in short-term recall tasks with deaf adolescents, and Hanson, Goodell, and Perfetti (1991) demonstrated tongue-twister effects in a semantic judgment task. All of these findings suggest that deaf readers can acquire phonological coding, implying phonemic awareness. However, some studies have indicated that this function develops primarily in deaf children who have intelligible speech (Hanson, 1986). Given that such children have also been shown to have good implicit phonological awareness at an earlier age (Harris & Beech, 1998), it is possible that there is a continuity between the two processes, with one facilitating the development of the other.

The relationship between phonological coding and reading has led to an emphasis on oral skills in deaf education. Some authors, however, have questioned this traditional approach, arguing that the relative inaccessibility of phonological information makes such an emphasis unworkable for the majority of deaf children. Grushkin (1998) claims that, "deaf readers, like hearing readers, can and do use other strategies for word recognition that are not dependent on phoneme-grapheme relations" (p. 186). He argues for a paradigm shift in deaf education, advocating a whole word approach that emphasizes reading for meaning, "instead of forming connections between speech and print" (p. 193).

Certainly, phonological coding is not the only factor to predict reading ability. Several studies have identified a number of other variables that are consistently related to literacy skills. Studies from the United States have shown a relationship between fingerspelling and literacy (Hirsh-Pasek, 1987). Furthermore, children who come from Deaf families tend to achieve more academic success, and have better literacy skills, than deaf children of hearing parents. It is possible that this difference is at least partly the result of social–emotional factors linked to esteem and cultural acceptance. However, it is also the case that general differences in language competence, such as vocabulary development, are closely related to literacy skills because a breadth of language experience allows children to draw on their previous knowledge and make educated guesses when encountering novel words. In the Harris and Beech (1998) study described earlier, reading success was correlated not only with phonological awareness, but also with single-word language comprehension, which in turn was correlated with signing skills but *not* with oral skills. This finding indicates that general language abilities are important precursors of reading progress. Deaf children raised in signing environments are likely to have experienced greater breadth of vocabulary, by virtue of the perceptual accessibility of sign language, and this factor may account for the superior educational attainment commonly reported for deaf children raised in Deaf signing families.

This hypothesis is supported by findings from a large-scale study by Strong and Prinz (1997) involving 160 deaf children. They showed a positive correlation between signing skills and English literacy skills, which persisted even when both age and IQ (intelligence quotient) were controlled for. Using statistical techniques to examine a range of factors, they concluded that the most likely explanation was a beneficial effect of signing fluency on the development of English literacy, rather than a causal relationship in the opposite direction, or the attendant effects of confounding variables such as age or IQ. Furthermore, when ASL fluency was held constant, the traditional superiority in literacy skills of children from deaf families disappeared, suggesting that this difference is not merely an artefact of social–emotional factors but is primarily the result of relatively poorer signing (and therefore language) skills in deaf children of hearing parents. This finding reflects a generic benefit to learning and academic achievement from a strong first language foundation and suggests that early exposure to fluent signing may be as important for literacy as training in phonological skills.

IMPLICATIONS FOR PRACTICE IN EDUCATIONAL AND ASSESSMENT SETTINGS

Assessing Working Memory in Deaf Children

Attempts to measure cognitive functioning in deaf individuals are fraught with pitfalls. Potential difficulties include finding appropriate measures, the relevance of comparisons with hearing peers, and questions over appropriate methodologies for administering tests. These issues have significant implications for professionals seeking a fair and equitable way to assess the WM capabilities of deaf children.

In the past, deaf people have been labeled as cognitively and linguistically inferior to hearing people as a result of their relatively poor performance on standardized tests. It is now becoming clear, however, that many tests developed for use with hearing people are, for a variety of reasons, partly or wholly unsuitable for use with deaf participants. For example, many existing tests are audiocentric and languagecentric and use paradigms designed to elicit verbal-sequential coding, which is known to be an area of weakness in deaf people.

We know from historical experience with other minority populations that the misapplication of tests has social consequences that are potentially serious, both for individuals and for the population as a whole. Such inappropriate use of tests may have indirectly resulted from a traditional view of deaf people as "hearing" people with a "deficient" auditory sense (Lane, 1992). In sharp contrast to this philosophy, a number of authors have argued that deaf people are best conceptualized as "linguistically different, not deficient, resulting from a need to learn primarily through a modality and language different from English" (Grushkin, 1998, p. 180). On the basis of this perspective, it might be more appropriate to consider the cognitive *strengths* of deaf people when selecting measures of memory performance.

We have already mentioned one key difference between signed and spoken languages, which arises from the simultaneous nature of the visuo-spatial modality and the sequential nature of the vocal–auditory domain (Penney, 1989). Whereas speech entails serially ordered sounds that unfold sequentially in time, signs comprise concurrently produced components occurring in parallel within space. The superior memory among deaf signers for simultaneously presented stimuli probably arises from this difference (Todman & Cowdy, 1993; Todman & Seedhouse, 1994).

This clearly has implications for the deployment of serial recall paradigms for measuring short-term memory function. Deaf signing children, although at a disadvantage on serial recall tasks (such as traditional span tasks), may show equivalent or better memory for simultaneously presented information or under free recall conditions. Spoken language, however, confers a relative advantage to sequentially presented material even among deaf people, and this factor can produce inequitable comparisons between deaf children who may come to an assessment situation with differing degrees of oral training. Thus, it is important to consider the type of memory code that an individual is likely to use when selecting a measure of short-term memory and to have a range of measures available to tap different strengths.

One major issue for standardized tests is the validity of comparisons between deaf individuals and hearing norms for performance. There is a conspicuous lack of norms available for deaf populations. Among those tests that do provide them, the validity of the information is often dubious. Sample sizes are small, and there is little comparison between different deaf subgroups, such as signers and nonsigners, even though (as we have seen) this factor can influence WM functions. Even where deaf norms are available for standardized tests developed for hearing populations, construct validity is inevitably flawed because different psychometric properties are being tested in each population—that is, the test may not measure in deaf people what it claims to measure in hearing people (Maller, 2003).

Another concern is the matter of how well standardized tests can represent the huge diversity among deaf people. As we have said elsewhere, deaf children constitute an even more diverse population than hearing children, and such individual differences make it difficult to formulate absolute assertions about cognitive performance. Maller (1999) found that 35.5% of deaf children show unique cognitive profiles on the WISC III (Wechsler Intelligence Test for Children), compared with only 5% of hearing children. This finding not only reveals the greater diversity among the deaf population, but also suggests that the test does not measure the construct of intelligence in deaf children in the same way that it purports to in hearing children.

To obtain some recommendations for good practice in the arena of memory assessment, we carried out an informal survey of practicing educational and clinical psychologists who have extensive experience of working with deaf children. We asked these professionals for some general guidelines for good practice for administering standardized tests.

A general recommendation that came through universally was to use, where possible, nonverbal measures of memory. Deaf people often have a limited English vocabulary and have difficulties with syntax. Importantly for assessment, these common weaknesses occur independently of general cognitive functioning. It is therefore important that performance on any measure does not depend on verbal abilities, or it may substantially underestimate the individual's true level of functioning. Performance-based measures were universally recommended over verbal measures for this reason. Nevertheless, it is always important to critically evaluate precisely what kinds of cognitive functions are likely to be engaged by a given task. It should not be assumed, for example, that a test that is ostensibly nonverbal does not implicitly tap verbal abilities.

Another crucial point is to ensure that the deaf child understands all directions given. Even on performance-based measures, the use of verbal instructions, either written or spoken, could cause difficulties for deaf participants. However, where the test allows little departure from the standard administration procedure, any attempt to introduce other formats for instructions may introduce unpredictable issues for comparing performance with the normative sample. Adaptations to tests, such as signed instructions, translations from English to sign, or the use of interpreters, may render the tests nonequivalent. The issue of using interpreters is further complicated by the likelihood that the interpreter will not have expertise in psychometric testing procedures. It is therefore important to discuss the general aims and approach of the test, as well as individual test items, with the interpreter both before and after the assessment session, to identify potential misunderstandings that may need to be considered when interpreting the results. Such issues highlight the need for assessors who are skilled in both sign language and psychometrics. Unfortunately, few qualified educational and clinical psychologists in the United Kingdom are fluent in BSL.

It was recommended that standardized assessment scores and comparisons with norms should never be cited in reports without detailed caveats explaining the difficulties of accurate assessment of deaf children, and assessment results should be treated as a minimum benchmark of actual aptitude on a test. In addition, clinicians may consider collecting baseline data against which to measure improvement or deterioration in individual children.

Our informants were generally reluctant to make firm recommendations for standardized tests, largely because of a lack of validation with deaf samples (they added frequent cautions about the difficulties of administering such tests with deaf children). However, one test that has been rigorously validated for use with a deaf population is the individually administered Universal Nonverbal Intelligence Test (UNIT). Maller (2000) administered the UNIT to 104 deaf children aged 5–17 to assess whether any of the test items functioned differently for this population, relative to the standardization sample of hearing children. She examined four subtests of the UNIT: Symbolic Memory, Spatial Memory, Analogic Reasoning, and Object Memory. Maller found that none of the items exhibited differential item functioning, indicating that hearing status does not significantly affect test responses. This type of rigorous assessment is welcome, if relatively rare, because it provides an empirical basis for selecting appropriate and unbiased assessment instruments for deaf populations (although further replication of such findings is always desirable).

Issues for Teaching and Learning

The difficulties that many deaf children face with literacy skills are a perennial cause for concern among educators. Harris and Beech (1998) describe learning to read as "one of the most difficult educational tasks to confront children with a severe or profound hearing loss" (p. 205). Several different variables have been implicated in these difficulties, including both WM factors (such as phonological processing skills and memory span) and other, more broad-ranging linguistic abilities (such as vocabulary size or knowledge of discourse and syntactic rules). Although most educational methods focus on developing phonological skills in young deaf readers, some authors suggest that such approaches should be reassessed. Grushkin (1998) claims that "the search for a phonological basis in the reading skills of deaf individuals represents an ethnocentric perspective that is not entirely applicable or useful in the case of most deaf (and some hard of hearing) readers, due to the biological need of this population to relate to the world visually" (p. 186). As an alternative to the traditional emphasis on phonological methods, Grushkin (1998) advocates a whole-language approach to teaching reading and literacy skills. This paradigm deemphasizes phonology in favor of whole-word recognition through visual or orthographic processes. His approach emphasizes reading for meaning, rather than attempting to form associations between spoken and printed words.

Grushkin (1998) suggests a number of pedagogical activities that represent a shift away from a primary focus on grapheme–phoneme correspondence. He argues for the use of visual devices to increase vocabulary, such as color-coded word grids showing the semantic relationships between words. To help students use alternative (nonphonological) strategies for decoding meaning from text, he advocates activities such as teaching skills of inference and interpretation based on context and background knowledge, bringing common orthographic patterns to students' attention to increase their metacognitive awareness about language, and teaching about word origins and associated morpheme patterns. Grushkin's recommendations include practicing speeded word identification with orthographically similar words; using visuo-spatial devices (flowcharts, boxes, diagrams) to make sense of expository passages; identifying anomalous words intentionally inserted into texts; using fingerspelling as a link to the orthographic structure of written words when introducing new vocabulary; and learning new similarly spelled words to help students understand the importance of letter arrangement.

Although Grushkin's paradigm for teaching literacy remains largely untested, his general emphasis on using visuo-spatial methods in the classroom may have some validity. Converging evidence suggests that the visuo-spatial modality is likely to be the stronger suit for many deaf learners, and it therefore seems logical to use pedagogical methods that support visuo-spatial coding. Representational formats such as diagrams, flow charts, visual media, and the spatial organization of information are likely to be more accessible, and facilitate better understanding, than methods that require verbal sequential coding, such as dictation, rote or list learning, or reciting information aloud.

CONCLUSIONS

Research with deaf children has revealed a complex and varied picture of WM functioning, with many factors interacting to create a unique cognitive profile for each child. It should be noted, however, that much of the research is open to criticism. Many studies, especially those claiming to assess WM capacity, may not compare like with like, in terms of both stimuli and participants. When comparing deaf and hearing children a number of confounds are difficult to control, including the criteria on which these populations are matched, the comparability of printed and signed material, and fluency in language of presentation.

Overall, the literature supports an individual differences approach to understanding WM functioning in children who are deaf. Those with better speech skills, or who are orally educated, are likely to rely more heavily on phonological coding in memory tasks. By contrast, those who are less reliant on speech may use alternative strategies. Such differences in underlying memory codes give rise to differing patterns of performance on standardized tests and highlight the difficulty of establishing fair and equitable ways of assessing memory functioning. Quantitative and qualitative differences on memory tasks should therefore be carefully interpreted. While it is possible that they reflect different cognitive *capabilities,* it is equally plausible that they actually reflect different cognitive *preferences* or *strategies.* These two alternative interpretations have very different implications.

The question of memory capabilities in deaf children is a critical and recurring theme in the classroom. As one educational psychologist put it: "Memory is an issue we are often asked to assess because 'the child does not remember what he learned in class.' " Educators need to understand the confluence of factors that affect WM development in deaf children and appreciate how this in turn affects learning. Achieving these goals will help move away from past patterns of looking for deficits among deaf children and instead seek educational approaches that work with the cognitive strengths of each deaf child.

Summary Box

- Deaf children are not all alike. Many factors interact to create a unique cognitive profile for each child. Some writers argue that there is more variability in the deaf population than in the hearing population.
- Among the most important factors for WM development are as follows: degree of hearing impairment, age of onset (prelingual or postlingual), family environment (deaf or hearing), primary language mode (speech or sign), and schooling.

- Sign language is a true language form, and it is represented in WM via mechanisms analogous to those for speech. Early exposure to sign language gives rise to cognitive adaptations that permit the internal representation of signs.
- Sign language experience also produces adaptations to visuo-spatial WM. Many visuo-spatial functions are enhanced among deaf (and hearing) native signers, probably as a result of the spatial properties of the language.
- Literacy is often an area of difficulty for deaf children. Success in learning to read is moderated by (among other factors) phonological awareness and general language competence. Phonological awareness is correlated with better speech articulation and lipreading skills. General language competence is usually greater for children raised in fluent signing environments.
- Not all deaf children represent information using the same underlying memory code, and some deaf children have access to a variety of memory codes. Understanding the type of code used by an individual child on a given task is important for selecting appropriate methods for learning and assessment.
- Standard memory assessment techniques are often not appropriate for use with children who are deaf. Because of the heterogeneity of the deaf population, it can even be inappropriate to compare two deaf children on the same test.
- Teaching methods should seek to tap into a deaf child's strengths. Educational approaches that rely heavily on verbal sequential coding are generally less appropriate for deaf children.

Acknowledgments

Thanks to Clive Mason and Trudi Collier for demonstrating the signs shown in Figure 7.1 and to Davis Fretwell for help with manuscript preparation.

References

Arnold, P., & Kopsel, A. (1996). Lipreading, reading and memory of hearing and hearing-impaired children. *Scandinavian Audiology, 25(1)*, 13–20.

Arnold, P., & Murray, C. (1998). Memory for faces and objects by deaf and hearing signers and hearing nonsigners. *Journal of Psycholinguistic Research, 27(4)*, 481–497.

Atkinson, J., Campbell, R., Marshall, J., Thacker, A., & Woll, B. (2004). Understanding "not": Neuropsychological dissociations between hand and head markers of negation in BSL. *Neuropsychologia, 42(2)*, 214–229.

Atkinson, J., Marshall, J., Thacker, A., & Woll, B. (2002). When sign language breaks down: Deaf people's access to language therapy in the UK. *Deaf Worlds, 18*, 9–21.

Baddeley, A. D. (1986). *Working memory*. Oxford: Oxford University Press.

Baddeley, A. D., & Hull, A. (1979). Prefix and suffix effects: Do they have a common basis? *Journal of Verbal Learning and Verbal Behaviour, 18*, 129–140.

Bavelier, D., Corina, D. P., Jezzard, P., Padmanabhan, S., Clark, V. P., Karni, A., et al. (1997). Sentence reading: a functional MRI study at 4 Tesla. *Journal of Cognitive Neuroscience, 9(5)*, 664–686.

Beech, J. R., & Harris, M. (1997). The prelingually deaf young reader: A case of reliance on direct lexical access? *Journal of Research in Reading, 20(2)*, 105–121.

Bellugi, U., Klima, E., & Siple, P. (1975). Remembering in signs. *Cognition, 3(2)*, 98–125.

Bettger, J., Emmorey, K., McCullough, S., & Bellugi, U. (1997). Enhanced facial discrimination: Effects of experience with American Sign Language. *Journal of Deaf Studies and Deaf Education, 2(4)*, 223–233.

Blair, F. X. (1957). A study of the visual memory of deaf and hearing children. *American Annals of the Deaf, 102*, 254–263.

Campbell, R. (1992). Speech in the head? Rhyme skill, reading, and immediate memory in the deaf. In D. Reisberg (Ed.), *Auditory Imagery*. Hillsdale, NJ: Lawrence Erlbaum Associates.

Campbell, R., & Dodd, B. (1980). Hearing by eye. *Quarterly Journal of Experimental Psychology, 32*, 85–99.

Conrad, R. (1970). Short-term memory processes in the deaf. *British Journal of Psychology, 61(2)*, 179–195.

Conrad, R. (1972). Short-term memory in the deaf: A test for speech coding. *British Journal of Psychology, 63(2)*, 173–180.

Conrad, R., & Hull, A. J. (1964). Information, acoustic confusion, and memory span. *British Journal of Psychology, 55*, 429–432.

Conrad, R., & Rush, M. L. (1965). On the nature of short-term memory encoding by the deaf. *Journal of Speech and Hearing Disorders, 30(4)*, 336–343.

Corina, D. P. (1997). Sign language aphasia. In P. Coppens (Ed.), *Aphasia in atypical populations*. Hillsdale, NJ: Lawrence Erlbaum Associates.

Corina, D. P. (1998). Studies of neural processing in deaf signers: Toward a neurocognitive model of language processing in the deaf. *Journal of Deaf Studies and Deaf Education, 3(1)*, 35–48.

Corina, D. P., Poizner, H. P., Feinberg, T., Dowd, D., & O'Grady, L. (1992). Dissociations between linguistic and non-linguistic gestural systems: A case for compositionality. *Brain and Language, 43*, 414–447.

Dodd, B. (1980). The spelling abilities of profoundly prelingually deaf children. In U. Frith (Ed.), *Cognitive Processes in Spelling* (pp. 423–440). New York: Academic Press.

Dodd, B., & Hermelin, B. (1977). Phonological coding by the prelinguistically deaf. *Perception and Psychophysics, 21*, 413–417.

Dodd, B., Hobson, P., Brasher, J., & Campbell, R. (1983). Deaf children's short-term memory for lip-read, graphic and signed stimuli. *British Journal of Developmental Psychology, 1(4)*, 353–364.

Emmorey, K. (1996). The confluence of space and language in signed languages. In P. Bloom, M. Peterson, L. Nadel, & M. Garrett (Eds.), *Language and space* (pp. 171–209). Cambridge, MA: MIT Press.

Emmorey, K., Corina, D., & Bellugi, U. (1995). Differential processing of topographic and referential functions of space. In K. Emmorey & J. Reilly (Eds.), *Language, gesture, and space* (pp. 43–62). Hillsdale, NJ: Lawrence Erlbaum Associates.

Emmorey, K., Klima, E., & Hickok, G. (1998). Mental rotation within linguistic and non-linguistic domains in users of American Sign Language. *Cognition, 68*, 221–246.

Emmorey, K., Kosslyn, S. M., & Bellugi, U. (1993). Visual imagery and visual-spatial language: Enhanced imagery abilities in deaf and hearing ASL signers. *Cognition, 46*, 139–181.

Feldman, H., Goldin-Meadow, S., & Gleitman, L. (1978). Beyond Herodotus: the creation of language by linguistically deprived children. In A. Lock (Ed.), *Action, gesture and symbol: The emergence of language*. London: Academic Press.

Gardiner, J. M., Gathercole, S. E., & Gregg, V. H. (1983). Further evidence of interference between lipreading and auditory recency. *Journal of Experimental Psychology, 9*, 328–333.

Grushkin, D. A. (1998). Why shouldn't Sam read? Toward a new paradigm for literacy and the deaf. *Journal of Deaf Studies & Deaf Education, 3(3)*, 179–204.

Hamers, J. F., & Blanc, M. H. A. (1989). *Bilinguality and bilingualism*. Cambridge: Cambridge University Press.

Hamilton, H., & Holzman, T. G. (1989). Linguistic encoding in short-term memory as a function of stimulus type. *Memory & Cognition, 17(5)*, 541–550.

Hanson, V. (1982). Short-term recall by deaf signers of American Sign Language: Implications of encoding strategy for order recall. *Journal of Experimental Psychology: Learning, Memory and Cognition, 8(6)*, 572–583.

Hanson, V. L. (1986). Access to spoken language and the acquisition of orthographic structure: Evidence from deaf readers. *Quarterly Journal of Experimental Psychology, 38A*, 193–212.

Hanson, V. L., Goodell, E. W., & Perfetti, C. A. (1991). Tongue-twister effects in the silent reading of hearing and deaf college students. *Journal of Memory and Language, 30*, 319–330.

Hanson, V. L., & Lichtenstein, E. H. (1990). Short-term memory coding by deaf signers: The primary language coding hypothesis reconsidered. *Cognitive Psychology, 22(2)*, 211–224.

Harris, M., & Beech, J. R. (1995). Reading development in prelingually deaf children. In K. E. Nelson & Z. Reger (Eds.), *Children's Language* (Vol. 8, pp. 181–202). Hillsdale, NJ: Lawrence Erlbaum Associates.

Harris, M., & Beech, J. R. (1998). Implicit phonological awareness and early reading development in prelingually deaf children. *Journal of Deaf Studies & Deaf Education, 3(3)*, 205–216.

Hermelin, B., & O'Connor, N. (1973). Ordering in recognition memory after ambiguous initial or recognition displays. *Canadian Journal of Psychology, 27*, 191–199.

Hickok, G., Bellugi, U., & Klima, E. S. (1996). The neurobiology of sign language and its implications for the neural basis of language. *Nature, 381*(6584), 699–702.

Hirsh-Pasek, K. (1987). The metalinguistics of fingerspelling: An alternate way to increase reading vocabulary in congenitally deaf readers. *Reading Research Quarterly, 22*, 455–474.

Klima, E., & Bellugi, U. (1979). *The signs of language*. Cambridge, MA: Harvard University Press.

Kosslyn, S. M., Cave, C. B., Provost, D. A., & von Gierke, S. M. (1988). Sequential processes in image generation. *Cognitive Psychology, 20*, 319–343.

Krakow, R. A., & Hanson, V. (1985). Deaf signers and serial recall in the visual modality: Memory for signs, fingerspelling, and print. *Memory & Cognition, 13(3)*, 265–272.

Kyle, J. G. (1981). Signs and memory: The search for the code. In B. Woll, J. G. Kyle, & M. Deuchar (Eds.), *Perspectives in British Sign Language and deafness* (pp. 71–88). London: Croom Helm.

Kyle, J. G. (1994). Understanding bilingualism: Some applications to the development of deaf children. In J. G. Kyle (Ed.), *Growing Up in Sign and Word* (pp. 126–140). Bristol: Centre for Deaf Studies/Deaf Studies Trust.

Lane, H. (1992). *The mask of benevolence: Disabling the deaf community*. New York: Alfred A. Knopf.

Lane, H., Boyes-Braem, P., & Bellugi, U. (1979). A feature analysis of handshapes. In E. Klima & U. Bellugi (Eds.), *The signs of language* (pp. 164–180). Cambridge, MA: Harvard University Press.

Lichtenstein, E. H. (1998). The relationships between reading processes and English skills of deaf college students. *Journal of Deaf Studies & Deaf Education, 3(2)*, 80–134.

Locke, J. L., & Locke, V. W. (1971). Deaf children's phonetic, visual, and dactylic coding in a grapheme recall task. *Journal of Experimental Psychology, 89*, 142–146.

Lundberg, I., Frost, J., & Peterson, O. P. (1988). Effects of an extensive program for stimulating phonological awareness in preschool children. *Reading Research Quarterly, 23*, 263–284.

MacSweeney, M., Campbell, R., & Donlan, C. (1996). Varieties of short-term memory coding in deaf teenagers. *Journal of Deaf Studies & Deaf Education, 1(4)*, 249–262.

Maller, S. J. (1999). *The validity of WISC-III sub-test analysis for deaf children.* Paper presented at the Annual General Meeting of the American Educational Research Association, Montreal.

Maller, S. J. (2000). Item invariance in four subtests of the Universal Nonverbal Intelligence Test (UNIT) across groups of deaf and hearing children. *Journal of Psychoeducational Assessment, 18*(3), 240–254.

Maller, S. J. (2003). Intellectual assessment of Deaf people—A critical review of core concepts and issues. In M. Marschark & P. E. Spencer (Eds.), *Deaf Studies, Language and Education.* New York: Oxford University Press.

Marschark, M. (1993). *Psychological development of deaf children.* New York: Oxford University Press.

Marschark, M. (1996). *Influences of signed and spoken language on memory span.* Paper presented at the Annual Meeting of the Psychonomics Society (Nov 1996), Chicago.

Marschark, M., & Mayer, T. S. (1998). Interactions of language and memory in deaf children and adults. *Scandinavian Journal of Psychology, 39*(3), 145–148.

Marshall, J., Atkinson, J., Thacker, A., & Woll, B. (2004). Stroke in users of BSL: Investigating sign language impairments. In S. Austen & S. Crocker (Eds.), *Deafness in Mind: Working Psychologically with Deaf People Across the Lifespan.* London: Whurr.

Mayberry, R. I., Lock, E., & Kazmi, H. (2002). Linguistic ability and early language exposure. *Nature, 417* (6884, May 2002), 38.

McCullough, S., & Emmorey, K. (1997). Face processing by deaf ASL signers: Evidence for expertise in distinguishing local features. *Journal of Deaf Studies and Deaf Education, 2(4),* 212–222.

McGuire, P. K., Robertson, D., Thacker, A., David, A. S., Kitson, N., Frackowiak, R. S. J., et al. (1997). Neural correlates of thinking in sign language. *Neuroreport, 8,* 695–698.

Merrills, J. D., Underwood, G., & Wood, D. J. (1994). The word recognition skills of profoundly, prelingually deaf children. *British Journal of Developmental Psychology, 12*(3), 365–384.

Miles, D. (1988). *British Sign Language: A beginner's guide.* London: BBC Books.

Miller, G. A., & Nicely, P. E. (1955). An analysis of perceptual confusions among some English consonants. *Journal of the Acoustical Society of America, 27,* 339–352.

Moores, D. F. (1996). *Educating the deaf: Psychology principles and practices.* Boston: Houghton Mifflin.

Morford, J. P., & Mayberry, R. I. (2000). A reexamination of "early exposure" and its implications for language acquisition by eye. In C. Chamberlain & J. P. Morford (Eds.), *Language acquisition by eye* (pp. 111–127). Mahwah, NJ: Lawrence Erlbaum Associates.

Morgan, G., Herman, R., & Woll, B. (2002). The development of complex verb constructions in British Sign Language. *Journal of Child Language, 29*(3), 655–676.

National Deaf Children's Society (2002). *Deaf children: Positive practice standards in social services.* NDCS Report.

Neville, H. J., Coffey, S. A., Lawson, D. S., Fischer, A., Emmorey, K., & Bellugi, U. (1997). Neural systems mediating American Sign Language: Effects of sensory experience and age of acquisition. *Brain and Language, 57*(3), 285–308.

Neville, H. J., & Lawson, D. (1987). Attention to central and peripheral visual space in a movement detection task: An event-related potential and behavioral study: II. Congenitally deaf adults. *Brain Research, 405,* 268–283.

Newman, A. J., Bavelier, D., Corina, D., Jezzard, P., & Neville, H. J. (2002). A critical period for right hemisphere recruitment in American Sign Language processing. *Nature Neuroscience, 5(1),* 76–80.

O'Connor, N., & Hermelin, B. (1972). Seeing and hearing and time and space. *Perception and Psychophysics, 11,* 46–48.

Parasnis, I., & Samar, V. J. (1985). Parafoveal attention in congenitally deaf and hearing young adults. *Brain & Cognition, 4(3),* 313–327.

Parasnis, I., Samar, V. J., Bettger, J. G., & Sathe, K. (1996). Does deafness lead to enhancement of visual spatial cognition in children? Negative evidence from deaf nonsigners. *Journal of Deaf Studies & Deaf Education, 1(2),* 145–152.

Penney, C. (1989). Modality effects and the structure of short-term verbal memory. *Memory & Cognition, 17(4)*, 398–422.

Poizner, H., Bellugi, U., & Tweney, R. D. (1981). Processing of formational, semantic, and iconic information in American Sign Language. *Journal of Experimental Psychology: Human Perception and Performance, 7(5)*, 1146–1159.

Poizner, H., Fok, A., & Bellugi, U. (1989). The interplay between perception of language and perception of motion. *Language Sciences, 11*, 267–287.

Poizner, H., Klima, E. S., & Bellugi, U. (1987). *What the hands reveal about the brain*. Cambridge: MIT Press.

Rettenbach, R., & Diller, G. S., Ruxandra. (1999). Do deaf people see better? Texture segmentation and visual search compensate in adult but not in juvenile subjects. *Journal of Cognitive Neuroscience, 11(5)*, 560–583.

Shand, M. A., & Klima, E. S. (1981). Nonauditory suffix effects in congenitally deaf signers of American Sign Language. *Journal of Experimental Psychology, 7*, 464–474.

Siple, P. (1997). Modules and the informational encapsulation of language processes. In M. Marschark & P. Siple (Eds.), *Relations of language and thought: The view from sign language and deaf children* (pp. 163–171). London: Oxford University Press.

Soderfeldt, B., Ronnberg, J., & Risberg, J. (1994). Regional cerebral blood flow in sign language users. *Brain and Language, 46*, 59–68.

Stokoe, W. C. (1960). *Sign language structure* (Vol. 8). Buffalo: University of Buffalo Press.

Stokoe, W. C. (1978). *Sign language structure: The first linguistic analysis of American Sign Language* (Revised ed.). Silver Spring, MD: Linstock Press, Incorporated.

Stokoe, W. C. (2001). Deafness, cognition, and language. In M. Karchmer (Ed.), *Context, cognition, and deafness* (pp. 6–13). Washington, DC: Gallaudet University Press.

Strong, M., & Prinz, P. M. (1997). A study of the relationship between American Sign Language and English literacy. *Journal of Deaf Studies & Deaf Education, 2(1)*, 37–46.

Sutton-Spence, R., & Woll, B. (1999). *The linguistics of British Sign Language*. Cambridge: Cambridge University Press.

Tharpe, A. M., Ashmead, D. H., & Rothpletz, A. M. (2002). Visual attention in children with normal hearing, children with hearing aids, and children with cochlear implants. *Journal of Speech, Language, & Hearing Research, 45(2)*, 403–413.

Todman, J., & Cowdy, N. (1993). Processing of visual-action codes by deaf and hearing children: Coding orientation or M-capacity? *Intelligence, 17(2)*, 237–250.

Todman, J., & Seedhouse, E. (1994). Visual-action code processing by deaf and hearing children. *Language & Cognitive Processes, 9(2)*, 129–141.

Wilson, M., Bettger, J. G., Niculae, I., & Klima, E. S. (1997). Modality of language shapes working memory: Evidence from digit span and spatial span in ASL signers. *Journal of Deaf Studies and Deaf Education, 2(3)*, 150–160.

Wilson, M., & Emmorey, K. (1997a). A visuospatial "phonological loop" in working memory: Evidence from American Sign Language. *Memory & Cognition, 25(3)*, 313–320.

Wilson, M., & Emmorey, K. (1997b). Working memory for sign language: A window into the architecture of the working memory system. *Journal of Deaf Studies and Deaf Education, 2(3)*, 121–130.

Wilson, M., & Emmorey, K. (1998). A "word length effect" for sign language: Further evidence for the role of language in structuring working memory. *Memory & Cognition, 26(3)*, 584–590.

CHAPTER

8

Working Memory in the Classroom

SUSAN E. GATHERCOLE, EMILY LAMONT, AND
TRACY PACKIAM ALLOWAY

University of Durham

There have been many claims by cognitive psychologists that working memory (WM) plays a role in learning during childhood, supported by studies demonstrating close links between WM skills and measures of learning and academic achievement. An important shortcoming of this approach is that it does not illuminate how and why WM is needed in the everyday classroom activities that form the basis for learning. This is unfortunate because this is the information needed by teachers and other education professionals wishing to improve the learning outcomes for children with WM problems.

The aim of this chapter is to begin to redress this situation by investigating some of the ways in which WM may contribute to the process of acquiring knowledge and complex skills in school. Following a review of relevant research evidence, findings are reported from a study in which children with poor WM skills were observed in the course of their normal classroom activities. Activities that demand WM were found to be common in all classes observed and were particularly frequent in literacy and mathematics lessons. Children with poor WM skills experienced particular problems in carrying out complex tasks that required both memory storage and effortful processing such as writing and counting and in remembering instructions. They had difficulties in keeping track of their place in complex task structures, particularly when writing. Poor episodic memory for the relatively recent past was also observed in this group.

The possible psychological mechanisms linking WM failures to impairments in the acquisition of knowledge and complex skills are considered in this chapter. We also discuss the implications of these findings for classroom practice, and in particular for minimizing the learning difficulties that result from WM failures.

WORKING MEMORY AND EDUCATIONAL ACHIEVEMENT: A REVIEW

Over the past two decades cognitive psychologists have intensively investigated the possible causes of low educational achievement. A consistent finding from a large number of studies is a close relationship between children's performance on indicators of scholastic attainments and their WM skills. Young people with low scores on standardized assessments of reading and mathematics usually score poorly on complex memory span tasks that involve both the processing and temporary storage of verbal reading material (e.g., Bull & Scerif, 2001; de Jong, 1998; Gathercole & Pickering, 2000a; McLean & Hitch, 1999; Passolunghi & Siegel, 2001; Swanson, 1994). A typical example of such a task is listening span, in which the participant makes a judgment about the meaning of each of a series of spoken sentences and then attempts to recall in sequence the final word of each sentence.

Complex memory span tasks have been suggested to depend on WM. One popular view of WM is that it is a limited capacity system that operates as a kind of mental workspace in which material can be both processed and maintained (Case, Kurland, & Goldberg, 1982; Daneman & Carpenter, 1980; Engle, Cantor, & Carullo, 1992; Just & Carpenter, 1992). According to this view, activities that place heavy burdens on either processing or storage are likely to place excessive demands on limited resources and therefore will overload the system and result in task failure.

An alternative account is associated with the more detailed WM model of Baddeley and Hitch (1974), elaborated by Baddeley (1986, 2000). This model consists of three components. The central executive is an attentional system responsible for a range of regulatory functions including attention, the control of action, and problem solving. This component is supplemented by two limited-capacity slave systems. The phonological loop is a slave system specialized for the temporary storage of material that can be represented in a sound-based form. The visuo-spatial sketchpad stores and maintains visual or spatial information for brief periods. It has been suggested that, whereas the processing component of verbally based complex span tasks such as listening span is supported by the central executive, the storage needs are met by the phonological loop (Baddeley & Logie, 1999; Duff & Logie, 2001).

The learning problems associated with poor WM skills are substantial. In England, children with low scores on WM assessments have been found to perform poorly on national curriculum assessments at the ages of 7, 11, and

14 years (Gathercole & Pickering, 2000b; Gathercole, Pickering, Knight, & Stegmann, 2003; Jarvis & Gathercole, 2003). In some cases, the learning difficulties of children with below-average WM function are sufficiently severe to warrant special educational support in school (Alloway, Gathercole, Adams, & Willis, in press; Gathercole, 2002; Gathercole & Pickering, 2001; Pickering & Gathercole, 2004). More generally, many studies have shown that weak WM function is a characteristic of children with learning disabilities in literacy or numeracy or in both areas (Bull & Scerif, 2001; de Jong, 1998; Mayringer & Wimmer, 2000; Siegel & Ryan, 1989; Swanson, 1994; Swanson, Ashbaker, & Sachse-Lee, 1996).

What, then, is the underlying basis for the association between WM and learning? Two main types of explanations have been advanced and are represented in Figure 8.1. One possibility (Model 1) is that WM limitations result from difficulties in a particular processing domain. By this account, children with poor skills in processing spoken language may obtain low listening span scores because they are unable to meet the processing demands of listening to a sentence and making a semantic decision, and this leads to task failure. They would also be expected to struggle to learn to read as a consequence of their weak language processing skills. In this situation, neither the low listening span scores nor poor levels of academic achievement are a result of poor WM capacity *per se*; instead, they are both consequences of a primary language processing problem.

The evidence in support of this model is not compelling. Many studies have demonstrated that the relationships between WM measures and high-level cognitive skills such as reading and mathematics are not explicable simply in terms of the processing element of specific WM tasks (e.g., see Engle, Tuholski, Laughlin, & Conway, 1999, for a review). It appears that it is the general capacity of WM that is crucial, and not skill within a particular processing domain.

The alternative view (Model 2 in Figure 8.1) is that WM capacity directly constrains the ability to learn complex skills and to acquire knowledge. The detailed processes by which WM contributes to the acquisition of complex skills and knowledge during the school years are not, however, well understood. Statistical associations between WM assessments and outcome measures of learning (e.g., reading, mathematics) do not cast light on these processes because these measures tap the endpoints of scholastic attainment and thus provide no information regarding the nature of failed individual learning episodes that led to poor attainment levels.

The contribution of WM to mental arithmetic in particular has been investigated more directly using experimental methods. Consistent with the view that WM is used to support storage and processing in the course of mental arithmetic, mathematic calculations have been found to be more accurate when the numbers in the problem are visible throughout calculation, hence alleviating the WM burden (Adams & Hitch, 1997). Other studies have used dual-task procedures to impair selectively the operation of specific com-

Model 1   Model 2

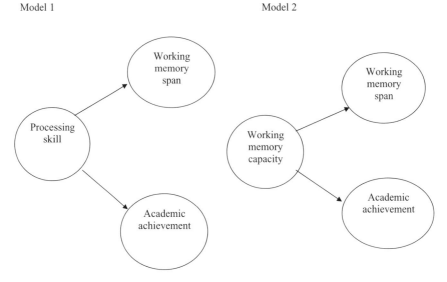

FIGURE 8.1
Alternative models of the relationship between working memory
and achievement.

ponents of WM during arithmetic calculations. This research has yielded strong evidence for central executive involvement in mental addition (De Rammelaere, Stuyven, & Vandierendonck, 2001; Furst & Hitch, 2000; Logie, Gilhooly, & Wynn, 1994) and for the contribution of the phonological loop to the storage of problem information (Furst & Hitch, 2000; Logie et al., 1994). The loop may also play a more specific role in supporting multiplication (Lee & Kang, 2002).

Although these studies provide valuable insights into how mental arithmetic may be limited by poor WM function, it should be noted that because participants were adults in most cases, the results reflect the cognitive processes involved in skilled mathematic functioning rather than the acquisition of mathematic skills. There have been no investigations, to our knowledge, either of the WM loads of real-life learning activities, or of the specific difficulties experienced by children with poor WM function in the classroom. This limits the practical applications of the substantial evidence that WM plays a crucial role in supporting the acquisition of knowledge and complex skills during the school years. To provide effective remedial support for children with poor WM skills, it is necessary to anticipate, alleviate, and compensate for these problems in school. These questions can only start to be answered effectively if the role of WM in the classroom is known.

OBSERVING WORKING MEMORY IN THE CLASSROOM

Our study investigated WM and learning directly, by observing and analyzing the WM constraints of routine classroom activities. The aim of the study was to bridge the gap between educational practice and the empirical evidence that WM is a conduit to academic learning during the school years, complementing the outcome-based studies that form the scientific foundations for the study. Our specific objectives were to provide a detailed analysis of the learning situations in which WM demands are sufficient to impair progress toward learning goals in some children and to begin identifying means by which the learning difficulties that may arise from poor WM function can be alleviated.

The WM demands of regular activities across the range of curricular and noncurricular activities in the course of a normal school week were observed in classes of 5- and 6-year-old children in four state primary schools in an urban area of northeast England. The observations focused on 3 boys who had been identified 1 year earlier as having poor WM test scores shortly after commencing full-time schooling, as part of a large-scale screening study of memory and more general cognitive function of children in reception classes (Alloway, Gathercole, Willis, & Adams, 2004). In what follows, the 3 children are referred to using the pseudonyms of David, Philip, and Joshua.

The children's scores on standardized ability tests are summarized in Table 8.1. Testing occasion 1 was the original screening study; at this time, the children's ages ranged between 4 years 10 months and 5 years 2 months. Testing occasion 2 took place between 9 and 12 months later, when the children were in year 1 classes. These children were selected on the

TABLE 8.1
Standardized Scores on the Cognitive and Behavioral Assessments, for Each Child

Area of Assessment	Test	Testing Occasion	David	Philip	Joshua
Working memory/	Backwards digit recall	1	56	71	56
central executive	Counting recall	1	67	70	70
	Listening recall	2	73	73	55
Phonological loop	Nonword recall	1	98	78	86
		2	89	85	89
	Word recall	1	92	108	81
		2	101	101	105
	Digit recall	1	97	83	86
Nonverbal ability*	Object assembly	1	7	10	8
	Block design	1	11	5	8
		2	11	5	9

*Scaled scores (mean = 10, SD = 3).

basis of low scores on the first occasion (=>2 *SD* below the mean) on 2 complex span measures (Backward Digit Recall and Counting Span) from the Working Memory Test Battery for Children (WMTB-C; Pickering & Gathercole, 2001). Their average standardized scores on 3 phonological loop measures (the Children's Test of Nonword Repetition, Gathercole & Baddeley, 1996; Word List Recall and Digit Recall from the WMTB-C) fell within 1 *SD* of the mean. The mean scaled scores on 2 performance sub-tests (block design and object assembly) of the Wechsler Preschool and Primary Scale of Intelligence—Revised (WPPSI—R; Wechsler, 1990) fell within a standard deviation of the population mean for each child.

Each child was observed in the course of normal classroom activities for 3 or 4 days. At the end of this period, the children were reassessed on 2 phonological loop tests and 1 complex span test from the Working Memory Test Battery for Children. They were also given the block design test of the WPPSI—R. Test scores on this second testing occasion are shown in Table 8.1. In addition, the class teachers rated the children's behavior using the Conners' Rating Scale for Teachers (Conners, 1997), a measure devised to detect attentional problems. Responses are scored on 4 scales—opposi-tional, cognitive problems/inattention, hyperactivity, and the Conners' ADHD (attention deficit/hyperactivity disorder) index.

The aim of the observations was to identify the learning situations in which the WM demands have detectable consequences on a child's ability to complete a task satisfactorily. The observer was seated in a position allow-ing a clear view of the target child but in a location that did not disrupt ongoing individual and group activities and that did not alert the child to the ongoing observation. Observations were recorded in note form at the time of observation. The following operational definition of WM demands was adopted to guide the observations:

> The requirement of temporary mental storage, or temporary storage combined with ongoing processing, that is sufficiently demanding to lead, on occasion, to failures to complete target activities.

Although the primary focus of the observer was the target child, WM loads in other classroom activities that did not include the target child were also observed and recorded where possible. Note was also taken of methods used spontaneously by the child, teacher, or any other person to alleviate the WM demands of specific activities, with the aim of identifying good practice where possible.

Profiles

Characteristics of the behavior of each child and his or her performance on cognitive assessments are provided in the following. The behavioral profiles of the children are based both on teacher reports and the observer's own impressions of the academic and social functioning of each child.

David

David's scores on the complex memory span tests fell considerably below the population mean at the times of both the original assessments of Backwards Digit Recall and Counting Recall at 4 years of age and the Listening Recall test at 5 years. Performance on phonological loop measures was normal for age at both points in time, as was David's performance on the nonverbal ability tests. Scores on the Conners' Teaching Rating Scale (Conners, 1997) indicated significant attentional difficulties on one scale, Cognitive Problems/Inattention. According to the test material, high scorers on this scale may be inattentive, have more academic difficulties than most individuals of their age, have problems organizing their work, have difficulty completing tasks or schoolwork, and appear to have trouble concentrating on tasks that require sustained mental effort.

David was a reserved, well-behaved child who was observed to be reasonably well-liked by his classmates. He rarely contributed to class discussions unless asked directly and was generally reticent about offering information. At the time of observation he was placed in the lowest ability group in the class for numeracy. In literacy he had just been moved up from the lowest ability group to the next group up to minimize contact with another child who was considered to be a bad influence.

Joshua

Joshua performed very poorly on the complex memory span measures on both occasions, but he scored within the normal range on the phonological loop tests. His performance on the nonverbal ability tests was also normal for age at both times of testing. Joshua's scores on the Conners' Rating Scale for Teachers identified no significant behavioral problems.

Joshua was observed to be a quiet child who was obedient in the classroom and was well-liked by his peers. He had a characteristic style of responding slowly in all tasks. Joshua often failed to follow general class instructions and required frequent reminders. His teacher described him as being in a world of his own. During observation he rarely contributed to class discussions and, at the time of observation, was in the lowest ability groups in both numeracy and literacy. Joshua frequently showed overt signs of frustration, including pulling faces and banging his head with his hands, during activities at which he was struggling.

Philip

Philip obtained very low scores on all three assessments of complex memory span, with phonological memory scores falling within the average range. Philip's performance on the object assembly test from the WPPSI was normal for his age, although he did perform at low levels on the block design test on both testing occasions.

Philip had a very pleasant and cheery personality. He was well behaved and popular in his class. His performance was poor in the areas of both numeracy and literacy and, at the time of observation, was in the lowest ability group in literacy. He frequently became frustrated by the difficulties that he experienced, particularly in writing. Philip did not often participate in class discussions, and on several occasions he was observed to be unable to respond even after he had raised his hand in response to a question by the teacher. Philip showed awareness of his memory problems, making comments such as, "I forget everything, me." No behavioral problems were identified for Philip on the Conners' Rating Scale for Teachers.

Observed Memory Failures

David, Joshua, and Philip struggled in many of their classroom activities, reflecting their generally low levels of academic ability. Task failures that appeared to be the result in part, at least, of failure to meet the WM demands of the situation were observed in all three cases and were particularly common in the daily numeracy and literacy sessions. These failures were many times more common than those observed in two further children selected on the basis of very poor phonological short-term memory but normal complex memory span performance. The main categories of memory-related failure observed in David, Joshua, and Philip are described in the following.

Forgetting Instructions

The most commonly observed memory-related failure in all three children was an inability to follow instructions from the teacher. This failure appeared to be the result of forgetting the content of the instruction, particularly when it was fairly lengthy and did not represent a routine classroom activity. Some examples are provided in the following.

> *"Put your sheets on the green table, put your arrow cards in the packet, put your pencil away and come and sit on the carpet."*

David failed to put his sheet on the green table. The teacher asked David if he could remember where he was supposed to put it; he could not and needed reminding.

> *"Put your arrow cards in their packets and come and sit in a circle on the floor."*

David put the cards away and then sat at his desk with arms folded.

> *"Can you collect the books in from the yellow and green table, please, and put them on the shelf?"*

Having collected the books, Joshua had to ask where to put them.

Joshua was handed his computer login cards and told to go and work on computer number 13. He failed to do this because he had forgotten which computer he had been told to use.

Philip was asked to go back and put an "n" in the word *bean*. He went back and asked the classroom assistant what he had been asked to do.

In each of these instances, the child has to process linguistic information that includes some fairly arbitrary content. Such material has been found to place substantial demands on short-term memory, which is needed to support off-line linguistic analysis (Baddeley & Wilson, 1994). Poor short-term memory capacity would be expected to lead to failures to process such instructions adequately and may explain the difficulties experienced by each of these children in grasping the structure of many classroom activities.

Failing to Cope with Simultaneous Processing and Storage Demands

David, Joshua, and Philip all frequently struggled in structured activities whose successful completion involved engaging in a relatively demanding processing activity at the same time as storage of information. Many of these activities involved counting. Although all three children were capable of counting accurately in the context of a simple task, many classroom activities combined counting with other cognitive processes. One frequent activity in literacy sessions involved counting the numbers of words in a sentence, often prior to writing the sentence down. Joshua was unable to recall the sentence, isolate each word, and count it without assistance from the teacher. A group activity in Philip's class was to count the number of sentences in a text. Philip was unable to keep track of the tally number while reading aloud the text. In both cases, the task failure appeared to result from combining the memory demands of counting (keeping track of the tally number) in the context of a concurrent and fairly demanding processing activity. ▬

There was frequent use in each classroom of number aids, designed to facilitate children's grasp and mastery of counting and basic arithmetic. Examples included number lines, number fans, and "Unifix" blocks. In each case, the device provides a means of representing number physically. The children in the low WM group struggled to take full advantage of the support potentially provided by these number aids. Number lines are designed to facilitate counting by allowing the child to jump one step at a time from a starting number. Joshua was encouraged to use a number line when counting up the number of ducks shown on two cards, but he struggled to coordinate the act of jumping along the line with counting up to the second number. He abandoned the attempt, solving the sum instead by counting up the total number of ducks on the two cards. Similarly, Philip was observed to choose not to use the number line when available; instead he counted on his fingers.

In both cases, the unfamiliar activity of counting along the points of the number line to a stored target number appeared to impose a greater WM load than simple counting of the physical events.

Further failures were observed in tasks that involved the detection of target items in spoken or written text. These tasks imposed significant processing demands (analysis and comprehension of spoken language, or text reading) in conjunction with the storage of multiple items. For example, the children in Joshua's class were asked to identify the rhyming words in a text read aloud by the teacher. They had to wait until all four lines had been read before telling the teacher the two words that rhymed: *tie* and *fly*. This task involves matching the sound structures of a pair of words and storing them. Joshua was unable to do this. A related activity in David's class involved the teacher writing number sequences on the white board with some numbers missing. She counted the numbers aloud and asked the class what numbers she had left out. In each case, there was more than one number missing (e.g., 0, 1, 2, 4, 5, 7, 8). Here, the child had to use his or her number knowledge to identify each missing number and store them. David was unable to tell the teacher which numbers she had missed out on any of the occasions.

All of the tasks discussed here share the common feature of imposing significant processing demands on the child at the same time as creating a storage load. In themselves, the storage loads do not appear to be particularly excessive. In the case of counting-based activities, the child simply has to retain the tally number and sometimes the target number to which he must count, and, in the examples of the detection tasks supplied listed previously, the child had only to store two items in each case. In isolation, it seems likely that the child would be able to meet these storage requirements without difficulty. The task failures appear to arise from the combining storage with the significant processing demands of the task. These task features are, of course, also shared by the complex memory span tasks on which David, Joshua, and Philip scored so poorly and have been strongly associated with general WM capacity.

Losing Track in Complex Tasks

David, Joshua, and Philip experienced marked difficulties in writing a sentence either generated by the child himself or provided by the teacher. The task structure of writing a sentence accurately consists of a hierarchy involving three levels—letters, words, and the sentence. If the sentence is internally generated by the child or spoken by the teacher, its surface form needs to be maintained to guide the writing of the words and their individual letters, and the child has to keep track of the position in the sentence while writing. If the task involves copying a sentence, the burden of sentence representation in WM is reduced, but the child still needs to keep track of his position while writing.

Two types of failure were observed in writing. The first type of error involved the child forgetting either some or all of the sentence content. This was relatively easy to identify because it was common practice for teachers to check with children in lower-ability groups if they were able to repeat the sentence before beginning to write it. David, Joshua, and Philip all demonstrated on occasion that they were unable to do this. The second type of error involved the child losing track of his position in the sentence. This resulted in omission of words, repetition of words (when the child forgot that the word had already been written), intrusion of words that were not in the target sentence, and (frequently) abandonment of the task.

David provided an example of both types of writing failure when he was working with his teacher and the rest of the low-ability group. The teacher decided that the children should write "He had 36 barrels of gunpowder." The sentence was repeated until the children appeared to remember it. David successfully wrote "he" and "had" and then could not remember what to write next. The teacher asked him to read what he had already written and then to say what word came next, but he could not. The teacher reminded him of the sentence. David then got stuck after writing several letters of the word "gunpowder," attempted and failed to get the teacher's attention to help him, and then forgot that the word needed completing.

A further example of a place-keeping error was provided by Philip. The teacher wrote on the board "*Monday 11th November*" and underneath, "*The Market*," which was the title of the piece of work. Philip lost his place in the laborious attempt to copy the words down letter-by-letter, writing "*moNemarket*." It appeared that he had begun to write the date, forgot what he was doing, and began writing the title instead.

One of the reasons that place-keeping failures were particularly common in the WM group even when copying from a board or card was that the children wrote the letters on a one-by-one basis rather than in a larger group or word. This strategy presumably reflected the children's poor knowledge of spelling patterns, reducing the opportunity for chunking letter groups. As a consequence, the child had to remember not only his place in the word sequence of the sentence, but the letter sequence of each word. Effectively, this means that the children with low WM skills were working with a more complex task structure (a hierarchy involving three levels of unit—letter, word, and sentence) than more able children for whom task hierarchies were reduced to two levels (word and sentence), imposing a commensurately greater place-keeping load.

Episodic Forgetting

The main focus of the observations was on task failures that may have been the result of excessive WM loads for this group of children. Longer-term memory failures were, however, also frequently observed in this group, with all three children failing on several occasions to remember information that they had encountered in an earlier activity in the day. Memory for specific events in the relatively recent past is known as "episodic memory" (Tulving, 1983) and traditionally represents a functionally distinct system from WM or short-term memory (Baddeley & Warrington, 1970).

The following examples illustrate the poor episodic remembering of the three children. David's teacher discussed bonfire night and read the story of Guy Fawkes to the class. When David was asked, "*What might you see in the sky tomorrow night?*" he failed to answer *fireworks*. He was also unable to say what Guy Fawkes planned to do, even after writing the sentence in answer to the question. Similarly, in a class activity involving the teacher and class together reading from a big book, Joshua was unable to answer any questions asked about the text.

A number of episodic memory failures were also observed for Philip. For example, he failed to remember the three vegetables that a character had bought in a book read by the class together. As reported earlier, Philip showed considerable awareness of his poor memory abilities. When the teacher told them to learn their spellings that night ready for a test the next day, Philip responded by slapping himself on the forehead and saying, "*If I remember!*"

These observations raise the interesting possibility that episodic memory is based in part at least on records from the more temporary storage systems corresponding to WM. Baddeley (2000) has made a similar suggestion based on the identification of a new component of WM, the episodic buffer. The function of the buffer is to integrate multiple sources of memory information, effectively binding representations from different modalities and representational domains (e.g., other components of WM as well as more durable memory systems) in a way that may generate the experience of consciousness. Furthermore, Baddeley suggested that the episodic buffer is linked to episodic memory. The current observations of frequent episodic forgetting in children with poor WM function fit well with this proposal.

Other Observations

Despite their contrasting personalities, there were a number of interesting commonalities in the classroom behavior of David, Philip, and Joshua. First, all three children were reserved in group and class discussions, rarely volunteering information or raising their hand in answer to questions. This was notable particularly in the case of Philip, who was outgoing and humorous by nature in more informal social interactions. Because teachers often asked the children questions about recent activities as part of these discussions, it is possible that the poor episodic remembering of these children (possibly resulting from a primary problem in WM) prevented them from participating in these exercises.

A further similarity between all three children was their preference for simplifying tasks where possible. An example of this was provided earlier for Philip, who would not use a number line to add the two numbers corresponding to the number of ducks on two cards together. Instead, he counted the ducks individually. It was argued that in doing so Philip was avoiding the additional processing load involved in jumping along a number line a specific number of times (which had to be stored). His preference was for simple counting of physical objects—a more highly practiced activity that imposes reduced processing and storage loads.

Joshua also demonstrated a tendency to simplify tasks in a way that was likely to reduce memory loads. Children in his class were taught a five-stage process for learning spellings, known as "look, say, cover, write, check." Joshua avoided the memory test element of this procedure of covering the spelling and chose instead simply to copy the word down a second time with the target word in full view.

It is notable that in both of the examples, the learning benefits associated with the specified learning activity are likely to be reduced by the children's simplification of the tasks. Joshua's choice not to cover the original spelling when copying the word a second time is likely to have prevented him from valuable retrieval practice and the subsequent opportunity for self-correction in the case of an error. In the case of Philip, his dependence on simple counting rather than use of an external memory aid would potentially have increased the WM load of the task. It is possible that the tendency to simplify complex tasks reflects the children's avoidance of situations in which they lose their place in task hierarchies. Paradoxically, the consequence for the child is likely to be increased, rather than reduced, rates of learning failure.

LEARNING IS BASED ON SUCCESS

In the previous sections we described some of the learning failures observed in common classroom activities that can be attributable failures of WM resulting from excessive memory demands of the tasks or from the very poor WM capacities of some children. Could these failures underlie the difficulties experienced by some children in making normal educational progress through the school years? Certainly, the poor performance on WM assessments of David, Philip, and Joshua predated their failures to progress normally in the crucial scholastic domains of literacy and numeracy.

Some insight into why classroom failures may compromise learning in this way is provided by research comparing learning under conditions where errors are prevented ("errorless learning") with learning in situations in which the participant learns by trial and error ("errorful learning"). Studies of individuals with memory deficits resulting from acquired brain damage have consistently shown a substantial benefit to errorless learning (e.g., Baddeley & Wilson, 1994; Clare, Wilson, Carter, Roth, & Hodges, 2002; Parkin, Hunkin, & Squires, 1998). One explanation for this finding is that responses in specific situations are based on long-term memories from previous related episodes. The probability of a correct response being generated in a particular situation is, therefore, greater if the participant has consistently made correct responses in the past than if prior responses were inconsistent.

This analysis may provide a simple explanation for why children with poor WM abilities experience difficulties in learning during the school years. The frequent WM-related errors that these children were observed to make in the course of complex learning activities may have impeded their chances of acquiring crucial skills in the domains of literacy and numeracy because they prevented the successful completion of relevant tasks. Task errors and failures to complete target activities constitute exactly the type of errorful learning situations previously shown to compromise learning achievements. If a child has poor WM, it is therefore extremely important to minimize chances of task failure resulting from WM overload.

IMPLICATIONS FOR CLASSROOM PRACTICE

To manage WM loads effectively in the course of classroom activities, it is important to be aware of the memory capacities for that age group. It is not in the interests of the smooth running of the classroom that children engage in activities in which many of them will fail because of excessive memory demands. This situation will result in frequent requests by children for reminders that will disrupt the lesson and also in some children abandoning activities because they cannot remember what is required of them. These situations represent lost learning opportunities.

The data plotted in Figure 8.2 are taken from the standardization data for the Working Memory Test Battery for Children (Pickering & Gathercole, 2001; see also Gathercole, Pickering, Ambridge, & Wearing, 2004). This battery provides multiple assessments of each of the main components of the Baddeley & Hitch (1974) WM model and is suitable for use with children aged 4–15 years of age (see Chapter 9 for a detailed description of this test). Phonological loop assessments include Digit Recall, Word List Recall, Nonword List Recall, and Word List Matching. Visuo-spatial tests are Block Recall, Visual Patterns Test (Della Sala, Gray, Baddeley, & Wilson, 1997), and Mazes Memory. Central executive measures are Listening Recall, Counting Recall, and Backward Digit Recall. The data points were obtained by calculating z-scores for each subtest across the standardization sample as a whole and then averaging the scores across different subtests tapping each component of WM to produce composite scores.

The figure shows that WM capacity develops steadily across the primary and secondary school years. Children's abilities to cope with the memory demands of particular activities will therefore depend very much on their age. The likelihood of WM-related failures is greatest in the early school

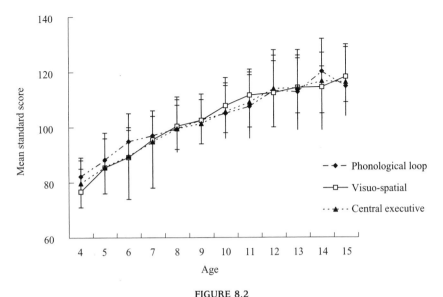

FIGURE 8.2

Mean standard scores as a function of aspect of working memory, with 10th and 90th centiles.

years, diminishing gradually in older age groups. As a rule, most children's scores on WM assessments are close to those of the average adult by 14 years of age. At the age of 6 years, they are approximately half of this on measures associated with the central executive and visuo-spatial sketchpad and about three-fourths of this on measures of the phonological loop. This marked reduction in WM capacity in younger children should be borne in mind when planning their learning activities.

It is also important to recognize that some children in a class will have much poorer WM than others. There is a substantial degree of individual variability in WM abilities, as demonstrated by the difference between 10th and 90th centile plots in Figure 8.2. A typical class of 9-year-old children is therefore likely to include individuals whose WM capacities vary from that of the average 7–12 year old.

We now turn to the issue of when one might consider the possibility of a WM deficit in a child who is failing to progress well in class. The case studies reported here give some indication of the behavioral and cognitive profiles that are associated with WM deficits. The children we observed did not usually exhibit overt behavioral problems, and they showed reasonable social adjustment. They were, however, reserved in school and unwilling to participate in class discussions. In all aspects of the classroom, they often had difficulties following instructions that involved unfamiliar or arbitrary sequences of actions. Their learning difficulties were manifest in frequent failures to complete activities involving significant cognitive processing loads in the course of more complex tasks involving memory storage. Examples include attempting to spell an unfamiliar word while writing a sentence from memory and carrying out a numeric calculation abstracted from a question expressed in everyday language. In these situations, children with poor WM function are likely to lose their place in the complex task structure, resulting in frequent repetitions, place-skipping, or task abandonment.

WM deficits are not easy to detect on the basis of informal contact alone and can easily be misclassified either as attentional problems or more pervasive cognitive impairments. Comments made to us by teachers about children with poor WM abilities include: *"He doesn't seem to listen to what I say"* and *"It's in one ear and out the other."*

A notable finding of our observational study was that children seem to be capable of considerable insight into their memory failures. Philip, a child with very poor WM function, commented to the classroom assistant, *"I forget everything, me!"* On other occasions, we observed failures that were likely the result of high WM demands in children with normal WM skills for their age. One child was given a long series of task instructions by her teacher and failed to complete the activity. When asked why, she commented, *"Mrs. McGregor told me a lot and I forgot."* In another class-based activity in which children had to clap one more time than the preceding child in a circle, many children failed to clap the correct number of times. Two children spontaneously exclaimed, *"I forgot the number!"* One valuable strategy for identifying children with WM problems may therefore be, quite simply, to ask them why they have failed in a particular activity: Insight appears to be reliable.

In considering the possibility that a child has a WM deficit, it is worth bearing in mind that there are a number of crucial differences in the behavioral and cognitive profiles associated with poor WM, attentional problems, and general cognitive deficits. First, children with low WM usually score in the normal range on systematic assessments for attentional deficits or show problems only related to inattention. The nature of the link between ADHD and WM is not yet completely clear (as indicated in Chapter 6 of this book). Children with low WM do not seem to have the problems of social integration with peers that are characteristic of ADHD. Second, individuals with general cognitive impairments are distinguished by across-the-board deficits in cognitive tests that include both WM and nonverbal ability measures, and they show comprehension problems. In contrast, children with poor WM perform at normal levels on nonverbal assessments and are less likely to have problems with comprehension.

The best way to identify WM deficits is to assess them directly using tests standardized for use with children (e.g., the Working Memory Test Battery for Children). When assessing WM capacity, it is important to use a number of tasks with varying processing demands. This is necessary to determine whether a low WM score is the result of a processing impairment in a particular domain or a more general decrement in WM capacity. For example, some children have specific difficulties with numbers. These individuals inevitably will score very poorly on WM tasks that involve counting as the processing activity (as in the case of Counting Recall, for example) because the level of task difficulty will be higher for them than for other children. In these cases, a low counting span score may reflect a specific counting problem rather than a general WM deficit. To distinguish between these two possibilities, it is necessary to test the child on other WM tasks that do not tax the same processing activity. Listening Recall, in which the processing activity involves making a decision about a spoken sentence, would be a good alternative measure. A child with poor WM capacity would be expected to score poorly on this task, too, whereas a child with only a counting problem would not.

Minimizing Working Memory Failures in Learning Situations

Once it has been detected that a child has poor WM abilities, the next step is to identify the learning activities that will place heavy memory demands. There are two broad classes of WM-loaded activities. In the first, the child has to store a considerable amount of material that may be arbitrary in structure (such as a series of numbers or the precise wording of a fairly lengthy sentence). The second type of activity involves the child storing material while being engaged in another activity that is demanding for him or her (such as spelling or reading a new word or making an arithmetic calculation).

In the following section we discuss ways of managing and reducing the WM demands of such learning situations. Some of these methods are based on good practice by teachers and classroom assistants observed in the course of our study. Other techniques have been derived from current understanding of the cognitive processes of WM. We recommend a remedial approach for children with WM deficits that combines multiple methods as appropriate for particular learning situations. In each case, the aim is to reduce the frequency of occasions in which the child fails a learning activity and so misses a crucial learning opportunity because he or she is unable to meet the WM demands of the situation.

Ensure That the Child Can Remember the Task

To achieve learning success, it is crucial that the child can remember the task set by the teacher. The child's memory for instructions will be enhanced by keeping the instructions as brief and linguistically simple as possible. Because instructions that are too lengthy will not be remembered, it is advisable to break them down into smaller constituents where possible. This will also have the advantage of reducing task complexity, another factor influencing learning success in children with low WM (see later).

One effective strategy for improving memory for task instructions is frequent repetition of instructions. For tasks that take place over an extended time period, reminding of crucial information rather than repetition of the original instruction is likely to be most useful. Probably the best way to ensure that the child has not forgotten crucial information is to ask them to repeat it back. Children have good insight into their WM failures and are able to say they have forgotten if given the opportunity. It has also been shown that attempting to remember information boosts memory performance on subsequent retrieval attempts.

Use External Memory Aids

The child's performance in activities that have a complex structure, or that impose significant processing as well as storage loads, will be aided by the use of external memory aids. These are already in widespread usage within many classrooms. They include number aids such as "Unifix" blocks and number lines that are designed to reduce processing demands.

However, it was apparent in our observational study that children with poor WM function often choose not to use such devices in the context of relatively complex tasks and gravitate instead toward lower-level strategies whose processing requirements may be lower (such as simple counting) but less efficient (e.g., more error-prone and time-consuming). To encourage children's uptake of such aids, we recommend regular periods of practice in the use of the aids in the context of simple activities.

Relevant spellings also function as useful memory aids in writing activities. Reducing the processing load and opportunity for error in spelling individual words will increase the child's success in completing the sentence as a whole. However, reading off information from such external aids was observed, in itself, to be a source of error in children with low WM skills, with children often losing their place within either the word or the sentence. Making available spellings of key words on the child's own whiteboard placed on his or her desk rather than a distant class board will reduce these errors by making the task of locating key information easier and reducing opportunities for distraction. Methods for marking the child's place in word spellings may also be useful because loss of position within a word while copying was a frequent source of error and task abandonment.

Reduce Processing Loads

In complex learning situations that place significant processing and storage demands on the child, the chances of WM failures can be reduced by cutting down the processing load of the task. This will reduce the possibility of task failure as a result of a combination of excessive storage and processing demands. In many situations, this may be achieved easily. Consider, for example, the sentence-writing activity that was a source of difficulty for all of the children with low WM that we observed. Processing loads can be diminished by reducing the linguistic complexity of the sentence—in terms either of the vocabulary (common versus lower frequency words) or of the syntactic structures (simple subject–verb–object constructions rather than relative clauses). The planned sentences could also be reduced in length. If the child has to work with lengthy sentences and difficult words, the chances of task failure will increase dramatically and an opportunity for task success, and hence for learning, is lost. Provided that the modified learning activity successfully meets the desired learning outcomes identified by the teacher, this strategy of simplifying processing requirements is likely to be highly effective in promoting successful completion of complex tasks.

SUMMARY

There is substantial evidence that low scores on tests of WM skills are associated with poor attainments in the key curricular areas of English and mathematics. To illuminate the specific nature of the failed learning episodes that may be contributing to the failure of such children to make normal scholastic progress, we observed the classroom behavior of three children with poor WM abilities. Four different kinds of learning failure were observed with high frequency in each of these children that could be attributed to the children failing to meet the WM demands of the activity: forgetting instructions, failing to meet combined processing and storage demands, losing track in complex tasks, and forgetting from episodic long-term memory at high rates.

We propose that these learning failures impair the children's chances of abstracting knowledge and skills that form the basis for functioning in the complex cognitive activities associated with the domains of literacy and mathematics. It is therefore important to identify WM problems as a source of learning difficulty in individual children and to reduce the opportunities for learning failures by minimizing WM demands in classroom activities. In a WM intervention study, we are applying the principles from cognitive psychology to achieve these goals. Children with WM impairments are identified using standardized tools derived from the WM model, such as the Working Memory Test Battery for Children (Pickering & Gathercole, 2001) and the Automated Working Memory Assessment (Alloway, Gathercole, & Pickering, 2004). Classroom staff receive guidance that allows them to identify WM failures in the classroom and shows them how to minimize them for individual children. The children will also be encouraged to use their own strategies to overcome their WM limitations. It is hoped that this approach will enhance learning outcomes for children struggling to cope with poor WM function.

Summary Box

- There is wide individual variation in WM skills during the childhood years.
- Children with poor WM skills typically make poor academic progress in the areas of literacy and mathematics.
- Children with WM impairments frequently fail in classroom activities that impose significant WM loads.
- The most common types of classroom failure involved forgetting instructions, losing place in complex tasks, and struggling in tasks that involved both processing and storage loads.
- Although children with WM impairments have some awareness of their memory problems, in our study their teachers did not and attributed their problems to lack of attention.
- It is proposed that effective management of WM loads in classroom activities may minimize the learning difficulties that typically accompany impairments of WM.

Acknowledgment

This research was supported by the Medical Research Council core grant for the Co-operative group on Human Memory and Learning: A Working Memory Approach.

References

Adams, J. W., & Hitch, G. J. (1997). Working memory and children's mental addition. *Journal of Experimental Child Psychology, 67*, 21–38.

Alloway, T. P., Gathercole, S. E., Adams, A.-M., Willis, C. S. (2005). Working memory abilities in children with special educational needs. *Educational and Child Psychology, 22*, 56–67.

Alloway, T. P., Gathercole, S. E., & Pickering, S. J. (2004). *Automated Working Memory Assessment*. Available from the authors on request.

Alloway, T. P., Gathercole, S. E., Willis, C. S., & Adams, A.-M. (2004). A structural analysis of working memory and related cognitive skills in young children. *Journal of Experimental Child Psychology, 87*, 85–170.

Baddeley, A. D. (1986). *Working memory*. Oxford: Oxford University Press.

Baddeley, A. D. (2000). The episodic buffer: A new component of working memory? *Trends in Cognitive Sciences, 4*, 417–422.

Baddeley, A. D., & Hitch, G. (1974). Working memory. In G. Bower (Ed.), *The Psychology of Learning and Motivation, 8*, 47–90. New York: Academic Press.

Baddeley, A. D., & Logie, R. (1999). Working memory: The multiple component model. In A. Miyake & P. Shah (Eds.), *Models of Working Memory: Mechanisms of Active Maintenance and Executive Control* (pp. 28–61). Cambridge: Cambridge University Press.

Baddeley, A. D., & Warrington, E. K. (1970). Amnesia and the distinction between long- and short-term memory. *Journal of Verbal Learning and Verbal Behavior, 9*, 176–189.

Baddeley, A. D., & Wilson, B. A. (1994). When implicit learning fails: Amnesia and the problem of error elimination. *Neuropsychologia, 32*, 53–68.

Bull, R., & Scerif, G. (2001). Executive functioning as a predictor of children's mathematics ability: Inhibition, task switching, and working memory. *Developmental Neuropsychology, 19*, 273–293.

Case, R., Kurland, D. M., & Goldberg, J. (1982). Operational efficiency and the growth of short-term memory span. *Journal of Experimental Child Psychology, 33*, 386–404.

Clare, L., Wilson, B. A., Carter, G., Roth, I., & Hodges, J. R. (2002). Relearning face-name associations in early Alzheimer's disease. *Neuropsychology, 16*, 538–547.

Conners, C. K. (1997). *Conners' Teacher Rating Scale—Revised (S)*. New York: Multi-Health Systems Inc.

Daneman, M., & Carpenter, P. A. (1980). Individual differences in working memory and reading. *Journal of Verbal Learning and Verbal Behaviour, 19*, 450–466.

de Jong, P. F. (1998). Working memory deficits of reading disabled children. *Journal of Experimental Child Psychology, 70*, 75–96.

De Rammelaere, S., Stuyven, E., & Vandierendonck, A. (2001). Verifying simple arithmetic sums and products: Are the phonological loop and the central executive involved? *Memory and Cognition, 29*, 267–273.

Della Sala, S., Gray, C., Baddeley, A. D., & Wilson, L. (1997). *Visual Patterns Test*. Bury St Edmonds: Thames Valley Test Company.

Duff, S. C., & Logie, R. H. (2001). Processing and storage in working memory span. *Quarterly Journal of Experimental Psychology, 54A*, 31–48.

Engle, R. W., Cantor, J., & Carullo, J. J. (1992). Individual differences in working memory and comprehension: A test of four hypotheses. *Journal of Experimental Psychology: Learning, Memory and Cognition, 18*, 972–992.

Engle, R. W., Tuholski, S. W., Laughlin, J. E., & Conway, A. R. A. (1999). Working memory, short-term memory and general fluid intelligence: A latent variable approach. *Journal of Experimental Psychology: General, 128*, 309–331.

Engle, R. W., Kane, M. J., & Tuholski, S. W. (1999). Individual differences in working memory capacity and what they tell us about controlled attention, general fluid intelligence, and functions of the prefrontal cortex. In A. Miyake & P. Shah (Eds.), *Models of Working Memory*, (pp 102–134). Cambridge: Cambridge University Press.

Furst, A. J., & Hitch, G. J. (2000). Separate roles for executive and phonological components of working memory in mental arithmetic. *Memory and Cognition, 28*, 774–782.

Gathercole, S. E. (2002). Working memory in the classroom. *Special!* Summer 2002, 54–55.

Gathercole, S. E., & Baddeley, A. D. (1996). *The Children's Test of Nonword Repetition*. London: Psychological Corporation Europe.

Gathercole, S. E., & Pickering, S. J. (2000a). Working memory deficits in children with low achievements in the national curriculum at seven years of age. *British Journal of Educational Psychology, 70*, 177–194.

Gathercole, S. E., & Pickering, S. J. (2000b). Assessment of working memory in six- and seven-year-old children. *Journal of Educational Psychology, 92*, 377–390.

Gathercole, S. E., & Pickering, S. J. (2001). Working memory deficits in children with special educational needs. *British Journal of Special Education, 28*, 89–97.

Gathercole, S. E., Pickering, S. J., Ambridge, B., & Wearing, H. (2004). The structure of working memory from 4 to 15 years of age. *Developmental Psychology, 40*, 177–190.

Gathercole, S. E., Pickering, S. J., Knight, C., & Stegmann, Z. (2003). Working memory skills and educational attainment: Evidence from National Curriculum assessments at 7 and 14 years of age. *Applied Cognitive Psychology, 17*, 1–16.

Jarvis, H. L., & Gathercole, S. E. (2003). Verbal and nonverbal working memory and achievements on national curriculum tests at 11 and 14 years of age. *Educational and Child Psychology, 20*, 123–140.

Just, M. A., & Carpenter, P. A. (1992). A capacity theory of comprehension: Individual differences in working memory. *Psychological Review, 99*, 122–149.

Lee, K.-M., & Kang, S.-Y. (2002). Arithmetic operation and working memory: differential suppression in dual tasks. *Cognition, 83*, B63–68.

Logie, R. H., Gilhooly, K. J., & Wynn, V. 1994. Counting on working memory in arithmetic problem solving. *Memory and Cognition, 22*, 395–410.

Mayringer, H., & Wimmer, H. (2000). Pseudoname learning by German-speaking children with dyslexia: Evidence for a phonological learning deficit. *Journal of Experimental Child Psychology, 75*, 116–133.

McLean, J., & Hitch, G. J. (1999). Working memory impairments in children with specific arithmetic learning difficulties. *Journal of Experimental Child Psychology, 74*, 240–260.

Parkin, A. J., Hunkin, N. M., & Squires, E. J. (1998). Unlearning John Major: The use of errorless learning in the reacquisition of proper names following herpes simplex encephalitis. *Cognitive Neuropsychology, 15*, 361–375.

Passolunghi, M. C., & Siegel, L. S. (2001). Short-term memory, working memory, and inhibitory control in children with difficulties in arithmetic problem solving. *Journal of Experimental Child Psychology, 80*, 44–57.

Pennington, B. F., & Ozonoff, S. (1996). Executive functions and developmental psychopathology. *Journal of Child Psychology and Psychiatry, 37*, 51–87.

Pickering, S. J., & Gathercole, S. E. (2001). *Working Memory Test Battery for Children.* London: Psychological Corporation Europe.

Pickering, S. J., & Gathercole, S. E. (2004). Distinctive working memory profiles in children with special educational needs. *Educational Psychology, 24*, 393–408.

Siegel, L. S., & Ryan, E. B. (1989). The development of working memory in normally achieving and subtypes of learning disabled children. *Child Development, 60*, 973–980.

Swanson, H. L. (1994). Short-term memory and working memory—Do both contribute to our understanding of academic achievement in children and adults with learning disabilities? *Journal of Learning Disabilities, 27*, 34–50.

Swanson, H. L., Ashbaker, M. H., & Lee, C. (1996). Learning disabled readers working memory as a function of processing demands. *Journal of Experimental Child Psychology, 61*, 242–275.

Swanson, H. L., & Sachse-Lee, C. (2001). Mathematical problem solving and working memory in children with learning disabilities: Both executive and phonological processes are important. *Journal of Experimental Child Psychology, 79*, 294–321.

Tulving, E. (1983). *Elements of episodic memory.* Oxford: Oxford University Press.

Vallar, G., & Baddeley, A. D. (1984). Phonological short-term store, phonological processing and sentence comprehension: A neuropsychological case study. *Cognitive Neuropsychology, 1*, 121–141.

Wechsler, D. (1990). *Wechsler Pre-school and Primary Scale of Intelligence–Revised UK edition.* London: Psychological Corporation.

CHAPTER

9

Assessment of Working Memory in Children

SUSAN J. PICKERING
University of Bristol

In 1927 Robert S. Woodworth noted the following in his book *Psychology: A Study of Mental Life*:

> So much depends on a good memory in all walks of life . . . that perhaps it is no wonder that many students and business professional men become so worried about their memories and resort to "memory training courses" in the hope of improvement. (p. 332)

Today this assertion is no less valid. At the time of writing this chapter it is hard to find a conference presentation or publication in the field of psychology or special education that does not make some mention of memory, particularly "working memory," somewhere. Increasingly, researchers and practitioners in a range of fields are coming to the view that many of the behavioral phenomena we are interested in understanding, measuring, and perhaps manipulating are linked to working memory (WM) functioning in one way or another. It is for this reason, therefore, that now more than ever the detailed and accurate assessment of WM is becoming an issue with which many are concerning themselves.

In this chapter I aim to provide the reader with an overview of the assessment of WM, beginning with a look at how WM has been assessed in earlier times. In the following sections of the chapter I introduce a theoretically based battery of WM tests, the *Working Memory Test Battery for Children* (WMTB-C; Pickering & Gathercole, 2001); discuss the process by which the test was created and the uses to which it is being put; and present some research findings from children with different educational difficulties. In the final sections of the chapter I discuss a computerized and extended version of the WMTB-C, the Automated Working Memory Assessment (AWMA) battery (Alloway, Gathercole, & Pickering, 2004), and some recent research findings from this test. The chapter closes with some thoughts on the link between WM assessment and remediation.

ASSESSING WORKING MEMORY IN THE 20TH CENTURY

Although philosophers have speculated about memory for more than 2 millennia, the scientific study of this aspect of cognition only began about 100 years ago, with a German scholar named Herman Ebbinghaus (Baddeley, 1997). His approach to studying memory has left a lasting legacy for anyone now interested in WM and its assessment. Ebbinghaus chose to study memory in an extremely rigorous way that avoided many of the complexities of human mental functioning. He created simple artificial materials—nonsense syllables—and investigated how such materials were learned and forgotten by a single adult participant—himself. Although a number of researchers have since protested against the lack of "ecological validity" in this experimental approach to studying memory performance (e.g., Neisser, 1978), the dominant method for measuring WM (or short-term memory [STM], as it is also referred to) today is still based on the memorization and recall of simple, relatively meaningless information, such as lists of numbers, unrelated words, or nonsense words.

The first recorded attempt to measure STM for educational purposes was carried out by a schoolmaster from London named Joseph Jacobs. Jacobs was interested in the mental capacity of his pupils and therefore devised a technique in which the child was presented with a sequence of items, such as numbers, and asked to repeat them back exactly as they had been heard. This technique is what we now call the *memory span procedure*. An important feature of this procedure is that assessment of memory performance can begin with very short sequences, which can then be increased systematically (usually by one item) until the participant cannot recall the sequences correctly. The sequence length (number of items in the list) at which the participant can recall correctly on 50% of the trials is then referred to as his or her memory span (Jacobs, 1887, cited in Baddeley, 1997).

The concept of memory span has been a very powerful one, invoking the notion of a particular mental space, or capacity, by which the participant is limited in his or her intellectual processing. This concept is far more complex than first imagined, however; capacity is often found to be different for varying types of information. Moreover, active processing of stimuli in a memory span test can increase the amount of information that can be retained at any one time. A college student studied by Ericsson and colleagues (Ericsson, Chase, & Faloon, 1980) was able to achieve a digit span of 79 items. This figure of 79 stands in stark contrast to "The magic number seven, plus or minus one," the title of the classic paper by George Miller in 1956. In this paper Miller argued that, in adults, memory span was limited to between 6 and 8 pieces of information. He did, however, say that this magic number related to the amount of "chunks" that could be held in mind temporarily. The question of what constitutes a "chunk" is determined by a whole range of factors, including one's familiarity with the information to be remembered and the extent to which such information is actively divided into meaningful chunks. Many of the long numbers that we have to deal with in everyday life, such as telephone numbers and credit card details, are often arranged in chunks of 3 or 4 digits that form the crucial number. The recall of 79 digits was achieved using strategic approaches that involved chunking and increasing the meaningfulness of the digits (see Ericsson, Delaney, Weaver, & Mahadevan, 2004, for an account of the mechanisms involved in retaining large numbers of digits)—plus a great deal of practice.

The Digit Span Task

Given that it is clear that factors such as meaningfulness, chunking, and other forms of strategic activity can affect performance on memory span tests, how has this influenced the approaches that have been used to measure WM in children? The answer to this question lies with the selection of the *digit span* task as the most commonly used measure of short-term verbal memory over the last century. Digits lend themselves well to the assessment of STM capacity: They are acquired early in life, highly over-learned, and easily presented. Digit span tasks typically utilize the numbers 1–9, thus providing the user of the test with a small pool of memory items that can be combined and recombined in a number of different ways. Many digit span tests aim to include each digit only once in each sequence (although this is only possible with sequences of 9 items or less) and avoid the use of predictable sequences (such as 3, 2, 1). In doing so, the extent to which strategic activity such as chunking can be used during the task is minimized. Moreover, although each digit in the sequence has inherent meaning in the sense that it represents magnitude, it might be argued that the richness of meaning of individual digits is not as great as that for individual words, for example. Thus, memory span tasks that involve digits have become very popular measures of STM capacity in both adults and children.

  In a typical digit span task care is taken to standardize presentation procedures; digits in the sequence are read to the participant in an even monotone, so as to discourage any likelihood of chunking the items on the basis of intonation and prosodic information. Digits are presented at a steady and even pace; in many cases this is one item per second, although some versions of the digit span procedure recommend faster rates, such as two items per second (e.g., the Recall of Digits Forward subtest of the British Ability Scales II; Elliot, 1996). The procedures for administration of the Digits Forward subtest of the Wechsler Intelligence Scale for Children III-UK (WISC

III-UK; Wechsler, 1992, p. 209) bear out what was described earlier in this chapter:

> Read the digits at the rate of one per second, dropping voice inflection slightly on the last digit in a series. After each sequence, pause to allow the child to respond.

For the British Ability Scales II, the instructions for the Recall of Digits Forward subtest stress the lack of intonation in the voice and include reference to the faster rate of presentation (British Ability Scales II Administration and Scoring Manual, or BAS II; Elliot, 1996, p. 302):

> Read digits in an even monotone at half-second intervals. Drop your voice slightly on the last digit . . .

Exactly what effect the difference in presentation rate may have for these two versions of the digit span task is not immediately clear. When presentation rates are set at one item per second, participants have more time between memory items to rehearse the sequence to aid recall. However, it is also true that the entire list takes twice as long to be presented, possibly leading to greater decay of memory items from the temporary store that is thought to hold them. In contrast, faster presentation rates are likely to reduce the opportunities for between-item rehearsal, but the entire list will be presented more quickly, which may limit the degree of memory loss as a result of decay.

Thus, we can see that the memory span task designed more than a century ago by Joseph Jacobs has found a central place in the assessment of WM, both as a single test and as part of a larger assessment of overall intellectual functioning (or intelligence quotient) as embodied by tests such as the WISC III-UK or BAS II. In the case of the WISC and the BAS, scores on the memory span task have been standardized for children of different ages. This tells us something important about the performance of children on the memory span task: It is expected that it will change with age.

Indeed, one intriguing feature of children's performance on a task such as digit span is the extent to which span appears to increase as children get older. A great deal of research has been dedicated to the study of this memory span development with the aim of understanding what factors promote increases in memory span and what consequences this might have for the everyday functioning of children of different ages (see, for example, Gathercole, 1999 or Cowan, 1997).

From our own data (Pickering & Gathercole, 2001) we have found that more than 80% of children between the ages of 4:7 and 5:6 years had a digit span of between 4 and 5 items. In contrast, a significant proportion of children of 14:9 to 15:9 years of age obtained digit spans of 5 items (37%), 6 items (27%), and 7 items (23%). Of the older age group, 2% recorded digit spans of 9 items, whereas none of the youngest group managed to obtain a digit span of greater than 6 items. Why do the older children seem to have more "space" to hold digits temporarily than the younger children? One suggestion concerns the development of subvocal rehearsal at around the age of 7 years (e.g., Gathercole & Hitch, 1993).

Those who have experience administering digit span tasks to children of different ages may have found that children appear to deal with the task in different ways depending on their age. Children of around 4–5 years of age are often found to take a relatively passive approach to the task: listening to the lists of digits without attempting to carry out any active processing of the items during presentation or prior to recall. This approach contrasts sharply with that of children of around 7 years of age and older. These children can often be seen to repeat items in the sequence to themselves during presentation, either silently (the efforts of which are often visible for the tester to see in the form of lip, head, and eye movements) or out loud. The use of rehearsal appears to increase over childhood (Flavell, Beach, & Chinsky, 1966), and the quality of rehearsal shows developmental changes too (Cowan, 1997). For example, in the period during which children are becoming aware of the usefulness of rehearsal and becoming skilled in its use, children can often be observed carrying out a rudimentary form of the strategy in which the child repeats each digit after it has been said by the tester. What children often fail to do, however, is to string the list items together and rehearse them as a sequence—a process known as cumulative rehearsal (Gathercole & Hitch, 1993).

Thus, we can see that performance on a digit span task increases significantly over childhood, and much of this increased capacity for digits appears to be dependent on the use of a cumulative rehearsal strategy after the age of about 7 years. The process of rehearsal of memory items has also been linked to speed of articulation (Cowan et al., 1998; Hulme, Thomson, Muir, & Lawrence, 1984) whereby faster articulation rates (the speed at which words can be spoken) have been found to be related to greater memory spans. This is thought to be because rate of rehearsal of items in memory is linked to speed of articulation—and speed of articulation appears to increase as children get older (Hulme et al., 1984).

The digit span task is a simple, easy-to-administer measure of the STM of an individual. It is used widely in psychological, educational, medical, and other settings to gauge the capacity of a person to hold information in mind temporarily. However, the digit span task is not without limitations, some of which are inherent in the basic structure of the task, whereas others are related to the particular design of specific versions of the task.

One obvious limitation of the digit span task is that it restricts the assessment of STM to verbal information, and in this sense the test may be more accurately described (according to the Baddeley and Hitch model of WM) as a test of phonological loop function, rather than as a measure of STM *per se*. In addition to this, the use of digits in the task means that the information in the phonological loop is already well established in long-term memory (LTM), a feature that means that immediate memory performance can be supported by the activity of LTM. This process has been termed "redintegration" (Hulme, Maughan, & Brown, 1991) and provides support for short-term recall by allowing one to compare the partially decayed memory trace in STM with possible candidates in LTM. Thus, the restricted pool of items (the digits 1–9), plus significant familiarity with these numbers, increases the potential for variables other than the basic capacity of the phonological loop to contribute to the digit span obtained.

Other factors that may affect the performance of an individual on a digit span task include the: the extent to which they are paying attention when the list of items is presented, their hearing ability, and their capacity for spoken output. Many versions of the digit span task involve both spoken presentation and recall, although the task can be presented visually and recall can be written. The transient nature of the task stimuli poses a problem for any situations in which the participant's attention is distracted away from the stimuli. A digit sequence that was not attended to, either because the child's attention wandered, or because of some form of external distraction (such as a door slamming nearby), will not easily be recalled. In cases like this, errors may not reflect the fact that the sequence had exceeded the child's capacity for holding digits in memory. One way to overcome this problem is to include a relatively large number of trials at each difficulty level. By doing this, one is able to obtain a number of responses to sequences of a particular length and thus obtain a more robust indication of the child's digit span.

Digit Span and Beyond

In this section of the chapter we have examined the historical basis of WM assessment by focusing on the memory span procedure, first used by Joseph Jacobs, and charting the widespread use of the digit span task as a measure of STM capacity. Although the digit span task has contributed—and continues to contribute—significantly to our understanding of the WM functioning of individuals in a wide range of settings, the limitations of the procedure outlined earlier suggest the need for a broader approach to the assessment of WM. The digit span task measures phonological loop function for a restricted pool of highly familiar material. What are the consequences for memory functioning when the pool of items is unrestricted, as in the case of words? How can we measure visuo-spatial WM functioning? Is there a way of measuring WM without the contribution of LTM? Finally, what processes can we attribute to the central executive (CE) component of Baddeley and Hitch's WM model, and how do we go about measuring these? These questions are considered in the next section where the assessment tool known as the Working Memory Test Battery for Children (WMTB-C) is introduced.

ASSESSING WORKING MEMORY USING A BATTERY OF TESTS

Memory test batteries are far from being a new concept; a number of such batteries have existed for some time. These include tests such as the Rivermead Behavioural Memory Test for Children (Wilson, Ivani-Chalian, & Aldrich, 1991), The Wechsler Memory Scale III-UK (Wechsler, 1997), the Test of Memory and Learning (Reynolds & Bigler, 1994), the Wide Range Assessment of Memory and Learning (Sheslow & Adams, 1990), and the Children's Memory Scale (Cohen, 1997). Each of these tests provides the user with a range of subtests with which a child's memory performance can be measured. The Children's Memory Scale, for example, includes subtests that have been designed to measure immediate verbal memory, delayed verbal memory, general memory, immediate visual memory, and delayed visual memory in children from 5 to 16 years of age. Thus we can see that this test, like many of the others listed here, provides the user with a measure of a range of different types of memory including both LTM and STM. Clearly, some test users will be interested in such a range of memory scores, and for those users a test like this will be of great use. However, for those users particularly interested in measuring the *working memory* performance of a child, it might be argued that a test such as this will be of more limited use. At least two factors contribute to this view.

The first point to note is that by including subtests that measure aspects of memory other than WM, the number of subtests that are devoted to the measurement of immediate memory is necessarily limited. Second, the theoretical basis of many of the tests is not immediately clear. In other words, tests that base their structure and content on well-established, intensively researched, and well-understood models of memory functioning appear to be rare. This point is important because when we look at a child's scores on a memory battery, we want to be able to understand the cognitive structures and processes that may have contributed to performance, and what the consequences of these scores might be.

One memory battery that has based itself on a well-established and intensively researched model of WM is the WMTB-C (Pickering & Gathercole, 2001). This test was designed to measure the WM performance of children between the ages of 4:6 and 15:9 years using the WM model originally proposed by Baddeley and Hitch in 1974 (with subsequent modifications) as its theoretical basis. As other chapters in this book have described in varying degrees of detail, the Baddeley and Hitch model departed from previous conceptualizations of STM (e.g., the "modal model," Atkinson & Shiffrin, 1968) by specifying a multi-component structure and a dynamic "working" set of functions. For many years the model was proposed to consist of three major components—a central executive and two "slave systems," the phonological loop and the visuo-spatial sketchpad. In 2000 a fourth component was hypothesized to be part of the system: the episodic buffer (e.g., Baddeley, 2000). Work on this additional component had not begun at the time that the WMTB-C was being constructed, and even now there are few tests in existence that are thought to be able to measure the functioning of this component (Baddeley, personal communication, 2005).

Thus, the WMTB-C is a battery of WM tests based on the tripartite structure of the WM model. One of the characteristics of WM, as embodied by this model, is the extent to which, although related in the sense of being a coherent system of immediate memory functioning, the activities of the three components of WM have been demonstrated to be largely separable. Data from experimental studies in which participants are asked to carry out, for example, a phonological loop task (e.g., digit recall), while simultaneously engaging in a secondary task designed to use the visuo-spatial sketchpad (e.g., spatial tapping) has shown little decrement in the primary task performance (e.g., Pickering, Gathercole, Hall, & Lloyd, 2001). This finding contrasts sharply with the results of studies in which the secondary task uses the phonological loop (e.g., articulatory suppression). Here we see significant impairments in performance (e.g., Baddeley, Lewis, & Vallar, 1984).

Other research findings support the separability of the three WM components. Research with neuropsychological patients, for example, has revealed individuals with specific impairments in one component of WM but spared performance in other components (see, for example, Henson, 2001, for a review). In addition to this, developments in the technology available for brain scanning have provided neuroanatomical evidence that activities associated with the three WM components appear to be located in different areas of the brain (e.g., Henson, Burgess, & Frith, 2000; Owen, Evans, & Petrides, 1996; Smith & Jonides, 1997).

Confirmation that the subtests selected for use in the WMTB-C fitted well with the Baddeley and Hitch model came from factor analyses that were carried out on the data collected during the standardization process for the battery. Although there were some minor, but interesting, variations in the relationships between the different subtests in the battery for children in different age groups (see Gathercole, Pickering, Ambridge, & Wearing, 2004, for a more detailed discussion of this analysis), a three-factor structure gave a good fit to the data and provided further support for both the validity of the subtests chosen and the WM model itself.

Selection of the WMTB-C Subtests

The selection of subtests for inclusion in the WMTB-C was based on a number of factors. The first was an understanding of the literature on the structures and processes of WM as identified by the extensive research activity that has been devoted to the study of this aspect of cognition over the last 30 years in locations all over the globe. The second was a review of what we know about the development of WM and the factors that influence such development. Research in this area has been most significant in relation to the phonological loop component of WM. Much less is known about

TABLE 9.1
Subtests Included in the Prototype Version of the WMTB-C

Working Memory Component	Subtest
Phonological loop	Digit Recall
	Word List Recall
	Nonword List Recall
	Word List Matching
	Nonword List Matching
	Children's Test of Nonword Repetition
Visuo-spatial sketchpad	Matrices Static
	Matrices Dynamic
	Mazes Static
	Mazes Dynamic
Central executive	Listening Recall
	Counting Recall
	Backward Digit Recall

the development of the visuo-spatial sketchpad and CE components, although research in these areas is increasing.

In the early stages of the development of the test battery we added to our knowledge of children's WM by carrying out a range of experimental studies designed to fill in some of the gaps in our knowledge (e.g., Gathercole, Pickering, Hall, & Peaker, 2001; Pickering et al., 2001). The findings from such studies allowed us to design new tasks for inclusion in the battery or to better understand tasks that had already existed in the experimental literature but had not been used with children to any significant degree. On this basis we chose a number of tasks for inclusion in a prototype version of the WM battery. This battery included 12 subtests: some tests with a long-history in the STM world, such as the recall of digits; some tasks that had been adapted from experimental work with adults, such as listening recall; some new tasks that emerged from our own experimental work, such as the matrices and mazes tasks. Finally, an already-standardized test of phonological loop function, the Children's Test of Nonword Repetition (CNRep; Gathercole & Baddeley, 1996) was added.

The total set of 13 tests included in the prototype battery is shown in Table 9.1.

The prototype WM battery was administered to 87 children of 6 and 7 years of age, along with a series of standardized tests of performance in receptive language, literacy, and arithmetic. A number of interesting findings emerged from this study; these are described in detail by Gathercole and Pickering (2000a, 2000b, & 2001), along with descriptions of the subtests and their administration procedures. In summary, the battery appeared to provide an easy-to-administer and reliable way of measuring WM performance in children of this age. Moreover, performance on the tests was found to be linked to scores on the standardized attainment tests and to performance in Key Stage 1 National Curriculum Standard Attainment Tests. Test performance also provided the ability to distinguish between children with and without Special Educational Needs (SEN) with a high degree of accuracy.

Not all subtests of the prototype battery proved equally valuable, however, and for the purposes of constructing the final version of the WMTB-C, a number of modifications were made to the test. These modifications are described in detail in Pickering and Gathercole (2001) and included the removal of some subtests from the battery (such as the Nonword List Matching task) and the modification of others (such as the Mazes task). The Nonword List Matching subtest was removed because it was found that it did not provide any additional information that could not be obtained from the sole use of the Word List Matching task. In the course of experimental work we discovered that the "lexicality effect," our superior recall of words over nonsense words, did not appear to operate in the same way when participants were required to match sequences of items rather than recall them (Gathercole et al., 2001).

The final number of subtests included in the standardization of the WMTB-C was 10. However, one of the subtests actually existed as a published psychometric test prior to the publication of the WMTB-C. The Visual Patterns Test (Della Sala, Gray, Baddeley, & Wilson, 1997) was originally designed as a neuropsychological test of visual memory in adults. However, in the course of our research we found that it could be administered easily to children as young as age 4 years. Because this test provided us with an excellent measure of visuo-spatial sketchpad functioning (the specifics of which will be discussed in the next section) we decided to include it the final version of the battery in place of the Matrices Static task, to which it is closely related. The major difference between the two tasks is that the Matrices task is computer administered and the Visual Patterns Test uses a pencil and paper format—something that can make test administration much easier for users without access to a computer.

Thus nine subtests can be found in the WMTB-C battery, and the standard scores for all of these tests, plus the Visual Patterns Test, are provided in the accompanying manual. The Visual Patterns Test can be bought separately and added to the battery, if a user so requires.

What Do Each of the WMTB-C Subtests Measure?

Having made the claim that the WMTB-C represents a theoretically based tool for measuring WM, it is important to specify what that theoretical basis is. In this section, each of the 10 WMTB-C subtests is discussed with respect to its relationship to our understanding of the structure and function of WM. The set of 10 subtests is listed in Table 9.2.

TABLE 9.2
Subtests Included in the WMTB-C

Working Memory Component	Subtest
Phonological loop	Digit Recall
	Word List Recall
	Nonword List Recall
	Word List Matching
Visuo-spatial sketchpad	Block Recall
	Visual Patterns Test
	Mazes Memory
Central executive	Listening Recall
	Counting Recall
	Backward Digit Recall

Digit Recall

Much has already been said about the recall of digits in this chapter and elsewhere in this book. On this basis, we know that this phonological loop task requires the immediate recall of numbers and that for a response to be correct, the right numbers need to be recalled in the right order. The Digit Recall subtest measures a child's capacity for storing and outputting sequences composed of highly familiar numbers. Sequences are presented verbally (at the rate of one item per second), and the child is required to respond in spoken form. As discussed earlier, the familiarity of digits means that some support from LTM would be expected when carrying out this task. In addition, the phonological form of the numbers 1–9 is distinct: None of the digit names sounds much like the other (certainly in English anyway), and with the exception of the number 7, all of the digit names are mono-syllabic. Using our knowledge of factors that have been shown to influence the operation of the phonological loop, we can see that digits are concrete (i.e., not abstract), familiar, short, phonologically distinct, selected from a closed set, and relatively easily articulated. Children of 7 years of age and older would be very likely to approach a digit recall task in an active way and to rehearse the digits to maximize their chances of recall. On this basis, we can see that performance on the Digit Recall subtest of the WMTB-C provides us with an indication of the capacity of the phonological store of WM, with additional contributions from LTM and, in older children, active rehearsal processes.

Word List Recall

The Word List Recall subtest shares some structural similarities with the Digit Recall subtest, the key difference being that the to-be-remembered information is now words rather than numbers. Examination of the characteristics of the stimuli selected for this subtest reveals that each of the items in the sequences has a consonant–vowel–consonant (CVC) structure, contains phonemes from a restricted pool (avoiding the use of late-acquired sounds), and includes words that are likely to be within the vocabulary of even very young children. Many of the stimuli in the subtest derive from our earlier experimental work on word and nonword recall (e.g., Gathercole & Pickering, 1999). Thus, this test was designed to measure recall of memory items that form part of a much larger and notionally unrestricted pool of stimuli—in the sense that no item in this subtest occurs more than once. The stimuli are again monosyllabic, and care was taken to avoid putting phonologically similar words together in the same list.

It could be argued that words are more semantically rich than digits; many of the items in the lists may link to images, feelings, and other forms of information that are already stored in LTM and thus might be invoked during the subtest. In Chapter 1 we saw that the "Levels of Processing" framework proposed by Craik and Lockheart (1972) was very helpful in describing the phenomenon whereby information processed at a deeper and more meaningful level is more likely to be recalled.

During presentation of the Word List Recall task children may attempt to link items in the memory lists together and create mental images of them. In the case of the two-item sequence, "lip, bag," there is scope for creating the image of a bag with a picture of some lips on it. However, children are not specifically instructed to use this strategy, nor are they instructed not to use it. Moreover, not all sequences lend themselves to the strategy as well as this example does, partly because not all of the words in the subtest are concrete and readily imageable.

Thus, the specific design of the Word List Recall subtest of the WMTB-C provides the user with a measure of the capacity of the phonological store of WM with potential additional support from other aspects of the cognitive system including long-term semantic and visual memory, visual WM, plus the active rehearsal processes available during the digit span task.

Nonword List Recall

As with Digit and Word List Recall, Nonword List Recall requires the immediate spoken recall of a series of verbally presented items. In this case, however, the memory items are CVC nonsense words—that is, each item in the list does not have any meaning in the English language. Care has also been taken to make sure that none of the items actually forms a homophone for a real word. The use of nonsense words in the measurement of phonological loop function has a long history stretching all the way back to the work of Ebbinghaus more than 100 years ago. One of the proposed advantages of testing phonological STM with nonsense words is that no support is available from LTM, and therefore, this type of test has been seen as a purer measure of immediate memory capacity than those that use familiar items as their stimuli (see, for example, Gathercole et al., 2001).

This issue has subsequently proved to be much more complex than first imagined, however. As described in Chapter 1 of this volume, work by Gathercole and colleagues (e.g., Gathercole, Frankish, Pickering, & Peaker, 1999) has indicated that nonsense words can vary in their "wordlikeness"— that is, the extent to which they are perceived to resemble real words. One way that the concept of wordlikeness has been operationalized is through the use of phonotactic probabilities (Gathercole & Pickering, 1999; Gathercole et al., 1999). Pairs of phonemes cooccur to a greater or lesser extent in any given language. Research by Gathercole and colleagues found that nonsense words composed of phoneme pairs that had high phonotactic probabilities in English (e.g., bip) were significantly better recalled than those made up of pairs with low phonotactic probabilities (e.g., vook). This suggests that as well as being able to benefit from the effects of lexicality (i.e., better recall of words over nonsense words), children were able to use information stored in LTM at the sublexical level—that is, long-term knowledge about the statistical properties of our language appears to support recall of memory items that are not even known words.

On this basis, tests of phonological loop function can vary in the extent to which they draw on the contents of LTM depending on the way that the nonsense words are constructed. In the WMTB-C, nonsense words were constructed using the same restricted pool of phonemes that were used to create the words in the Word List Recall subtest. However, because we wanted to create a sufficient pool of nonsense words to allow us to include each item only once in the whole subtest, the possibility of manipulating the phonotactic probabilities of the test items was not open to us. Thus, the extent to which knowledge of the sublexical properties of the English language can help with recall of these memory items is not specifically known. A quick scan of the items that are included in the test suggests that the phonotactic probability of most of the items is neither particularly high nor particularly low. A sequence such as "gach, mup, coom, terl" appears to contain some items that appear wordlike and some that appear less wordlike. Further research will inform us of the precise phonotactic structure of the nonsense words in this task.

One particularly interesting feature of this subtest is its relationship with the Word List Recall subtest. The two tests were designed to be identical to one another except for the fact that in one case the combinations of phonemes in each memory item formed words and in the other they formed nonsense words. In all other respects the two subtests are the same. This means that a systematic comparison of the scores achieved on the two subtests is possible, allowing us to get a sense of the extent to which a child was able to draw on knowledge in LTM—be it lexical or sublexical—to support recall.

Word List Matching

The same pool of memory items was used in the construction of the Word List Matching subtest and the Word List Recall subtest. The key difference between the two subtests lies in the process by which the memory sequences are administered and the response that is required from the child. The Word List Recall subtest is an example of a *serial recognition* (as opposed to serial recall) task (Gathercole et al., 2001). Based on measures developed in the course of our experimental work, these tasks involve the verbal presentation of a sequence, the repetition of the sequence (either in exactly the same way as before, or with two of the list items transposed), and then a response by the child as to whether the second list was the same or different from the first list. An example from the WMTB-C is as follows:

> *cut, mob, fell, teach, pad*   *cut, fell, mob, teach, pad*   "*different*"

In this example, the second sequence is different from the first because the second and third words in the sequence have been swapped with each other. In Chapter 1 Alan Baddeley discusses research evidence from studies that have used a serial recognition paradigm and suggests that such tasks provide a good measure of the phonological store of the phonological loop that appears to be free of the influence of our stored knowledge of, and facility with, language. He also suggests that performance on such tasks can be carried out without much contribution from the phonological rehearsal mechanism of the phonological loop (unlike performance on serial recall tasks). Support for this view comes from our studies of serial recognition of words and nonsense words (Gathercole et al., 2001), which revealed no significant advantage for serial recognition of word sequences over nonsense word sequences.

So, the Word List Matching subtest appears to be a measure of the capacity of the phonological store of WM without much contribution from language knowledge and ability. One other important feature of the task is the simple response of "same" or "different" that is required from the child. In most cases this response is obtained verbally, but if a child does experience speech output difficulties, the response can be given nonverbally by pointing to the words "same" or "different" printed on a card placed in front of the child, for example. In this way children without *any* spoken language can complete the task, something that cannot often be achieved with tests of phonological loop function. The Word List Matching subtest therefore provides users with a measure of phonological loop performance that is free from any limitations with spoken language that a child might be experiencing.

Block Recall

The Block Recall subtest of the WMTB-C is based on the test of visuo-spatial memory originally devised by Corsi (e.g., Milner, 1971). This task is administered using a board on which nine identical cubes (blocks) are fixed in a random arrangement. The board is placed on a table and the administrator of the test and the child sit opposite one another, with the board between them. On one side of each block a number (from 1 to 9) is printed; this is the side of the board that the administrator can see. Using these numbers, the administrator taps out a sequence on the blocks, and the child is required to repeat the sequence, touching the same blocks in the same order as they have been shown.

The Corsi blocks task has been used in experimental and neuropsychological work for some time and has provided users with a simple measure of recall of sequences of a nonverbal nature. In recent years the task has been specifically conceptualized as a measure of a *spatial* subcomponent of visuo-spatial WM (e.g., Logie, 1995). Findings from both experimental and neuropsychological studies of visuo-spatial WM have provided support for a fractionation of this component of the Baddeley and Hitch model, although the specific characteristics of the two suggested subcomponents are still a matter for some debate (see Pickering, 2001, for a detailed discussion of this issue). For the purposes of our analysis of the theoretical basis of the WMTB-C subtests, two important points are worth noting about the Block Recall subtest. The first is that it appears to be a measure of the capacity of some form of spatial immediate memory, and the second is that, unlike many purported measures of visuo-spatial memory, it does not lend itself well to phonological recoding. Development of good measures of visuo-spatial memory has proved particularly difficult because of the tendency to phonologically recode (i.e., name, label, describe) information to ourselves when it is presented in visual form. Children begin to do this from the age of about 8 years of age (e.g., Hitch, Halliday, Schaafstal, & Schraagen, 1988), making any test that has nameable items potentially more of a phonological memory test than a visuo-spatial one. Evidence from interference task studies suggests that tasks like Block Recall are relatively free from the effects of phonological recoding (e.g., Farmer, Berman, & Fletcher, 1986), as demonstrated when performance on these tasks is combined with something that ties up phonological loop activity, such as articulatory suppression. In this way, therefore, the Block Recall subtest provides users with a relatively "pure" measure of the more spatial aspect of visuo-spatial WM performance.

Visual Patterns Test

As mentioned earlier in the chapter, the Visual Patterns Test was designed by Della Sala and colleagues (1997) for use with adult neuropsychological patients. Both experimental and neuropsychological research with this test has indicated that it appears to measure a different aspect of visuo-spatial WM functioning from the Corsi blocks task. Using Logie's (1995) conceptualization of visuo-spatial WM as being composed of a visual and a spatial subcomponent, the visual patterns test is suggested to measure the former, rather than the latter (see also Pickering, 2001). The task involves the recall of two-dimensional matrix patterns. Each pattern is formed by the combination of equal numbers of black and white squares in a matrix. After having seen a pattern for 3 seconds, the participant is asked to recall the location of the black squares by marking onto an empty matrix of the same size. Patterns increase in complexity as the number of black and white squares increases. This allows the user to measure visual pattern span—the number of target (black) squares that can be held in immediate memory.

It was noted earlier that the tendency to phonologically recode visually presented stimuli has been a problem in the development of "pure" measures of visuo-spatial WM. One study (Miles, Morgan, Milne, & Morris, 1996) has suggested that older children and adults may use a phonological recoding strategy when carrying out a visual patterns test. However, in our own research we found no evidence to support this view (Pickering et al., 2001). At present, therefore, although it is impossible to say that no participant uses such a strategy when carrying out this task, it appears that it is by no means universal and, perhaps more importantly, does not necessarily confer major benefits on performance. Thus, the Visual Patterns Test seems to provide us with a simple measure of the visual subcomponent of visuo-spatial WM.

Mazes Memory

The Mazes Memory subtest was developed from the Mazes (static and dynamic) task used in our earlier experimental work (Pickering et al., 2001). The test consists of two-dimensional mazes presented using a pencil-and-paper format. A route is shown through the maze in red, and the administrator of the test traces the route with their finger. Following this, the child is asked to draw the exact route that they have seen into an identical, but empty, maze.

The specific administration process for the Mazes Memory subtest combines the two presentation formats from the static and dynamic Mazes tasks from our earlier work. Children are shown information in static (visual) form—as a red line on paper—and in dynamic (spatial) form—as the sequence traced by the moving finger of the administrator. Thus, the two major forms of information thought to be processed by the two subcomponents of visuo-spatial WM are brought together in one subtest (Pickering, 2001). This was done for two reasons. One is that, although it might be possible to dissociate visual (static) and spatial (dynamic) information in carefully controlled psychological experiments, it is likely that these two types of information continually interact in the real world. Logie's model of visuo-spatial WM specifies the existence of a "visual cache" for storing visual information about shape, color, and so on and an "inner scribe" for dealing with spatial sequential information, which may also be involved in the rehearsal of information in visuo-spatial WM. The Mazes Memory test therefore provides a measure of the whole visuo-spatial WM system.

The second reason why performance on this subtest may be interesting for WMTB-C users is that given the opportunity to use both static visual and dynamic spatial information in WM, some children may show a preference for one type of information over another or may exhibit particular problems with either visual or spatial information. On this basis, therefore, it is interesting to look at the performance of a child across all three of the visuo-spatial subtests of the WMTB-C to see whether evidence for such a dissociation in performance exists. In this way, the WMTB-C allows the user to develop a detailed description of visuo-spatial WM for each child.

Listening Recall

Both the Listening Recall and the Counting Recall subtests of the WMTB-C are examples of what has been referred to as "complex span" tasks (see other chapters of this book, particularly Chapters 1 and 2, for discussion of this type of task). Such tasks can be contrasted from "simple" span tasks on the basis that, whereas simple span tasks require a participant to encode and immediately recall information in immediate memory, complex span tasks require that some additional processing is carried out while information is maintained.

The Listening Recall subtest of the WMTB-C used a procedure originally developed for use with adults (Daneman & Carpenter, 1980) and adapted it to be more suitable for children. In the task the child hears a series of short sentences and is asked to decide whether the sentences make sense by responding either "true" or "false." For example, they might hear:

> Cars have wheels.
> Rabbits have long ears.
> Bicycles eat grass.

to which the child would have responded "true" after the first and second sentence and "false" after the third. The next part of the task requires the recall of each of the final words in the sentences in the order that they were heard. Thus, the child would respond "wheels, ears, grass."

We can see, therefore, that complex span tasks such Listening Recall measure much more than the simple storage of information and, in doing so, appear to draw heavily on the resources of the CE of WM. After the child has heard the first sentence in each trial, they must hold the final word of that sentence in mind while they listen to, and judge the veracity of, the next sentence, and so on. This subtest is particularly demanding, and even adults find trials with more than three or four sentences challenging.

Can other cognitive processes or strategic activities affect performance on this task? Possibly. It seems highly likely that children old enough to rehearse memory items in a phonological loop task will apply this strategy to the final words of each sentence in the Listening Recall task. Similarly, the type of semantic and visual processing that was discussed with reference to the Word List Recall task might also be possible here. Preliminary findings from the application of this task to children with and without dyslexia revealed some surprising patterns of performance (Pickering & Gathercole, 2006). Children with dyslexia seemed to score particularly well on this task—a finding that might be explained by the greater tendency of individuals with dyslexia to code information in WM visually and semantically, rather than phonologically (Byrne & Shea, 1979; Rack, 1985).

Overall, therefore, we can see that the Listening Recall subtest of the WMTB-C provides users with a measure of an important aspect of CE functioning, namely the ability to store and process information simultaneously in immediate memory. Performance on this task will almost certainly depend on the ability of the CE and the phonological loop, given the verbal presentation and response requirement of the task. However, children skilled in the use of semantic and visual recoding of phonologically presented information may also benefit from the use of such strategies.

Counting Recall

The Counting Recall subtest of the WMTB-C differs from the Listening Recall subtest in that children are asked to recall dot tallies while counting other arrays of dots (see Case, Kurland, & Goldberg, 1982). Specifically, the child is presented with a card on which there are either four, five, six, or seven dots. They are instructed to count the dots one at a time by placing their finger on the dot and counting out loud. This process is repeated until all of the dot cards are counted, at which point the child is asked to recall each of the tallies in the order in which they were encountered (e.g., "5, 4, 6, 7, 4"). In a similar way to that for the Listening Recall task, the child is holding and processing information at the same time.

The Counting Recall task is a measure of CE function, but children may also use both phonological loop and visuo-spatial sketchpad resources to carry it out. Given the verbal nature of the counting and recall process, it seems likely that phonological processes play a major role in the performance of this task, however. Thus, as with the Listening Recall task, the Counting Recall subtest of the WMTB-C provides a measure of the storage and processing function of the CE with a heavy emphasis on phonological coding. It also seems likely that a child's facility with counting will play a role in this task. Older and more able children can count faster, although the specific administration procedures for the counting part of this task are designed to preclude the use of subitizing (merely looking at an array and identifying the numbers of dots immediately) and to standardize the speed of counting for younger and older participants as much as possible.

Backward Digit Recall

A task that involves the repetition of digit sequences in *reverse* order is far from new; backward digit recall tasks have been included in many digit span assessments. What is interesting, however, is the way that performance on both forward and backward recall of digits has often been lumped together to form one measure of digit span (e.g., in the Wechsler intelligence tests). The cognitive processes involved in the recall of digit sequences in reverse order (e.g., 9, 5, 1, 4, 2 becomes 2, 4, 1, 5, 9) seem quite different to those involved in the recall of digits forward. Specifically, when carrying out a backward digit recall task, participants need to hold the sequence that they have just heard in mind while they reverse it ready for output. In other words, they need to carry out some form of processing of the information while storing the information in immediate memory. Here we can see that tasks involving the recall of digits in reverse order have many of the characteristics of the Listening Recall and Counting Recall tasks described earlier. For this reason, we and many others have come to view this task as a measure of CE function, rather than a simple phonological storage task.

There is no doubt that phonological coding will be very likely in the Backward Digit Recall task, given the verbal presentation and response requirement. What is interesting, however, is the range of strategic approaches that participants appear to use in carrying out this task. For example, in our studies, some children have been observed to use verbal rehearsal to maintain the presented sequence in mind while systematically attempting to recall each item in the sequence, beginning with the final item and working back. Other children can be seen to be looking upward to a virtual visual array of digits, so as to be able to read off backward from it. Some children may use a range of approaches to this task. What does seem to be clear, however, is that this task is more complex than the recall of digits in forward order and therefore much more than a simple phonological loop task.

Some Comments on the General Organization of the WMTB-C

Having described the nature of the theoretical basis of the 10 subtests of the WMTB-C, it is also worth giving some consideration to some of the overarching features of the test and the rationale for these. One of the first points to note is that the test provides a comprehensive standardized assessment of WM function and in doing so allows the user to systematically compare a child's performance across the three related, but separable, components of WM. This is done by calculating *component scores* for the phonological loop, visuo-spatial sketchpad, and CE from the three or four subtests that represent each of those components. By including a range of measures of each component, we are able to increase the robustness of each of these three scores. In addition, within each of the three components it is possible to make a detailed comparison of scores of each of the different subtests, while taking into account the specific features of those subtests as described earlier (e.g., comparing recall of words and nonsense words, or visual and spatial recall). Standard scores obtained on the test can be plotted as a WMTB-C profile, giving a good visual impression of the performance of a child relative to children of his or her age, and of the strengths and weaknesses demonstrated in the three different areas of WM functioning.

Two other features of the test offer practical advantages. The first is that the child is given six opportunities to demonstrate their memory capacity at each difficulty level, of which only four of the six trials need to be correct. This allows for distractions and lapses of attention to occur during testing without having devastating consequences for the scores obtained by the child. Second, testing can be discontinued when the child fails to recall three trials correctly at a particular difficulty level, and for older and more able children, each subtest can actually begin at a point other than the first trial. These two features of the subtests mean that testing time can be significantly reduced, and moreover, children are not required to continue with a subtest once it is clear that their own level of performance has been exceeded.

HOW HAS THE WMTB-C BEEN USED?

Since publication in 2001, more than 300 copies of the WMTB-C have been sold worldwide. The list of those who have purchased the battery includes educational psychologists, special needs teachers, and academic researchers, among others. How do these individuals and organizations use the test? A questionnaire study of the WMTB-C asked this very question, and some of the responses are outlined below.

A number of respondents indicated that they use the WMTB-C as a diagnostic tool for the purpose of building up a pupil profile prior to referral for assessment by an Educational Psychologist. Others have used it with children as a baseline test. Some have used it with children with specific learning difficulties to find out about children's areas of strength and weakness. Some respondents have used the WMTB-C for research or teaching purposes. Many of the users of the WMTB-C told us that they found the profiles of performance across the three components useful in their work. As an academic researcher, I have used the battery extensively since 2001. One of my research interests is the study of developmental disorders such as dyslexia, developmental coordination disorder, attention deficits, autistic spectrum disorders, and other specific educational problems that manifest during childhood. Given the significant debate that surrounds these conditions in terms of their definition, diagnosis, and comorbidity, I was keen to apply a systematic assessment of WM to these populations. As indicated throughout this chapter, one of the advantages of giving a battery of WM tests to children with learning problems is that their scores can be related back to what we already know about WM structures and functions. Thus, studies of this type may help us to understand more about the nature of both the deficits found in these populations and the areas in which they do not experience impairments. This is a very important point because much of the research on learning problems has focused on what individuals cannot do, but it has said very little about what they can do. These findings have enormous implications for understanding the learning problems themselves and for the design and delivery of learning support activities for individuals who experience them.

Research Findings from the WMTB-C

One possible outcome from the application of a standardized battery of WM tasks to groups with particular learning problems is that a "signature" WM profile would be found for each group. This would allow us to use WM in the assessment of children with learning problems to understand more about the type of problem they were experiencing (e.g., "the profile looks like this. . . . therefore, this child has problems of . . . type"). This is an ambitious idea and very unlikely to be borne out so simplistically in the research findings, not least because within and between various learning problems there is much overlap and much variation. Dyslexia, for example, is a hugely heterogeneous condition. Might it be possible to establish a WM profile for dyslexia in the face of all this individual variation?

The WMTB-C and Dyslexia

Several studies have been carried out in which children identified as having problems of a dyslexic nature have been administered a battery of WM tests (see Pickering, 2004 and Pickering, in press, for a more detailed description of some of this research). The first study involved the prototype version of the WMTB-C (Pickering & Gathercole, 2006). When this battery was administered to children with dyslexia, chronological age (CA) controls, and reading age (RA) controls, it was found that the scores of the dyslexic group were relatively poor on the measures of phonological loop and CE function but largely unimpaired on the tests of visuo-spatial sketchpad function. Subsequent studies using the WMTB-C have provided additional support for this finding (e.g., Pickering & Chubb, in prep), including a study carried out in Greece using a modified version of the WMTB-C suitable for administration to Greek children (Pickering & Zacharof, in prep). Inspection of the WM profiles of individual children with dyslexia indicates quite a wide range of profiles of WM performance, which may relate to a range of factors including the nature of their dyslexia (e.g., whether problems appear to be of a primarily verbal or visual nature) and the nature and extent of any remedial help that the child has already received. Nonetheless, at a group level, children with dyslexia appear to have weaknesses in phonological loop

functioning and possibly even more significant problems with CE functioning (see Chapter 2 of the this volume for a more detailed discussion of this
issue). Unless phonological recoding is likely to benefit performance, visuo-
spatial sketchpad functioning appears to be unimpaired in this group
(although this issue needs to be examined more closely in children with
visual dyslexic problems). More research is required to investigate these
findings yet further.

The WMTB-C and Developmental Coordination Disorder

Developmental coordination disorder (DCD) is a problem that affects about
6% of children and is defined as a marked impairment in the development
of motor coordination that significantly interferes with academic achievement or activities of daily living and is not the result of a general medical
condition. Individuals with DCD (the terms DCD and dyspraxia are often
used interchangeably, but there is debate about their equivalence) may
exhibit marked delays in achieving motor milestones, such as walking, and
may appear to be "clumsy" (see, for example, Portwood, 2000). One major
problem for many involved in the assessment of developmental problems
such as DCD is the extent to which the problems associated with this disorder are also found in individuals with other developmental disorders, such
as dyslexia and attention disorders. One study (see Pickering, in press, for
further details) allowed us to investigate the WM performance of children
with DCD and dyslexia. In this study, one group of children had been identified as having dyslexia but also manifested DCD problems. A second group
had been identified as having the converse pattern of problems—that is, a
diagnosis of dyslexia with a cooccurrence of motor skills problems. When
these children were tested with the WMTB-C it was found that children with
primarily movement problems appeared to show one WMTB-C profile (with
poor visuo-spatial sketchpad functioning but unimpaired phonological loop
and CE functioning), whereas children with primarily dyslexic problems
showed a different profile (relatively poor phonological loop and CE performance but unimpaired visuo-spatial sketchpad performance). Again, at the
level of the individual child, there was some variation in memory performance, but across groups, children with motor skills and literacy skills problems seemed to experience different strengths and weaknesses in their WM
performance. These findings are supported by studies by Jeffries and Everatt
(Jeffries & Everatt, 2003, 2004), who found similar WM profiles to those
described previously in adults with motor skills problems.

The WMTB-C and Attention Deficits

When the WMTB-C was administered to children with a diagnosis of attention deficit/hyperactivity disorder (ADHD), relatively poor performance was
found across a range of subtests including Digit Recall, Word List Matching,

Block Recall, Listening Recall, Counting Recall, and Backward Digit Recall. As Chapter 6 of this volume indicates, attention deficits appear to be linked to problems with CE functioning. This view was supported in our own research, but children also appeared to score poorly on tests other than those that measured CE function. It is interesting that 4 of the 18 children with ADHD in this study also had a diagnosis of dyslexia—a cooccurrence of learning problems that appears to be common in our schools. Problems of a dyslexic nature may go some way to accounting for the poor scores on tests of phonological loop function that were found in this study. More research clearly is needed to understand how WM functions in children with attention problems. Nonetheless, the WMTB-C may offer detailed information about the cognitive strengths and weaknesses of individual children with attention problems, either with or without other comorbid conditions.

The WMTB-C and Autistic Spectrum Disorders

A small-scale study involved administering the WMTB-C to children with autism spectrum disorders (ASD). The performance of the children on the WMTB-C was highly variable, both across subtests and across individual children. What did seem to be relatively consistent across the group of children studied, however, were poor scores on the CE subtests of the battery. CE— or executive function deficits in ASD have been proposed by a number of researchers, although there is still much debate and discussion about this issue (e.g. Russell, 1997). Again, further research clearly is needed to establish whether WM deficits are a key feature of ASD. The WMTB-C may allow those working with children with ASD to learn more about the cognitive strengths and weaknesses that these children experience and the implications that they might have for their educational progress.

Limitations of the WMTB-C

The WMTB-C was the first theoretically driven WM assessment tool for children. It provides users with a range of features that had not been available to them before. However, the test battery is not without its limitations. Indeed, it has already been pointed out that, whereas the WMTB-C is based on a tripartite model of WM, the Baddeley and Hitch model now contains four components. This issue is something that will be addressed in the coming years, as more knowledge becomes available about the new "episodic buffer" component and tests to measure its function increase in number.

A potentially more important limitation of the WMTB-C centers on the range of subtests used to measure CE function. Although these tests are based on extensive literature on the processes associated with CE functioning, they do not capture all of the different types of processing associated with the CE. More specifically, although each test measures the capacity to store and process information simultaneously, none of the tests is able to provide specific information about the attention-based functions that have also been attributed to the CE. This may not matter so much if we are merely asking if the CE is impaired because the three CE subtests in the battery almost certainly draw on a range of CE functions, including the focusing, dividing, and switching of attention. However, because evidence is beginning to develop (see Chapters 1, 2, and 6 of this book) that CE functions can be fractionated, and moreover may be differentially affected in different individuals and populations, more precise measures of the different CE functions may be deemed to be useful in the future.

One other feature of the CE tasks included in the WMTB-C is worthy of note—that is, all three of the subtests are very strongly loaded on the phonological loop component of WM. The Listening Recall, Counting Recall, and Backward Digit Recall subtests all involve verbal responses, and the stimuli included in each subtest lend themselves very well to phonological (re)coding. One consequence of this strongly verbal CE assessment is that children who have problems with processing information in phonological form may well find these tasks difficult, not so much because they are CE tasks but because they use phonological information. The obvious solution is to include nonverbal measures of CE function; however, tasks of this sort were not available to us when the WMTB-C was developed. This has now changed, and a small number of nonverbal CE tasks have come into existence. These will be discussed further in the next section.

One final comment regarding the limitations of the WMTB-C concerns the use of the test outside the country in which it was designed and standardized. This issue is not just difficult for the WMTB-C; it has an impact on any standardized test that is used outside of its country of origin. We know from the responses to the questionnaire study that individuals outside of the United Kingdom, including those based in countries whose dominant language is not English, have bought the battery. What implications does this have for the use and interpretation of WMTB-C scores? The fact that WM has been studied internationally means that we already have some idea about how different languages affect performance on tasks designed to measure WM functioning. For example, in the case of digit recall, it has been shown that when digits are presented and recalled in Welsh, scores tend to be lower than for English (Ellis & Hennelly, 1980), but when the language being used is Chinese, digits spans tend to be higher than in English (Hoosain & Salili, 1987). These findings have been linked to the articulatory duration of numbers in the different languages. In Welsh, numbers tend to have longer vowel sounds, whereas the spoken duration of numbers in Chinese is very short. So, the language in which a child's WM is tested may have significant consequences for the interpretation of their performance. It is interesting that some recent research in our laboratories involving the administration of the WMTB-C to children in Hong Kong found that, although the sequences in the Digit Recall task were administered in English, some children responded in English, some in Cantonese, and some used a mixture of the two languages. The precise mechanisms by which different languages influence WM performance require further investigation. The findings of future studies may be able to tell us how language affects WM performance and may also help us to understand further the structure and function of WM as a whole.

Differences in language use are not the only factors that might need to be taken into consideration when administering a test like the WMTB-C outside of the United Kingdom. Cultural differences may mean that a child in one country may have differing experiences on which to draw when completing the various subtests. Two particular examples have been drawn to my attention, both of which relate to the experiences of children in China. The first concerns the differences in practices that are common in schools in China and the United Kingdom. In China, there is a strong emphasis on developing rote memory in children of school age, and many activities are devoted to the development of this skill. What implications does this have for children's memory development in China? Does children's WM performance benefit from such training? A second example concerns the subject matter of the Mazes Memory subtest. Anecdotal reports suggest that children in China do not usually have experience with mazes in the way that children in the United Kingdom may have. Does experience with mazes contribute to a child's ability to carry out this task efficiently? Further research is needed to answer this and other related questions. Work is in progress to tackle issues concerning the cultural and language implications for WM. WM test batteries are being developed in countries outside of the United Kingdom (e.g., Greece), and experimental investigations of WM performance in non-English children are under way. As this research develops, we should be in a better position to understand how to assess the WM of children all across the world.

A COMPUTER-BASED WORKING MEMORY ASSESSMENT TOOL: THE AWMA

In the previous section it was noted that the three subtests that measure CE function in the WMTB-C were very verbal in nature as a consequence of the lack of nonverbal tests available at the time that the test was developed. Since that time, however, a small number of more nonverbal CE tests have been developed, and these tests have been combined with many of the original subtests of the WMTB-C into a computer-administered version of the WMTB-C, known as *Automated Working Memory Assessment* battery (or AWMA; Alloway et al., 2004).

The AWMA contains 12 subtests. Six tests measure the ability to hold information temporarily (without any processing demands) including Digit Recall, Word List Recall, Nonword List Recall, Dot Matrix task (adapted from the Visual Patterns Task), Mazes Memory, and Block Recall. It can be seen that, whereas the first three subtests measure phonological loop function, the second three measure visuo-spatial sketchpad function. Six further tests measure the child's ability to hold and process information at the same time: Listening Recall; Counting Recall; Backward Digit Recall; and three newer tests, the Odd-One-Out task (adapted from Russell, Jarrold, & Henry, 1996), the Mr X. task (adapted from Hamilton, Coates, & Heffernan, 2003), and the Spatial Span task (adapted from Jarvis & Gathercole, 2003). The final three tests just listed are all conceptualized as visuo-spatial (i.e., non-phonological) CE tasks, whereas, as discussed earlier, the first three tasks in this list appear to tap mainly phonological processes (Alloway, Gathercole, & Pickering, in prep). Computerized presentation of WM tasks brings with it some procedural advantages, not least the standardization of presentation of the subtests (although experience suggests that computer presentation may also pose minor problems for some WM subtests, particularly those that involve the requirement to hear a precise pronunciation of a memory item, such as a nonword). However, perhaps the most significant contribution that the AWMA can make to the assessment of WM is the availability of nonverbal CE tasks. Such tasks allow us to develop our understanding of the specific nature of CE functioning in children, both with and without recognized learning problems.

This issue has particular relevance for our understanding of WM functioning in children with dyslexia. As outlined earlier, poor performance on both phonological loop and CE tasks has been found across a number of studies of WM in this group (see Chapter 2 of this volume and Pickering, 2004, for reviews). One problem with the assertion that CE deficits are found in dyslexia hinges on the largely verbal nature of many of the CE tests that have been used in these studies. By including tests of nonphonological CE function we are able to establish whether the pattern of results obtained so far can be explained by a general problem with the maintenance and processing of all information in phonological form or whether the deficits observed also extend to tests of nonphonological CE function. Preliminary findings from our own research suggest that children with dyslexia find verbal CE tasks more difficult than visuo-spatial CE tasks. Our next task is to establish whether performance on the visuo-spatial tasks is at age-appropriate levels. Further research is needed to clarify these initial findings and thus increase our understanding of the nature of WM in this group.

ASSESSMENT OF WORKING MEMORY AND CONSEQUENCES FOR REMEDIATION

A question that is often asked when information about WM assessment batteries is presented is as follows: "What do we do once the assessment has been carried out?" This is a very valid question and one that should command the attention of educators and psychologists interested in WM. So far, however, very little has been written specifically about how to help children with problems in WM, although advances are being made in this area. The remediation of WM is discussed in two chapters of this book—in Chapter 8 in the context of WM in the classroom setting and in Chapter 10 in an account of research that has attempted to develop remedial approaches for WM problems. On this basis, a detailed discussion of WM remediation will not be presented here. Rather, this final section of the chapter will concern itself with the remedial implications that derive specifically from the use of the WM assessment batteries described earlier.

One of the envisaged strengths of the WMTB-C was the ability to sample across the whole of WM in a standardized way. Thus, users of the battery can look at a child's performance in the three WM components (phonological loop, visuo-spatial sketchpad, and CE), both in comparison to children of the same age and across different memory components. This WM profiling appears to have been found to be useful for many of the WMTB-C users that took part in the questionnaire study. Indeed, one of the strengths of a WM profile is that it allows the user to understand where the child's weaknesses lie and where they show a relative strength. Such information can be important when devising teaching and learning approaches for children, both with and without recognized learning problems.

Although we are not yet at the stage where a dedicated WM remediation program that links with the assessment batteries has been developed, we are steadily moving toward this goal (see Chapter 8 for a discussion of current research in this area). In the meantime, there are many useful sources of information that we can draw on to help children with WM problems. Some of these approaches are described in Chapters 8 and 10. In many cases, experienced teachers will have been using approaches such as these in their classrooms for many years. Teaching approaches based on "multi-sensory" techniques have been popular for a long time with those working with children with dyslexia. Similar approaches may work well with children who manifest uneven profiles on the WM batteries. For these children, WM profiles can provide important information about what type of information (phonological or visuo-spatial) is causing the most significant problems. Teaching to the strengths to overcome areas of weakness is a well-established remedial approach for many specialist teachers. This method is just one of a number of remedial approaches that may be used by those wishing to support the educational activities of children with WM problems.

SUMMARY

This chapter has examined the assessment of WM in children, beginning with an examination of the methods first used more than 100 years ago to measure immediate memory capacity. It is clear from this review that many of the basic features of the early assessment of WM are still critical today. However, advances in our theoretical understanding and, in particular, the development of the multi-component model of memory originally proposed by Baddeley and Hitch, have allowed us to create more varied and increasingly specific tools for measuring the range of processes carried out by the WM system.

The Working Memory Test Battery for Children and the Automated Working Memory Assessment battery are two examples of detailed tools for WM assessment. Although the specific features of each test battery vary to some degree, both tests are capable of providing a user with a standardized profile of performance across different aspects of the WM system. Information of this type may assist in the identification and understanding of children with different and sometimes cooccurring developmental disorders, such as dyslexia, DCD, attention problems, and ASD. WM profiles may also help in the design and delivery of remedial help to children.

Summary Box

- The assessment of WM (or STM) has been of interest to educators for more than 100 years.
- Memory span for sequences of digits has remained a popular method of immediate memory assessment during this time.
- The Baddeley and Hitch (1974) WM model specified a three-component system of immediate memory functioning comprising a phonological loop, visuo-spatial sketchpad, and CE.
- The digit span task measures only the functioning of the phonological loop.
- In recent years, tests that measure the CE and visuo-spatial sketchpad have been developed; phonological loop tests other than digit span also have been developed.
- Experimental research has contributed to a much greater understanding of the factors that influence performance on a test of WM.
- A theoretically driven battery of WM tests for children, the WMTB-C, has been developed.
- When the test was administered to children with different developmental disorders, different profiles of WM performance were found.
- A computer-administered WM test battery (AWMA) combines subtests from the WMTB-C with new nonverbal measures of CE function.
- Remedial efforts with children with WM deficits may be usefully guided by the profiles obtained from tests such as the WMTB-C and AWMA.

References

Alloway, T. P., Gathercole, S. E., & Pickering, S. J. (2004). The Automated Working Assessment Battery. (Available from the authors on request.)

Alloway, T. P., Gathercole, S. E., & Pickering, S. J. (submitted). Verbal and visuo-spatial working memory in children: Are they separable? Child Development.

Atkinson, R. C., & Shiffrin, R. M. (1968). Human memory: A proposed system and its control processes. In K. W. Spence (Ed.), *The psychology of learning and motivation: advances in research and theory Vol. 2* (pp. 89–195). New York: Academic Press.

Baddeley, A. (1997). *Human memory: Theory and practice*. Hove, UK: Psychology Press.

Baddeley, A. D. (2000). The episodic buffer: A new component of working memory? *Trends in Cognitive Sciences, 4*, 417–423.

Baddeley, A. D., Lewis, V. J., & Vallar, G. (1984). Exploring the articulatory loop. *Quarterly Journal of Experimental Psychology, 36A*, 233–252.

Byrne, B., & Shea, P. (1979). Semantic and phonetic memory codes in beginning readers? *Memory and Cognition, 7*, 333–338.

Case, R. D., Kurland, M., & Goldberg, J. (1982). Operational efficiency and the growth of short-term memory span. *Journal of Experimental Child Psychology, 33*, 386–404.

Cohen, M. (1997). *Children's Memory Scale*. London: The Psychological Corporation.

Cowan, N. (1997). The development of working memory. In N. Cowan (Ed.), *The development of memory in childhood* (pp. 163–199). Hove, UK: Psychology Press.

Cowan, N., Wood, N. L., Wood, P. K., Keller, T. A., Nugent, L. D., & Keller, C. V. (1998). Two separate verbal processing rates contributing to short-term memory span. *Journal of Experimental Psychology: General, 127*, 141–160.

Craik, F. I. M., & Lockheart, R. S. (1972). Levels of processing: A framework for memory research. *Journal of Verbal Learning and Verbal Behavior, 11*, 671–684.

Daneman, M., & Carpenter, P. A. (1980). Individual differences in working memory and reading. *Journal of Verbal Learning and Verbal Behaviour, 19*, 450–466.

Della Sala, S., Gray, C., Baddeley, A., & Wilson, L. (1997). *Visual Patterns Test*. Bury St Edmunds: Thames Valley Test Company.

Elliot, C. D. (1996). *British Ability Scales II*. Windsor, UK: Nfer-Nelson.

Ellis, N. C., & Hennelly, R. A. (1980). A bilingual word-length effect: Implications for intelligence testing and the relative ease of mental calculation in Welsh and English. *British Journal of Psychology, 71*, 43–52.

Ericsson, K. A., Chase, W. G., & Faloon, S. F. (1980). Acquisition of a memory skill. *Science, 208*, 1181–1182.

Ericsson, K. A., Delaney, P. F., Weaver, G., & Mahadevan, R. (2004). Uncovering the structure of a memorist's superior "basic" memory capacity. *Cognitive Psychology, 49*, 191–237.

Farmer, E. W., Berman, J. V. F., & Fletcher, Y. L. (1986). Evidence for a visuo-spatial sketchpad in working memory. *Quarterly Journal of Experimental Psychology, 38A*, 675–688.

Flavell, J. H., Beach, D. H., & Chinsky, J. M. (1966). Spontaneous verbal rehearsal in a memory task as a function of age. *Child Development, 37*, 283–299.

Gathercole, S. E. (1999). Cognitive approaches to the development of short-term memory. *Trends in Cognitive Science, 3*, 410–418.

Gathercole, S. E., & Baddeley, A. D. (1996). *The Children's Test of Nonword Repetition*. The Psychological Corporation.

Gathercole, S. E., & Hitch, G. J. (1993). Developmental changes in short-term memory: A revised working memory perspective. In A. Collins, S.E. Gathercole, M.A. Conway, & P.E. Morris (Eds.), *Theories of memory* (pp. 189–210). Hove, UK: Lawrence Erlbaum Associates.

Gathercole, S. E., Frankish, C. R., Pickering, S. J., & Peaker, S. (1999). Phonotactic influences on short-term memory. *Journal of Experimental Psychology—Learning, Memory & Cognition, 25*, 84–95.

Gathercole, S. E., & Pickering, S. J. (2000a). Assessment of working memory in six- and seven-year-old children. *Journal of Educational Psychology, 92*, 377–390.

Gathercole, S. E., & Pickering, S. J. (2000b). Working memory deficits in children with low achievements in the national curriculum at seven years of age. *British Journal of Educational Psychology*, *70*, 177–194.

Gathercole, S. E., & Pickering, S. J. (2001). Working memory deficits in children with special educational needs. *British Journal of Special Education*, *28*, 89–97.

Gathercole, S. E., Pickering, S. J., Hall, M., & Peaker, S. M. (2001). Dissociable lexical and phonological influences on serial recall and serial recognition. *Quarterly Journal of Experimental Psychology*, *54A*, 1–30.

Gathercole, S. E., Pickering, S. J., Ambridge, B., & Wearing, H. (2004). The structure of working memory from 4 to 15 years of age. *Developmental Psychology*, *40*, 177–190.

Hamilton, C. J., Coates, R. O., & Heffernan, T. (2003). What develops in visuo-spatial working memory development? *European Journal of Cognitive Psychology*, *15*, 43–69.

Henson, R. (2001). Neural working memory. In J. Andrade (Ed.), *Working memory in perspective* (pp. 151–173). Hove, UK: Psychology Press.

Henson, R., Burgess, N., & Frith, C. D. (2000). Recoding, storage, rehearsal and grouping in verbal short-term memory: An fMRI study. *Neuropsychologia*, *38*, 426–440.

Hitch, G. J., Halliday, M. S., Schaafstal, A. M., & Schraagen, J. M. C. (1988). Visual working memory in children. *Memory and Cognition*, *16*, 120–132.

Hoosain, R., & Salili, F. (1987). Language differences in pronunciation speed for numbers, digit span, and mathematical ability. *Psychologia*, *30*, 34–38.

Hulme, C., Thomson, N., Muir, C., & Lawrence, A. (1984). Speech rate and the development of short-term memory span. *Journal of Experimental Child Psychology*, *38*, 241–253.

Hulme, C., Maughan, S., & Brown, G. D. A. (1991). Memory for familiar and unfamiliar words: Evidence for a longer term memory contribution to short-term memory span. *Journal of Memory and Language*, *30*, 685–701.

Jarvis, H., & Gathercole, S. E. (2003). Verbal and non-verbal working memory and achievements on national curriculum tests at 11 and 14 years of age. *Educational and Child Psychology*, *20*, 123–140.

Jeffries, S. A., & Everatt, J. E. (2003). Differences between dyspraxics and dyslexics in sequence learning and working memory. *Dyspraxia Foundation Professional Journal*, *2*, 12–21.

Jeffries, S., & Everatt, J. (2004). Working memory: its role in dyslexia and other specific learning difficulties. *Dyslexia*, *10*, 196–214.

Logie, R. H. (1995). *Visuo-spatial working memory*. Hove: Lawrence Erlbaum Associates.

Miles, C., Morgan, M. J., Milne, A. B., & Morris, E. D. M. (1996). Developmental and individual differences in visual memory span. *Current Psychology*, *15*, 53–67.

Miller, G. A. (1956). The magic number seven, plus or minus two: Some limits on our capacity for processing information. *Psychological Review*, *63*, 81–97.

Milner, B. (1971). Interhemispheric differences in the localisation of psychological processes in man. *British Medical Bulletin*, *27*, 272–277.

Neisser, U. (1978). Memory: What are the important questions? In M. M. Gruneberg, P. E. Morris, & R. N. Sykes (Eds.), *Practical aspects of memory*. London: Academic Press.

Owen, A. M., Evans, A. C., & Petrides, M. (1996). Evidence for a two-stage model of spatial working memory processing within the lateral frontal cortex: A positron emission tomography study. *Cerebral Cortex*, *6*, 31–38.

Pickering, S. J. (2001). Cognitive approaches to the fractionation of visuo-spatial working memory. *Cortex*, *37*, 457–473.

Pickering, S. J. (2004). Verbal working memory in the learning of literacy. In M. Turner & J. Rack (Eds.), *The study of dyslexia*. New York: Plenum Publishers.

Pickering, S. J. (in press). Working memory in dyslexia. In T. P. Alloway & S. E. Gathercole (Eds.), *Working memory and neurodevelopmental condition*. Hove, UK: Psychology Press.

Pickering, S., & Gathercole, S. (2001). *The Working Memory Test Battery for Children*. London: The Psychological Corporation.

Pickering, S. J., Gathercole, S. E., Hall, M., & Lloyd, S. A. (2001). Development of memory for pattern and path: Further evidence for the fractionation of visuo-spatial memory. *Quarterly Journal of Experimental Psychology, 54A*, 397–420.

Pickering, S. J., & Gathercole, S. E. (2006). Working memory deficits in dyslexia: Are they located in the phonological loop, visuo-spatial sketchpad or central executive? Found in text on p 258 & p 261.

Pickering, S. J., & Chubb, R. (in prep). Working memory in dyslexia: A comparison of performance of dyslexics and reading age controls on the WMTB-C.

Pickering, S. J., & Zacharof, C. (in prep). Identifiable patterns of working memory performance in Greek children with developmental dyslexia.

Portwood, M. (2000). *Understanding developmental dyspraxia*. London: David Fulton Publishers.

Rack, J. (1985). Orthographic and phonetic coding in normal and dyslexic readers. *British Journal of Psychology, 76*, 325–340.

Reynolds, C. R., & Bigler, E. D. (1994). *Test of memory and learning*. Austin: Pro-Ed.

Russell, J. (1997). Autism as an executive disorder. New York: Oxford University Press.

Russell, J., Jarrold, C., & Henry, L. (1996). Working memory in children with autism and with moderate learning difficulties. *Journal of Child Psychology and Psychiatry and Allied Disciplines, 37*, 673–686.

Sheslow, D., & Adams, W. (1990). *Wide Range Assessment of Memory and Learning*. London: The Psychological Corporation.

Smith, E. E., & Jonides, J. (1997). Working memory: A view from neuroimaging. *Cognitive Psychology, 33*, 5–42.

Wechsler, D. (1992). *Wechsler Intelligence Scale for Children—Third Edition UK*. London: The Psychological Corporation.

Wechsler, D. (1997). *Wechsler Memory Scale—Third UK Edition*. London: The Psychological Corporation.

Wilson, B. A., Ivani-Chalian, R., & Aldrich, F. (1991). *The Rivermead Behavioural Memory Test for Children*. Bury St Edmunds: Thames Valley Test Company.

Woodworth, R. S. (1927). *Psychology: A Study of Mental Life*. London: Methuen & Co.

CHAPTER

10

Sources of Working Memory Deficits in Children and Possibilities for Remediation

MEREDITH MINEAR
Washington University

PRITI SHAH
University of Michigan

Much of our childhood is spent developing complex cognitive skills that as adults we may take for granted, including language, reading, mathematics, and reasoning. These are the very skills that allow us to reap the greatest benefits from education and from life in general. Psychologists have long been interested in trying to identify general cognitive mechanisms that may underlie such complex cognitive activities. One promising candidate is working memory (WM), most generally defined as the ability to actively maintain task-relevant information during the performance of a cognitive task (Baddeley & Hitch, 1976; Shah & Miyake, 1999).

WM has evolved from the earlier concept of short-term memory. Short-term memory provides temporary on-line storage of information that decays rapidly unless rehearsed. A standard measurement of short-term memory capacity is the digit span task, in which an individual is read a string of digits and is asked to repeat them back. The longest series of digits that can be accurately repeated is that individual's digit span. However, in the real world, short-term storage of information is frequently not so static. For example, when performing mental arithmetic one must not only store the numbers, but also transform them into a new number while still remembering the old numbers. WM measures are designed to assess an individual's ability to simultaneously store and process information. An example of a WM measure is the reading span task, in which an individual reads and judges the veracity of a series of sentences while at the same time remembering the last word from each sentence. The number of sentences for which an individual can both correctly judge the sentences and remember all of the words is that person's reading span score. Individual differences in WM measures such as reading span have been shown to predict performance on a wide variety of tasks including vocabulary acquisition (Gathercole & Baddeley, 1993), language comprehension (Daneman & Merikle, 1996), mathematics, (Bull, Johnston, & Roy, 1999), and reasoning (Kyllonen & Christal, 1990). Based on its predictive power, WM has been proposed to play an essential role in many school-based cognitive activities (Gathercole & Baddeley, 1993; Gathercole, Pickering, Knight, & Stegmann, 2004).

In the course of normal development, children show large increases in their WM capacity (Gathercole, 1999; Pickering, 2001). However, there are many children in whom the expected progression of some portion of WM appears to be either delayed or disrupted. WM deficits have been reported in a diverse array of populations ranging from children with developmental disorders with known etiologies such as Down syndrome (Hulme & Mackenzie, 1992), to those with specific learning disabilities (Swanson & Sachse-Lee, 2001a), to children who have survived chemotherapy treatments (Schatz, Kramer, Albin, & Matthay, 2000). Although these groups differ widely in the exact nature and the degree of cognitive impairment experienced, poor WM function has often been identified as playing an important role in these children's overall performance and as a target process in which to attempt remediation. Given the power of WM measures in predicting various indices of future educational achievement (Gathercole, Brown, & Pickering, 2003; Gathercole et al., 2004), even small increases in the efficacy of WM skills may significantly improve these children's performance in the classroom and in their daily lives.

In this chapter, we provide a broad overview of the different approaches taken in rehabilitating cognitive functioning that either target WM function directly or have been shown to improve WM function. We then examine the types of WM deficits identified in different populations of children who are learning impaired and the extent to which different forms of remediation have been attempted in each. Finally, we conclude with a summary of the general principles for remediation that can be drawn from the current evidence and suggest future directions for research.

THEORETICAL APPROACHES TO WORKING MEMORY REMEDIATION

The standard model of WM proposed by Baddeley and Hitch (1976) is a three-part system consisting of a central executive (CE) and two peripheral systems: the phonological loop and the visuo-spatial sketchpad. The phonological loop and visuo-spatial sketchpad are temporary storage systems responsible for maintaining verbal and visuo-spatial information, respectively. Each can be divided into two basic subcomponents: a limited capacity store, which holds only a few items and decays rapidly without being refreshed by the second subcomponent, a rehearsal process (Baddeley, 1986). The CE has been broadly defined as the supervisory system that oversees and regulates the cognitive processes involved in WM performance (Baddeley, 1986). So-called "executive" processes thought to reflect the functioning of the CE include various forms of attentional control such as focusing attention, switching attention, and dividing attention as well as the ability to inhibit unwanted thoughts or actions and the ability to stay focused on a particular goal (Baddeley, 2002; Duncan, 1995; Miyake et al., 2000).

Therefore, within the Baddeley model, deficits in WM function have multiple possible origins, including differences in the size of the phonological or visuo-spatial stores, the efficiency of the rehearsal processes, or the integrity of higher-level processes of the CE. As a result, a continuum of WM measures exists, with very simple storage tasks at one end and complex problem-solving tasks at the other. Tasks along this continuum differ in the amount and type of CE processes required. An example of a task low in executive demand would be a simple span task in which an individual must remember a series of letters, movements, or sounds and repeat them back. An example of a task that requires one aspect of CE functioning, the inhibition of prepotent responses, is the Stroop task. The Stroop task requires participants to view color words written in different colors of ink and inhibit the well-practiced response of reading the words, instead of naming the color of the ink (Stroop, 1935). Finally, an example of a task that involves multiple executive processes would be a problem-solving task such as the Tower of London/Hanoi, which consists of a puzzle in which a person must move a series of disks across a series of pegs. Such problem-solving tasks require storage of information in memory along with focusing attention, inhibitory processing, and maintaining and updating goals and subgoals.

Although most WM theorists usually agree on the existence of peripheral systems that process relatively domain-specific information (e.g., visual as opposed to verbal information), as well as centralized control mechanisms that may be more domain general, there are differences amongst theoretical approaches as to the source of individual variations in WM performance. For example, a number of researchers have proposed that capacity differences in the amount of "WM resources" or "controlled attention capacity" possessed by individuals predict individual differences in performance on a variety of WM measures, independent of the specific processing domain (Just & Carpenter, 1992; Kane & Engle, 2002; Daily, Lovett, & Reder, 2001). Although these theories of WM acknowledge that acquired knowledge and experience may have an impact on performance of individual tasks, they suggest a large proportion of the individual variability on many novel, intelligence-demanding tasks relevant for schooling may be accounted for by this general factor (Engle, Tuholski, Laughlin, & Conway, 1999). Therefore any intervention that could increase this capacity should have general effects on WM and tasks thought to require it.

However, other theories such as long-term WM (Ericsson and Kintsch, 1995) and connectionist approaches (MacDonald and Christiansen, 2002; O'Reilly, Braver, & Cohen, 1999) emphasize the role of domain-specific knowledge and the importance of strategies in the performance of complex cognitive tasks that rely on WM. Individual differences in performance on WM tasks may not solely result from differences in capacity limitations; they also may result from differences in long-term memory and processing strategies gained through experience. These theories assume performance on tasks that demand WM can be improved but that this improvement is highly strategic and specific to the task practiced. For example, through training, one individual expanded his *digit* span to 79 continuous items by devising strategies to quickly remember numbers. This well exceeds the capacity limits of the phonological store (Ericsson, Chase, & Faloon, 1980). However, this extra capacity was not seen when the same individual was asked to remember a series of *letters,* in which he did no better than an average span. A more common example is experienced restaurant servers who may excel at remembering customer orders without writing them down but then may perform no better than anyone else on another WM demanding task, even if it is another verbal one (Ericsson & Polson, 1988).

There then exist multiple possible reasons why WM may be impaired and multiple routes by which intervention may be attempted. Damage may be localized to one of the peripheral systems, or it may have a more general effect through a failure of the CE. Within a system, possible underlying problems include reduced processing capacity, poor knowledge representations in long-term memory, failures to use efficient and appropriate strategies, or any combination with one deficit possibly causing or exacerbating another. For example, children with poor attentional capacity may have more difficulty self-initiating a rehearsal strategy that would improve their performance. Although training these children to use rehearsal strategies may improve WM performance, it may not be as effective as treating the underlying cause of the deficit. Therefore the success of a remediation attempt may depend on correctly targeting the locus or loci of impairment in a particular population of children.

Remediation of Peripheral Impairments

Specific impairments of peripheral systems have been hypothesized in a number of different developmental learning disorders ranging from severe intellectual disabilities to very specific learning difficulties without any other obvious intellectual impairment, such as dyslexia. The selective nature of many of these conditions has been used as evidence in support of the separability of the different peripheral systems such as the phonological loop and the visuo-spatial sketchpad (Wang & Bellugi, 1994). In light of these patterns of impairment, a number of remedial approaches for children with developmental disorders have focused on the improvement of storage and processing in one or other of the peripheral WM components.

Of the two peripheral systems, the phonological loop has received the greatest amount of research both as a locus of deficit and as a target for remediation. Phonological WM is hypothesized to consist of two components: a phonological store, which holds only a few items and decays rapidly without being refreshed by the second component, a subvocal rehearsal process (Baddeley, 1986). This rehearsal process is also responsible for translating visual or written materials into phonologically based representations through a process known as phonological recoding (Gathercole & Baddeley, 1993; Palmer, 2000b). The visuo-spatial sketchpad has received comparatively less attention in terms of being specifically damaged and even fewer attempts at remediation. However, it is thought to be similar to the phonological loop in that there is also a store and rehearsal processes (Logie, 1995).

Strengthening Storage Representations

One proposed source of deficits specific to either the phonological or visuo-spatial storage systems is poor long-term memory representations or the inability to retrieve long-term representations. In the context of phonological representations, where this issue has been most extensively studied, listeners must code acoustic information into phonological codes that rely on the quality of information in long-term memory. Thus, crisp, highly distinguishable memory representations lead to greater WM capacity (Cowan, 1996). Conversely, poor and indistinct memory representations result in reduced WM capacity.

Auditory temporal processing deficits are frequently proposed as an underlying source of poor phonological representations (Tallal, 2003; Veale, 1999). Auditory temporal processing skills involve the ability to process rapidly presented stimuli. To develop distinct neural representations of phonemes in any language, the listener must first be able to distinguish between auditory input that is rapidly changing, often in less than 40 milliseconds (Tallal, 2003). Children who process speech sounds too slowly to identify and distinctly represent different phonemes (such as children with specific language impairment and dyslexia) also have impairments in phonological WM and other language skills (Montgomery, 2003). Thus, one approach to remediation has been to train children to process acoustic changes in speech more rapidly (Merzenich et al., 1996; Tallal et al., 1996; Veale, 1999). Although there has been little investigation as to whether improving the speed of auditory processing in children leads to improved performance on WM tasks *per se* (but see Deutsch, Miller, Merzenich, & Tallal, 1999), we include it nonetheless as a possible method for remediation in children with poor phonological WM, in light of the theoretical links between temporal processing, phonological representations, and WM (Downie, Jakobson, Frisk, & Ushycky, 2002). The fact that temporal training has also been shown to affect language processing and reading comprehension tasks that are problematic for children with poor WM is also promising (Tallal, 2003; Veale, 1999).

Phonological awareness is the conscious knowledge of the phonological structure of language and describes an individual's ability to recognize and manipulate the various components of words such as syllables and phonemes. Thus, phonological awareness has been identified as a construct highly related to phonological WM, with a number of studies demonstrating a correlation between phonological awareness and phonological WM (Gillam & van Kleeck, 1996; Leather & Henry, 1994; Oakhill & Kyle, 2000). One explanation is that phonological awareness tasks usually require active maintenance of information in WM to compare and process phonological information. Gillam & van Kleek (1996) argue that because phonological awareness tasks are demanding of phonological WM, training on phonological awareness may lead to improvements in WM. Another possibility is that better phonological awareness is a result of high-quality phonological representations in long-term memory that allow for easier storage and processing in WM. Phonological awareness training generally consists of repeated practice on a series of phonological awareness tasks such as judging the initial sound in a word, categorizing a particular sound, blending two phonemes together, and deleting a phoneme from a word. Such training has been shown to improve performance on a large number of related phonological awareness tasks (Downie et al., 2002; Torgesen & Davis, 1996) and on reading ability (Maridaki-Kassotaki, 2002; Wright & Jacobs, 2003).

Rehearsal

Deficits in WM may also arise from failures to use appropriate rehearsal strategies. Before the age of 7 years, children do not appear to use rehearsal consistently, and it is the development of rehearsal and other strategies that is thought to be at least partly responsible for increased WM span (Gathercole, 1999). Evidence that some children fail to develop rehearsal, or have poor organizational strategies, has led some to attempt to remediate WM by explicitly teaching children to rehearse or to use other strategies such as chunking words or digits into larger units, which are easier to remember. The training of even simple rote rehearsal strategies has been shown to improve WM performance in adults with low memory spans (McNamara & Scott, 2001; Turley-Ames & Whitfield, 2003). However, there is also evidence that, for these individuals, the teaching of more complex strategies may be less effective given the greater difficulty in mastering them (Turley-Ames & Whitfield, 2003). It may be that differences in strategy use may be more centrally based, with some individuals simply being more strategic overall, regardless of the processing domain (McNamara & Scott, 2001). However, rehearsal training has frequently been undertaken in the service of improving WM in the context of specific impairments in a peripheral system.

Centrally Based Processing and Remediation Approaches

A second approach to the remediation of WM difficulties in children has focused on possible impairments in the functioning of the CE. Three basic approaches have been proposed to remediate CE deficits in WM: the direct training of planning and metacognitive strategies, process specific training, and the use of pharmacologic agents intended to increase attentional capacity.

One method proposed to improve cognitive performance in children believed to have more global attentional or CE problems has been to teach them various planning strategies and better metacognitive awareness of their own performance (Marlowe, 2000; Ylvisaker & DeBonis, 2000). Although these interventions are not thought to have a direct effect on WM capacity (Mateer, Kerns, & Eso, 1996), they may allow children who are impaired to better manage the diminished attentional resources they do possess. In addition, such training has the potential to improve the efficacy of other remediation attempts when used in tandem. Training may include helping students to be more aware of which situations require executive processes and the teaching of strategies such as the verbal mediation of performance, in which children are taught a sequence of orienting questions that allow them to identify the current goal and to benefit more from feedback (Sohlberg, Mateer, & Stuss, 1993). Although there is little evidence on how effective these approaches are for direct measures of WM performance such as the reading span, there is some work showing improvement on various educational measures such as reading comprehension and arithmetic performance, which are thought to rely on WM (Singer & Bashir, 1999).

A second approach to remediation is process-specific training, in which the repeated practice of a particular cognitive process is hypothesized to lead to an improvement and reorganization of that process. This approach was originally developed for the rehabilitation of cognitive deficits in adults with brain injury and was thought to be especially useful for the rehabilitation of attentional abilities (Sohlberg & Mateer, 1987). Attention process training (APT) is a process-specific approach in which individuals receive repeated practice on tasks in five areas of attention: focusing, selecting, sustaining, switching, and dividing attention (Sohlberg & Mateer, 1987). A number of studies have reported improvements in attention or executive function in adults who have been brain injured (Park, Proulx, & Towers, 1999; Sohlberg & Mateer, 1987; Sohlberg et al., 2000) and in adults with schizophrenia (Lopez-Luengo & Vazquez, 2003). However, many of these studies have been criticized for the small sample size and limited generality of the improvements reported (Park & Ingles, 2001). Although APT was originally developed for adults, there is a growing interest in adapting this procedure for use in children.

A third approach to the remediation of the CE has been to try to improve the underlying efficiency of the neural systems involved by targeting the neurotransmitter systems on which they are thought to depend. Drugs that act on the catecholamine system have been shown to affect WM performance both in animals (Solanto, 2002) and humans (Mehta et al., 2000). Several studies have demonstrated improvements in the visuo-spatial WM performance of adults with the administration of methylphenidate (Ritalin) and other agents that increase dopaminergic and cholinergic function (Elliott et al., 1997; Furey, Peietrini, & Haxby, 2000; Kempton et al., 1999; Mehta et al., 2000). Therefore, for children in whom WM difficulty may have a clear neurochemical basis, pharmacological approaches to remediation may hold a great deal of promise.

REMEDIATION APPROACHES IN DIFFERENT WORKING MEMORY IMPAIRED POPULATIONS

In the next section of the chapter we shall examine the types of remediation approaches taken in different populations of children with WM impairment. WM impairments are reported in a number of different developmental disorders and conditions. However, the exact nature of the deficit in a particular disorder is frequently a source of great debate. Naturally, understanding the source of a deficit would seem to lead to better interventions. However, it may be that the type of interventions that are successful will also be informative about the type of deficit present in a given population of children.

Children Who Are Intellectually Disabled

In the United States, individuals are classified as having intellectual disability (ID) if their IQ (intelligence quotient) is measured as being below 70. This includes individuals for whom the source of their disability is known, such as those individuals with Down syndrome, and those for whom there is no clear etiology. A number of studies have found that children with ID appear to be disproportionately impaired in measures of verbal WM, whereas their performance on visuo-spatial WM measures is relatively spared (Jarrold, Baddeley, & Hewes, 1999; Rosenquist, Conners, & Roskos-Ewoldsen, 2003; Wang & Bellugi, 1994). One hypothesis for this pattern of impaired and spared abilities is that children with ID fail to develop verbal rehearsal. A frequently cited piece of evidence indicating a lack of rehearsal in these children is a reduced or absent word-length effect compared to age-matched, or vocabulary-matched, controls (Hulme & Mackenzie, 1992). The word-length effect is the finding that immediate recall is usually better for words that take less time to pronounce than longer words, even when the number of syllables is held constant (e.g., "bishop" is recalled better than "harpoon") (Baddeley, Thomson, & Buchanan, 1975). A failure to find the word-length effect has been reported both in children with Down syndrome (Hulme & Mackenzie, 1992; Jarrold, Baddeley, & Hewes, 2000) and with individuals whose ID is of unknown origin (Rosenquist et al., 2003). Given the evidence for a specific deficit in rehearsal, a number of studies have examined the possibility of improving verbal WM performance in these children by training them explicitly in the use of rehearsal (Broadley, MacDonald, & Buckley, 1994; Comblain, 1994; Hulme & Mackenzie, 1992; Laws, MacDonald, & Buckley, 1996) and other organizational strategies, such as chunking (Broadley et al., 1994). Such remediation programs have been shown to significantly improve WM performance (Conners, Rosenquist, & Taylor, 2001), although the gains have been criticized for being fairly small in magnitude, with only a half to one memory item improvement (Jarrold et al., 2000). There is also some question as to how long these improvements are maintained once the training is completed, with some studies reporting sustained benefits weeks and months later (Bowler, 1991; Broadley et al., 1994), whereas others found these benefits to diminish with time (Comblain, 1994, Laws et al., 1996).

Although rehearsal training does appear to be helpful, at least in the short term, there is growing evidence that a lack of rehearsal alone does not explain the WM deficits reported. Jarrold, Baddeley, & Hewes (2000) found that children with Down syndrome had poorer verbal WM scores even when compared with matched children with learning disabilities. In this study, neither group was observed to be using a rehearsal strategy, but the children with Down syndrome still showed significantly greater impairment. Similar findings were reported by Vicari, Marotta, & Carlesimo (2004) using a control group matched for mental age. They concluded that lack of rehearsal was not a sufficient explanation for the differences between the two groups (neither of which used rehearsal) and that other possibilities, such as reduced capacity in the phonological store or a more general impairment of the CE, must be examined. Indeed, a study of the structure of WM in individuals with ID identified a general WM factor composed of performance on CE measures and dissociable from a separate phonological factor (Numminen et al., 2000). This general factor was related to performance on an intelligence test and various academic measures such as reading, writing, and mathematic performance. The phonological factor, however, was related to reading, writing, and sentence comprehension, but not with intelligence or measures of everyday cognitive performance. The authors interpreted these results as indicative of a separate CE deficit in ID that appears to be relatively independent of impairments in the phonological loop (Numminen et al., 2000). Unfortunately, to date there have been no attempts to apply more general capacity–based remediation methods to the proposed CE deficits in ID.

Specific Language Impairment

Specific language impairment (SLI) is a term used to describe children who exhibit a delayed development of language, both in comprehension and production, without other obvious intellectual impairments (Bishop, 2004). Related to their specific language impairments, these children have also been found to be impaired on various WM tasks, especially those thought to measure the effectiveness of the phonological loop (Dollaghan & Campbell, 1998; Gathercole & Baddeley, 1990; Montgomery, 1995).

It has been hypothesized that the phonological loop plays an important role in language acquisition because it allows auditory input to be transformed into a phonological representation and then held temporarily for analysis and transferred to long-term memory (Gathercole, Baddeley, & Papagno, 1998). Phonological WM capacity in children has been shown to predict their ability both to acquire (Gathercole, Hitch, Service, & Martin, 1997; Gathercole, Service, Hitch, Adams, & Martin, 1999) and produce language (Adams & Gathercole, 1995). Thus, one specific hypothesis about the role of WM in the language deficits seen in children with SLI is that they have some impairment in the functioning of the phonological loop. Explanations of the role of phonological problems in children with SLI have focused on the capacity of the short-term phonological store rather than the rehearsal process because deficits in the use of rehearsal do not appear to be present in children with SLI (Gathercole & Baddeley, 1990; Montgomery, 1995). This view of SLI leads to a number of possible interventions, which include giving children practice with encoding and maintaining phonological representations and encouraging the use of strategies that use long-term memory, or other components of WM, to compensate for the reduced storage (Gathercole, 1993; Montgomery, 2003). For example, Gill and colleagues (Gill, Klecan-Aker, Roberts, & Fredenburg, 2003) found significant and lasting improvements in the ability to follow instructions in children who were taught a rehearsal strategy that involved visualizing the different instructions.

It has also been suggested that the phonological store may be impaired in SLI because the phonological representations to be stored in memory suffer from a lack of distinctiveness and are therefore difficult to distinguish from one another (Elbro, 1996). One reason that these representations may be incomplete is the presence of a deficit in phonological awareness, the conscious knowledge of phonological structure (Gillam & van Kleeck, 1996). Therefore, training of phonological awareness is another form of remediation frequently used in children with SLI. However, although such training has been shown to lead to improvements on tests of phonological awareness, only one study has found any evidence of transferable improvement to a measure of phonological WM. In this study, Gillam & van Kleeck (1996) reported improvements after a course of phonological awareness training in children's performance on nonword repetition tasks that are frequently used to measure the performance of the phonological loop. They hypothesized that the training was beneficial for two reasons. First, the intervention improved the children's ability to translate a phonological representation into WM, and second, the phonemic awareness tasks themselves were WM demanding and thus the phonological intervention provided direct practice on WM.

A related hypothesis concerning the quality of phonological representations is that poor representations in children with SLI may result from a deficit in processing and producing brief sequential events in sensory domains such as vision and audition (Tallal, 1998). According to this model of SLI, slow auditory processing speed may lead to the inability to encode phonemic information rapidly and accurately. Tallal and colleagues (Tallal et al., 1996) have developed a computer-based intervention called "Fast ForWord" for children hypothesized to have slowed auditory processing; it consists of a number of video games, primarily designed to improve processing speed and accuracy. In a typical task, children are presented with artificially slowed speech, allowing them to detect relevant information and distinguish between phonemes in the context of a computer game. As children get better at performing the task, the duration of the presentation of the sounds is reduced. "Fast ForWord" has been highly successful in improving the performance of children with SLI on a wide variety of language comprehension and reading measures (Tallal, 2003). Furthermore, in the one preliminary study that we are aware of, children's performance in WM was improved after participation in the training program (Deutsch et al., 1999).

It should be noted that it is not clear which aspects of the "Fast ForWord" program lead to children's improvements and, specifically, whether increasing auditory processing speed benefited children on WM tasks. In addition to tasks designed specifically to support temporal processing of auditory information, "Fast ForWord" also includes language comprehension tasks that involve listening to phrases of increasing syntactic complexity and short-term storage tasks that involve remembering phonemes for brief periods of time. Thus, any improvements in WM seen after training using "Fast ForWord" may directly result from practice on the comprehension and storage tasks, rather than improved auditory processing.

A final view of SLI is that WM deficits may be the result of more centrally based processing limitations (Ellis Weismer, 1996; Montgomery, 2002), as evidenced by studies demonstrating disproportionate impairment on tasks with high executive processing demands (Ellis Weismer, 1996; Montgomery, 2003). If the WM deficits in children with SLI are the result of a more general executive deficit, then remediation approaches that have been effective in improving the function of the CE may also be helpful for

SLI. However, to date there have been no attempts at remediating central attentional processing capacity in these children.

Reading Disability

Reading disabilities have long been associated with WM impairments (Cain, Oakhill, & Bryant, 2004; Chiappe, Siegal, & Hasher, 2002; Smith-Spark, Fisk, Fawcett, & Nicolson, 2003; Swanson & Howell, 2001, and Chapters 2 and 3 of this book). This is true both in individuals identified as dyslexic (in whom poor reading performance is not accompanied by any other intellectual difficulties) and in "garden variety" poor readers (in whom intellectual performance is poor overall). Although there have been many attempts at improving the reading performance of these children, only a few studies have examined the possible role of WM in the remediation of reading disability by including WM tasks as either part of the training or as an outcome measure. Those that have fall into two basic categories: remediation targeting the properties of the phonological loop and the remediation of deficits in more general attentional processing.

Children with reading disorders are most commonly hypothesized to have problems specifically in the phonological loop component of WM because they evidence impaired performance on tasks such as digit or letter span (Cain et al., 2004; Smith-Spark et al., 2003; Swanson & Howell, 2001). Therefore attempts at remediation in these children have frequently focused on improving the function of the phonological loop in ways similar to the intervention programs seen in children with specific language disorders, such as improving auditory temporal processing, phonological awareness, and repeated practice on phonological WM tasks.

Deficits in both auditory temporal processing and phonological awareness have been reported in children with reading impairments (Cacace & McFarland, 2000; Carroll & Snowling, 2004; Cormier & Dea, 1997; Goswami & Bryant; 1990); training in auditory temporal processing as typified by the "Fast ForWord" program and training targeting phonological awareness alone have both been shown to be effective in improving reading performance in children with dyslexia (Lovett et al., 1994; O'Shaughnessy & Swanson, 2000, Temple et al., 2003). In addition, there is evidence that patterns and activity levels of brain areas hypothesized to play a role in WM processing are affected by such training manipulations, with improved frontal and temporoparietal activity seen in children with dyslexia after auditory temporal process training (Temple et al., 2003) and changed activity seen in the left occipitotemporal areas of children with dyslexia after training on phonological awareness (Shaywitz et al., 2004). However, the little research that has directly examined the effect of phonological awareness training on WM performance is equivocal. O'Shaughnessy & Swanson (2000) reported significant improvements in the verbal WM of children with reading disabilities after lengthy training on phonological awareness using two measures of verbal WM (recall of similar sounding words and reading span). However, a second study reported no improvement on a verbal WM task as measured by reading span after a similar course of phonological awareness training (Gonzalez, Espinel, & Rosquete, 2002).

Only one study has investigated the extent to which training directly on a phonological WM task will lead to improvements in reading performance. Maridaki-Kassotaki (2002) gave schoolchildren a course of training on phonological WM using repeated practice on nonword repetition. Training was administered 15 minutes a day, 4 days a week, for the duration of a school year (7 months). Both a training and control group were tested pre- and post-training on nonword repetition and on a measure of reading comprehension. There were no group differences before the training intervention. However, post-training, the training group showed significantly better performance on both nonword repetition and reading comprehension. Although these results are preliminary, they do suggest that children who are reading impaired may benefit from interventions that provide direct practice on verbal WM tasks. However, the extent to which this is true for tasks other than nonword repetition is unclear.

Other researchers have focused on the possibility of deficits in the CE component of WM and have hypothesized that at least in some children who are reading disabled, more general attentional capacity limitations underlie deficits in reading performance (Palmer, 2000a; Swanson, 1999). For example, dyslexic readers have been shown to be impaired on a number of executive tasks including the Wisconsin Card Sorting Task (WCST), a measure of inhibitory processing and switching (Palmer, 2000a); reading span (Cain et al., 2004; Chiappe et al., 2002; Swanson & Sachse-Lee, 2001b; Swanson & Howell, 2001); and letter updating (Smith-Spark et al., 2003). Therefore remediation approaches targeting CE processing constitute another means by which performance may be improved in children who are reading disabled.

Deficits in the ability to inhibit have been hypothesized as one source of executive impairment in reading disability (Chiappe et al., 2002; Palmer, 2000a), with some researchers proposing that reading problems in dyslexia may be the result of impaired spatial attention processing ultimately derived from an inhibitory deficit (Facoetti, Lorusso, Paganoni, Umilta, & Mascetti, 2003). For example, Facoetti et al. (2003) found that children with dyslexia failed to demonstrate normal inhibitory processing in a covert visual attention task. They then used an intervention called "visual hemisphere specific function" (VHSS; developed by Bakker, 1992), in which they stimulated either the right or left hemisphere (depending on the type of dyslexia) with words presented in the left or right visual field for 32 training sessions across 4 months. Participants in the intervention performed better on spatial attention tasks at post-test compared to a control group, who received a traditional intervention for dyslexia, such as phonological awareness training or individual reading tutoring. Furthermore, they were also better on measures of reading accuracy and reading speed.

A final possibility is that WM difficulties in at least some children with reading disorders may result in part from a lack of vocabulary knowledge. In general, children with reading disorders tend to have less knowledge about print, story structure, and vocabulary (Cain et al., 2004; Hecht, Burgess, Torgesen, Wagner, & Rachotte, 2000). In addition, McDougall & Donohoe (2002) found that children with reading difficulties performed equally as well as children without reading difficulties on span tasks that used high-frequency words, but they performed worse than children without reading difficulties on span tasks that used low-frequency words. This result is in line with results from studies of long-term WM that show a relationship between how much information can be actively maintained and the organization and quantity of long-term knowledge (Ericsson & Kintsch, 1995). Results such as these suggest another possible approach to remediation may be to expand these children's knowledge bases.

Attention Deficit/Hyperactivity Disorder

Attention deficit/hyperactivity disorder (ADHD) is a developmental disorder characterized by inattention, overactivity, and impulsive behavior (see also Chapter 6 of this volume). It is believed to be fairly common, with estimates as high as 3–5% of all children affected (American Psychiatric Association, 1994). Whereas a number of WM and executive function deficits have been reported in children with ADHD, the primary impairment has widely been hypothesized to be a failure of inhibitory processing (Barkley, 1997; Schachar, Tannock, & Logan, 1993), which is then believed to lead to poor performance on WM and executive function tasks. Deficits have been reported for both verbal and visuo-spatial measures of WM (Karatekin & Asarnow, 1998; Mariani & Barkley, 1997; McInnes, Humphries, Hogg-Johnson, & Tannock, 2003, but see Pennington & Ozonoff, 1996; Shue & Douglas, 1992) and a wide array of executive tasks including WCST (Pineda et al., 1998; Reeve & Schandler, 2001; Seidman et al., 1997), verbal fluency (generating as many items that meet some criterion, such as starting with the letter R or belonging to the category flower, in a short time frame; Pineda et al., 1998), the Stroop Task (Reeve & Schandler, 2001; Seidman et al., 1997), switching between tasks (Cepeda, Cepeda, & Kramer, 2000), and Tower of London (Cornoldi, Barbieri, Gaiani, & Zocchi, 1999).

Naturally, clinical interventions often focus on the remediation of the behavioral problems seen in children with ADHD. However, there is evidence that the WM problems seen in these children may also be responsive to treatment. Three major approaches have been proposed in the remediation of WM and executive function impairments in ADHD. These are process-specific training, instruction in metacognitive strategies, and medication.

In process-specific training, a damaged cognitive process is rehabilitated by repeated practice on tasks that exercise the damaged processes. One example is the APT described earlier, which was developed originally to help rehabilitate adults with brain injuries with attentional and executive function deficits (Sohlberg & Mateer, 1987). However, several preliminary studies have begun to examine the potential of modified forms of APT in children with ADHD. In Kerns, Eso, & Thomson (1999), children with ADHD aged 5–10 years were given training on both visual and auditory versions of sustained, selective, alternating, and divided attention tasks for two 30-minute sessions a week for 8 weeks. Each task used materials that had been modified from earlier APT work so that they would be more interesting and appropriate for children. The performance of the trained children was compared to a control group pre- and post-training on 6 tasks thought to reflect attentional and executive abilities. Although not all the measures used showed evidence of transfer, the authors did report training-related improvements on a measure of sustained auditory attention, a measure of sustained visual attention, and a variant of the Stroop task commonly thought to require inhibition and selective attention. However, they did acknowledge that the small sample size (7 children) and the lack of follow-up testing limited the conclusions that could be drawn.

A second study investigating the effectiveness of APT in ADHD used a combination of metacognitive and process-specific methods. Semrud-Clikeman et al. (1999) trained a group of children with ADHD on two tasks taken from the APT program (Sohlberg & Mateer, 1987)—a visual attention task in which children had to find a target in an array of distracters and an auditory task in which they counted targets presented in an auditory stream of stimuli such as certain letters of words beginning with a specific sound. They were also given specific guidance and practice on the use of effective strategies and goal setting in the performance of the training tasks. The training intervention consisted of two 1-hour training sessions a week, for a total of 18 weeks. At the end of the training period, the children who had been trained showed significantly more improvement on both an unpracticed selective visual attention measure and an unpracticed auditory divided attention measure, in comparison to a control group of children with ADHD who had not received the training. Although this study found clear improvements, the extent to which the training benefits would generalize was uncertain and the contribution of each form of remediation (process specific and learning of strategies) to the gains seen was unclear. Additionally some of the children were taking medication at the time of training, and others were not. Unfortunately, as noted by the authors, there were not enough children taking traditional stimulant medications to be able to compare the efficacy of this form of training in children both undergoing and not undergoing pharmacological therapy (Semrud-Clikeman et al., 1999).

A third study by Klingberg, Forssberg, & Westerberg (2002) combined basic principles from both process-specific training and sensory discrimination training in training WM in children with ADHD. In this program, children were given repeated practice on a computerized version of a visuo-spatial WM task, Backward Digit Span, Letter Span, and a go/no-go reaction time task (in which participants must inhibit a frequent response given a "no-go" signal). The difficulty for each individual subject was adaptable on a trial-by-trial basis, with each child receiving 20 minutes of training a day, 4–6 days a week, for 5 weeks. A control group of children received a lesser version of the same training tasks in which the difficulty was not adjusted, but it was for less than 10 minutes a day. Group differences in pre- and post-training improvement between training and control groups were reported on an untrained visuo-spatial WM task; Raven's Progressive Matrices, a common measure of fluid intelligence; and the Stroop task (Klingberg et al., 2002). In a later neuroimaging study, Olesen, Westerberg, & Klingberg (2004) found increases in prefrontal and parietal areas associated with WM after a similar course of WM training in normal young adults.

Another form of remediation proposed to have possible effects on WM and executive performance in children with ADHD is the teaching of organizational strategies such as self-monitoring, verbal mediation, and various higher level problem-solving strategies (Marlowe, 2000; Wasserstein & Lynn, 2001). No studies have directly examined the extent to which such a program alone would remediate WM. However, such training has been proposed as an important addition to process-specific training and other forms of remediation (Sohlberg & Mateer, 2001) as seen in Semrud-Clikeman et al. (1999).

A third possibility in the remediation of WM and executive deficits may lie in the stimulant medications traditionally used to reduce hyperactivity in ADHD because there is growing evidence that they may also improve certain aspects of WM function. Methylphenidate is the most commonly prescribed stimulant medication used to treat ADHD and has been shown to increase dopamine levels in normal subjects (Solanto, 2002; Volkow, Fowler, Wang, Ding, & Gatley, 2001). Behaviorally, treatment with methylphenidate appears to reduce problems in children with ADHD (Whalen et al., 1987), and it has also been reported to improve performance on a number of school-related activities (Douglas, Barr, O'Neill, & Britton, 1986). A number of studies have reported improvements with the use of methylphenidate on both WM and executive tasks. Two studies comparing children treated with methylphenidate to unmedicated children and normal controls found no difference between the medicated and control groups' performance on spatial WM and executive function tasks, whereas unmedicated children were impaired on both (Barnett et al., 2001; Kempton et al., 1999). Other studies have directly compared the performance of children with ADHD, both taking and not taking medication, and found better performance while medicated on measures of verbal WM (Tannock, Ickowicz,

& Schachar, 1995), visuo-spatial WM (Bedard, Martinussen, Ickowicz, & Tannock, 2004), focused and sustained attention (Konrad, Gunther, Hanisch, & Herpertz-Dahlmann, 2004), and task switching (Kramer, Cepeda, & Cepeda, 2001).

Another pharmacological agent that has shown promise in improving WM function is modafinil. This drug is different from methylphenidate and related compounds in that it is not thought to affect dopaminergic systems; instead, it affects an individual's level of arousal. Therefore it is often used in the treatment of narcolepsy. However, two studies have reported improvements of clinical features of ADHD with modafinil use in children (Rugino & Copley, 2001) and adults with ADHD (Taylor & Russo, 2000). Although the direct action of modafinil on cognitive dysfunction in ADHD has not been directly tested, it has been shown to improve cognitive performance in animals (Beracochea et al., 2001) and in humans, with enhanced performance on tasks requiring WM and inhibitory processing (Turner et al., 2003).

As we have seen, there are several approaches targeting the CE that appear to hold promise in the remediation of the WM and CE deficits seen in ADHD. However, one factor that has not been considered in the remediation attempts to date is the large comorbidity of ADHD with other learning impairments and conditions such as reading disability (Dykman & Ackerman, 1991) and anxiety disorders (Tannock et al., 1995). The extent to which the efficacy of these different programs of remediation is changed in these subpopulations of children with ADHD is a topic for further research.

Childhood Schizophrenia

Schizophrenia is another relatively common disorder in which WM impairment has been hypothesized to constitute a core deficit. Poor WM performance, in both the verbal and spatial domains, has been reported in children with schizophrenia (Asarnow et al., 1994; Karatekin & Asarnow, 1998) and adults (Barch & Csernansky, 2002; Goldman-Rakic, 1994; Huguelet, Zanello, & Nicastro, 2000; Silver, Feldman, Bilker, & Gur, 2003). Individuals diagnosed with schizophrenia also perform poorly on a variety of executive function measures including the WCST (Goldman-Rakic & Selemon, 1997), verbal fluency (Bokat & Goldberg, 2003), and the Tower of London (Andreasen et al., 1992; Morris, Rushe, Woodruffe, & Murray, 1995). Although the remediation of WM has yet to be attempted in children with schizophrenia, there are a growing number of studies in which the amelioration of WM deficits has been undertaken in adults, using cognitive training techniques or new pharmacological treatments.

Two cognitive training programs that have shown promise in the remediation of WM deficits in schizophrenia are the frontal/executive program (FEP) developed by Delahunty and Morice (1996) and neurocognitive enhancement therapy (NET) developed by Bell et al. (2001). In the first program, FEP, patients with schizophrenia are given targeted training on a series of paper and pencil tasks in three different domains of executive function: cognitive flexibility, WM, and planning (Delahunty & Morice, 1996). Training in each of these domains emphasizes errorless learning, immediate feedback, and explicit instruction in various strategies for each domain. Wykes et al. (Wykes, Reeder, Corner, Williams, & Everitt, 1999) trained schizophrenic individuals using this program for approximately 40 days, with three to five 1-hour sessions of training per week. They measured a variety of cognitive and social measures, both before and after the training, and compared the amount of improvement seen to a control group of patients who received a more traditional occupational therapy. They found improvements in performance in a planning task, digit span, and WCST for both therapies, with a significantly larger advantage for the group receiving the FEP. In addition, there is early evidence that this training may have demonstrable effects on areas of the brain shown to be involved in WM processing. In a preliminary study, Wykes et al. (2002) reported increased frontal activation during the performance of an untrained WM task after an extended course of FEP training in several patients with schizophrenia. However, although increased activation was seen in areas associated with WM processing, it was not correlated with any improved performance on the task.

A second approach to the remediation of WM deficits in schizophrenia has been more process specific in nature because patients are given repeated practice with an increasing level of difficulty on various tasks but are not explicitly taught any particular strategy for improvement. This approach has been termed neurocognitive enhancement therapy (or NET; Bell et al., 2001). Two studies have compared the cognitive benefits of a course of work therapy to a course of work therapy *augmented* with a course of NET training, in which patients were given lengthy training (up to 5 hours a week for 26 weeks) on 4 computer-based programs, 2 visual tracking tasks requiring sustained attention, practice at a computerized versions of digit and word spans, and a planning task similar to the Tower of London (Bell et al., 2001; Bell, Bryson, & Wexler, 2003). In the first study, the group that received neurocognitive training in addition to work therapy showed greater levels of improvement on both an executive measure (WCST) and a common measure of WM (Backward Digit Span) (Bell et al., 2001). This was replicated in a later study, with the same benefit found for the training group on the Backward Digit Span (Bell et al., 2003), and training benefits enduring for at least 6 months after training had concluded (Fiszdon, Bryson, Wexler, & Bell, 2004). There is evidence that this form of remediation also has the potential to affect patterns of brain activity measurably. In a study in which verbal WM was targeted for training, 8 patients with schizophrenia were scanned while performing an auditory serial position memory task both before and after 10 weeks of intensive training on auditory verbal serial position memory tasks (Wexler, Anderson, Fulbright, & Gore, 2000). Although not all of the patients showed significant improvements with training, those who did showed increased task-related activity in the left inferior frontal cortex, shown to be active in normal control participants in performance of the task. One patient who received an additional 5 weeks of training was shown to have a normalization of brain activity after training, so that his pattern of activation was virtually the same as that of the controls.

Although the efficacy and the generalizability of cognitive remediation in schizophrenia is debated (Krabbendam & Aleman, 2003; Pilling et al., 2002), there is growing evidence that, in the treatment of WM and executive problems, it can have some positive impact. However, the degree to which WM can be remediated, and improvements generalized to real-life activities, is still unknown. In addition, the effect of these programs on children with schizophrenia, which is thought to be more severe in nature than adults, is still not yet known.

Another approach that holds promise for the remediation of cognitive deficits, and WM dysfunction in particular, lies in new drug therapies being developed to treat schizophrenia. Although early descriptions of schizophrenia emphasized the importance of the cognitive dysfunction seen in patients (Andreasen, 1999), traditional drug treatments such as haloperidol have focused on relieving the positive symptoms of schizophrenia, such as hallucinations. These early treatments were not effective in treating the cognitive deficits of the disease and may have, in fact, worsened WM performance (Castner, Williams, & Goldman-Rakic, 2000). However, there is growing evidence that some of the newer drug therapies, the so-called "atypical" neuroleptics, may improve WM performance by increasing dopaminergic activity in the prefrontal systems identified as being important for WM performance (Gemperle, McAllister & Olpe, 2003; Hertel et al., 1996). Abnormal activity in these same areas has been found repeatedly in neuroimaging studies of schizophrenia and WM (Barch & Csernansky, 2002; Callicot et al., 2003; Manoach et al., 2000). One drug, risperidone, has been shown to improve WM performance (Green et al., 1997; Harvey, Green, McGurk, & Meltzer, 2003) as well as increase activation in several brain areas associated with WM, including the right prefrontal cortex (Honey et al., 1999). Three other "atypical" drugs that have shown some promise in treating WM deficits are clozapine (Meltzer & McGurk, 1999), olanzapine (Harvey et al., 2003), and iloperidone (Gemperle et al., 2003). In addition to direct improvements in WM and executive performance, another possible benefit to these drug treatments is that they may enhance the effectiveness of other forms of remediation, such as cognitive training (Wykes et al., 1999).

Cognitive remediation of WM deficits is an important goal in the treatment of schizophrenia, especially in light of the evidence that it is the resolution of these deficits rather than more dramatic symptoms (such as hallucinations) that best predict a patient's long-term social outcome (Green et al., 2000). Another possible area of investigation is in the remediation of deficits in children who are genetically at greater risk of developing schizophrenia because they have been shown to have poorer WM function (Davalos, Compagnon, Heinlein, & Ross, 2004; Erlenmeyer-Kimling et al., 2000), and the extent of the deficit has been shown to be predictive of the likelihood of their later developing the disorder (Erlenmeyer-Kimling et al., 2000). Therefore, it is possible that early intervention and improvement of cognitive function may have some effect on whether and how severely the disease manifests itself. Although this proposition is highly speculative, given the devastating effects of schizophrenia, it is worth future investigation.

Autism

Autism is another developmental condition in which executive function has been hypothesized as playing an important role (Pennington & Ozonoff, 1996) and for which the remediation of the CE has been proposed as a treatment strategy (Ozonoff, 1998). However, the exact nature of the WM and executive deficits seen in autism is not entirely clear and is currently the topic of some debate. Several studies have reported finding WM deficits in children with autism (Bennetto, Pennington, & Rogers, 1996; Luna et al., 2002; Minshew & Goldstein, 2001; Pennington & Ozonoff, 1996), whereas others have not (Russell, Jarrold & Henry, 1996). A similar situation exists for different measures of executive function, with some studies reporting impaired performance (Ozonoff, 1998), and others not (Griffith, Pennington, Wehner, & Rogers, 1999). One explanation for these inconsistent findings is that children with autism have impaired development and use of organizational strategies and that their performance suffers in situations where planning and strategy are important for optimal performance (Minshew & Goldstein, 2001).

Minshew & Goldstein (2001) studied WM span in individuals with autism using letter sequences, word sequences, and a sequence of directions. The subjects with autism were not significantly impaired on the letter sequences but were significantly worse for both word and direction sequences, with performance decreasing as opportunity to benefit from strategy use increased. The authors interpreted this as support for the hypothesis that as the complexity of the material increases and lends itself more to strategies, the more impaired individuals with autism are. A related proposition is that individuals with autism have poor or nonexistent inner speech, which would curtail any attempts to verbally mediate an organizational approach to the material, and that performance deficits will be the greatest on tasks in which there are arbitrary rules that must be followed, such as in planning tasks like WCST and the Tower of London/Hanoi (Russell et al., 1996). This theory may also help to explain the findings of Griffith et al. (1999), who reported finding no differences between autistic and age- and ability-matched children on eight separate measures of executive function. The children in this study were tested between the ages of 4 and 5 years, before reliable rehearsal and strategy use appears to develop in children (Gathercole, 1999). If poor performance on executive tasks in children with autism results in part from a failure to use organizational strategies, differences may not become apparent until children are older.

Although little has been attempted in the specific remediation of WM and executive function deficits, some of the same approaches used in other impaired populations have been proposed for children with autism. These have included stimulant medications such as methylphenidate, metacognitive training to increase organizational skills and strategies, and process-specific training in areas such as cognitive flexibility (Ozonoff, 1998). Currently there are no published studies evaluating the effectiveness of each of these approaches in children with autism. However, in addition to the possible rehabilitative benefits of such interventions being tested, there is also the possibility that the success or failure of different remediation attempts may be informative about the underlying deficits in autism. One prediction is that if the main deficit is the organization and utilization of strategies, then the direct instruction in the development and use of metacognitive strategies may be most effective.

Traumatic Brain Injury

WM and executive function deficits are frequently reported outcomes of traumatic brain injury in both adults and children (Levin et al., 1988; Levin et al., 2004; Roncadin, Guger, Archibald, Barnes, & Dennis, 2004; Slomine et al., 2002; Thompson et al., 1994). Although traumatic brain injuries can result from several different causes, such as infections, vascular accidents, and tumors, the most common cause is closed head injury, to which the frontal lobes appear to be especially vulnerable (Levin et al., 1997). The remediation of WM deficits has thus focused on the executive processes theorized as relying on frontal integrity. In a similar manner to that for developmental disorders in which the nature of WM impairments is hypothesized as lying in the CE, three forms of intervention have been presented as methods by which the attentional functions of the CE in individuals who have been brain injured can be improved. These are process-specific training, metacognitive approaches, and the use of stimulant medications.

Several studies have attempted to assess the extent to which patients who have been brain injured can benefit from process-specific training and the degree to which the improvements seen will generalize to new tasks. Interventions using programs such as APT (Sohlberg et al., 2000) and other forms of repeated practice on executive tasks, such as random number generation (which requires participants to generate a list of random, unrelated digits and inhibit well-learned sequences and recent responses), dual task performance, and n-back (which requires participants to remember and update a sequence of digits or letters and judge whether a particular item is the same as one presented a certain number of items previously) (Cicerone, 2002), have shown some limited promise in adult patients. However, a recent meta-analysis of the effectiveness of different attentional rehabilitation programs for patients with brain injuries found little evidence of generalized benefits from direct retraining efforts such as APT (Park & Ingles, 2001). A similar situation exists in the research on APT in children with brain damage, with preliminary results suggesting possible improvements with training (Mateer, Kerns, & Eso, 1996). Further controlled research is necessary to thoroughly assess the benefits of this approach in children.

Metacognitive deficits have also been reported in children with severe traumatic brain injuries (Dennis, Barnes, Donnelly, Wilkinson, & Humphreys, 1996; Hanten, Bartha, & Levin, 2000; Hanten, Levin, & Song, 1999). In adults with brain damage, the ability to improve with practice has been linked to their ability to develop and use strategies (Dirette, Hinojosa, & Carnevale, 1999). Therefore metacognitive training may be of benefit to children who are brain injured and may allow them to benefit more from other forms of training. A program attempting to rehabilitate memory and attention in children with brain injuries used a combination of process-specific and metacognitive training (van't Hooft, Andersson, Sejersen, Bartfai, & von Wendt, 2003). The Amsterdam Memory and Attention Training program has been formulated as a multi-pronged approach in which children are given both process-specific training on various attentional and memory tasks and metacognitive training focusing on the learning of specific performance strategies. In addition, children also receive social and therapeutic counseling. Pilot data obtained from three children with traumatic brain injuries who completed this program of training found weak evidence for improvements on selective attention as measured by the Stroop task and WM as measured by digit span (van't Hooft et al., 2003). However, considerably more research is necessary to establish the effectiveness of this program and the extent to which any improvements will generalize to other tasks.

The attentional deficits frequently seen in patients who are brain injured have led to investigations of the efficacy of stimulant medications such as methylphenidate in remediating these impairments. However, both the pediatric and the adult literatures are mixed, with some studies reporting improvement in attention and memory function after treatment with methylphenidate in children with brain injuries (Hornyak, Nelson, & Hurvitz, 1997; Mahalick et al., 1998) and in adults with brain injuries (Kaelin, Cifu, & Matthies, 1996; Plenger et al., 1996), and other studies with no such reports (Speech, Rao, Osmon, & Sperry, 1993; Williams, Ris, Ayyangar, Schefft, & Berch, 1998). A review of methylphenidate use in treating brain injuries concluded that, although there is evidence to support the effectiveness of the drug on behavioral problems such as impulsivity, the support for cognitive improvements is weak (Jin & Schachar, 2004).

Unlike adults, children may appear to have recovered from a brain injury only to manifest deficits months or even years later (Mateer & Williams, 1991; Thompson et al., 1994). This phenomenon by which children appear to grow into a deficit is likely to be a result of the increased WM and executive function demands of school and other activities as children age. Therefore, it is possible that successful remediation given shortly after the injury may help prevent or alleviate these later impairments. Although the possibility of such benefits is only speculative at this time, given the cognitive difficulties faced by these children, it is worth further investigation.

Chemotherapy and Cranial Radiation Treatments

Children treated with chemotherapy and cranial radiation therapy manifest a pattern of WM and executive impairments similar to children with traumatic brain injuries, including the delayed onset of deficits, which may not appear until 2 or 3 years after a child begins treatment (Butler, Kerr, & Marchand, 1999; Copeland et al., 1988; Mulhern & Palmer, 2003; Schatz et al., 2000). This unintended side effect to these life-saving measures is thought to arise from radiation damage to white matter and other subcortical areas such as the basal ganglia (Mulhern et al., 1999).

In light of the deficits suffered by these children, an ambitious rehabilitation program has been developed to treat them. Butler & Copeland (2002) have developed the cognitive remediation program in which children receive a combination of APT (Sohlberg & Mateer, 1987), explicit instruction in metacognitive strategies and cognitive-behavioral therapy in which children learn and practice strategies to resist distraction, and mnemonic strategies such as chunking. Training consists of 50 hours of treatment, with children receiving treatment 2 hours a week for 6 months. A pilot study of the effectiveness of this study found significant improvements on measures of WM (digit span and sentence memory) and sustained attention (the continuous performance test) for a group of young cancer survivors who completed the training, compared to a control group who did not receive treatment (Butler & Copeland, 2002). However, a fourth measure, a test of arithmetic achievement, did not show differential improvement. Although the lack of transfer to an academic measure correlated with WM performance was disappointing, the authors conceded that the data are preliminary and that more research is necessary before the true efficacy of the program can be evaluated. Therefore, they are conducting a large multi-site study to evaluate this program of cognitive remediation (Butler & Copeland, 2002). This is the most comprehensive and ambitious exploration of the possibilities of cognitive remediation to date.

CONCLUSION

In this chapter, we have documented an increasing interest in the remediation of WM impairments in children. Multiple forms of remediation have been attempted, with the type of intervention dependent on the hypothesized source of the deficit in a particular population of children. Taken as a whole, these studies suggest that at least some form of WM improvement is possible, although the specific mechanisms responsible for any changes have not been precisely identified. Thus, the extent to which different theoretical approaches to remediation are most appropriate in a given population of children is uncertain because there has so far been no systematic approach to research on cognitive remediation. There do, however, appear to be a few general principles that can be distilled and used in future attempts at remediation.

The first general principle is the importance of variability in training. Although not always desirable when trying to determine the possible causes of improvement in any given situation, it has been well established in the skill-acquisition literature that variability in training promotes greater transfer than training on a single task (Schmidt & Bjork, 1992). This also appears to be true when training is applied toward remediation, with the more successful programs reported here (such as Klingberg et al., 2002, Semrud-Clikeman et al., 1999, and Tallal et al., 1996) combining different tasks and types of training interventions. Two additional general principles for successful training are the length of training and the adaptability of difficulty. Most remediation programs reported here consisted of at least 1 hour of training a week for weeks or months. In addition, most programs had some form of difficulty adaptation. Klingberg, Forssberg, & Westerberg (2002) demonstrated the importance of difficulty manipulations and length of training by including a control group that received training on the same tasks for far less time and without trial-by-trial adaptations of difficulty and who then did not show improvement. A final general observation is that there is a growing use of neuroimaging techniques such as functional magnetic resonance imaging to demonstrate and measure the effects of training interventions on neural activity. However, until there is a clearer understanding and set of expectancies for how compensatory processing is accomplished in the brain, these results should be interpreted with caution.

It should be noted that the previous discussion of children with WM deficits is naturally limited by the extent to which attempts at remediating WM have so far been made. There are a number of additional populations of children who may also benefit from WM interventions including children with low birthweight (Harvey, O'Callaghan, & Mohay, 1999), phenylketonuria (Welsh, Pennington, Ozonoff, Rouse, & McCabe, 1990), fetal alcohol syndrome (Connor, Sampson, Bookstein, Barr, & Streissguth, 2000), arithmetic disability (Bull & Johnston, 1997), and epilepsy (Kadis, Stollstorff,

Elliott, Lach, & Smith, 2004). The inclusion of these different populations in future research will help to broaden our understanding of what types of WM remediation are possible and the mechanisms by which they can occur.

Summary Box

- Deficits in WM, the cognitive system involved in the active maintenance of task-relevant information, have been reported as a consequence of a diverse array of childhood disorders.
- WM ability may not be entirely fixed, and numerous interventions have shown promise in improving performance on different kinds of WM tasks.
- A number of approaches have been used to improve WM; these approaches include ones that focus on the ability to maintain specific kinds of information such as phonological or visuo-spatial information and those that focus on executive/attentional control skills.
- Children with intellectual disabilities such as Down syndrome have benefited from training in rehearsal strategies.
- Successful remediation of WM problems in children with language and reading impairments has often focused on teaching compensatory strategies, improving phonological awareness, and improving auditory processing speed.
- Children with ADHD suffer from impairments in executive functioning, and research suggests that such processes may be improved by process-specific training (repeated practice on impaired skills) and stimulant medications.
- Although remediation of children with schizophrenia has not been attempted, process-specific training and medications have improved executive functions in adult with schizophrenia; such approaches may be beneficial for childhood schizophrenia.
- Process-specific training and metacognitive strategy training have also been successfully used to treat WM deficits in children with traumatic brain injury and brain injury from chemotherapy and cranial radiation.
- Although our review of the literature suggests the potential for remediation of WM, much more research is necessary to establish the extent to which WM can be improved and what types of remediation are most effective for different populations.

References

Adams, A., & Gathercole, S. E. (1995). Phonological working memory and speech production in preschool children. *Journal of Speech & Hearing Research, 38*, 403–414.

Andreasen, N. C. (1999). A unitary model of schizophrenia: Bleuler's "fragmented phrene" as schizencephaly. *Archive of General Psychiatry, 56*, 781–787.

Andreasen, N. C., Rezai, K., Alliger, R., Swayze, V. W., Flaum, M., Kirchner, P., et al. (1992). Hypofrontality in neuroleptic-naive patients and in patients with chronic schizophrenia: Assessment with xenon 133 single-photon emission computed tomography and the Tower of London. *Archives of General Psychiatry, 49*, 943–958.

Asarnow, R. F., Asamen, J., Granholm, E., Sherman, T., Watkins, J. M., & Williams, M. E. (1994). Cognitive/neuropsychological studies of children with a schizophrenic disorder. *Schizophrenia Bulletin, 20*, 647–669.

American Psychiatric Association. (1994). *Diagnostic and statistical manual of mental disorders* (4th ed.). Washington, D.C.: Author.

Baddeley, A. (2002). Fractionating the central executive. In D. T. Stuss (Ed.), *Principles of frontal lobe function* (pp. 246–260). London: Oxford University Press.

Baddeley, A. D. (1986). *Working memory*. New York: Clarendon Press/Oxford University Press.

Baddeley, A. D., & Hitch, G. (1976). Verbal reasoning and working memory. *Quarterly Journal of Experimental Psychology, 28*, 603–621.

Baddeley, A. D., Thomson, N., & Buchanan, M. (1975). Word length and the structure of short-term memory. *Journal of Verbal Learning & Verbal Behavior, 14*, 575–589.

Bakker, D. J. (1992). Neuropsychological classification and treatment of dyslexia. *Journal of Learning Disabilities, 25*, 102–109.

Barch, D. M., & Csernansky, J. G. (2002). Working and long-term memory deficits in schizophrenia: Is there a common prefrontal mechanism? *Journal of Abnormal Psychology, 111*, 478–494.

Barkley, R. A. (1997). Behavioral inhibition, sustained attention, and executive functions: Constructing a unifying theory of ADHD. *Psychological Bulletin, 121*, 65–94.

Barnett, R., Maruff, P., Vance, A., Luk, E. S. L., Costin, J., Wood, C., et al. (2001). Abnormal executive function in attention deficit hyperactivity disorder: the effect of stimulant medication and age on spatial working memory. *Psychological Medicine, 31*, 1107–1115.

Bedard, A., Martinussen, R., Ickowicz, A., & Tannock, R. (2004). Methylphenidate improves visual-spatial memory in children with attention-deficit/hyperactivity disorder. *Journal of American Academy of Child Adolescent Psychiatry, 43*, 260–268.

Bell, M., Bryson, G., Greig, T., Corcoran C., & Wexler, B. E. (2001). Neurocognitive enhancement therapy with work therapy: Effects on neuropsychological test performance. *Archives of General Psychiatry, 58*, 763–768.

Bell, M., Bryson, G., & Wexler, B. E. (2003). Cognitive remediation of working memory deficits: Durability of training effects in severely impaired and less severely impaired schizophrenia. *Acta Psychiatrica Scandinavica, 108*, 101–109.

Bennetto, L., Pennington, B. F., & Rogers, S. J. (1996). Intact and impaired memory functions in autism. *Child Development, 67*, 1816–1835.

Beracochea, D., Cagnard, B., Celerier, A., le Merrer, J., Peres, M., & Pierard, C. (2001). First evidence of a delay-dependent working memory-enhancing effect of modafinil in mice. *Neuroreport: For Rapid Communication of Neuroscience Research, 12*, 375–378.

Bishop, D. V. M. (2004). Specific language impairment: Diagnostic dilemmas. In L. Verhoeven, & H. van Balkom (Eds.), *Classification of developmental language disorders: Theoretical issues and clinical implications* (pp. 309–326). Mahwah, NJ: Lawrence Erlbaum Associates.

Bokat, C. E., & Goldberg, T. E. (2003). Letter and category fluency in schizophrenic patients: A meta-analysis. *Schizophrenia Research, 64*, 73–78.

Bowler, D. M. (1991). Rehearsal training and short-term free-recall of sign and word labels by severely handicapped children. *Journal of Mental Deficiency Research, 35*, 113–124.

Broadley, I., MacDonald, J., & Buckley, S. (1994). Are children with Down's syndrome able to maintain skills learned from short-term memory training programme? *Down's Syndrome: Research and Practice, 2*, 112–116.

Bull, R., & Johnston, R. S. (1997). Children's arithmetical difficulties: Contributions from processing speed, item identification, and short-term memory. *Journal of Experimental Child Psychology, 65*, 1–24.

Bull, R., Johnston, R. S., & Roy, J. A. (1999). Exploring the roles of the visual-spatial sketchpad and central executive in children's arithmetical skills: Views from cognition and developmental neuropsychology. *Developmental Neuropsychology, 15*, 421–442.

Butler, R. W., & Copeland, D. R. (2002). Attentional processes and their remediation in children treated for cancer: A literature review and the development of a therapeutic approach. *Journal of the International Neuropsychological Society, 8*, 115–124.

Butler, R. W., Kerr, M., & Marchand, A. (1999). Attention and executive functions following cranial irradiation in children. *Journal of the International Neuropsychological Society, 5*, 108.

Cacace, A. T., & McFarland, D. J. (2000). Temporal processing deficits in remediation-resistant reading-impaired children. *Audiology & Neuro-Otology, 5*, 83–97.

Cain, K., Oakhill, J., & Bryant, P. (2004). Children's reading comprehension ability: Concurrent prediction by working memory, verbal ability, and component skills. *Journal of Educational Psychology, 96*, 31–42.

Callicot, J. H., Mattay, V. S., Verchinski, B. A., Marenca, S., Egan, M. F., & Weinberger, D. R. (2003). Complexity of prefrontal cortical dysfunction in schizophrenia: More than up or down. *American Journal of Psychiatry, 160*, 2209–2215.

Carroll, J. M., & Snowling, M. J. (2004). Language and phonological skills in children at high risk of reading difficulties. *Journal of Child Psychology & Psychiatry, 45*, 631–640.

Castner, S. A., Williams, G. V., & Goldman-Rakic, P. S. (2000). Reversal of antipsychotic-induced working memory deficits by short-term dopamine D1 receptor stimulation. *Science, 287*, 2020–2022.

Cepeda, N. J., Cepeda, M. L., & Kramer, A. F. (2000). Task switching and attention deficit hyperactivity disorder. *Journal of Abnormal Child Psychology, 28*, 213–226.

Chiappe, P., Siegel, L. S., & Hasher, L. (2002). Working memory, inhibition and reading skill. In S. P. Shohov (Ed); *Advances in Psychology Research* (Vol. 9, pp. 30–51). Hauppauge, NY: Nova Science Publishers, Inc.

Cicerone, K. D. (2002). Remediation of "working attention" in mild traumatic brain injury. *Brain Injury, 16*, 185–195.

Comblain, A. (1994). Working memory in Down's syndrome: Training the rehearsal strategy. *Down Syndrome: Research and Practice, 2*, 123–126.

Connor, P. D., Sampson, P. D., Bookstein, F. L., Barr, H. M., & Streissguth, A. P. (2000). Direct and indirect effects of prenatal alcohol damage on executive function. *Developmental Neuropsychology, 18*, 331–354.

Conners, F. A., Rosenquist, C. J., & Taylor, L. A. (2001). Memory training for children with Down syndrome. *Down Syndrome: Research & Practice, 7*, 25–33.

Copeland, D. R., Dowell, R. E., Fletcher, J. M., Sullivan, M. P., Jaffe, N., Frankel, L. S., et al. (1988). Neuropsychological effects of childhood cancer treatment. *Journal of Child Neurology, 3*, 53–62.

Cormier, P., & Dea, S. (1997). Distinctive patterns of relationship of phonological awareness and working memory with reading development. *Reading & Writing: An Interdisciplinary Journal, 9*, 193–206.

Cornoldi, C., Barbieri, A., Gaiani, C., & Zocchi, S. (1999). Strategic memory deficits in attention deficit disorder with hyperactivity participants: The role of executive processes. *Developmental Neuropsychology, 15*, 53–71.

Cowan, N. (1996). Short-term memory, working memory, and their importance in language processing. *Topics in Language Disorders, 17*, 1–18.

Daily, L. Z., Lovett, M. C., & Reder, L. M. (2001). Modeling individual differences in working memory performance: A source activation account. *Cognitive Science, 25*, 315–353.

Daneman, M., & Carpenter, P. A. (1980). Individual differences in working memory and reading. *Journal of Verbal Learning and Verbal Behavior, 19*, 450–466.

Daneman, M., & Merikle, P. M. (1996). Working memory and language comprehension: A meta-analysis. *Psychonomic Bulletin & Review, 3*, 422–433.

Davalos, D. B., Compagnon, N., Heinlein, S., & Ross, R. G. (2004). Neuropsychological deficits in children associated with increased familial risk for schizophrenia. *Schizophrenia Research, 67*, 123–130.

Delahunty, A., & Morice, R. (1996). Rehabilitation of frontal/executive impairments in schizophrenia. *Australian and New Zealand Journal of Psychiatry, 30*, 760–767.

Dennis, M., Barnes, M. A., Donnelly, R. E., Wilkinson, M., & Humphreys, R. (1996). Appraising and managing knowledge: Metacognitive skills after childhood head injury. *Developmental Neuropsychology, 12*, 77–103.

Deutsch, G. K., Miller, S. L., Merzenich, M. M., & Tallal, P. (1999). Improvements in auditory working memory after training of children with language impairments. Paper presented at the Cognitive Neuroscience Society.

Dirette, D. K., Hinojosa, J., & Carnevale, G. J. (1999). Comparison of remedial and compensatory interventions for adults with acquired brain injuries. *Journal of Head Trauma Rehabilitation, 14*, 595–601.

Dollaghan, C., & Campbell, T. (1998). Nonword repetition and child language impairment. *Journal of Speech, Language, and Hearing Research, 41*, 1136–1146.

Douglas, V. I., Barr, R. G., O'Neill, M. E., & Britton, B. G. (1986). Short term effect of methylphenidate on the cognitive, learning and academic performance of children with attention deficit disorder in the laboratory and the classroom. *Journal of Child Psychology and Psychiatry, 27*, 191–221.

Downie, A. L. S., Jakobson, L. S., Frisk, V., & Ushycky, I. (2002). Auditory temporal processing deficits in children with periventricular brain injury. *Brain and Language, 80*, 208–225.

Duncan, J. (1995). Attention, intelligence and the frontal lobes. In M. S. Gazzaniga (Ed.), *The Cognitive Neurosciences* (pp. 721–733). Cambridge, MA: The MIT Press.

Dykman, R., & Ackerman, P. T. (1991). ADD and specific reading disability: Separate but often overlapping disorders. *Journal of Learning Disabilities, 24*, 96–103.

Elbro, C. (1996). Early linguistic abilities and reading development: A review and a hypothesis. *Reading & Writing, 8*, 453–485.

Elliott, R., Sahakian, B. J., Matthews, K., Bannergia, A., Rimmer, J., & Robbins, T. W. (1997). Effects of methylphenidate on spatial working memory and planning in healthy young adults. *Psychopharmacology, 131*, 196–206.

Ellis Weisemer, S. (1996). Capacity limitations in working memory: The impact on lexical and morphological learning by children with language impairment. *Topics in Language Disorders, 17*, 33–44.

Engle, R. W., Tuholski, S. W., Laughlin, J. E., & Conway, A. R. A. (1999). Working memory, short-term memory, and general fluid intelligence: A latent variable approach. *Journal of Experimental Psychology: General, 128*, 309–331.

Ericsson, K. A., Chase, W. G., & Faloon, S. F. (1980). Acquisition of a memory skill. *Science, 208*, 1181–1182.

Ericsson, K. A., & Kintsch, W. (1995). Long-term working memory. *Psychological Review, 102*, 211–245.

Ericsson, K. A., & Polson, P. G. (1988). An experimental analysis of a memory skill for dinner-orders. *Journal of Experimental Psychology: Learning, Memory, and Cognition, 14*, 305–316.

Erlenmeyer-Kimling, L., Rock, D. R., Roberts, S. A., Janal, M., Kestenbaum, C., Cornblatt, B., et al. (2000). Attention, memory, and motor skills as childhood predictors of schizophrenia-related psychoses: the New York high-risk project. *American Journal of Psychiatry, 157*, 1416–1422.

Facoetti, A., Lorusso, M. L., Paganoni, P., Umilta, C., & Mascetti, G. G. (2003). The role of visuospatial attention in developmental dyslexia: Evidence from a rehabilitation study. *Cognitive Brain Research, 15*, 154–164.

Fiszdon, J. M., Bryson, G. J., Wexler, B. E., & Morris, M. D. (2004). Durability of cognitive remediation training in schizophrenia performance on two memory tasks at 6-months and 12-months follow-up. *Psychiatry Research, 125,* 1–7.

Furey, M. L., Peietrini, P., & Haxby, J. V. (2000). Cholinergic enhancement and increased selectivity of perceptual processing during working memory. *Science, 290,* 2315–2318.

Gathercole, S. E. (1993). Word learning in language-impaired children. *Child Language Teaching & Therapy, 9,* 187–199.

Gathercole, S. E. (1999). Cognitive approaches to the development of short-term memory. *Trends in Cognitive Sciences, 3,* 410–419.

Gathercole, S. E., & Baddeley, A. D. (1990). Phonological memory deficits in language disordered children: Is there a causal connection? *Journal of Memory & Language, 29,* 336–360.

Gathercole, S. E., & Baddeley, A. D. (1993). Phonological working memory: A critical building block for reading development and vocabulary acquisition? *European Journal of Psychology of Education, 8,* 259–272.

Gathercole, S. E., Baddeley, A. D., & Papagno, C. (1998). The phonological loop as a language learning device. *Psychological Review, 105,* 158–173.

Gathercole, S. E., Hitch, G. J., Service, E., & Martin, A. J. (1997). Phonological short-term memory and new word learning in children. *Developmental Psychology, 33,* 966–979.

Gathercole, S. E., Brown, L., & Pickering, S. J. (2003). Working memory assessments at school entry as longitudinal predictors of National Curriculum attainment levels. *Educational & Child Psychology, 20,* 109–122.

Gathercole, S. E., Pickering, S. J., Knight, C., & Stegmann, Z. (2004). Working memory skills and educational attainment: Evidence from national curriculum assessments at 7 and 14 years of age. *Applied Cognitive Psychology, 18,* 1–16.

Gathercole, S. E., Service, E., Hitch, G. J., Adams, A., & Martin, A. J. (1999). Phonological short-term memory and vocabulary development: Further evidence on the nature of the relationship. *Applied Cognitive Psychology, 13,* 65–77.

Gemperle, A. Y., McAllister, K. H., & Olpe, H. R. (2003). Differential effects of iloperidone, clozapine, and haloperidol on working memory of rats in delayed non-matching-to-position paradigm. *Psychopharmacology, 169,* 354–364.

Gill, C. B., Klecan-Aker, J., Roberts, T., & Fredenburg, K. A. (2003). Following directions: Rehearsal and visualization strategies for children with specific language impairment. *Child Language Teaching & Therapy, 19,* 85–104.

Gillam, R. B., & van Kleeck, A. (1996). Phonological awareness training and short-term working memory: Clinical implications. *Topics in Language Disorders, 17,* 72–81.

Goldman-Rakic, P. S. (1994). Working memory dysfunction in schizophrenia. *Journal of Neuropsychiatry & Clinical Neurosciences, 6,* 348–357.

Goldman-Rakic, P. S., & Selemon, L. D. (1997). Functional and anatomical aspects of prefrontal pathology in schizophrenia. *Schizophrenia Bulletin, 23,* 437–458.

Gonzalez, M., Espinel, A. I. G., & Rosquete, R. G. (2002). Remedial interventions for children with reading disabilities: Speech perception an effective component in phonological training? *Journal of Learning Disabilities, 35,* 334–342.

Goswami, U., & Bryant, P. (1990). *Phonological skills and learning to read.* London: Erlbaum.

Green, M. F., Marshall, B. D., Wirshing, W. C., Ames, D., Marder, S. R., McGurk, S., et al. (1997). Does risperidone improve verbal working memory in treatment-resistant schizophrenia? *American Journal of Psychiatry, 154,* 799–804.

Griffith, E. M., Pennington, B. F., Wehner, E. A., & Rogers, S. J. (1999). Executive functions in young children with autism. *Child Development, 70,* 817–832.

Hanten, G., Bartha, M., & Levin, H. S. (2000). Metacognition following pediatric traumatic brain injury: A preliminary study. *Developmental Neuropsychology, 18,* 383–398.

Hanten, G., Levin, H. S., & Song, J. X. (1999). Working memory and metacognition in sentence comprehension in severely head-injured children: A preliminary study. *Developmental Psychology, 16,* 393–414.

Harvey, J., O'Callaghan, M. J., & Mohay, H. (1999). Executive function of children with extremely low birthweight: A case control study. *Developmental Medicine and Child Neurology, 41,* 292–297.

Harvey, P. D., Green, M. F., McGurk, S. R., & Meltzer, H. Y. (2003). Changes in cognitive functioning with risperidone and olanzapine treatment: A large-scale, double blind, randomized study. *Psychopharmacology, 169,* 404–411.

Hecht, S. A., Burgess, S. R., Torgesen, J. K., Wagner, R. K., & Rashotte, C. A. (2000). Explaining social class differences in growth of reading skills from beginning kindergarten through fourth-grade: The role of phonological awareness, rate of access, and print knowledge. *Reading & Writing, 12,* 99–127.

Hertel, P., Nomikos, G. G., Iurlo, M., & Svensson, T. H. (1996). Risperidone: Regional effects in vivo on release and metabolism of dopamine and serotonin in the rat brain. *Psychopharmacology, 124,* 74–86.

Honey, G. D., Bullmore, E. T., Soni, W., Varatheesan, M., Williams, S. C. R., & Sharma, T. (1999). Differences in frontal cortical activation by a working memory task after substitution of risperidone for typical antipsychotic drugs in patients with schizophrenia. *Proceeding of the National Academy of Sciences, 96,* 13432–13437.

Hornyak, J. E., Nelson, V. S., & Hurvitz, E. A. (1997). The use of methylphenidate in pediatric traumatic brain injury. *American Journal of Physical Medicine & Rehabilitation, 76,* 440–450.

Huguelet, P., Zanello, A., & Nicastro, R. (2000). A study of visual and auditory verbal working memory in schizophrenic patients compared to healthy subjects. *European Archives of Psychiatry & Clinical Neuroscience, 250,* 79–85.

Hulme, C., & Mackenzie, S. (1992). *Working memory and severe learning difficulties.* Hove, U.K.: Lawrence Erlbaum Associates.

Jarrold, C., Baddeley, A. D., & Hewes, A. K. (1999). Genetically dissociated components of working memory: Evidence from Down's and Williams syndrome. *Neuropsychologia, 37,* 637–651.

Jarrold, C., Baddeley, A. D., & Hewes, A. K. (2000). Verbal short-term memory deficits in Down syndrome: A consequence of problems in rehearsal? *Journal of Child Psychology and Psychiatry, 40,* 233–244.

Jin, C., & Schachar, R. (2004). Methylphenidate treatment of attention-deficit/hyperactivity disorder secondary to traumatic brain injury: a critical appraisal of treatment studies. *CNS Spectrums, 9,* 217–226.

Just, M. A., & Carpenter, P. A. (1992). A capacity theory of comprehension: Individual differences in working memory. *Psychological Review, 99,* 122–149.

Kaelin, D. L., Cifu, D. X., & Matthies, B. (1996). Methylphenidate effect on attention deficit in the acutely brain-injured adult. *Archives of Physical Medicine & Rehabilitation, 77,* 6–9.

Kadis, D. S., Stollstorff, M., Elliott, I., Lach, L., & Smith, M. L. (2004). Cognitive and psychological predictors of everyday memory in children with intractable epilepsy. *Epilepsy & Behavior, 5,* 37–43.

Kajs-Wyllie, M. (2002). Ritalin revisited: does it really help in neurological injury? *Journal of Neuroscience Nursing, 34,* 303–313.

Kane, M. J., & Engle, R. W. (2002). The role of prefrontal cortex in working memory capacity, executive attention, and general fluid intelligence: An individual differences perspective. *Psychonomic Bulletin and Review, 9,* 637–671.

Karatekin, C., & Asarnow, R. F. (1998). Working memory in childhood-onset schizophrenia and attention-deficit/hyperactivity disorder. *Psychiatry Research, 80,* 165–176.

Kempton, S., Vance, A., Maruff, P., Luk, E., Costin, J., & Pantelis, C. (1999). Executive function and attention deficit hyperactivity disorder: stimulant medication and better executive function performance in children. *Psychological Medicine, 29,* 527–538.

Kerns, A. K., Eso, K., & Thomson, J. (1999). Investigation of a direct intervention for improving attention in young children with ADHD. *Developmental Neuropsychology, 16,* 273–295.

Klingberg, T., Forssberg H., & Westerberg, H. (2002). Training of working memory in children with ADHD. *Journal of Clinical and Experimental Neuropsychology, 24*, 781–791.

Konrad, K., Gunther, T., Hanisch, C., & Herpertz-Dahlmann, B. (2004). Differential effects of methylphenidate on attentional functions in children with attention-deficit/hyperactivity disorder. *Journal of American Academy of Child Adolescent Psychiatry, 43*, 191–198.

Krabbendam, L., & Aleman, A. (2003). Cognitive rehabilitation in schizophrenia a quantitative analysis of controlled studies. *Psychopharmacology, 139*, 376–382.

Kramer, A. F., Cepeda, N. J., & Cepeda, M. L. (2001). Methylphenidate effects on task-switching performance in attention-deficit/hyperactivity disorder. *Journal of American Academy of Child Adolescent Psychiatry, 40*, 1277–1284.

Kyllonen, P. C., & Christal, R. E. (1990). Reasoning ability is (little more than) working-memory capacity? *Intelligence, 14*, 389–433.

Laws, G., MacDonald, J., & Buckley, S. (1996). The effects of a short training in the use of a rehearsal strategy on memory for words and pictures in children with Down syndrome. *Down Syndrome: Research & Practice, 4*, 70–78.

Leather, C. V., & Henry, L. A. (1994). Working memory span and phonological awareness tasks as predictors of early reading ability. *Journal of Experimental Child Psychology, 58*, 88–111.

Levin, H. S., Hanten, G., Zhang, L., Swank, P. R., Ewing-Cobbs, L., Dennis, M., et al. (2004). Changes in working memory after traumatic brain injury in children. *Neuropsychology, 18*, 240–247.

Levin, H. S., High, W. M. Jr., Ewing-Cobbs, L., Fletcher, J. M., Eisenberg, H. M., Miner, M. E., et al. (1988). Memory functioning during the first year after closed head injury in children and adolescents. *Neurosurgery, 22*, 1043–1052.

Levin, H. S., Song, J., Scheibel, R. S., Fletcher, J. M., Harward, H., Lilly, M., et al. (1997). Concept formation and problem-solving following closed head injury in children. *Journal of the International Neuropsychological Society, 3*, 598–607.

Logie, R. H. (1995). *Visuo-spatial working memory*. Hove, UK: Lawrence Erlbaum Associates Ltd.

Lopez-Luengo, B., & Vazquez., C. (2003). Effects of attention process training on cognitive functioning of schizophrenic patients. *Psychiatry Research, 119*, 41–53.

Lovett, M. W., Borden, S. L., DeLuca, T., Kacerenza, L., Benson, N. J., & Brackstone, D. (1994). Treating the core deficits of developmental dyslexia: Evidence of transfer of learning after phonologically- and strategy-based reading training programs. *Developmental Psychology, 30*, 805–822.

Luna, B., Minshew, N. J., Garver, B. A., Lazar, N. A., Thulborn, K. R., Eddy, W. F., et al. (2002). Neocortical system abnormalities in autism: An fMRI study of spatial working memory. *Neurology, 59*, 834–840.

MacDonald, M. C., & Christiansen, M. H. (2002). Reassessing working memory: Comment on Just and Carpenter (1992) and Waters and Caplan (1996). *Psychological Review, 109*, 35–54.

Mahalick, D. M., Carmel, P. W., Greenberg, J. P., Molofsky, W., Brown, J. A., Heary, R. F., et al. (1998). Psychopharmacologic treatment of acquired attention disorders in children with brain injury. *Pediatric Neurosurgery, 29*, 121–126.

Manoach, D. S., Gollub, R. L., Benson, E. S., Searl, M. M., Goff, D. C., Halpern, E., et al. (2000). Schizophrenia subjects show aberrant fMRI activation of dorsolateral prefrontal cortex and basal ganglia during working memory performance. *Biological Psychiatry, 48*, 99–109.

Mariani, M. A., & Barkley, R.A. (1997). Neuropsychological and academic functioning in preschool boys with attention deficit hyperactivity disorder. *Developmental Neuropsychology, 13*, 111–129.

Maridaki-Kassotaki, K. (2002). The relation between phonological memory skills and reading ability in Greek-speaking children: Can training on phonological memory contribute to reading development? *European Journal of Psychology of Education, 17*, 63–73.

Marlowe, W. B. (2000). An intervention for children with disorders of executive functions. *Developmental Neuropsychology, 18*, 445–454.

Mateer, C. A., Kerns, K. A., & Eso, K. L. (1996). Management of attention and memory disorders following traumatic brain injury. *Journal of Learning Disabilities, 29*, 18–32.

Mateer, C. A., & Williams, D. (1991). Effects of frontal lobe injury in childhood. *Developmental Neuropsychology, 7*, 359–376.

McDougall, S. J. P., & Donohoe, R. (2002). Reading ability and memory span: Long-term memory contributions to span for good and poor readers. *Reading & Writing, 15*, 359–387.

McInnes, A., Humphries, T., Hogg-Johnson, S., & Tannock, R. (2003). Listening comprehension and working memory are impaired in attention-deficit hyperactivity disorder irrespective of language impairment. *Journal of Abnormal Child Psychology, 31*, 427–443.

McNamara, D. S., & Scott, J. L. (2001). Working memory capacity and strategy use. *Memory & Cognition, 29*, 10–17.

Mehta, M. A., Owen, A. M., Sahakian, B. J., Mavaddat, N., Pickard, J. D., & Robbins, T. W. (2000). Methylphenidate enhances working memory by modulating discrete frontal and parietal lobe regions in the human brain. *The Journal of Neuroscience, 20*, RC65.

Meltzer, H. Y., & McGurk, S. R. (1999). The effects of clozapine, risperidone, and olanzapine on cognitive function in schizophrenia. *Schizophrenia Bulletin, 25*, 233–255.

Merzenich, M. M., Jenkins, W. M., Johnston, P., Schreiner, C., Miller, S. L., & Tallal, P. (1996). Temporal processing deficits of language-learning impaired children ameliorated by training. *Science, 271*, 77–81.

Minshew, N. J., & Goldstein, G. (2001). The pattern of intact and impaired memory functions in autism. *Journal of Child Psychology and Psychiatry, 42*, 1095–1101.

Miyake, A., Friedman, N. P., Emerson, M. J., Witzki, A. H., Howerter, A., & Wager, T. (2000). The unity and diversity of executive functions and their contributions to complex "frontal lobe" tasks: A latent variable analysis, *Cognitive Psychology, 41*, 49–100.

Montgomery, J. W. (1995). Sentence comprehension in children with specific language impairment: The role of phonological working memory. *Journal of Speech & Hearing Research, 38*, 187–199.

Montgomery, J. W. (2002). Understanding the language difficulties of children with specific language impairments: Does verbal working memory matter? *American Journal of Speech-Language Pathology, 11*, 77–91.

Montgomery, J. W. (2003). Working memory and comprehension in children with specific language impairment: what we know so far. *Journal of Communication Disorders, 36*, 221–231.

Morris, R. G., Rushe, T., Woodruffe, P. W. R., & Murray, R. M. (1995). Problem solving in schizophrenia: A specific deficit in planning ability. *Schizophrenia Research, 14*, 235–246.

Mulhern, R. K., & Palmer, S. L. (2003). Neurocognitive late effects in pediatric cancer. *Current Problems in Cancer, 27*, 177–197.

Mulhern, R. K., Reddick, W., Palmer, S. L., Glass, J. O., Elkin, T. D., Kun, L. E., et al. (1999). Neurocognitive deficits in medulloblastoma survivors and white matter loss. *Annals of Neurology, 46*, 834–841.

Numminen, H., Service, E., Ahonen, T., Korhonen, T., Tolvanen, A., Patja, K., et al. (2000). Working memory structure and intellectual disability. *Journal of Intellectual Disability Research, 44*, 579–590.

Oakhill, J., & Kyle, F. (2000). The relation between phonological awareness and working memory. *Journal of Experimental Child Psychology, 75*, 152–164.

Olesen, P. J., Westerberg, H., & Klingberg, T. (2004). Increased prefrontal and parietal activity after training of working memory. *Nature Neuroscience, 7*, 75–79.

O'Reilly, R. C., Braver, T. S., & Cohen, J. D. (1999). A biologically based computational model of working memory. In A. Miyake & P. Shah (Eds.), *Models of Working Memory: Mechanisms of Active Maintenance and Executive Control* (pp. 375–411). New York: Cambridge University Press.

O'Shaughnessy, T. E., & Swanson, H. L. (2000). A comparison of two reading interventions for children with reading disabilities. *Journal of Learning Disabilities, 33*, 257–277.

Ozonoff, S. (1998). Assessment and remediation of executive dysfunction on autism and Asperger syndrome, *Asperger Syndrome or High-functioning Autism?* (pp. 263–289). New York: Plenum Press.

Palmer, S. (2000a). Phonological recording deficit in working memory of dyslexic teenagers. *Journal of Research in Reading, 23,* 28–40.

Palmer, S. (2000b). Working memory: A development study of phonological recoding. *Memory, 8,* 179–193.

Park, N. W., Proulx, G. B., & Towers, W. M. (1999). Evaluation of the attention process training programme. *Neuropsychological Rehabilitation, 9,* 135–154.

Park, W. P., & Ingles, J. L. (2001). Effectiveness of attention rehabilitation after an acquired brain injury: A meta-analysis. *Neuropsychology, 15,* 199–210.

Pennington, B. F., & Ozonoff, S. (1996). Executive functions and developmental psychopathology. *Journal of Child Psychology and Psychiatry, 37,* 51–87.

Pickering, S. J. (2001). The development of visuo-spatial working memory. *Memory, 9,* 423–432.

Pilling, S., Bebbington, P., Kuipers, E., Garety, P., Geddes, J., Martindale, B., et al. (2002). Psychological treatments in schizophrenia: II. Meta-analyses of randomized controlled trials of social skills training and cognitive remediation. *Psychological Medicine, 32,* 783–791.

Pineda, D., Ardila, A., Rosselli, M., Cadavid, C., Mancheno, S., & Mejia, S. (1998). Executive dysfunctions in children with attention deficit hyperactivity disorder. *International Journal of Neuroscience, 96,* 177–196.

Plenger, P. M., Dixon, C. E., Castillo, R. M., Frankowski, R. F., Yablon, S. A., & Levin, H. S. (1996). Subacute methylphenidate treatment for moderate to moderately severe traumatic brain injury: a preliminary double-blind placebo-controlled study. *Archives of Physical Medicine & Rehabilitation, 77,* 536–540.

Reeve, W. V., & Schandler, S. L. (2001). Frontal lobe functioning in adolescents with attention deficit hyperactivity disorder. *Adolescence, 36,* 749–765.

Roncadin, C., Guger, S., Archibald, J., Barnes, M., & Dennis, M. (2004). Working memory after mild, moderate or severe childhood closed head injury. *Developmental Neuropsychology, 25,* 21–36.

Rosenquist, C., Conners, F. A., & Roskos-Ewoldsen, B. (2003). Phonological and visuo-spatial working memory in individuals with intellectual disability. *American Journal on Mental Retardation, 108,* 403–413.

Rugino, T. A., & Copley, T. C. (2001). Effects of modafinil in children with Attention-Deficit/Hyperactivity Disorder: An open-label study. *Journal of the American Academy of Child & Adolescent Psychiatry, 40,* 230–235.

Russell, J., Jarrold, C., & Henry, L. (1996). Working memory in children with autism and with moderate learning difficulties. *Journal of Child Psychology & Psychiatry & Allied Disciplines, 37,* 673–686.

Schachar, R. J., Tannock, R., & Logan, G. (1993). Inhibitory control, impulsiveness, and attention deficit hyperactivity disorder. *Clinical Psychology Review, 13,* 721–739.

Schatz, J., Kramer, J. H., Albin, A., & Matthay, K. K. (2000). Processing speed, working memory and IQ: A developmental model of cognitive deficits following cranial radiation therapy. *Neuropsychology, 14,* 189–200.

Schmidt, R. A., & Bjork, R. A. (1992). New conceptualizations of practice: Common principles in three paradigms suggest new concepts for training. *Psychological Science, 3,* 207–217.

Seidman, L. J., Biederman, J., Faraone, S. V., Weber, W., & Ouellette, C. (1997). Toward defining a neuropsychology of attention deficit-hyperactivity disorder: Performance of children and adolescents from a large clinically referred sample. *Journal of Consulting and Clinical Psychology, 65,* 150–160

Semrud-Clikeman, M., Nielsen, K. H., Clinton, A., Sylvester, L., Parle, N., & Connor, R. T. (1999). An intervention approach for children with teacher- and parent-identified attentional difficulties. *Journal of Learning Disabilities, 32,* 581–590.

Shah, P., & Miyake, A. (1999). Models of working memory: An introduction. In A. Miyake & P. Shah (Eds.), *Models of Working Memory: Mechanisms of Active Maintenance and Executive Control.* New York: Cambridge University Press.

Shaywitz, B. A., Shaywitz, S. E., Blachman, B. A., Pugh, K. Fulbright, R. K., Skudlarski, P., et al. (2004). Development of left occipitotemporal systems for skilled reading in children after a phonologically-based intervention. *Biological Psychiatry, 55,* 926–933.

Shue, K. L., & Douglas, V. I. (1992). The role of frontal lobe maturation in cognitive and social development. *Brain & Cognition, 20,* 104–124.

Silver, H., Feldman, P., Bilker, W., & Gur, R. C. (2003). Working memory deficit as a core neuropsychological dysfunction in schizophrenia. *American Journal of Psychiatry, 160,* 1809–1816.

Singer, B. D., & Bashir, A. S. (1999). What are executive functions and self-regulation and what do they have to do with language-learning disorders? *Language, Speech and Hearing Services in Schools, 30,* 265–273.

Slomine, B. S., Gerring, J. P., Grados, M. A., Brady, K. D., Christensen, J. R., & Denckla, M. B. (2002). Performance on measures of 'executive function' following pediatric traumatic brain injury. *Brain Injury, 16,* 759–772.

Smith-Spark, J. H., Fisk, J. E., Fawcett, A. J., & Nicolson, R. I. (2003). Investigating the central executive in adult dyslexics: Evidence from phonological and visuospatial working memory performance. *European Journal of Cognitive Psychology, 15,* 567–587.

Sohlberg, M. M., & Mateer, C. A. (2001). Improving attention and managing attentional problems: Adapting rehabilitation techniques to adults with ADHD. *Annals New York Academy of Sciences, 931,* 359–375.

Sohlberg, M. M., Mateer, C. A., & Stuss, D. T. (1993). Contemporary approaches to the management of executive control dysfunction. *Journal of Head Trauma Rehabilitation, 81,* 45–58.

Sohlberg, M. M., McLaughlin, K. A., Pavese, A., Heidrich, A., & Posner, M. I. (2000). Evaluation of attention process training and brain injury education in person with acquired brain injury. *Journal of Clinical and Experimental Neuropsychology, 22,* 656–676.

Solanto, M. V. (2002). Dopamine dysfunction in AD/HD: Integrating clinical and basic neuroscience research. *Behavioral Brain Research, 130,* 65–71.

Speech, T. J., Rao, S. M., Osmon, D. C., & Sperry, L. T. (1993). A double-blind controlled study of methylphenidate treatment in closed head injury. *Brain Injury, 7,* 333–338.

Stroop, J. R. (1935). Studies of interference in serial verbal reactions. *Journal of Experimental Psychology, 18,* 643–662.

Swanson, H. L. (1999). Reading comprehension and working memory in learning-disabled readers: Is the phonological loop more important than the executive system? *Journal of Experimental Child Psychology, 72,* 1–31.

Swanson, H. L., & Howell, M. (2001). Working memory, short-term memory, and speech rate as predictors of children's reading performance at different ages. *Journal of Educational Psychology, 93,* 720–734.

Swanson, H. L., & Sachse-Lee, C. (2001a). Mathematical problem solving and working memory in children with learning disabilities: Both executive and phonological processes are important. *Journal of Experimental Child Psychology, 79,* 294–321.

Swanson, H. L., & Sachse-Lee, C. (2001b). A subgroup analysis of working memory in children with reading disabilities. *Journal of Learning Disabilities, 34,* 249–263.

Tallal, P. (2003). Language learning disabilities: Integrating research approaches. *Current Directions in Psychological Science, 12,* 206–211.

Tallal, P. (1998). Language learning impairment: Integrating research and remediation. *Scandinavian Journal of Psychology, 39,* 195–197.

Tallal, P., Miller, S. L., Bedi, G. Wang, X., Nagarajan, S. S., Schreiner, C., et al. (1996). Language comprehension in language-learning impaired children improved with acoustically modified speech. *Science, 271,* 81–84.

Tannock, R., Ickowicz, A., & Schachar, R. (1995). Differential effects of methylphenidate on working memory in ADHD children with and without comorbid anxiety. *Journal of the American Academy of Child & Adolescent Psychiatry, 34,* 886–896.

Taylor, F. B., & Russo, J. (2000). Efficacy of modafinil compared to dextroamphetamine for the treatment of attention deficit hyperactivity disorder in adults. *Journal of Child & Adolescent Psychopharmacology, 10*, 311–320.

Temple, E., Deutsch, G. K., Poldrack, R. A., Miller, S. L., Tallal, P., Merzenich, M. M., et al. (2003). Neural deficits in children with dyslexia ameliorated by behavioral remediation: Evidence from functional MRI. *Proceedings of the National Academy of the Sciences, 100*, 2860–2865.

Thompson, N. M., Francis, D. J., Stubing, K. K., Fletcher, J. M., Ewing-Cobbs, L., Miner, M. E., et al. (1994). Motor, visual-spatial, and somatosensory skills after closed head injury in children and adolescents: A study of change. *Neuropsychology, 8*, 333–342.

Torgesen, J. K., & Davis, C. (1996). Individual difference variables that predict response to training in phonological awareness. *Journal of Experimental Child Psychology, 63*, 1–21.

Turley-Ames, K. J., & Whitfield, M. M. (2003). Strategy training and working memory task performance. *Journal of Memory & Language, 49*, 446–468.

Turner, D. C., Robbins, T. W., Clark, L., Aron, A. R., Dowson, J., & Sahakian, B. J. (2003). Cognitive enhancing effects of modafinil in healthy volunteers. *Psychopharmacology, 165*, 260–269.

van't Hooft, I., Andersson, K., Sejersen, T., Bartfai, A., & von Wendt, L. (2003). Attention and memory training in children with acquired brain injuries. *Acta Paediatrics, 92*, 935–940.

Veale, T. K. (1999). Targeting temporal processing deficits through Fast ForWord: Language therapy with a new twist. *Language, Speech and Hearing Services in Schools, 30*, 353–362.

Vicari, S., Marotta, L., & Carlesimo, G. A. (2004). Verbal short-term memory in Down's syndrome: An articulatory loop deficit? *Journal of Intellectual Disability Research, 48*, 80–92.

Volkow, N. D., Fowler, J. S., Wang, G., Ding, Y., & Gatley, S. J. (2001). Mechanism of action of methylphenidate: Insights from PET imaging studies. *Journal of Attention Disorders, 6*, S-31–S-43.

Wang, P. P., & Bellugi, U. (1994). Evidence from two genetic syndromes for a dissociation between verbal and visual-spatial short-term memory. *Journal of Clinical & Experimental Neuropsychology, 16*, 317–322.

Wasserstein, J., & Lynn, A. (2001). Metacognitive remediation in adult ADHD: Treating executive function deficits via executive functions. *Annals New York Academy of Sciences, 931*, 376–384.

Welsh, M. C., Pennington, B. F., Ozonoff, S., Rouse, B., & McCabe, E. R. B. (1990). Neuropsychology of early-treated phenylketonuria: Specific executive function deficits. *Child Development, 61*, 1697–1713.

Wexler, B. E., Anderson, M., Fulbright, R. K., & Gore, J. C. (2000). Preliminary evidence of improved verbal working memory performance and normalization of task-related frontal lobe activation in schizophrenia following cognitive exercises. *American Journal of Psychiatry, 157*, 1694–1697.

Whalen, C. K., Henker, B., Swanson, J. M., Granger, D., Kliewer, W., & Spencer, J. (1987). Natural social behaviors in hyperactive children: Dose effects of methylphenidate. *Journal of Consulting and Clinical Psychology, 55*, 187–193.

Williams, S. E., Ris, M. D., Ayyangar, R., Scheftt, B. K., Berch, D. (1998). Recovery in pediatric brain injury: Is psychostimulant medication beneficial? *Journal of Head Trauma Rehabilitation, 13*, 73–81.

Wright, J., & Jacobs, B. (2003). Teaching phonological awareness and metacognitive strategies to children with reading difficulties: A comparison of the two instructional methods. *Educational Psychology, 23*, 17–45.

Wykes, T., Brammer, M., Mellers, J., Bray, P., Reeder, C., Williams, C., et al. (2002). Effects on the brain of a psychological treatment: cognitive remediation therapy. *British Journal of Psychiatry, 181*, 144–152.

Wykes, T., Reeder, C., Corner, J., Williams, C., & Everitt, B. (1999). The effects of neurocognitive remediation on executive processing in patients with schizophrenia. *Schizophrenia Bulletin, 25*, 291–307.

Ylvisaker, M., & DeBonis, D. (2000). Executive function impairment in adolescence: TBI and ADHD. *Topics in Language Disorders, 20*, 29–57.

Subject Index